Effectuating Free Movement in the EU through Recognition of Qualifications

Lavinia S.J. Kortese

Effectuating Free Movement in the EU through Recognition of Qualifications

A Question of Our Time, A Question of All Times?

Springer

Lavinia S.J. Kortese
International and European Law
Utrecht University
Utrecht, The Netherlands

ISBN 978-3-032-21334-1 ISBN 978-3-032-21335-8 (eBook)
https://doi.org/10.1007/978-3-032-21335-8

This Springer imprint is published by the registered company Springer Nature Switzerland AG
The registered company address is: Gewerbestrasse 11, 6330 Cham, Switzerland

Competing Interests The author has no competing interests to declare that are relevant to the content of this manuscript.

Contents

Abbreviations

CJEU	Court of Justice of the European Union
ECTS	European Credit Transfer and Accumulation System
EEA-2025	European Education Area
EESC	European Economic and Social Committee
EHEA	European Higher Education Area
EPC	European Professional Card
EQF	European Qualifications Framework for lifelong learning
ESG	Standards and guidelines for quality assurance in the European Higher Education Area
EU	European Union
LRC	Lisbon Recognition Convention
OMC	Open Method of Coordination
PQD	Professional Qualifications Directive
QF-EHEA	Qualifications Framework for the European Higher Education Area
TEU	Treaty on European Union
TFEU	Treaty on the Functioning of the European Union
VET	Vocational Education and Training

Introduction

1 Setting the Scene: Recognition of Qualifications and the Freedom of Movement

An individual's career path may take a myriad of different forms. After secondary education, one may decide to enrol in vocational education and training aimed at learning a profession. However, a person may later change their mind and continue their education by pursuing studies at higher education level commencing with a bachelor's degree, perhaps followed by a master's degree, and a doctorate after that. And when an individual decides that his or her educational career has ended after obtaining a certain diploma, career opportunities are plentiful. Nevertheless, the human learning process never ends. Even after concluding formal education, some professionals may decide to pursue further studies whilst working to switch career paths. Other professionals may be content remaining in their respective fields of work, but will nevertheless continue to learn, grow and acquire experience in their daily activities.

Needless to say, options are plentiful and become even more widespread—perhaps even endless—when adding mobility into the mix. In the European Union (EU), the free movement of persons is considered one of the four fundamental freedoms guaranteed by the Treaty on European Union (TEU) and the Treaty on the Functioning of the European Union (TFEU).[1] Ever since the 1992 Maastricht Treaty introduced European citizenship, "the right to move and reside freely within the territory of the Member States" has become one of the essential rights connected to that status.[2] Moreover, the freedom of movement is also considered a fundamental right in light of the EU Charter of Fundamental Rights.[3] Keeping with the focus on fundamental

[1] More specifically Article 3(2) Treaty on European Union (TEU) and Title IV (particularly Articles 45, 49 and 56) Treaty on the Functioning of the European Union (TFEU).

[2] See Articles 20 and 21 TFEU.

[3] Article 45 Charter of Fundamental Rights of the European Union.

L. S.J. Kortese, *Effectuating Free Movement in the EU through Recognition of Qualifications*, https://doi.org/10.1007/978-3-032-21335-8_1

rights, the topic of the recognition of qualifications obviously also concerns the right to education as well as the freedom to seek and engage in work, both also fundamental rights under the Charter.[4] The right to education and to free movement are furthermore fundamental rights under the European Convention on Human Rights.[5]

Against this background it is clear that mobility between EU Member States for purposes of either work or studies is not merely something to be desired. For EU citizens in particular, it is their right. In this context, the principle of non-discrimination on the grounds of nationality plays a crucial role in the realisation of free movement. When this principle—and ultimately freedom of movement—function optimally, citizens of the Union can be confident that their qualifications are not only understood, but also recognised beyond the borders of their nation-state.[6] Recognition of qualifications, encompassing the process through which foreign qualifications are interpreted in the context of the host Member State's education system or labour market, is an important prerequisite for the mobility of both students and professionals.[7] Considering the fact that the mobility of individuals may depend on recognition in a host Member State, the process of recognition being carried out smoothly is of paramount importance. Following this reasoning, recognition is capable of positively contributing to intra-EU mobility. Indeed, increased recognition of foreign qualifications has been found to be linked to better attracting EU migrants, meaning enhanced recognition has a positive effect on intra-EU mobility.[8] Moreover, qualifications play an important role in consolidating the areas of education and the labour market, since trusted education structures are able to guarantee labour market relevance.[9]

2 Effectuating Recognition of Qualifications in the EU: Who Does What?

While there are of course many ways in which to recognise qualifications, legislation and policy inevitably play a crucial role in making recognition processes succesful. For example, legislation and policy can be used to create frameworks to enhance common understanding of qualifications among employers, educational institutions, and competent authorities. Such common understanding can be enhanced by

---

[4] Articles 14 and 15 Charter of Fundamental Rights of the European Union (CFREU).

[5] Article 2 Protocol to the Convention for the Protection of Human Rights and Fundamental Freedoms, Paris 20 March 1952; Article 2 Protocol No. 4 to the Convention for the Protection of Human Rights and Fundamental Freedoms securing certain rights and freedoms other than those already included in the Convention and in the First Protocol thereto, Strasbourg 16 September 1963.

[6] Jefferies and Evetts (2000, p. 99).

[7] Rauhvargers (2009, p. 111).

[8] Capuano and Migali (2017, p. 771).

[9] Lettmayr and Martin (2013, p. 19).

improving transparency of foreign education systems, professions, and qualifications. However, legislation and policy can also be employed to create procedures for recognition and streamline practices across Member States. Considering the multitude of qualifications that is amplified by the freedom of movement in the EU context, legislation and policy are essential to achieve recognition. Nevertheless, as the terms legislation and policy already suggest, there are various approaches to recognising qualifications. In the EU, recognition is achieved through both legislative instruments as well as policy initiatives.

However, contrary to what the EU-oriented focus of this contribution may suggest, it is not exclusively the EU that has adopted relevant legislation and policy on recognition applicable in the EU's Member States. While this contribution therefore seeks to approach the topic of recognition from an EU law perspective, it seeks to provide an encompassing image—which includes initiatives beyond the EU. Indeed, relevant legal instruments have not only been created by the EU, but also by the Council of Europe. Furthermore, legislative instruments have also been adopted at the regional level to advance recognition. While several such examples can be provided,[10] the focus here will be on the Benelux. Apart from legislative action, policies affecting recognition of qualifications also originate from different actors. We can again mention the EU here, but reference should also be made to the Bologna Process. Though responsible for some of the biggest changes in higher education seen in European countries, the initiative itself is located outside the EU legal framework and progress achieved through intergovernmental cooperation (i.e. action that is legally non-binding). Taking these actors—and their respective instruments—on recognition of qualifications into consideration, we arrive at the overview in Table 1.

Those well-versed in the area of recognition of qualifications, professional regulation, education, or other related fields will likely remark that not all the instruments mentioned above concern recognition as such. Indeed, this contribution strives to take a broad view to matters related to recognition. As mentioned previously, recognition can be improved by enhancing understanding of foreign qualifications. Instruments increasing familiarity and trust in other Member states' education systems and professions therefore play an important role in ultimately effectuating recognition. Next to this, however, there are of course instruments containing procedures laying down rights and duties for individuals undergoing recognition and the authorities recognizing them. For this reason, the present contribution includes instruments beyond recognition procedures such as provisions on qualifications frameworks, common documentation formats, and quality assurance. While each of these constitute areas of study in their own right, the present contribution examines these instruments for their role in contributing to the recognition of qualifications.

[10] For example, the Benelux, Baltic States, and Nordic Countries.

Table 1 Overview of actors on recognition and their instruments & initiatives

European Union
• Professional Qualifications Directive[11] • Proportionality Test Directive[12] • European Qualifications Framework for lifelong learning (EQF)[13] • Europass[14] • 2020 VET Recommendation[15] • Automatic Recognition Recommendation[16] • Micro-credentials Recommendation[17] • Proposal for a recommendation on a European quality assurance and recognition system in higher education[18] • Communication on a European degree[19]

(continued)

[11] In this contribution, the term "Professional Qualifications Directive" is used to refer to Directive 2005/36/EC of the European Parliament and of the Council of 7 September 2005 on the recognition of professional qualifications, [2005] OJ L 255/22 *as amended by* Directive 2013/55/EU of the European Parliament and of the Council of 20 November 2013 amending Directive 2005/36/EC on the recognition of professional qualifications and Regulation (EU) No 1024/2012 on administrative cooperation through the Internal Market Information System ('the IMI Regulation'), [2013] OJ L 354/132. The consolidated version of the Professional Qualifications Directive can be accessed at: https://eur-lex.europa.eu/legal-content/EN/TXT/?uri=CELEX%3A02005L0036-20251029.

[12] In this contribution, the term "Proportionality Test Directive" is used to refer to Directive (EU) 2018/958 of the European Parliament and of the Council of 28 June 2018 on a proportionality test before adoption of new regulation of professions, [2018] OJ L 173/25.

[13] Council Recommendation of 22 May 2017 on the European Qualifications Framework for lifelong learning and repealing the recommendation of the European Parliament and of the Council of 23 April 2008 on the establishment of the European Qualifications Framework for lifelong learning, [2017] OJ C 189/15.

[14] Decision (EU) 2018/646 of the European Parliament and of the Council of 18 April 2018 on a common framework for the provision of better services for skills and qualifications (Europass) and repealing Decision No 2241/2004/EC, [2018] OJ L 112/42.

[15] In this contribution, the term "2020 VET Recommendation" is used to refer to Council Recommendation of 24 November 2020 on vocational education and training (VET) for sustainable competitiveness, social fairness and resilience, [2020] OJ C 417/1.

[16] In this contribution, the term "Automatic Recognition Recommendation" is used to refer to Council Recommendation of 26 November 2018 on promoting automatic mutual recognition of higher education and upper secondary education and training qualifications and the outcomes of learning periods abroad, [2018] OJ C 444/1.

[17] In this contribution, the term "Micro-credentials Recommendation" is used to refer to Council Recommendation of 16 June 2022 on a European approach to micro-credentials for lifelong learning and employability, [2022] OJ C 243/10.

[18] Proposal for a Council Recommendation on a European Quality Assurance and Recognition System in Higher Education, COM(2024) 147 final.

[19] Communication from the Commission to the European Parliament, the Council, the European Economic and Social Committee and the Committee of the Regions—a blueprint for a European degree, COM(2024) 144, p. 3.

Table 1 (continued)

Council of Europe & UNESCO
• Lisbon Recognition Convention (LRC)[20]
Bologna Process
• The framework of qualifications for the European Higher Education Area (QF-EHEA) • Diploma Supplement • European Credit Transfer and Accumulation System (ECTS)[21] • Standards and guidelines for quality assurance in the EHEA (ESG)
Regional Initiatives
• Benelux Decisions on Automatic Mutual Generic Level Recognition[22]

3 Challenges to Recognition

It is therefore clear that recognition of qualifications has the potential to positively affect mobility *and* that much action has been undertaken to make recognition a reality. However, this does not mean the topic is without fault since attention given to the recognition of qualifications is unfortunately oftentimes negative. Recognition often carries negative associations as it is frequently considered an obstacle to mobility, rather than a facilitator. Proof can be found of both students as well as professionals being confronted with recognition-related challenges. For example, students in the European region were previously found to perceive recognition procedures as problematic—and to have high expectations regarding their mobility.[23] Indeed, expectations of individuals regarding their opportunities for mobility may be more advanced than legislation and policy currently permit. As far as professionals are concerned, the case law of the Court of Justice—with cases on recognition of professional qualifications running in the hundreds—can serve as testament that they too experience issues with recognition.[24] More generally speaking, issues have been found to exist in relation to different phases of the recognition process. For example, issues exist before entering the recognition process (e.g. insufficient awareness of

[20] In this contribution, the term "Lisbon Recognition Convention" is used to refer to the Convention on the Recognition of Qualifications concerning Higher Education in the European Region, Council of Europe and UNESCO, 11 April 1997, ETS—No. 165.

[21] As taken up in: EHEA, Bologna Process and European Commission, *ECTS Users' Guide* (Publications Office of the European Union, 2015).

[22] Beschikking van het Benelux Comité van Ministers betreffende de automatische wederzijdse generieke niveauerkenning van diploma's hoger onderwijs, M(2015) 3; Beschikking van het Benelux Comité van Ministers tot aanvulling van beschikking M(2015) 3 betreffende de automatische wederzijdse generieke niveauerkenning van diploma's hoger onderwijs, M(2018) 1; Verdrag betreffende de automatische erkenning van diploma's in het hoger onderwijs (14 September 2021).

[23] EHEA Pathfinder Group on Automatic Recognition, Report by the EHEA Pathfinder Group on Automatic Recognition: To present to Ministers of the European Area of Higher Education for the Bologna Ministerial Conference 14–15 May 2015, Yerevan, Armenia, January 2015, pp. 14–15.

[24] See also European Court of Auditors (2024) The recognition of professional qualifications in the EU: An essential mechanism, but used sparsely and inconsistently, Special Report 10.

relevant information on recognition, understanding how these systems work), during procedures (e.g. long duration of procedures, difficulties in understanding foreign qualifications), and after recognition (e.g. insufficient evidence on effects of recognition).[25] These sources are but few examples of issues associated with the recognition of qualifications in practice.

Considering the extensive action taken in the area of recognition, we may pose the question where these issues come from. For an answer to this question we can point to two main challenges of the recognition of qualifications. Though each of these challenges is ultimately related to multitude, they manifest themselves in different ways. First, we find multitude in the qualifications subject to recognition. Differences in education systems lead to different diplomas and certificates. Differences which make qualifications incompatible or harder to comprehend—and therefore recognise—across borders. Beyond differences in education systems, professions are also composed differently across Member States. Something which challenges the immediate exercise thereof across the EU. Indeed, recognition in the context of exercising professions is often necessary to ensure a person is sufficiently qualified to work safely in the context of the host Member State. To summarise here, differences in national education systems and professions directly create the need for recognition.

Second, we may also find multitude in the legislation and policy contributing to or effectuating recognition. Table 1 above is a testament of this. Such multitude of instruments is an attempt to bridge differences in national education systems and professions to ultimately effectuate freedom of movement in the EU. Nevertheless, we may question whether the multitude of instruments contributing to or effectuating recognition may itself not be a challenge to freedom of movement. Since such instruments ultimately seek to effectuate free movement for individuals, we may ask whether such an elaborate recognition system is sufficiently comprehensible and ultimately supportive of their ambitions for mobility.

In summary, the complexity in relation to recognition of qualifications comes from (1) differences in national education systems and professions which necessitates recognition in the first place and (2) from the extensive legislative and policy response seeking to bridge those differences and which directly concerns recognition. The successful improvement of recognition is more likely to occur by advancing legislation and policy on topics concerning recognition (challenge number 2), rather than seeking to tackle the multitude of educational systems and professions (challenge number 1). Naturally, the need for recognition could be diminished or even removed by making national education systems and professions more similar. Viewed from the perspective of EU law such ambitions would, however, either require legislative harmonisation imposed top-down or bottom-up voluntary harmonisation between Member States—both of which may be equally difficult to achieve.[26] Compelling reasons are nevertheless the cause of the improbability of large-scale harmonisation

[25] V. Donlevy et al. (2016, pp. 100–101).

[26] Indeed, prior attempts at voluntary harmonisation have yielded limited results. For example, in the 2024 report by Mario Draghi "soft forms of coordination" were found to have led to limited results due to a lack of willingness among Member States. Although these comments were made in

of education systems and professions. Indeed, the organisation of national education systems and professions is closely related to the national identity and culture of Member States, and accordingly something they tend to be protective over. Education policy, for example, has been considered as "high politics" explaining the protectiveness of Member States and corresponding fear of homogenization that could lead to loss of national identity.[27] In particular, education has been considered a remnant of identity politics through which national governments can, among others, create social legitimacy, promote political socialisation, develop democratization, and ultimately preserve national identity.[28]

In EU law, we see a consideration for this importance solidified in the foundational Treaties: the Treaty on European Union (TEU) and the Treaty on the Functioning of the European Union (TFEU). In the TEU, Article 4(2) prescribes that the EU shall respect Member States' national identities as formed by their political and constitutional structures. In that same Article, we may read in paragraph 1 that competences not conferred on the EU remain with the Member States. The principle of conferral laid down in Article 5(1)(2) TEU confirms this and limits EU action to what is explicitly prescribed in the Treaties. Article 5 TEU also sets out the principles of subsidiarity and proportionality. Subsidiarity ensures that EU action is only undertaken if it cannot be sufficiently achieved by the Member States. Proportionality, in turn, limits EU action to what is necessary to achieve the Treaty objectives.

In line with these principles, any EU action therefore starts with the conferral of a competence. Competences can subsequently be categorised in three categories: exclusive, shared, and ancillary. Whereas education constitutes an ancillary competence meaning Member States are in charge while the EU supports them, the internal market is a shared competence meaning that once the EU has become active on a topic it is transferred from the national to the EU level.[29] When it comes to recognition of qualifications, we can see the manifestation of this in Articles 53 and 165 TFEU. Whereas Article 53 TFEU on internal market enables the EU to adopt directives on recognition for professionals, Article 165 TFEU on education prescribes EU action on education-related recognition is aimed at encouraging mobility of students and teachers—thereby excluding any harmonisation of national law.[30]

The protection of national identity serves as an important incentive to argue that action on recognition is to be focused on improving legislation and policy on recognition, rather than to argue for harmonisation of national education systems and professions. In turn, accepting the reality of diverse education systems and professions requires us to divert our attention to the legislation and policy on recognition of qualifications. The recognition of qualifications is the quintessential area where education meets the internal market. Accordingly, the area of education interacts

respect to skills policy, similar approaches may be expected when seeking to coordinate education systems and/or professions; see Draghi (2024b, p. 267).

27 Walkenhorst (2008, p. 567; and the literature cited).

28 Walkenhorst (2005, p. 2).

29 See Articles 2(2)(5), 4(a) and 6(e) TFEU.

30 See in particular paragraph 4 of Article 165 TFEU.

with more economic areas such as the EU internal market and the freedom of movement. Some have found this interaction to result in favour of the internal market, to the detriment of education. For example, Tavares and Sin described the internal market-education relationship as "the visible hand of the market in European (higher) education".[31] However, discussions on the role of economic thinking in education have been taking place more generally. Walkenhorst, for example, noted that policy developments such as the Bologna Process and Lisbon Strategy led to a change in (higher) education policy direction towards economization and functionalization.[32] Therefore, the recognition of qualifications gives rise to questions regarding demarcation between the areas of the internal market and education—and more legally speaking between the respective EU competences in this area (notably in Articles 53 and 165 TFEU). How has the balance been struck between the two areas? How have these competences been employed to contribute to intra-EU mobility? How should the corresponding competences be understood and employed to develop a comprehensive recognition system? Questions such as these are central to the current contribution—and become more important to ask at present in relation to recognition considering some crucial and ambitious plans that have been drawn up in relation to both the internal market and education.

4 Ambitions for the Future: Recognition of Qualifications in Light of the Future Development of the Internal Market and European Education Area

The EU in recent years has been confronted with large scale political, economic and societal developments affecting its way of functioning. For example, the twin transitions require more awareness on regulating the digital spheres and encouraging sustainability through legal and policy action. Simultaneously, changing geopolitical developments are also responsible for a shift away from openness. In turn, this shift leads to a reconsideration of the EU's relationship with the rest of the world[33]—and how it performs in comparison to other world parties. By 2024, these developments led to the introduction of several reports and communications presenting visions of a competitive, resilient, and innovative EU. While visions such as these concern the EU in general, we may find connections to the recognition of qualifications—often described as a means to contribute to the achievement of the ambitions foreseen.

For example, 2024 saw the publication of the report by former Italian Prime Minister and EU rapporteur Enrico Letta. In his report, Letta designates steps urgently needed to propel the Single Market into the future in a sustainable and prosperous manner. The importance of recognition is emphasised in the context of a call to create a sustainable Single Market for all. In particular, the report indicates that, despite

[31] Tavares and Sin (2018).

[32] H. Walkenhorst (2008, p. 567).

[33] See for example Van der Wende (2023).

its successes, the free movement of persons is still the least developed of the four freedoms—and, more importantly, that the opportunities it provides remain limited to a minority of EU citizens.[34] Accordingly, the report calls for a reduction of barriers to occupational mobility, most notably by extending the system of automatic recognition of professional qualifications, reviewing the need for professional regulation, and gaining better understanding of labour shortages and surpluses.[35] It also remarks that skills and labour shortages are a decisive theme for the future of the Internal Market and mentions that the recognition of academic qualifications needs to be simplified and accompanied by the introduction of a European Degree.[36]

While the Letta report reinforced prior actions related to recognition of qualifications, it presented a new vision when it introduced the fifth freedom. Understood to be the freedom to enhance research, innovation, and education in the Single Market, this fifth freedom is foreseen to encourage frontier research and new business models allowing the development of new technologies to ultimately embed research and innovation into the core of the Single Market.[37] The report designates education (and the European Education Area) as a crucial dimension of this fifth freedom. Accordingly, exchanges such as Erasmus are to be enhanced,[38] funding for the European University Alliances to be increased, and the aforementioned European Degree introduced, all to help realise this fifth freedom.[39]

Similar calls were made later that year in the report composed by former president of the European Central Bank Mario Draghi. The report makes note of a marked shift in geopolitics causing former dependencies to turn into vulnerabilities. This combined with speeding technological advances and slowed economic development leads to a need for productivity growth to not only remain competitive in the world, but to also uphold the EU's fundamental values of prosperity, equity, freedom, peace, and democracy in a sustainable environment.[40] The report makes suggestions to advance growth along three lines: closing the innovation gap, creating a joint plan for decarbonisation and competitiveness, and increasing security and reducing dependencies. In the context of the first line consistency in regulation is proposed to advance innovation and allow it to be translated to commercialisation. Part of the proposals also includes ambitious suggestions on advancing skills and

[34] Letta (2024, p. 102).

[35] Ibid.

[36] Ibid.

[37] Ibid., pp. 19–20.

[38] In relation to Erasmus, the report mentions that mobility should be extended to every student, thereby also covering Erasmus under the age of 18. While this initiative serves to level the playing field, it is also paired with an interesting future objective. The report reads: *"By 2030, our goal is to normalise high school student mobility*, underpinned by harmonised educational systems, *enhanced teacher training programs, and increased EU funding. This strategy not only cultivates a more inclusive society but also lays the groundwork for continuous innovation and unity within the EU"*. Considering the known limitations in terms of competences, the elaboration of the point on harmonisation will make for a particularly interesting development to follow.

[39] Letta (2024, pp. 23–24).

[40] Draghi (2024a, p. 1).

education at all ages. Closing the skills gap is primarily presented with the objective of making education and training systems more responsive to changing skills needs. Issues identified concern, for example, the deterioration of the European education systems, limited adult learning, and low labour mobility.[41] In this context, recognition of qualifications and professional regulation again feature as barriers to free movement.

While the main focus of the Draghi report is on the development of adequate skills, the aforementioned elements also touch upon recognition thereof. In terms of proposals, the report remarks that a rethinking of European skills policies needs to include a move from the delivery of diplomas to equipping students and learners with the right skills for the evolving labour market.[42] Soft coordination is to be replaced by greater substantive coordination in terms of the governance models on skills whereby mention is even made of harmonisation of the certification of skills and the revision of curricula where a great role is reserved for higher education institutions in responding to labour market needs. Regarding recognition this should become less focused on formal qualifications and more flexible allowing skills to be validated through diverse pathways.[43]

While it is clear that the Letta and Draghi reports have sketched ambitious visions for the future of the Internal Market, the same can be said in relation to education in the EU. While the initial goal set for the creation of the European Education Area was 2025 (hereinafter: EEA-2025), ambitions have since been strengthened. The development of the EEA-2025 was to focus on six dimensions: quality of education, inclusion & gender, green & digital transitions, teachers & trainers, higher education, and a geopolitical dimension.[44] Recognition of qualifications features as an important objective in the context of several of these dimensions and serves to support the achievement of intra-EU mobility.[45] In particular, the desire is expressed to move towards automatic recognition of qualifications and study periods in the context of higher education as well as the development of a common approach towards micro-credentials as a means to recognise shorter learning moments.[46]

---

[41] Draghi (2024b, pp. 262–266).

[42] Ibid., p. 270.

[43] Ibid., pp. 270–273.

[44] Communication from the Commission to the European Parliament, the Council, the European Economic and Social Committee and the Committee of the Regions on achieving the European Education Area by 2025, COM(2020) 625 final, p. 5.

[45] See for example point 14 Council resolution on the European Education Area: Looking to 2025 and beyond, [2023] OJ C 185/35.

[46] Communication from the Commission to the European Parliament, the Council, the European Economic and Social Committee and the Committee of the Regions on achieving the European Education Area by 2025, COM(2020) 625 final, pp. 11, 15–16 and 20–23; point 1(d)(e), priority area 2(vii)(ix), priority area 4(vi) Council Resolution on a strategic framework for European cooperation in education and training towards the European Education Area and beyond (2021–2030), [2021] OJ C 66/1; Communication from the Commission to the European Parliament, the Council, the European Economic and Social Committee and the Committee of the Regions on progress towards the achievement of the European Education Area, COM(2022) 700 final, pp. 13–14; point 10 and

Visions as ambitious as these regarding the way European citizens are educated and maintain their skills have effects on existing instruments for recognition of qualifications. Indeed, despite their differences in focus pertaining to either the Internal Market or the EEA-2025, some commonalities can be deduced in relation to recognition of qualifications. Most importantly, these ambitions show that the topic continues to be seen as an obstacle to free movement. Furthermore, automatic recognition is to be advanced in both the educational as well as Internal Market contexts. Regarding the latter, professional regulation is furthermore considered a particular obstacle in both the Letta as well as Draghi reports. In the educational context, a call for simplification of recognition has been issued in the Letta report paired with the expression of a desire for a European Degree—something also mirrored in the visions for the EEA-2025. The latter furthermore shares a commonality with the Draghi report when it comes to making learning more flexible, for example in relation to micro-credentials. Such a change from the delivery of diplomas to learning relevant skills and recognition thereof also leads to questions regarding the suitability of the system for qualifications currently in place. Questions can even be raised in relation to legal basis since some of these visions for the future (most notably the Draghi report) foresee revisions of curricula and harmonisation of skills certifications. While matters related to recognition typically concerned articles 53 and 165 TFEU, these proposed activities bring new legal bases into the mix, most notably Articles 145–150 TFEU on employment.[47] To conclude here, it can be said that ambitious visions have been set out for the future of the Internal Market and European Education Area. Despite obviously being broad in scope these visions nevertheless also include plans affecting the current system for recognition of qualifications. Summarising the above, visions for the future on recognition centre on three objectives: more automatic recognition, less (unnecessary) regulation, and more flexibility of learning pathways.[48]

5 Focus of Analysis & Outline

The existence of a multitude of actors together with the level of ambition related to the future of the Internal Market and EEA-2025 require reflection on the current state of the system for recognition of qualifications in the EU. Indeed, the system for the recognition of qualifications was previously subject to an extensive analysis

---

14 Council resolution on the European Education Area: Looking to 2025 and beyond, [2023] OJ C 185/35.

[47] Draghi (2024b, p. 266; footnote 7).

[48] It will be particularly interesting to follow developments in these areas in the upcoming years. At the time of conclusion of this manuscript, the Commission had just launched consultations for an upcoming Skills Portability Initiative bringing together efforts on digitalisation, increased transparency, and improved recognition procedures in relation to skills and qualifications. The adoption of the Skills Portability Initiative was planned for Q3 of 2026.

regarding its coherence.[49] However, in light of the considerable changes in terms of societal context, increased ambitions for the EU internal market and EEA-2025, and legislation and policy contributing to or effectuating recognition it is necessary to revisit the system for recognition. The previous sections give rise to many questions in relation to recognition. For example, we may ask whether the current system for recognition facilitates free movement while providing legal certainty for those needing recognition or whether lacuna can be perceived in the system. In relation to the future ambitions of the EU affecting recognition of qualifications we may ask to which extent the current system for recognition is future proof and capable of advancing the objectives set.

This dual focus on the current functioning of the system for recognition as well as the potential to achieve objectives set for the Internal Market and EEA-2025 are central to the present contribution. In this context, particular attention will be given to the position of mobile EU citizens. Circling back to the start of this introduction, it may be recalled that the freedom of movement is a right all EU citizens have.[50] These free movement rights related to EU citizenship mean that EU citizens should be able to study or work in Member States other than their own. Furthermore, it is important to remark that when recognition is considered an obstacle such a finding usually follows on the experiences of individuals undergoing recognition procedures. In such situations, issues on recognition serve as a direct obstacle to the free movement right of individuals.

Furthermore, in addition to free movement it is important to examine recognition procedures closely in light of legal certainty. A general principle under EU law, it follows that individuals that are undergoing recognition procedures should know precisely which obligations they have under the recognition process and what their rights are during such procedures.[51] Should a person's rights not be respected, the right to an effective remedy means access to justice should be available in such situations.[52] Accordingly, each of these principles covers a different phase in the recognition process. The right to free movement can be considered as the facilitator and initial catalyst in relation to recognition of qualifications (i.e. what enables mobility and therefore makes recognition necessary). Next, legal certainty is what protects individuals during the recognition process. Finally, access to justice ensures individuals can represent their interests in the event that their rights were not respected during a recognition procedure.

In exploring these different aspects of the recognition of qualifications some delineations are to be made to the scope of the analysis. To start, this contribution is primarily oriented towards the EU and approaches the topic from the perspective of

---

[49] See L. Kortese (2020) The Recognition of Qualifications in the EU: Blurring the Lines of Competences between the Internal Market and Education, Doctoral Thesis, Maastricht University.

[50] See Article 3(2) TEU and Articles 20, 21, 45, 49, and 56 TFEU.

[51] See for example Case C-345/06 *Gottfried Heinrich*, ECLI:EU:C:2009:140, para. 44 and Case C-160/20 *Stichting rookpreventie Jeugd v. Staatssecretaris van Volksgezondheid, Welzijn en Sport*, ECLI:EU:C:2022:101, para. 41.

[52] Article 47 CFREU.

the freedom of movement. Instruments included are therefore those that concern the EU and/or the Member States, meaning instruments on recognition originating from international law not aimed at the European region, the EU or the Member States are excluded from the scope of this contribution.[53] The same largely applies for third country nationals and qualifications originating from outside the EU. Although undeniably important and generally under researched, EU citizens and qualifications are the primary focus in this contribution since these are the main addressees of the instruments included for analysis.[54]

Apart from these general delineations, some concepts are of central importance in this contribution and should accordingly be defined. Earlier in this chapter recognition of qualifications was already defined as the process through which foreign qualifications are interpreted in the context of a host Member State's education system or labour market – and ultimately approved for use in that Member State.[55] As indicated previously, a broad scope is adopted in relation to the term recognition which ranges beyond procedures laying down rights and duties for recognition to also include instruments that contribute to recognition by enhancing transparency. In this context, this contribution also includes instruments concerning qualifications frameworks, credit systems, common documentation formats, and quality assurance. As mentioned earlier in Sect. 2 of this chapter, each of these topics constitute areas of study in their own right. However, the present contribution examines these instruments for the role they play in recognizing qualifications. The term qualifications is thereby understood to comprise any diploma, certificate or attestation attesting to certain education completed or professional experience.[56] Although this definition is limited since it places the focus primarily on qualifications obtained in a formal setting, such delineation is necessary for reasons of feasibility. This limitation is however offset by a broader focus in terms of education types. Accordingly, this contribution concerns instruments aimed at both vocational education and training (VET) and higher education.

To examine the current system for recognition and the extent to which it is future-proof this contribution is divided into three parts. Part I focuses on deepening understanding of the system for recognition of qualifications in the EU. Chapter "The Long History of the Recognition of Qualifications in the EU" accordingly discusses the long history of the recognition of qualifications in the EU. Indeed, the topic has been included in the Treaties and subject to EU action since the inception of European cooperation. Chapter "Challenging Convention: Theory, Competences & The Grey Area of Recognition" subsequently examines the current system for recognition by first discussing the theory surrounding recognition. Indeed, recognition of qualifications has long been explained by a typology centred on the different purposes

[53] See Sect. 2, Table 1 for an overview of the instruments included.

[54] Some provisions on recognition are nevertheless provided for non-EU citizens and qualifications issued by third countries. These are explored where appropriate throughout this contribution.

[55] Rauhvargers (2009, p. 111).

[56] This definition largely follows that of the Professional Qualifications Directive. See Article 3(b)(c) of the directive.

for which recognition may be necessary (study or work). Attention is subsequently given to explaining how this typology has been expressed in EU competences and how these ultimately resulted in the current system for recognition. However, this chapter also shows that the typology and related competences do not result in a black and white delineation, arguing that a grey area may be defined challenging our current understanding of recognition types—and their associated competences under EU law. Part II subsequently shifts the focus to the instruments for the recognition of qualifications in the EU. Chapter "Professional Recognition" thereby discusses instruments on recognition related to the exercise of a profession, while Chapter "Academic Recognition" elaborates on instruments related to recognition for educational purposes. Part III subsequently concludes this contribution by assessing in Chapter "Re-Imagining the System for the Recognition of Qualifications in the EU" which strengths and weaknesses the current system for recognition has and how recognition may be optimized to facilitate free movement and make the system for recognition future-proof.

References

Capuano S, Migali S (2017) The migration of professionals within the EU: Any barriers left? Rev Int Econ 25:760–773

Donlevy V, Curtarelli, M, McCoshan, A, Meierkord A (2016) Study on obstacles to recognition of skills and qualifications: final report. Publications Office of the European Union, Luxembourg

Draghi, M. (2024a) The future of European competitiveness: Part A – A competitiveness strategy for Europe

Draghi, M. (2024b) The future of European competitiveness: Part B – In-depth analysis and recommendations

Jefferies D, Evetts J (2000) Approaches to the international recognition of professional qualifications in engineering and the sciences. Eur J Eng Educ 25:99–107

Letta, E. (2024) Much more than a market: speed, security, solidarity – empowering the Single Market to deliver a sustainable future and prosperity for all EU citizens

Lettmayr CF, Martin L (2013) The role of qualifications in governing occupations and professions. Cedefop Working Paper No. 20

Rauhvargers A (2009) Recognition and qualifications frameworks. Assess Educ Princ Policy Pract 16(2009):111–125

Tavares O, Sin C (2018) The visible hand of the market in European higher education policies. In: Sin C et al (eds) European Higher Education and the internal market: tensions between European policy and national sovereignty. Palgrave Macmillan, Cham, pp 363–375

Van der Wende M (2023) "How open can it be?" The promise of open systems and open science under siege. In: Engwall L (ed) Internationalization in higher education and research. Springer, Cham, pp 97–115

Walkenhorst H (2005) The changing role of eu education policy – a critical assessment. Paper for the EUSA 9th Biennal International Conference

Walkenhorst H (2008) Explaining change in EU education policy. J Eur Publ Policy 15:567–587

Understanding the Status Quo of the Recognition of Qualifications

The Long History of the Recognition of Qualifications in the EU

1 Introduction

The introduction to this contribution showed that recognition of qualifications is an area characterised by multitude, whether it be in terms of courses of study and professions, or in terms of the legislation and policy on recognition adopted by various actors. Recognition of qualifications in the EU has a long history since it was one of the areas included in the Treaties at the start of European cooperation. While EU action was initially economically motivated and aimed at professionals (in the context of the free movement of workers, services, and establishment), it later also focused on enabling mobility in an educational context. Indeed, over the course of time, EU action has been adopted to facilitate recognition in both the contexts of work and study to ultimately improve the freedom of movement. However, the EU is not the sole actor improving recognition of qualifications since such action has also been taken in the context of the Bologna Process, Council of Europe and UNESCO, and even regionally such as in the Benelux. Looking back at the development of recognition is necessary to contribute to a better understanding of the system as it stands today. The present chapter therefore serves as a basis for the explanation of the theory and ultimately examination of the current system for recognition in Chapter 3 "Challenging Convention: Theory, Competences & The Grey Area of Recognition".

L. S.J. Kortese, *Effectuating Free Movement in the EU through Recognition of Qualifications*, https://doi.org/10.1007/978-3-032-21335-8_2

2 EU Action on Recognition

2.1 Recognition in the Early Days of European Integration

The recognition of qualifications in the EU started with the 1957 Treaty of Rome that, among others, established the free movement rights of citizens in the European Economic Community (EEC). Article 57 EEC Treaty[1] was placed under the chapter on the freedom of movement, the right of establishment to be exact. From that point onwards, work started on recognition related to the exercise of professions, i.e. professional recognition. The early days of European cooperation can be considered a search for a suitable legislative approach to professional recognition. Between the 1960s and 1990s we can indeed observe an evolution from a transitional approach to a vertical one, and ultimately to a horizontal approach—the legacy of which we still find in today's Professional Qualifications Directive.[2]

The 1960s transitional approach involved the creation of numerous directives that concerned recognition of professional qualifications in sectors such as commerce, industry, and small crafts industries.[3] Under these directives, professionals could exercise their professional activity in all other Community Member States. From the start, it was however clear that this was due to be a temporary approach: these directives were supposed to apply for a limited period of time only (hence the denomination of the transitional period). In particular, these directives applied for the period in which harmonisation of the conditions for the exercise of certain professional activities was pending.[4] Since they were created at a time when no harmonisation had yet been attempted in this area and the direct effect of the relevant Treaty Articles had not yet been established, the transitional approach resulted in directives that were fairly ineffective and rarely challenged before the Court of Justice.[5]

It may therefore come as no surprise that this approach was soon abandoned in favour of a vertical approach taken in the 1970s. The vertical approach was the European institutions' attempt at liberalising the regulated professions of medical doctors, nurses, dentists, veterinarians, midwives and pharmacists by establishing minimum harmonisation of education and their mutual recognition.[6] These vertical

[1] Current Article 53 TFEU.

[2] In this research, the term "Professional Qualifications Directive" is used to refer to Directive 2005/36/EC of the European Parliament and of the Council of 7 September 2005 on the recognition of professional qualifications, [2005] OJ L 255/22 *as amended by* Directive 2013/55/EU of the European Parliament and of the Council of 20 November 2013 amending Directive 2005/36/EC on the recognition of professional qualifications and Regulation (EU) No 1024/2012 on administrative cooperation through the Internal Market Information System ('the IMI Regulation'), [2013] OJ L 354/132. The consolidated version of the Professional Qualifications Directive can be accessed at: https://eur-lex.europa.eu/legal-content/EN/TXT/?uri=CELEX%3A02005L0036-20251029.

[3] Lettmayr and Martin (2013, p. 35).

[4] Hatzopoulos (2012, p. 238).

[5] Ibid., pp. 238–239.

[6] Claessens (2008, p. 25).

directives consisted of two complementary directives per profession: one containing harmonised educational standards and the other containing procedural standards for recognition.[7] The vertical approach was only maintained for a relatively short period of time due to its complexity. Indeed, reaching unanimity on the content of the directives was a lengthy process and the administrative burden that was paired with the regular revision of the different directives was bound to be very cumbersome.[8] Hatzopoulos furthermore notes that, apart from long negotiations, this approach also concerned areas which were subject to, among others, cultural and ideological prejudice and very much prone to corporatist control.[9]

The 1980s marked a shift in the approach to recognising professional qualifications. Due to its complexities, the Commission abandoned the vertical approach creating professional recognition legislation per profession and adopted a new approach in which mutual recognition without prior harmonisation was maintained.[10] While this system was much less cumbersome than the vertical approach, it did not lead to the promotion of a European identity of certain professions since no harmonised standards for education were involved in this approach.[11] In particular, the horizontal approach was based on the idea that—though different—programmes of study and training have equal validity across the Member States.[12] This era is ultimately marked by a change from harmonisation of education and training for certain professions to mutual recognition. Formulated differently, the focus shifted from attempting to harmonise education and training to create "European professions", to an approach which would lead to the mutual acceptance of qualifications in accordance with how these were issued in the Member States.

Though implemented in legislation, the change to the horizontal approach can be said to have been initiated through case law of the Court of Justice. The 1970s were the era in which the CJEU had issued several seminal cases on recognition and free movement. Apart from establishing the direct effect of the Treaty provisions on establishment and services,[13] the Court also abolished nationality, residence, and establishment requirements. For example, in *Reyners* the Court determined that a

---

[7] Doctors: Directive 75/362/EEC and Directive 76/363/EEC; Nurses: Directive 77/452/EEC and Directive 77/453/EEC; Dentists: Directive 78/686/EEC and Directive 78/687/EEC; Veterinarians: 78/1026/EEC and Directive 78/1027/EEC; Midwives; Directive 80/154/EEC and Directive 80/155/EEC; Pharmacists: Directive 85/432/EEC and Directive 85/433/EEC. Directives were also issued for the professions of lawyers (Council Directive 77/249/EEC and Directive 98/5/EC) and architects (Council Directive 85/384/EEC), although no minimum harmonisation of education was established for these professions. This means that the directives for lawyers and architects consisted only of procedural provisions on recognition as opposed to harmonised education. See Schneider and Claessens (2005, p. 138).

[8] Minor (1992, p. 3).

[9] Hatzopoulos (2012, p. 241).

[10] Schneider and Claessens (2005, p. 139).

[11] Minor (1992, p. 3).

[12] Schoenmaekers (2010, p. 89).

[13] See Case 2/74 *Reyners*, EU:C:1974:68, para. 24–30; Case 33/74 *Van Binsbergen*, EU:C:1974:131, para. 18 and 27; Case 11/77 *Patrick*, EU:C:1977:113, para. 9, 14–16.

nationality requirement was not consistent with the Treaty. Reyners had been prohibited from practicing as a lawyer in Belgium due to his Dutch nationality. This despite the fact that he had been trained as a lawyer in Belgium. At the time, Belgium maintained a nationality requirement meaning practicing lawyers had to be Belgian nationals. The Belgian State attempted at justifying its nationality requirement by arguing the profession was connected to the exercise of official authority, which the CJEU did not accept. In particular, the Court did not consider any of the activities of the lawyer profession to be connected to the exercise of official authority.[14] Following the Court's judgment, Reyners had to be able to exercise his profession in the Belgium.

Apart from nationality requirements, the Court also made short work of national requirements restricting establishment. In *Klopp*, for example, the Court determined that, although Member States are free to regulate professions, this does not mean they can limit professionals to having an establishment in only one Member State as that would clearly limit the freedom of establishment. Klopp was already a member of the Düsseldorf bar and sought to be admitted to the Paris bar association—a request that was denied due to the territorial limitation maintained in French law. The Court particularly considered that such a requirement would mean lawyers could only make use of their free movement if they would abandon their existing establishment, something the free movement provisions in the Treaty certainly did not intend.[15] While *Klopp* concerned a requirement regarding establishment, *Van Binsbergen* concerned a residence requirement. Van Binsbergen was a Dutch national living in the Netherlands who could not be represented by his Dutch lawyer who was residing in Belgium. Dutch law at the time required legal representatives to be established in the Netherlands, a practice again considered contrary to free movement by the CJEU.[16] Apart from ruling on the residence requirement, the Court in *Van Binsbergen* also laid the foundation for the development of a rule of reason in relation to the free movement of services which enables the justification of restrictions to free movement in the event that Member States have compelling interests.[17] Such a rule serves as a way to balance the achievement of free movement in the EU with Member States' interests. The development of this rule of reason in the context of the free movement of services can be considered to have paved the way for the introduction of the principle of mutual recognition which would become fundamental to the horizontal approach on recognition of qualifications.

[14] Case 2/74 *Reyners*, EU:C:1974:68, para. 51–55.

[15] Case 107/83 *Klopp*, EU:C:1984:270, para. 18–19.

[16] Case 33/74 *Van Binsbergen*, EU:C:1974:131.

[17] Claessens (2008, p. 16).

2.2 *Introducing Mutual Recognition to the Recognition of Qualifications*

Of course, mutual recognition was not new since it was already introduced in the 1970s when the Court issued its judgment in *Cassis de Dijon*. In that case, the Court held that additional requirements imposed by a Member State on products lawfully produced and marketed in another Member State were to be considered a restriction deemed incompatible with the Treaty.[18] Therefore, a product that was lawfully brought on the market in one Member State was to be considered as such in all Member States. To balance the effects of mutual recognition in the national legal systems, the Court also developed the rule of reason through which Member States could justify measures restricting free movement if there were pressing reasons in the public interest. While the principle of mutual recognition was therefore introduced in relation to the free movement of goods, it later also became relevant for qualifications. Indeed, the reasoning from *Cassis de Dijon* was extended to the recognition of qualifications in the *Vlassopoulou* case.[19]

The case concerned a Greek lawyer with a degree in German law who was denied access to practise as a lawyer in Germany for not having the relevant qualifications. However, Vlassopoulou was already practising law in Germany, be it under the responsibility of one of her German colleagues. The Court considered that, in the absence of harmonising legislation,[20] Member States were obliged to take all appropriate measures to attain the objective of freedom of establishment. National qualification requirements that did not take into account the knowledge and qualifications acquired in another Member State could hinder professionals in making use of their right of free movement,[21] thus constituting an infringement. Therefore, in order to ensure that the foreign diploma was at least equivalent to that of the host State, Member States had to "take into consideration the diplomas, certificates and other evidence of formal qualifications which the person concerned has acquired in order to exercise the same profession in another Member State by making a comparison between the specialised knowledge and abilities certified by those diplomas and the knowledge and qualifications required by the national rules", thereby focusing on the nature and duration of the studies and training.[22] If the foreign qualifications were then found to correspond to the national provisions, Member States had to recognise the diploma. The *Vlassopoulou* case therefore not only extended the principle of

---

[18] Case 120/78 *Rewe-Zentral AG (Cassis de Dijon)*, EU:C:1979:42, para. 14–15.

[19] Schneider and Claessens (2005, p. 139).

[20] The case was not assessed in the context of Directive 89/48/EEC because, at the time of the case, the implementation period had not yet passed. This meant that Vlassopoulou could not yet rely directly on the provisions of the Directive. Therefore, the case needed to be assessed on the basis of Article 52 EEC Treaty, which imposed a clear obligation on the Member States to attain freedom of establishment. See: Opinion of Advocate General Van Gerven in Case C-340/89 *Vlassopoulou*, EU:C:1991:426, para. 3; Case C-340/89 *Vlassopoulou*, EU:C:1991:193, para. 13.

[21] Case C-340/89 *Vlassopoulou*, EU:C:1991:193, para. 15.

[22] Ibid., para. 16–18.

mutual recognition to the area of qualifications, but also created a back-up system for all cases that did not fall within the scope of Union directives—a system that has been extended over the course of time and continues to apply present-day.[23]

From a legislative perspective, mutual recognition also soon became the core characteristic of the horizontal approach. The introduction of mutual recognition as a legislative approach was set in motion during the 1984 Fontainebleau European Council meeting. At the meeting, the Heads of State asked the Council and the Member States to conduct a study enabling the creation of "a general system for ensuring the equivalence of university diplomas, in order to bring about the effective freedom of establishment within the Community".[24] This request ultimately led to the adoption of Directive 89/48/EEC containing the general system based on mutual recognition and the comparability of levels of education and training (instead of their similarity as agreed in the vertical approach).[25] The scope of Directive 89/48/EEC was limited to those wishing to pursue a *regulated professional activity*,[26] a characteristic still present in today's Professional Qualifications Directive. Application of these directives has therefore always been limited to those professions for which qualification requirements are laid down in national legislation. Professionals exercising such professions will need to obtain recognition of their qualifications (i.e. approval by a competent authority) before they will be able to initiate the exercise of their profession. Apart from the focus on regulated professions, Directive 89/48/EEC would also apply only to those professionals that were not already subject to another directive establishing conditions for the mutual recognition of diplomas. Therefore, Directive 89/48/EEC co-existed with the sectoral directives adopted at the time of the vertical approach.[27] Directive 89/48/EEC would later be supplemented by two more directives: Directive 92/51/EEC which extended the scope of the general system to qualifications resulting from secondary education, and Directive 1999/42/EC which consolidated the directives adopted in the transitional approach.[28]

---

[23] See Chapter "Professional Recognition ", Sect. 6 of this contribution.

[24] European Council Meeting at Fontainebleau—Conclusions of the Presidency, 25 and 26 June 1984, p. 8.

[25] Council Directive of 21 December 1988 on a general system for the recognition of higher-education diplomas awarded on completion of professional education and training of at least three years' duration (89/48/EEC), [1989] OJ L 19/16.

[26] Article 2, first sentence Directive 89/48/EEC.

[27] White (2004, p. 67).

[28] Council Directive 92/51/EEC of 18 June 1992 on a second general system for the recognition of professional education and training to supplement Directive 89/48/EEC, [1992] OJ L 209/25; Directive 1999/42/EC of the European Parliament and of the Council of 7 June 1999 establishing a mechanism for the recognition of qualifications in respect of the professional activities covered by the Directives on liberalisation and transitional measures and supplementing the general systems for the recognition of qualifications, [1999] OJ L 201/77.

2.3 The Era of Consolidation in the 2000s: Introducing Directive 2005/36/EC and Its Modernisation Through Directive 2013/55/EU

It may come as no surprise that all action on the recognition of qualifications in the 2000s can be retraced to the 2000 Lisbon Strategy. That strategy is best-known for the EU's strategic goal "to become the most competitive and dynamic knowledge-based economy in the world capable of sustainable economic growth with more and better jobs and greater social cohesion" by 2010.[29] Accordingly, general system Directives 89/48/EEC and 92/51/EEC as well as the 12 directives regulating recognition for the sectoral professions[30] were updated through Directive 2001/19/EEC.[31] This latter Directive was nicknamed the SLIM Directive since it was adopted within the framework of the Commission's pilot project Simpler Legislation for the Internal Market (SLIM).[32] The SLIM Directive amended and introduced a vast array of provisions to the aforementioned Directives. Examples of updates include the incorporation of a requirement for Member States to consider professional experience, the updating of system for automatic recognition, and to a certain extent the clarification of the position of holders of third country qualifications.[33] The amendments made by the SLIM Directive nevertheless proved not to be sufficient since the subsequent proposal for legislative change was already introduced a year later in 2002.[34] This proposal would ultimately lead to the introduction of the main instrument on professional recognition we know today, namely the Professional Qualifications Directive.[35] The proposal for this directive sought to achieve greater liberalisation of service provision, increased automatic recognition, and more flexibility in the procedures allowing the directive to remain up-to-date and contribute to the knowledge-based economy. Furthermore, the new directive was also to consolidate all previous directives on recognition:

---

[29] Lisbon European Council, 23 and 24 March 2000—Presidency Conclusions.

[30] Doctors, general care nurses, dentists, veterinarians, midwives, architects, and pharmacists.

[31] Directive 2001/19/EC of the European Parliament and of the Council of 14 May 2001 amending Council Directives 89/48/EEC and 92/51/EEC on the general system for the recognition of professional qualifications and Council Directives 77/452/EEC, 77/453/EEC, 78/686/EEC, 78/687/EEC, 78/1026/EEC, 78/1027/EEC, 80/154/EEC, 80/155/EEC, 85/384/EEC, 85/432/EEC, 85/433/EEC and 93/16/EEC concerning the professions of nurse responsible for general care, dental practitioner, veterinary surgeon, midwife, architect, pharmacist and doctor, [2001] OJ L 206/1.

[32] Communication from the Commission to the Council and the European Parliament—Simpler Legislation for the Internal Market (SLIM): A Pilot Project, COM(96) 204 final.

[33] Recital 3, 5, 6 Directive 2001/19/EC. In relation to holders of third country qualifications, the SLIM Directive abandoned the case law of the Court of Justice in cases such as *Tawil Albertini* and *Haim I* where the Court ruled that a prior recognition of third country qualifications in one Member State had no effects on a subsequent recognition in a second Member State; Case C-154/93 *Tawil Albertini*, EU:C:1994:51, para. 12–13; Case C-319/92 *Haim I*, EU:C:1994:47, para. 19–22.

[34] Proposal for a Directive of the European Parliament and of the Council on the recognition of professional qualifications, COM(2002) 119 final.

[35] Directive 2005/36/EC of the European Parliament and of the Council of 7 September 2005 on the recognition of professional qualifications, [2005] OJ L 255/22.

i.e. Directives 89/48/EEC, 92/51/EEC, and 1999/42/EC, as well as the 12 sectoral directives adopted under the 1970s vertical approach.[36]

Nevertheless, the proposal also coincided with the 2004 accession, meaning it was also aimed at simplifying the administrative procedures on recognition to facilitate the addition of ten new education systems to the EU.[37] Moreover, the situation of the labour market and professions differed considerably in the new Member States. For example, Poland had high levels of unemployment and lower wages than the EU-15 States. These factors contributed to a high propensity for migration from Poland to Western Europe.[38] When focusing on the health sector, the strong push–pull factor increasing the probability of migration from the new Member States to the EU-15 States was furthermore fuelled by bad working conditions due to underfinanced medical institutions and low job satisfaction among healthcare professionals.[39] An adaptation of the recognition regime was therefore considered a suitable means to support the expected migration from the new Member States. However, this turned out not to be self-evident. D'Artillac-Brill noted that "for mutual trust to be the basis of recognition, there has to be some experience with the different foreign qualifications, and such experience can be slow to build up".[40] Indeed, mutual recognition and mutual trust are strongly interconnected although mutual trust is generally considered a prerequisite for well-functioning mutual recognition.[41] As far as the new Member States were concerned, the EU-15 States needed to first gain experience with these new qualifications.[42] The introduction of a new directive was considered to support such a process.

The changes made to the regime concerning the recognition of professional qualifications in the past two decades have quickly succeeded each other. After the implementation of Directive 2005/36/EC was finally completed in all Member States in 2010, the Commission did not hesitate to present a proposal for the modernisation of that same directive in the subsequent year.[43] The main reason for the modernisation of Directive 2005/36/EC was the demand for highly skilled workers being on the rise, thus leaving Europe with the task to meet that demand by filling the gaps in labour shortages through mobile and qualified EU professionals.[44] In the proposal,

[36] Recital 9 Directive 2005/36/EC of the European Parliament and of the Council of 7 September 2005 on the recognition of professional qualifications, [2005] OJ L 255/22.

[37] Van Riemsdijk (2013a, p. 54).

[38] Van Riemsdijk (2013b, p. 121).

[39] Gerlinger and Schmucker (2007, p. 187).

[40] D'Artillac Brill (2009, p. 19).

[41] Cambien (2017, p. 114).

[42] D'Artillac Brill (2009, p. 19).

[43] Proposal for a Directive of the European Parliament and of the Council amending Directive 2005/36/EC on the recognition of professional qualifications and regulation on administrative cooperation through the Internal Market Information System, COM(2011) 883 final.

[44] European Commission, Modernising the Professional Qualifications Directive will make it easier for professionals to find skilled jobs across Europe, 19 December 2011, Press release IP/11/1562.

it was noted that the recognition of professional qualifications was key to making the four freedoms a reality in the Internal Market.[45]

Directive 2013/55/EU was adopted in November 2013 and introduced certain innovative provisions to the benefit of the intra-EU mobility of professionals. Some of the key elements introduced by the modernising directive were the introduction of a European Professional Card, the introduction of an alert mechanism for healthcare professions, and the creation of common training principles as a way to extend the system for automatic recognition to professions currently not subject to it.[46] The directive also included an extensive mutual evaluation and transparency exercise with the objective of taking stock of which professions were regulated and how to initiate a dialogue about the need and motivation for certain qualification requirements. While such requirements may protect service recipients, their effect on mobility can be quite restrictive since they result in the application of the Professional Qualifications Directive and therefore need to undergo a recognition procedure before being able to carry out the profession.[47] Efforts related to the mutual evaluation exercise introduced by Directive 2013/55/EU ultimately resulted in the addition of the last legislative branch to the existing legislation on recognition of professional qualifications, namely Directive 2018/958. This Directive codified the Court's case law on proportionality tests[48] and serves to support Member States in making appropriate choices related to the regulation of their professions at the national level.[49]

Updates to the applicable EU legislation on recognition of professional qualifications have therefore quickly superseded each other—especially in recent years. Further changes may thereby be on the horizon since both Directive 2013/55/EU

[45] Proposal for a Directive of the European Parliament and of the Council amending Directive 2005/36/EC on the recognition of professional qualifications and regulation on administrative cooperation through the Internal Market Information System, COM(2011) 883 final, p. 2.

[46] These are professions currently subject to the general system of the Professional Qualifications Directive which will become subject to automatic recognition once a common training principle is adopted. Common training principles are discussed in more detail in Chapter "Professional Recognition" of this contribution.

[47] See Koumenta and Pagliero (2016).

[48] As previously developed in cases such as Case C-55/94 *Gebhard*, EU:C:1995:411. Gebhard was a German national who lived and practised law in Milan. At first, he worked in an Italian law firm assisting lawyers, but he later opened his own office to practise law under the Italian title of *avvocato*. He was sanctioned for using that title in contravention of national law. Carrying out a profession could be made conditional on other provisions laid down by national law, for example, stipulating that a profession is restricted to holders of a certain diploma, certificate or other evidence of professional qualifications. Nevertheless, the Court indicated that "national measures liable to hinder or make less attractive the exercise of fundamental freedoms guaranteed by the Treaty" had to pass the proportionality test, thus fulfilling four conditions not to infringe EU law: (1) national legislation setting conditions for the exercise of a profession had to be applied in a non-discriminatory manner, (2) had to be justified by imperative requirements in the general interest, (3) had to be suitable for attaining the pursued objective, and (3) needed to be proportionate.

[49] Directive (EU) 2018/958 of the European Parliament and of the Council of 28 June 2018 on a proportionality test before adoption of new regulation on professions, [2018] OJ L 173/25.

and the Proportionality Test Directive were recently subject to evaluation.[50] Furthermore, another evaluation from the Commission on the Professional Qualifications Directive appears to be underway,[51] meaning it will be interesting to follow such developments for their potential future amendments.

2.4 The Evolution of Action on Academic Recognition in the EU

While the typology for recognition will be discussed extensively in Chapter "Challenging Convention: Theory, Competences & The Grey Area of Recognition", the introduction to this contribution already indicated that instruments on recognition of qualifications are generally developed for either one of two purposes: work or study. The developments described in the previous sections concerned recognition in the context of work, i.e. professional recognition. These sections showed that the EU has undertaken extensive action in the field of professional recognition and that such action was primarily aimed at regulated professions. All action described in those sections took place in the context of the Internal Market and the fundamental freedoms and were therefore ultimately aimed at the taking up and pursuit of activities of self-employed persons and workers. This can be explained by the EU's initial focus being oriented strongly to achieving economic integration.

However, professional recognition is supplemented by academic recognition, a type of recognition which is considered less economically motivated and more strongly connected to education.[52] It may be recalled that education concerns a sensitive policy area due to its strong connection with national identity.[53] Action on

[50] Report from the Commission to the European Parliament, the Council, the European Economic and Social Committee and the Committee of the Regions on the implementation of certain new elements introduced by Directive 2013/55/EU of the European Parliament and of the Council of 20 November 2013 amending Directive 2005/36/EC on the recognition of professional qualifications and Regulation (EU) No 1024/2012 on administrative cooperation through the Internal Market Information System ('the IMI Regulation'), COM(2020) 191 final; European Court of Auditors (2024) The recognition of professional qualifications in the EU: An essential mechanism, but used sparsely and inconsistently, Special Report 10; Report from the Commission to the European Parliament and the Council on the implementation of Directive (EU) 2018/958 of the European Parliament and of the Council of 28 June 2018 on a proportionality test before adoption of new regulation of professions, COM(2024) 544 final.

[51] See, for example, European Commission, Minutes Meeting of the Group of Coordinators for the recognition of professional qualifications, 20 June 2024. At the time of completion of this manuscript (December 2025), the report had not yet been published. Nevertheless, new action which also concerns regulated professions was announced at that time in the form of the Skills Portability Initiative. At the time of conclusion of this manuscript, consultations for that initiative had just been initiated.

[52] Garben (2011a, p. 131).

[53] Walkenhorst (2008, p. 567; and the literature cited). See also Chapter "Introduction", Sect. 3 of this contribution.

academic recognition started at a later stage of European integration: it was only with the entry into force of the 1992 Maastricht Treaty that the EU gained an explicit competence on education. Before that time, the governments of the Member States could only discuss educational policy through intergovernmental cooperation.[54]

The fact that academic recognition was not expressly included in the Treaties did not mean that the EU undertook no action at all in this area. In fact, the development of Community action on education can also be traced to the 1957 Rome Treaty. That Treaty included Article 128 which stated that the Community would "lay down general principles for implementing a common vocational training policy capable of contributing to the harmonious development both of the national economies and of the common market". As the initial wording of the Community's competence on vocational training shows that the improvement of such training was held capable of supporting the economy and the common market, indicating that the Article's underlying motivation was economic in nature.

Despite the inclusion of vocational education and training in the Treaty of Rome, Community action on education can be considered to have started considerably later than professional recognition, namely in the 1970s and 1980s.[55] Although the EU refrained from adopting binding rules on education, it did adopt several resolutions and conclusions: all intergovernmental agreements adopted outside the Community legal framework. These primarily served as a means to express a political understanding. However, these measures were also considered to have the potential to lead to national policymaking and could therefore be considered as preparatory measures for larger-scale action.[56] In fact, one of the resolutions adopted during this phase concerned the mutual recognition of qualifications and expressed the desire to create directives on the right of establishment but emphasised that such directives were crucial in connection with education policies and should not impede efforts towards educational reform.[57] This resolution can serve as example of the interconnection of the areas of internal market and education where recognition of qualifications is concerned. In a similar vein, the Council of Ministers on Education,[58] identified a

[54] De Witte (1992, p. 85).

[55] For a detailed account on education as an emerging Community legislative and policy area see De Witte (1989).

[56] Lenaerts (1994, p. 9–10), De Witte (1992, p. 86).

[57] Council Resolution of 6 June 1974 on the mutual recognition of diplomas, certificates and other evidence of formal qualifications, [1974] OJ C 98/1.

[58] At this time, education was a topic at the periphery of Community competences. This meant that Education Ministers would first meet outside the Community structure thus providing for a cooperation that was truly intergovernmental. However, over the course of time the Ministers for Education started meeting less outside the Community framework and more within it until finally they met biannually in the meetings of the Council. There, they would meet in two capacities: once in the context of the Council meaning they could adopt formal decisions of the Council of Ministers and once in an intergovernmental capacity in which they could continue to adopt resolutions and conclusions that would express political commitments but without binding effects; see De Witte (1992, p. 86). For more on the legal nature of the resolutions adopted by the Education Ministers see Van Craeyenest (1989, pp. 127–128).

number of points of action in another resolution which included improved possibilities for academic recognition and encouragement of the freedom of movement and mobility of teachers, students and researchers.[59] In 1976, the Council adopted an Action Programme on education which can be considered a first step to the well-known Erasmus programme. When it was originally introduced, the programme aimed to improve cooperation in the field of higher education by, among others, promoting the free movement of teaching staff, students and researchers, and by increasing the possibilities for academic recognition.[60]

Nevertheless, the real impetus for the creation of the Erasmus programme came in the 1980s. At the 1984 Fontainebleau European Council Meeting, the Ministers not only discussed the creation of a general system for professional recognition as discussed in the sections above, they also established an *ad hoc* Committee aimed at ensuring that the Community responded to the expectations of the people of Europe.[61] The Adonnino Committee was accordingly concerned with a great number of topics, including improvements to be made to higher education and academic recognition.[62] In particular, it proposed an extensive exchange programme, examining the possibility of introducing a European system of academic credits transferable throughout the Community, and requesting academic authorities to recognise foreign diplomas as they would when assessing diplomas issued by other national higher education institutions.[63] These proposals ultimately led to the creation of the Comett[64] and the Erasmus Programmes.[65] Contrary to the Community's prior action on education, the adoption of the Comett and Erasmus decisions did fall within the scope of the

[59] Resolution of the Ministers of Education meeting within the Council, of 6 June 1974 on cooperation in the field of education, [1974] OJ C 98/2.

[60] Resolution of the Council and of the Ministers of Education meeting within the Council of 9 February 1976 comprising an action programme in the field of education, [1976] OJ C 38/1, pp. 3–4.

[61] European Council Meeting at Fontainebleau—Conclusions of the Presidency, 25 and 26 June 1984, p. 8.

[62] Dalichow (1987, p. 43).

[63] Ad hoc Committee "On a People's Europe" (the Adonnino Committee), Report to the European Council, pp. 18–19.

[64] The programme on cooperation between universities and enterprises regarding training in the field of technology (Comett) was adopted via a Council decision in 1986. Its most important objectives were to give a European dimension to the cooperation between universities and enterprises operating in the area of technology and to foster the joint development of training programmes and exchanging experience; see Articles 3(a)(b) Council decision of 24 July 1986 adopting the programme on cooperation between universities and enterprises regarding training in the field of technology (COMETT), [1986] OJ L 222/17.

[65] The European Community Action Scheme for the Mobility of University Students (Erasmus) came into force in 1987 and was specifically aimed at improving the mobility of teachers and students. Its main goals were to achieve a significant increase in the number of students studying in another Member State, to promote broad and intensive inter-university cooperation, increase mobility of teaching staff, strengthen interaction between citizens, and ensure the existence of a pool of university graduates with experience in intra-Community cooperation Articles 2(i)(ii)(iii)(iv)(v) Council Decision of 15 June 1987 adopting the European Community Action Scheme for the Mobility of University Students (ERASMUS), [1987] OJ L 166/20.

Community's legal framework.[66] The Comett and Erasmus Decisions were based on Articles 128 and 235 EEC Treaty. Article 128 constituted the competence on vocational training while Article 235 granted the possibility to adopt legislation on topics relating to the common market for which the Community did not have the necessary powers. However, the opportunity provided by Article 235 EEC Treaty was subject to the caveat of Council unanimity. Article 235 EEC Treaty was particularly controversial, since it both protected Member State interests by requiring unanimity and simultaneously granted the Community powers to extend its competences to areas not covered by the Treaties as long as it concerned the common market.[67] In the case of the Erasmus programme, the use of Article 235 EEC Treaty as a legal basis was subject to proceedings between the Commission and the Council before the CJEU.[68]

2.5 Creating Space for Academic Recognition: An Education Competence in the Maastricht Treaty

The Maastricht Treaty introduced a great deal of change in 1992. Not only did it establish the EU, it also introduced new concepts into the Treaties such as that of European citizenship and *education*. The road to the introduction of education into the Treaties was long and winding, as education was a typical policy area over which Member States wished to retain control. The reason for the sensitivity of the topic relates to the fact that education may be used to promote societal values, among others, and a loss of competence over education could go so far as to lead to a loss of national identity.[69] Education finally featured in the Treaties in 1992 by the efforts of Jacques Delors and his staff, an achievement they managed to accomplish by declaring the policy area of education to be a "co-ownership" of the Member States and the Union and by stating it would be governed by the principle of subsidiarity.[70]

The Treaty of Maastricht introduced Article 126 and renewed Article 127, which respectively dealt with education and vocational training. While the introduction of Article 126 ensured an explicit competence on education was now taken up in the Treaties, it also solidified the legal dichotomy between professional and academic recognition (i.e. recognition for work and study purposes). Action on professional recognition as was previously discussed in relation to the directives above had previously been based on Article 57 EEC Treaty, a provision which mentioned recognition but not specifically professional recognition. The division between the two types

[66] Indeed, decisions were explicitly mentioned in Article 189 EEC Treaty (current Article 288 TFEU).

[67] Blitz (2003, p. 203).

[68] Case 242/87 *Commission v. Council (Erasmus)*, EU:C:1989:217. The case is discussed more extensively in Chapter "Challenging Convention: Theory, Competences & The Grey Area of Recognition", Sect. 5.

[69] Walkenhorst (2008, pp. 567–568).

[70] Blitz (2003, p. 209).

of recognition became final since Article 126(2) EC Treaty mentioned the promotion of the mobility of students and teachers through, *inter alia*, academic recognition. Furthermore, the divide between the two types of recognition was strengthened because Article 126(4) also expressly excluded "any harmonisation of the laws and regulations of the Member States". Therefore, even if the policy objectives on education were formulated broadly, Union action in this area was limited in terms of the legal instruments to be used due to the prohibition of harmonisation.[71] Despite the solidification of a divide, some nuance is nevertheless to be made in relation to the Maastricht Treaty. In practice, the Maastricht Treaty this did not change much when it came to creating legislation on education. The pre-Maastricht era of education was just as much characterised by soft law instruments as the post-Maastricht era obliged it to be. According to Ertl, the post-Maastricht era of EU education and training policy of the early 1990s was dominated by subsidiarity-related restrictions, non-harmonisation, and ineffective administration and disproportionate bureaucracy related to the programmes adopted during that period.[72] However, what the new competence did was to establish a new and explicit legal basis, meaning that Article 235 EEC Treaty would no longer need to be used for issues concerning education.

As the end of the 1990s approached, the new millennium brought a new strategic goal for the Union that not only came to influence the EU's policy on the recognition of professional qualifications but also affected its approach to the field of education. Again, the Lisbon Strategy's goal of the EU becoming "the most competitive and dynamic knowledge-based economy in the world" also became the basis of the EU's action on education and training.[73] The 2002 Council Work Programme on education and training, also known as Education and Training 2010, set three main strategic objectives aimed at fulfilling the Lisbon Strategy ambition: (1) the quality and effectiveness of education and training systems in the EU had to be improved, (2) access to education and training had to be facilitated, and (3) education and training systems had to be opened up to the world.[74] In order to attain those goals the new Open Method of Coordination (OMC) was to be applied, meaning tools such as indicators, benchmarking, best practices, monitoring, evaluation, and peer review would be used to maintain a fully decentralised approach that would help Member States develop their own policies progressively.[75]

---

[71] De Witte (1992, p. 88).

[72] Ertl (2006, p. 14).

[73] Lisbon European Council, 23 and 24 March 2000—Presidency Conclusions.

[74] Council Detailed work programme on the follow-up of the objectives of education and training systems in Europe, [2002] OJ C 142/1, para. 1.2.

[75] Ibid., para. 4.1–4.2.

2.6 *After the Turn of the Millennium: The Copenhagen Process*

The turn of the millennium therefore saw the introduction of a new strategic goal as expressed in the Lisbon Strategy. The importance of the Lisbon Strategy for the EU's education policy should not be underestimated. Pépin indicated that the Strategy awarded education a central role and gave the EU's Ministers for Education the possibility to "make themselves heard" alongside the Ministers for Economy and the Ministers for Employment.[76] Strategic programmes such as the Education and Training 2010 and Education and Training 2020 continued to advance the EU's mission of improving education, lifelong learning, and active citizenship.[77] Currently, the EU is working towards the solidification of the European Education Area through its 2021–2030 strategic framework.[78] Apart from these activities, the Union also adopted a number of soft law instruments from 2000 onwards touching on the topic of the recognition of qualifications. It did so within the context of its own process for vocational education and training, which was inspired by the Bologna Process (focused on higher education—and discussed in Sect. 3 below).

The roots of the EU's Copenhagen Process can be traced to the 2002 Barcelona European Council in which the European Council requested that action similar to the Bologna Process be promoted in the area of vocational education and training. That same year, the Council of the EU adopted a Resolution on enhanced cooperation in the area of vocational education and training (VET).[79] In this context, the European VET Ministers and the European Commission adopted a Declaration to initiate the Copenhagen Process which, like the Bologna Process, was based on voluntary cooperation.[80] The purpose of this policy initiative was to "promote mutual trust,

[76] Pépin (2011, p. 26).

[77] Council Detailed Work Programme on the follow-up of the objectives of education and training systems in Europe, [2002] OJ C 142/1; Council conclusions of 12 May 2009 on a strategic framework for European cooperation in education and training ('ET 2020'), [2009] OJ C 119/2.

[78] Council Resolution on a strategic framework for European cooperation in education and training towards the European Education Area and beyond (2021–2030), [2021] OJ C 66/1.

[79] Council Resolution of 19 December 2002 on the promotion of enhanced European cooperation in vocational education and training, [2003] OJ C 13/2.

[80] Declaration of the European Ministers of Vocational Education and Training, and the European Commission, convened in Copenhagen on 29 and 30 November 2002, on enhanced European cooperation in vocational education and training—"The Copenhagen Declaration"; See, for example, Maastricht Communiqué on the Future Priorities of Enhanced European Cooperation in Vocational Education and Training (VET)—14 December 2004; The Helsinki Communiqué on Enhanced European Cooperation in Vocational Education and Training—Communiqué of the European Ministers of Vocational Education and Training, the European Social partners and the European Commission convened in Helsinki on 5 December 2006 to review the priorities and strategies of the Copenhagen Process.

transparency and recognition of competences and qualifications, and thereby establishing a basis for increasing mobility and facilitating access to lifelong learning".[81] Ultimately, the Copenhagen Process laid the basis for the creation of key tools for transparency and recognition.

One of the earliest Copenhagen Process instruments is the Europass Decision.[82] The objective of Europass was to establish a single Community framework for achieving transparency of qualifications and competences through common documentation.[83] Accordingly, the framework consisted of a number of document formats which would support the mobility of individuals by providing a way of presenting information that was common throughout the Community. Whereas arguably the most famous of these documents is the CV, Europass also consists of Europass Mobility, the Diploma Supplement, a Language Portfolio and the Certificate Supplement.[84] In 2018, the Europass framework was renewed in the context of the Commission Communication on the New Skills Agenda for Europe and was amended to primarily form an online service platform offering web-based tools to help make qualifications more insightful.[85]

Apart from Europass, the Copenhagen Process also covers the European Qualifications Framework for lifelong learning (EQF) which created "a common reference framework which should serve as a translation device between different qualifications systems and their levels, whether for general and higher education or for vocational education and training".[86] Facilitating translation between national qualification systems would lead to improved transparency, comparability, and portability of EU citizens' qualifications.[87] The EQF has been designed to cover every qualification from the most basic to the most advanced and allows those to be fitted into eight

[81] Declaration of the European Ministers of Vocational Education and Training, and the European Commission, convened in Copenhagen on 29 and 30 November 2002, on enhanced European cooperation in vocational education and training—"The Copenhagen Declaration".

[82] The decision was adopted following a Council Resolution in which the Council expressed the need for transparency, information and guidance; Council Resolution of 19 December 2002 on the promotion of enhanced European cooperation in vocational education and training, [2003] OJ C 13/2.

[83] Article 1 Decision No 2241/2004/EC of the European Parliament and of the Council of 15 December 2004 on a single Community framework for the transparency of qualifications and competences (Europass), [2004] OJ L 390/6.

[84] Article 2 io. Annexes II-VI Decision No 2241/2004/EC.

[85] Communication from the Commission to the European Parliament, the Council, the European Parliament, the European Economic and Social Committee and the Committee of the Regions, A new Skills Agenda for Europe: Working together to strengthen human capital, employability and competitiveness, COM(2016) 381 final, p. 11; Decision (EU) 2018/646 of the European Parliament and of the Council of 18 April 2018 on a common framework for the provision of better services for skills and qualifications (Europass) and repealing Decision No 2241/2004/EC, [2018] OJ L 112/42.

[86] Recital 12 Recommendation of the European Parliament and of the Council of 23 April 2008 on the establishment of the European Qualifications Framework for lifelong learning, [2008] OJ C 111/1.

[87] Ibid.

reference levels.[88] A new Recommendation was adopted in 2017, thereby striving to fulfil the goals of, among others, improved transparency, comparability and understanding of qualifications, and supporting flexible learning pathways and seamless transitions between systems of education and training and between education and employment.[89]

The final instruments part of the Copenhagen Process were the European Credit System for Vocational Education and Training (ECVET) and European Quality Assurance Reference Network for VET (EQAVET). When the ECVET was proposed in 2008, the Commission recognised that one of the biggest challenges to transnational mobility was the diversity and fragmentation of education, VET, and qualifications systems in Europe, necessitating a system to promote mutual trust and enable the transfer and recognition of learning outcomes in transnational mobility.[90] Next to ECVET, a Recommendation was adopted on quality assurance.[91] The EQAVET Recommendation was aimed at establishing a European Quality Assurance Reference Framework which would support Member States in promoting and monitoring the improvement of their VET systems.[92] Due to the prohibition of harmonisation of Article 165 TFEU and the principle of subsidiarity, the EQAVET does not create its own quality assurance system but instead supports Member States in the assessment of their VET systems by providing common principles, quality criteria, indicative descriptors and indicators.[93] Both initiatives however did not lead to the

[88] A. Rauhvargers (2009, p. 116); Annex II, Recommendation of the European Parliament and of the Council of 23 April 2008 on the establishment of the European Qualifications Framework for lifelong learning, [2008] OJ C 111/1.

[89] Proposal for a Council Recommendation on the European Qualifications Framework for lifelong learning and repealing the Recommendation of the European Parliament and of the Council of 23 April 2008 on the establishment of the European Qualifications Framework for lifelong learning, COM(2016) 383 final, p. 6; see also Council Recommendation of 22 May 2017 on the European Qualifications Framework for lifelong learning and repealing the recommendation of the European Parliament and of the Council of 23 April 2008 on the establishment of the European Qualifications Framework for lifelong learning, [2017] OJ C 189/15.

[90] Proposal for a Recommendation of the European Parliament and of the Council on the establishment of the European Credit system for Vocational Education and Training (ECVET), COM(2008) 180 final, p. 3.

[91] Recommendation of the European Parliament and of the Council of 18 June 2009 on the establishment of a European Quality Assurance Reference Framework for Vocational Education and Training, [2009] OJ C 155/1.

[92] Recital 9 Recommendation of the European Parliament and of the Council of 18 June 2009 on the establishment of a European Quality Assurance Reference Framework for Vocational Education and Training, [2008] OJ C 155/1.

[93] Recital 15 Recommendation of the European Parliament and of the Council of 18 June 2009 on the establishment of a European Quality Assurance Reference Framework for Vocational Education and Training, [2008] OJ C 155/1.

creation of a European credit system for vocational education and training, nor significantly impacted the transparency of quality assurance. Hence, both initiatives were consolidated in 2020 via a new Council recommendation.[94]

2.7 The EU's Action on Automatic Recognition, Micro-Credentials & More

The last element of EU action related to recognition to be mentioned here concerns its action on *automatic* recognition related to *academic* recognition. While automatic recognition is best known in relation to the Professional Qualifications Directive, the EU also took steps on automatic recognition of academic qualifications. The EU's action took place in light of other developments on automatic recognition in the context of the Bologna Process and Lisbon Recognition Convention.[95] In 2018, the European Commission's DG Education issued a Roadmap for a Council Recommendation promoting automatic mutual recognition of diplomas and study periods abroad.[96] This process was subsequently labelled the "Sorbonne Process" and became part of the EU's ambition to develop the European Education Area (hereinafter: EEA-2025).[97]

The initiative originated from a speech given by President Emmanuel Macron at the Sorbonne University in 2017. In it, he laid out his ambitious plans for the future of the EU and its education systems.[98] Macron called for the creation of European universities spanning multiple European countries and providing courses in multiple Member States and in multiple languages, thereby resulting in truly European diplomas. He also stated that the basis for this must be laid at secondary school, calling for harmonisation and mutual recognition of secondary school diplomas and a Sorbonne Process that would allow for exchanges and transitions throughout the European secondary system. Of course this is a far-reaching proposal and one may question whether it is realistic considering the high-stakes nature of education policy.

---

[94] Council Recommendation of 24 November 2020 on vocational education and training (VET) for sustainable competitiveness, social fairness and resilience, [2020] OJ C 417/1 (referred to in this contribution as the 2020 VET Recommendation).

[95] See Sect. 3 below.

[96] The Recommendation was proposed in the context of the Commission's Communication on 'Strengthening European Identity through Education and Culture', see Communication from the Commission to the European Parliament, the Council, the European Economic and Social Committee and the Committee of the Regions, Strengthening European Identity through Education and Culture—The European Commission's contribution to the Leaders' meeting in Gothenburg 17 November 2017, COM(2017) 673 final.

[97] Communication from the Commission to the European Parliament, the Council, the European Economic and Social Committee and the Committee of the Regions, Strengthening European Identity through Education and Culture—The European Commission's contribution to the Leaders' meeting in Gothenburg 17 November 2017, COM(2017) 673 final, p. 11.

[98] Macron (2017).

Nevertheless, the Commission's plans towards the EEA-2025 contained elements of these ideas.[99]

Ultimately, the Sorbonne Process had a somewhat different approach than that proposed by Macron, since it focused more on the aspect of recognition and less on harmonisation and exchanges and transitions in the secondary school system. Ultimately, a recommendation was adopted in which automatic recognition is essentially pursued by enhancing the application of instruments in the Bologna and Copenhagen Processes.[100] Member States had to put the necessary steps in place to achieve automatic recognition as intended under the Recommendation by 2025 (i.e. the deadline for the European Education Area).[101] Questions may be raised whether this deadline was to be met: the 2023 Commission evaluation of the Recommendation showed that, although key steps had been taken to achieve automatic recognition at national level, results differed between Member States meaning steps still needed to be taken to achieve the automatic recognition foreseen by the Recommendation.[102]

The most recent initiatives related to the EEA-2025 affecting recognition concern a common approach on micro-credentials, a proposed recommendation on quality assurance and recognition in higher education in the EU, and the development of a European degree. To start with micro-credentials, a common approach to micro-credentials was deemed necessary to enhance a culture of lifelong learning and to ensure reskilling throughout individuals' careers.[103] Micro-credentials span across education types and are aimed at certifying outcomes of small learning experiences to allow for more flexible learning paths. The micro-credentials recommendation is a way to enhance trust in these credentials. Trust is also central to another new initiative concerning recognition, namely the recommendation on quality assurance

[99] Communication from the Commission to the European Parliament, the Council, the European Economic and Social Committee and the Committee of the Regions, Strengthening European Identity through Education and Culture—The European Commission's contribution to the Leaders' meeting in Gothenburg 17 November 2017, COM(2017) 673 final, p. 12.

[100] Council Recommendation of 26 November 2018 on promoting automatic mutual recognition of higher education and upper secondary education and training qualifications and the outcomes of learning periods abroad, [2018] OJ C 444/1.

[101] Point 1 Council Recommendation of 26 November 2018 on promoting automatic mutual recognition of higher education and upper secondary education and training qualifications and the outcomes of learning periods abroad, [2018] OJ C 444/1.

[102] The Recommendation is especially targeted at upper secondary education qualifications giving access to higher education and higher education qualifications giving access to further higher education studies. Furthermore, the Recommendation is especially targeted at automatic recognition of the *level* of higher education degrees, meaning that the content may still be examined by higher education institutions; For the Commission's evaluation, see Report from the Commission to the Council on the implementation of the Council Recommendation on promoting automatic mutual recognition of higher education and upper secondary education and training qualifications and the outcomes of learning periods abroad, COM(2023) 91 final.

[103] Council Recommendation of 16 June 2022 on a European approach to micro-credentials for lifelong learning and employability, [2022] OJ C 243/10.

and recognition in higher education in the EU. Building on a previous recommendation on quality assurance,[104] the newest proposal clearly marks trust in education systems (as advanced by quality assurance) as the basis for automatic recognition of qualifications—and ultimately learning mobility.[105] Subsequently, we find a combination of enhancing trust and enhancing employability (through skills) in the last of the new initiatives, i.e. the communication on a European degree.[106] Following this initiative the European degree is a new type of qualification to be enshrined in national legislation. The European degree is to enable higher education institutions to more easily develop joint programmes leading to joint degrees—which should accordingly be easier to recognise in various Member States.

This section has therefore shown how extensive EU action is on academic recognition (i.e. as seen in the context of the instruments adopted based on the educational competence of Article 165 TFEU). While the sensitivity of the area of education means legislation in this area is characterised by soft law instruments such as recommendations, the ambitions foreseen in the context of the EEA-2025 are certainly great. The scaling up of ambitions has become particularly clear in recent years. Indeed, the EU used to mirror action taken in the Bologna Process with its own Copenhagen process which also came to comprise a qualifications framework, credit system, guidelines on quality assurance, and common documentation formats. Nevertheless, in recent years the EU has set itself the objective to become a front-runner in the implementation of the Bologna Process indicating the EEA-2025 is to become a "motor for the Bologna Process".[107] This can indeed be seen by looking at the latest initiatives related to recognition, namely the Automatic Recognition Recommendation, Micro-credentials Recommendation, proposal for a recommendation on quality assurance and recognition in the EU, and plans for a European degree. Nevertheless, the EU is not alone in its ambitions since action on academic recognition also continues outside the EU legal framework. Accordingly, attention needs to be turned to the Bologna Process and action by the Council of Europe.

---

[104] Recommendation of the European Parliament and of the Council of 15 February 2006 on further European cooperation in quality assurance in higher education, [2006] OJ L 64/60.

[105] Proposal for a Council Recommendation on a European Quality Assurance and Recognition System in Higher Education, COM(2024) 147 final, p. 1.

[106] Communication from the Commission to the European Parliament, the Council, the European Economic and Social Committee and the Committee of the Regions: a blueprint for a European degree, COM(2024) 144 final.

[107] Communication from the Commission to the European Parliament, the Council, the European Economic and Social Committee and the Committee of the Regions on achieving the European Education Area by 2025, COM(2020) 625 final, p. 11.

3 Extra-EU Action on Recognition

While it has become clear that the EU has adopted various measures aimed at improving both professional and academic recognition since its inception, the late 1990s also saw the introduction of equally ambitious parallel initiatives on higher education cooperation adopted outside the Union framework. In 1997, a new Convention was adopted in the framework of the Council of Europe and UNESCO.[108] This Lisbon Recognition Convention would become the most important legal text on academic recognition of higher education qualifications. A year after the introduction of the Convention, a number of the EU Member States' Ministers for education gathered to celebrate the anniversary of the Sorbonne University and to kick off a cooperation that would be responsible for the most drastic reform of higher education seen to this day. This cooperation was solidified in 1999 by a declaration through which the Bologna Process was born. The Lisbon Recognition Convention and Bologna Process are discussed in the following sections.

3.1 The Council of Europe and UNESCO: The Lisbon Recognition Convention

The introduction of the Council of Europe and UNESCO Convention on the Recognition of Qualifications concerning Higher Education in the European Region (the Lisbon Recognition Convention or LRC) followed on major changes that took place in higher education, such as the diversification of higher education and the rapid spread of both short- and long-term academic mobility.[109] These changes caused earlier Conventions adopted between the 1950s and 1960s to quickly become obsolete. Indeed, the early origins of the Lisbon Recognition Convention can be traced to the end of the Second World War when international and institutionalised cooperation was emphasised and organisations such as the Council of Europe, the United Nations (*in casu* UNESCO), and the European Coal and Steel Community were created.[110]

The LRC was therefore not the first instrument to be adopted in the context of the Council of Europe and UNESCO. The LRC consolidated a number of earlier conventions, the earliest of which dated back to 1953. These conventions were general in nature and did not take into account the rapid advances of higher education systems following, among others, on the accession of a number of new Parties to the Council of Europe as a consequence of the political changes that had taken place in central

[108] Convention on the Recognition of Qualifications concerning Higher Education in the European Region, Council of Europe and UNESCO, 11 April 1997, ETS—No. 165. The Convention is referred to in this research as the Lisbon Recognition Convention.

[109] Zgaga (2014, p. 22).

[110] Bergan (2014, p. 33).

and eastern Europe in the 1980s and 1990s.[111] Whereas these previous conventions concerned separate aspects of academic recognition such as the recognition of university qualifications and equivalence of periods of university study, the LRC made sure these aspects were all placed under one umbrella, in a single instrument.[112] As mentioned previously, the adoption of the 1997 Convention took place outside the Union framework, something that can be considered notable since all EU Member States have since ratified or acceded to the LRC. Nevertheless, it is important to remember that the LRC does not apply solely to the Member States, since a total of 53 States have ratified the Convention. Furthermore, the LRC has become closely intertwined with the Bologna Process.

3.2 The Bologna Process

Last, but certainly not least, in the line of historical developments on recognition in Europe is the Bologna Process. The Bologna Process is responsible for some of the most fundamental changes higher education systems in the EU have gone through, such as the introduction of the bachelor's/master's structure and the implementation of the European Credit Transfer and Accumulation System (ECTS). Like the LRC, the process is situated outside the Union's framework, although a link exists between the process and the EU because the European Commission has been actively involved in the Bologna Process since 1999.[113] Despite its successes, the Bologna Process' location outside the EU framework has also been contentious. The Bologna Process has, for example, been considered to constitute a renationalisation of higher education and has been described as a form of covert harmonisation.[114] Such critiques mainly find their origin in the fact that the Bologna Process was initiated by EU Member States who went outside the EU legal framework to create the Bologna Process—even when they may have had possibilities at their disposal to undertake action within it.[115] Over the course of time, the Process developed from a non-EU initiative established by Member States in their own capacities (i.e. independent of the EU and its legislative and policy framework), to a fully-fledged European Higher Education Area spanning 49 countries. This means that, like the LRC, the reach of the Bologna Process has become considerably wider than the EU's 27 Member States.

[111] Bergan and Rauhvargers (2005, p. 8).

[112] Over the course of time, the Convention and its principles have been elaborated by a number of subsidiary texts. In particular, Article X.2 of the Lisbon Recognition Convention realised the creation of a Committee which was tasked with overseeing the implementation of the Convention. In order to realise this, the Committee was granted the power to adopt recommendations, declarations, protocols and models of good practice. The instruments adopted by the Committee make up the Convention's subsidiary texts.

[113] In particular, the European Commission is a full member of the Bologna Follow-Up Group (i.e. the structure giving follow-up to the Bologna Process objectives).

[114] Garben (2011b), Verbruggen (2003, p. 204).

[115] See Garben (2011b).

Considering the fact that the Bologna Process is an intergovernmental cooperation initiative, this means that, originally, it did not include any legislation. Because of the non-EU nature of the Bologna Process, many of the advances made are non-legal in nature. Progress is achieved via voluntary cooperation by means of communiqués or declarations adopted after two- or three-yearly ministerial meetings. Over the course of time, follow-up to these ministerial meetings became the task of the Bologna Follow-up Group (BFUG). Since its inception, 13 ministerial conferences have taken place at which an equal number of communiques/declarations has been adopted. These conferences are the crucial drivers of the Bologna Process. In fact, the real value of the ministerial conferences was considered to not so much lie in new policy lines to be followed in subsequent years, but more in the high-profile follow-up the conferences provide.[116]

The Sorbonne and Bologna Declarations were the result of the first ministerial conferences. The former was adopted in 1998 when the Ministers for Education of France, Germany, Italy, and the United Kingdom first set out to harmonise the European higher education systems. Through the Sorbonne Declaration they called upon other EU Member States and European countries to join in on their newly established cooperation.[117] A year later in 1999, the Bologna Declaration was adopted in which 29 countries affirmed the principles of the Sorbonne Declaration and assured that they would coordinate their higher education policies in the short term. Currently, the Bologna Process includes all EU Member States along with 22 other States, the European Commission and several consultative members (including the Council of Europe and UNESCO). Through the Bologna Declaration the countries that were first party to the Bologna Process agreed on the creation of a European Higher Education Area (hereinafter: EHEA). In order to establish this area, the Ministers set six initial objectives: implementing the Diploma Supplement,[118] adopting a two-cycle system (undergraduate and graduate), establishing a system of credits (ECTS) mitigating obstacles to the exercise of free movement of students, teachers, researchers and administrative staff, promoting European cooperation in quality assurance, and stimulating the European dimensions in higher education.[119]

Since the 1990s, the Sorbonne and Bologna Declarations have been superseded by many conferences and communiqués/declarations whereby some focused on issues related to recognition more than others. One important development concerns the incorporation of the LRC into the Bologna Process as the Process' only legally

---

[116] Garben (2011b, p. 18).

[117] Sorbonne Joint Declaration on harmonisation of the architecture of the European higher education system, Paris 25 May 1998.

[118] The Diploma Supplement was to be issued from 2005 onwards to all students graduating from a university in the Bologna Process' countries; Towards the European Higher Education Area, Communiqué of the meeting of European Ministers in charge of Higher Education, Prague 19 May 2001; Realising the European Higher Education Area, Communiqué of the Conference of Ministers responsible for Higher Education in Berlin on 19 September 2003.

[119] Bologna Declaration of 19 June 1999—Joint declaration of the European Ministers of Education.

binding text at the 2005 Bergen Ministerial conference.[120] The incorporation of the LRC into the Bologna Process was mainly due to considerations related to simplification. Indeed, the legal framework for recognition, consisting of the EU Directives and the LRC, was largely in place and the limits of what could be regulated by law were considered to be reached for academic recognition due to the fact that the competences on recognition decisions in that area were mainly placed with higher education institutions for which direct state influence on their decision-making processes was limited.[121] Therefore, instead of opting for legislative amendments, recognition was to be improved by constant efforts in furthering the implementation of the Lisbon Recognition Convention's legal framework by ensuring that national legislation was in line with it.[122] This recommendation became the central policy line of the Bologna Process concerning recognition.

Other notable developments concern the development of a common framework of qualifications to improve the readability and comparability of European higher education degrees, and coherent quality assurance and accreditation mechanisms. Mentioned first in the 2001 Prague Communiqué, the idea came to fruition with the 2005 Bergen Ministerial Conference when Ministers formally adopted the EHEA overarching qualification framework consisting of generic descriptors based on learning outcomes, and credit ranges.[123] Whereas the EHEA initially comprised two cycles, by 2005 it had developed to a three cycle-system. The 2003 Berlin Communiqué played an important role here, since it called for the promotion of closer links between the EHEA (product of the Bologna Process) and the European Research Area (located within the EU legal framework) by including the doctoral level as the third Bologna Process cycle.[124] By 2005, the Bologna Process consisted of a three-cycle structure comprising bachelor's, master's *and* doctorate degrees, as well as general descriptions and credit ranges for each of the levels. For example, first cycle qualifications (i.e. bachelor's degrees) included 180 to 240 ECTS credits and indicated that a student had, among others, "demonstrated knowledge and understanding in a field of study that builds upon their general secondary education".[125] The framework itself was to be paired with national qualifications frameworks by 2010 and its compatibility with the European Qualifications Framework for lifelong learning was also to be ensured. By 2020 short cycle qualifications (of 90 to 120

[120] Zgaga (2014, p. 25); The European Higher Education Area—Achieving the Goals, Communiqué of the Conference of European Ministers Responsible for higher Education, Bergen 19–20 May 2005.

[121] ENIC/NARIC Network, Recognition issues in the Bologna Process—Final Report, 24 January 2001, p. 7.

[122] Ibid., pp. 7–8.

[123] The European Higher Education Area—Achieving the Goals, Communiqué of the Conference of European Ministers Responsible for Higher Education, Bergen 19–20 May 2005.

[124] Towards the European Higher Education Area, Communiqué of the meeting of European Ministers in charge of Higher Education, Prague 19 May 2001; Realising the European Higher Education Area, Communiqué of the Conference of Ministers responsible for Higher Education in Berlin on 19 September 2003.

[125] EHEA, The framework of qualifications for the European Higher Education Area.

ECTS) were also added within the qualifications framework of the EHEA to help facilitate access to higher education.[126]

In terms of recognition, the mid to late 2000s were a period of relative quiet in the Bologna Process when it came to recognition of qualifications. New impetus was nevertheless provided by 2010 when the Ministers for education met again to confirm their commitment to the Bologna Process, but mostly to celebrate the formal launch of the EHEA with the Budapest-Vienna Declaration.[127] Despite being mostly declaratory in nature, the Ministers did recognize in the declaration that implementation on the objectives of degree and curriculum reform, quality assurance, mobility, and *recognition* was not coherent across the participating countries—and thereby relied on the BFUG to propose measures. The subsequent 2012 Bucharest Ministerial Conference led to the formulation of a new ambitious goal in respect to recognition, namely cooperation towards automatic recognition.[128] The subsequent 2015 Yerevan Communiqué saw the formulation of a new strategy for 2020, including the achievement of automatic recognition. The Yerevan Communiqué particularly promised that automatic recognition of qualifications would be a reality by 2020 so students and graduates could move easily throughout the EHEA.[129]

In order to realise this goal, a pathfinder group was established to explore ways to achieve the automatic academic recognition of comparable degrees at the European level.[130] The concept of automatic recognition within the Bologna Process is to be understood by the quote “A Bachelor is a Bachelor is a Bachelor”, which signifies that the cycles—or rather, levels—adopted in the context of the Bologna Process’ qualifications framework are to be recognised automatically. Therefore, a bachelor’s degree from one country is referenced to the QF-EHEA as a bachelor’s degree, meaning that it can be equated to a bachelor’s degree in a second country also implementing the three-cycle structure. Following these developments, automatic recognition became an important objective on recognition next to the correct implementation of the LRC.[131] The 2018 Paris Communiqué accordingly called for further development of automatic recognition (i.a. by strengthening ECTS), sought to work on implementation of the LRC and the transparency of procedures, as well as create convergence between the LRC and Europass as regards the Diploma Supplement.[132] Subsequently the Rome and Tirana Communiqués (of 2020 and 2024),

[126] Paris Communiqué—Paris, May 25th 2018.

[127] Budapest-Vienna Declaration on the European Higher Education Area, 12 March 2010.

[128] Making the Most of Our Potential: Consolidating the European Higher Education Area, Bucharest Communiqué, 26–27 April 2012.

[129] Yerevan Communiqué, 14–15 May 2015.

[130] Making the Most of Our Potential: Consolidating the European Higher Education Area, Bucharest Communiqué, 26–27 April 2012.

[131] Rome Ministerial Communiqué, 19 November 2020; Tirana EHEA Ministerial Conference, 29–30 May 2024 (Tirana Communiqué).

[132] Paris Communiqué—Paris, May 25th 2018.

reaffirmed these objectives and also paid attention to issues such as the recognition of qualifications held by refugees and implementation of the UNESCO Global Convention on the Recognition of Qualifications concerning Higher Education.[133]

However, the Rome Communiqué is more interesting for those examining recognition in the EHEA from a legal perspective. While the 2020 Ministerial Conference was of course heavily influenced by the COVID-19 pandemic, the Ministers presented an ambitious view of the EHEA. In particular, they viewed the EHEA as "an area where students, staff and graduates can move freely to study, teach and do research" affirming that "the EHEA of our vision will fully respect the fundamental values of higher education and democracy and the rule of law".[134] This Communiqué can be seen as markedly different from the previous in light of these statements. Also because it included a section on fundamental values which centres on the commitment and protection of academic freedom, institutional autonomy, and integrity. Commitments to democracy, the rule of law, and respect of fundamental values are of course important, but the question may be raised how these are to be effectuated without legislation. The Rome Communiqué is novel in its consciousness of the previous lack of binding legislation related to the EHEA and calls for legislation to safeguard student rights developed in the national legal systems, guarantees for automatic recognition, and support of the fair recognition of qualifications held by refugees. It will be particularly interesting to see what follow-up will be given to these calls.

3.3 Regional Cooperation on Recognition: The Benelux

The commitment expressed in the 2020 Rome Communiqué shows awareness of the need for legislation at the national level to provide sufficient protection of individuals' rights when moving across Europe. While that Communiqué particularly pointed to *national* legal systems for the development of such legislation, some legal follow-up had already been given previously through regional cooperation in the Benelux. The Benelux already had a tradition of automatic recognition through several national initiatives prior to the introduction of new measures to this end from 2015 onwards. More specifically, the Netherlands and the Flemish Community of Belgium already automatically recognised the bachelor's or master's level of such degrees obtained in the respective countries/regions.[135] Luxembourg would automatically recognise the level of bachelor's and master's degrees from most European countries, and the Belgian Communities also automatically recognised the level of Belgian higher

[133] Rome Ministerial Communiqué, 19 November 2020; Tirana EHEA Ministerial Conference, 29–30 May 2024 (Tirana Communiqué).

[134] Rome Ministerial Communiqué, 19 November 2020.

[135] Treaty between the Flemish Community of Belgium and the Kingdom of the Netherlands concerning the accreditation of programmes within Flemish and Dutch higher education, 3 September 2003.

education degrees due to the omnivalence of diplomas, which originates from the Belgian Constitution.

However, the Benelux countries shared a desire to combat such fragmentation and decided to consolidate such practices into legislation. In May of 2015, the Benelux accordingly adopted a first Decision on the automatic mutual generic level recognition of higher education degrees in the Benelux.[136] While this initial Decision covered bachelor's and master's degrees, the scope of automatic recognition in the Benelux was soon extended to also cover short-cycle higher education degrees (i.e. associate degrees) and doctoral degrees through a second Decision adopted in 2018.[137] In 2021 this arrangement was even extended to the Baltic States by way of a Treaty that entered into force in May 2024.[138] These instruments therefore give legal power to the automatic level recognition developed in the Bologna Process.

4 Conclusion

This chapter has shown that recognition of qualifications in the EU has an extensive history underlying the current legislation and policy. It has shown that the EU has undertaken extensive action to improve recognition for both work and study purposes, whether through existing instruments such as the Professional Qualifications Directive and the Copenhagen Process instruments, or through new initiatives such as those on micro-credentials, quality assurance, and the European degree. Nevertheless, the chapter also showed the EU is not the only actor on academic recognition since important advances in this respect were made in the context of the Bologna Process and Council of Europe and UNESCO. The chapter shows that recognition is also improved at the regional level by referring to the Benelux Decisions on automatic mutual generic level recognition, instruments adopted to give legal power to principles of the Bologna Process. Apart from discussing the historical development of these different instruments, another aspect related to the discussion on recognition was equally touched upon in this chapter, namely the distinction in two recognition types depending on whether one needs recognition to work or study elsewhere. This distinction between recognition for work and study purposes gives way to a discussion on the corresponding typology associated with the recognition of qualifications where a distinction is made between professional and academic recognition. A typology that is subsequently connected to a distinction in competences (also briefly touched upon in this chapter) which has enabled the current pluriform legal and policy landscape to arise. Following this observation, attention should next be shifted to a more

[136] Beschikking van het Benelux Comité van Ministers betreffende de automatische wederzijdse generieke niveauerkenning van diploma's hoger onderwijs, M(2015) 3.

[137] Beschikking van het Benelux Comité van Ministers tot aanvulling van beschikking M(2015) 3 betreffende de automatische wederzijdse generieke niveauerkenning van diploma's hoger onderwijs, M(2018) 1.

[138] Verdrag betreffende de automatische erkenning van diploma's in het hoger onderwijs, Brussel 14 september 2021.

substantive discussion on the typology for recognition and corresponding competences. These elements are discussed in Chapter "Challenging Convention: Theory, Competences & The Grey Area of Recognition".

References

Bergan S (2014) Origins, history and evolution of the Lisbon Recognition Convention: a view of the past and a look at the future. In: Bergan S, Blomqvist C (eds) The Lisbon Recognition Convention at 15: making fair recognition a reality. Council of Europe Publishing, Strasbourg, pp 31–42

Bergan S, Rauhvargers A (2005) The Council Of Europe/UNESCO (Lisbon) Recognition Convention—what it is and how to use it. In: Bergan S, Rauhvargers A (eds) Standards for recognition: the Lisbon Recognition Convention and its subsidiary texts. Council of Europe Publishing, Strasbourg, pp 25–40

Blitz B (2003) From Monnet to Delors: Educational Co-operation in the European Union. Contemp Eur Hist 12:197–212

Cambien N (2017) Mutual recognition and mutual trust in the internal market. European Papers 2:93–115

Claessens S (2008) Free movement of lawyers in the European Union. Wolf Legal Publishers, Nijmegen

D'Artillac Brill L (2009) Experience of diploma recognition under EEC General System Directives in the Netherlands. Assessment in Education: Principles, Policy & Practice 16:13–23

Dalichow F (1987) Academic recognition within the European Community. Eur J Educ 22:39–58

De Witte B (1989) European community law of education. Nomos, Baden-Baden

De Witte B (1992) The influence of European Community law on national systems of higher education. In: Pertek J (ed) General Recognition of Diplomas and Free Movement of Professionals. European Institute of Public Administration, Maastricht, pp 73–90

Ertl H (2006) European Union policies in education and training: the Lisbon agenda as a turning point. Comp Educ 42:5–27

Garben S (2011a) On recognition of qualifications for academic and professional purposes. Tilburg Law Review 16:127–156

Garben S (2011b) EU higher education law: the Bologna process and harmonization by stealth. Kluwer Law International, Alphen aan den Rijn

Gerlinger T, Schmucker R (2007) Transnational migration of health professionals in the European Union. Cad Saude Publica 23:184–192

Hatzopoulos V (2012) Regulating services in the European Union. Oxford University Press, Oxford

Koumenta M, Pagliero M (2016) Measuring prevalence and labour market impacts of occupational regulation in the EU. European Commission, Brussels

Lenaerts K (1994) Education in European Community law after "Maastricht." Common Market Law Review 31:7–41

Lettmayr CF, Martin L (2013) The role of qualifications in governing occupations and professions. Cedefop working paper 20. Publications Office of the European Union, Luxembourg

Macron E (2017) Discours d'Emmanuel Macron pour une Europe souveraine, unie, démocratique. https://www.elysee.fr/emmanuel-macron/2017/09/26/initiative-pour-l-europe-discours-d-emmanuel-macron-pour-une-europe-souveraine-unie-democratique

Minor J (1992) Introductory lecture on the directive of 21 December 1988. In: Pertek J (ed) General recognition of diplomas and free movement of professionals. European Institute of Public Administration, Maastricht, pp 3–16

Pépin L (2011) Education in the Lisbon strategy: assessment and prospects. Eur J Educ 46:25–35

Rauhvargers A (2009) Recognition and qualifications frameworks. Assess Educ Principles Policy Pract 16(1):111–125

Schneider H, Claessens S (2005) The recognition of diplomas and the free movement of professionals in the European Union. In: Schneider H (ed) Migration, integration and citizenship: a challenge for Europe's future—Volume I. Forum Maastricht, Maastricht, pp 123–166

Schoenmaekers S (2010) The regulation of architects in Belgium and the Netherlands. Datawyse / Universitaire Pers Maastricht, Maastricht

Van Craeyenest F (1989) La nature juridique des resolutions sur la cooperation en matière d'éducation. In: De Witte B (ed) European community law of education. Nomos, Baden-Baden, pp 127–133

Van Riemsdijk M (2013a) Obstacles to the free movement of professionals: mutual recognition of professional qualifications in the European Union. Eur J Migr Law 15(1):47–68

Van Riemsdijk M (2013b) Politics of free movement in the European Union: recognition and transfer of professional qualifications. In: Maas W (ed) Democratic citizenship and the free movement of people. Martinus Nijhoff Publishers, Leiden, pp 115–142

Verbruggen MLW (2003) De Bolognaverklaring kritisch getoetst aan het Europees onderwijsbeleid. SEW 6:199–212

Walkenhorst H (2008) Explaining change in EU education policy. J Eur Publ Policy 15:567–587

White RCA (2004) Workers, establishment, and services in the European Union. Oxford University Press, Oxford

Zgaga P (2014) The Lisbon Recognition Convention as a paradigmatic shift and a change of the philosophy of recognition: between reflection and sentiments. In: Bergan S, Blomqvist C (eds) The Lisbon Recognition Convention at 15: making fair recognition a reality. Council of Europe Publishing, Strasbourg, pp 19–30

Challenging Convention: Theory, Competences & the Grey Area of Recognition

1 Introduction

At the root of the recognition of qualifications lies a fundamental theoretical distinction. The recognition of qualifications is generally understood to consist of two main types of recognition which are distinguished on the basis of the two main reasons individuals may need recognition for: work or study—or, expressed in terms of recognition types, professional and academic recognition. This theoretical distinction in terms of types of recognition has been solidified into separate EU competences which enable the existence of the present variety of actors and instruments: one on internal market and the other on education. The theory surrounding these recognition types and their associated EU competences are central to the present chapter. This chapter will nevertheless show that a grey area exists between recognition types, challenging the suitability of the division of competences between recognition types. Equally, the chapter will show how instruments on recognition can also be considered to challenge this divide by examining them in light of recognition theory and competences.

2 The Fundamentals of Recognition: A Typology

The main types of recognition are therefore distinguished based on the purpose for which recognition is necessary. Professional recognition is the type of recognition that concerns access to the labour market, meaning the recognition of educational qualifications for the purpose of taking up a job.[1] Academic recognition is aimed at facilitating student mobility, thereby making it possible for EU citizens to study in a State

[1] Dalichow (1992, p. 91).

L. S.J. Kortese, *Effectuating Free Movement in the EU through Recognition of Qualifications*, https://doi.org/10.1007/978-3-032-21335-8_3

other than their home Member State.[2] Whereas professional and academic recognition constitute the main subtypes of recognition typology, both types of recognition can be divided further into two more subtypes.

2.1 The Subtypes of Professional Recognition

Starting with professional recognition, this type of recognition can be subdivided into *de jure* and *de facto* professional recognition. *De jure* professional recognition concerns the exercise of a *regulated* profession in another Member State. In this case, the authorisation to carry out economic activities in a profession is legally subject to the professional possessing one or more relevant diplomas issued in the State in which the profession is to be carried out.[3] This situation means that the law stipulates specific requirements that indicate which qualifications a person needs to work in a certain profession. Typical examples of regulated professions are nurses, doctors, and lawyers. In this case, professionals will need to have their qualifications formally recognised by a competent authority before being able to take up employment in another Member State. *De jure* professional recognition is typically the EU's domain and the Professional Qualifications Directive (PQD) the main instrument.[4] This directive provides the rules that must be complied with when an EU citizen seeks to exercise his or her regulated profession in another Member State.

De facto professional recognition subsequently relates to the exercise of a profession in a Member State other than the home Member State. In this case, qualifications are recognised for *any* kind of labour market use.[5] In this case, it is usually the employer who needs to decide whether or not to recognise qualifications by accepting a person as an employee. In the EU, *de facto* professional recognition is

[2] West and Barham (2009, p. 25).

[3] Communication from the Commission on recognition of qualifications for academic and professional purposes, COM(94) 596 final, p. 5.

[4] In this research, the term "Professional Qualifications Directive" is used to refer to Directive 2005/36/EC of the European Parliament and of the Council of 7 September 2005 on the recognition of professional qualifications, [2005] OJ L 255/22 *as amended by* Directive 2013/55/EU of the European Parliament and of the Council of 20 November 2013 amending Directive 2005/36/EC on the recognition of professional qualifications and Regulation (EU) No 1024/2012 on administrative cooperation through the Internal Market Information System ('the IMI Regulation'), [2013] OJ L 354/132. Despite the fact that the Professional Qualifications Directive was introduced in 2005 and later amended in 2013, it does not mean that this was the first time that the EU Member States cooperated on the topic of *de jure* professional recognition. In fact, the EU already had a competence to legislate in this area ever since the early days of European cooperation through Article 57 of the 1957 Rome Treaty. Early cooperation on *de jure* professional recognition accordingly dates from the 1960s when the first directives on recognition were adopted. Important developments followed in the period between the 1970s and 1990s until the Professional Qualifications Directive in its current form was introduced in 2005. For more on the history on how the recognition of qualifications developed in the EU see Chapter "The Long History of the Recognition of Qualifications in the EU" of this contribution.

[5] Bergan (2009, p. 39).

subject to the Treaties. Article 45 TFEU on the free movement of workers, Article 49 TFEU on the right of establishment along with Article 56 TFEU on the freedom of services ensure that Union citizens exercising a non-regulated profession in principle have the right to go to another Member State to work there, move there to pursue activities as self-employed persons, and to temporarily provide services in a country other than the home Member State. The free movement rights enshrined in these Treaty provisions have prompted the Court of Justice of the EU to rule that all national measures "liable to hamper or to render less attractive the exercise [...] of fundamental freedoms guaranteed by the Treaty" are precluded by the Treaty unless they are sufficiently justified.[6]

Nevertheless, as the previous quote also shows, restrictions of free movement may still arise in practice on the labour market. Here, it is important to emphasise that, in the context of the internal market, competences not conferred to the EU remain with the Member States. While the definition for a regulated profession is determined at EU level, Member States remain free to decide how to organise their professions.[7] Within Member States other parties such as professional bodies may furthermore play an important role in determining requirements related to qualifications which are outside the scope of formal regulation (i.e. not subject to *de jure* professional recognition), yet may still constitute barriers. An example is the situation where there are no legal qualification requirements but professionals are in practice required to be members of certain professional organisations, whereby membership is determined on the basis of their qualifications. Alternatively, we may consider the situation of employers who recruit only those who possess a specific diploma.[8] In such situations there is no legislation governing access to the profession, but barriers nonetheless arise on the labour market. Unsurprisingly, these scenarios are more difficult to detect and to mitigate.

2.2 *The Subtypes of Academic Recognition*

Academic recognition, like professional recognition, also consists of two subtypes: academic recognition *by accumulation* and *by substitution*. Academic recognition by accumulation entails a person having completed one course of study by obtaining a diploma and wanting to progress to a subsequent course of study in another State

---

[6] Case C-19/92 *Kraus*, ECLI:EU:C:1993:125, para. 32. See also Case C-55/94 *Gebhard*, ECLI:EU:C:1995:411, para. 37; Case C-424/97 *Haim II*, ECLI:EU:C:2000:357, para. 57; Case C-285/01 *Burbaud*, ECLI:EU:C:2003:432, para. 95; Case C-575/11 *Nasiopoulos*, ECLI:EU:C:2013:430, para. 21.

[7] Case C-234/97 *Fernández de Bobadilla*, ECLI:EU:C:1999:367, para. 14; Case C-285/01 *Burbaud*, ECLI:EU:C:2003:432, para. 43; Case C-586/08 *Rubino*, ECLI:EU:C:2009:801, para. 23; Case C-372/09 and C-373/09 *Peñarroja Fa*, ECLI:EU:C:2011:156, para. 27.

[8] See Case C-164/94, *Aranitis*, ECLI:EU:C:1996:23.

which recognises the home State's qualifications.[9] Here, we can think of a student having completed a bachelor's degree in one Member State and moving to another to pursue a master's degree. We speak of academic recognition by substitution when a student travels abroad as part of his or her studies and the courses completed abroad are integral to the home Member State course of studies, meaning that the student can substitute the credits required by the home Member State by the credits he or she obtained abroad.[10] The most straightforward example of this are Erasmus exchanges where students temporarily study abroad and return to their home institution to complete their degrees. Both types of academic recognition, therefore, entail a change of educational institution. However, in the case of academic recognition by accumulation, the link with the home State institution is severed, whereas academic recognition by substitution entails retention of the link with the home Member State institution.[11]

Although the term academic recognition appears to apply only to higher education, it can also be understood to apply to other types of education. Here it is important to note that the most prominent advances in the area of academic recognition have been undertaken in the area of higher education. Nevertheless, action on academic recognition was also taken for qualifications originating from vocational education and training (VET). In the EU, academic recognition is in the hands of the EU, non-EU actors, and Member States. For higher education, the main instruments are the 1997 Lisbon Recognition Convention,[12] created by the Council of Europe and UNESCO, and the Bologna Process, which was created by European States on their own initiative.[13] The Benelux is also active in the area of academic recognition.[14] Furthermore, the EU has developed instruments for academic recognition in the context of the Copenhagen Process[15] as well as additional instruments ranging from the Automatic Recognition Recommendation to a blueprint for a European degree.[16]

---

[9] Communication from the Commission on recognition of qualifications for academic and professional purposes, COM(94) 596 final, p. 5.

[10] Garben (2011a, p. 135).

[11] Pertek (1998, p. 135).

[12] Convention on the Recognition of Qualifications concerning Higher Education in the European Region, Council of Europe and UNESCO, 11 April 1997, ETS—No. 165.

[13] Sorbonne Joint Declaration on harmonisation of the architecture of the European higher education system, Paris, 25 May 1998.

[14] Beschikking van het Benelux Comité van Ministers betreffende de automatische wederzijdse generieke niveauerkenning van diploma's hoger onderwijs, M(2015) 3.

[15] Declaration of the European Ministers of Vocational Education and Training, and the European Commission, convened in Copenhagen on 29 and 30 November 2002, on enhanced European cooperation in vocational education and training—"The Copenhagen Declaration".

[16] Council Recommendation of 26 November 2018 on promoting automatic mutual recognition of higher education and upper secondary education and training qualifications and the outcomes of learning periods abroad, [2018] OJ C 444/1; Council Recommendation of 16 June 2022 on a European approach to micro-credentials for lifelong learning and employability, [2022] OJ C 243/10; Proposal for a Council Recommendation on a European Quality Assurance and Recognition System in Higher Education, COM(2024) 147 final; Communication from the Commission to

3 The Basics of EU Competences and the Division into Types of Recognition

The typology between professional and academic recognition therefore logically reflects the distinction in different contexts in which persons may need recognition. This distinction as such nevertheless does not account for the amount of legislation and policy produced in this area. The answer to that question is rooted in the division of EU competences. For the EU, this issue is of particular importance since it only has the power to act on competences conferred on it by the Treaties and which are divided into three main categories: exclusive, shared, and supporting. For the topic of the recognition of qualifications, attention must be given to shared and supporting competences.

On the one hand, shared competences enable both Member States and the EU to legislate and adopt legally binding acts. However, under Article 2(2) TFEU, Member States can carry out their competence only "to the extent that the Union has not exercised its competence", meaning that their competence is restricted to that part of an issue on which the EU has not been active. Article 4 TFEU subsequently lays down the areas for which competences are shared. One area of which is the internal market, which also covers the topic of professional recognition. The exact competence on professional recognition can then be found in Article 53 TFEU.[17] This means that the EU has the power to adopt binding legislation on professional qualifications and the recognition thereof. At the same time, the Member States may also create binding legislation in this area, as long as it pertains to the area where the EU has not already done so. An example of the shared nature of this competence in relation to the recognition of qualifications can be seen in the existence of the PQD which provides harmonised procedures to effectuate recognition, while the decision to regulate professions and the form in which to do so remains with the Member States.

On the other hand, supporting competences can be found in Article 2(5) TFEU. In some areas, the Union has competence only to "support, coordinate or supplement the actions of the Member States, without thereby superseding their competence in these areas". Union action in such areas, found in Article 6 TFEU, is limited considering that within this third category of competences the use of harmonising measures is prohibited, as the second sentence of Article 2(5) TFEU expressly states that legislation in this area shall not entail harmonisation. Academic recognition can be found in Article 165(2) second indent of the TFEU, meaning EU action is limited to supporting, coordinating or supplementing Member State action.[18] The supporting nature of the Article 165 TFEU competence becomes clear when looking at the different instruments adopted on the basis of it. The vast majority of

---

the European Parliament, the Council, the European Economic and Social Committee and the Committee of the Regions—a blueprint for a European degree, COM(2024) 144.

[17] Although it had already been taken up in the Treaties ever since the 1957 Rome Treaty (Article 57). See Chapter "The Long History of the Recognition of Qualifications in the EU".

[18] Article 6(e) TFEU.

Table 1 Overview of the competences on recognition of qualifications in the TFEU

Article 53(1) TFEU	Article 165(1)(2)(4) TFEU
1. In order to make it easier for persons to take up and pursue activities as self-employed persons, the European Parliament and the Council shall, acting in accordance with the ordinary legislative procedure, issue directives for the mutual recognition of diplomas, certificates and other evidence of formal qualifications and for the coordination of the provisions laid down by law, regulation or administrative action in Member States concerning the taking-up and pursuit of activities as self-employed persons	1. The Union shall contribute to the development of quality education by encouraging cooperation between Member States and, if necessary, by supporting and supplementing their action, while fully respecting the responsibility of the Member States for the content of teaching and the organisation of education systems and their cultural and linguistic diversity … 2. Union action shall be aimed at: … – Encouraging mobility of students and teachers, by encouraging inter alia, the academic recognition of diplomas and periods of study, … 4. In order to contribute to the achievement of the objectives referred to in this Article: – The European Parliament and the Council, acting in accordance with the ordinary legislative procedure, after consulting the Economic and Social Committee and the Committee of the Regions, shall adopt incentive measures, *excluding any harmonisation* of the laws and regulations of the Member States, – The Council, on a proposal from the Commission, shall adopt recommendations

these concern soft law instruments such as recommendations.[19] Indeed, the particular nature of each competence (shared and supporting) is reflected in both TFEU provisions respectively, as seen in Table 1:

A few comments are to be made based on the respective competences for professional and academic recognition above. First, the internal market competence never explicitly related to professional recognition exclusively—nor does article 53 TFEU above. The categorisation of Article 53 TFEU as professional recognition can be considered to have occurred by default once the education competence was formally introduced including its explicit reference to academic recognition in the Maastricht Treaty. Several authors have commented that the exclusion of academic recognition from the scope of Article 53 TFEU and its earlier versions was neither apparent

[19] The only exception being Decision 2018/646 of the European Parliament and of the Council of 18 April 2018 on a common framework for the provision of better services for skills and qualifications (Europass) and repealing Decision no 2241/2004/EC, [2018] OJ L 112/42. See Table 2 below for an overview of all instruments adopted on the basis of the academic recognition competence of Article 165 TFEU.

nor convincing.[20] Indeed, the division of competences and recognition types was certainly less pronounced in the past than it is present-day. Previous versions of Article 53 TFEU left more room for discussion as to its scope. For example, this can be seen in Article 47 of the EC Treaty and Article 57 of the Treaty of Rome in which paragraph 1 of both of these provisions concerned the issuance of "directives for the mutual recognition of diplomas, certificates and other evidence of formal qualifications" for the purpose of making it easier for persons to use their right of free movement. Paragraph 2 subsequently concerned the issuance of "directives for the coordination of the provisions laid down by law, regulation or administrative action in Member States concerning the taking-up and pursuit of activities as self-employed persons".[21] These separate elements were merged by the Lisbon Treaty. Following this previous division in two separate paragraphs we can deduce that that paragraph 1 could have been wider in scope than its present use (i.e. beyond *de jure* professional recognition), while paragraph 2 concerned coordination of the regulation of a profession.

The Lisbon Treaty ultimately led to the current formulation of Article 53 TFEU which combines the two aspects of mutual recognition and coordination into one paragraph. Nevertheless, the former existence of the general system directives (i.e. the directives based on the principle of mutual recognition which functioned without prior harmonisation of education and training),[22] teaches us that the elements of recognition of qualifications and coordination of education and training can still develop separately. What is more important concerning the use of Article 53 TFEU is that its use as a legal basis has been limited to cover only those professions carrying a regulated status, i.e. *de jure* professional recognition. These observations regarding Article 53 TFEU nevertheless lead to questions regarding how Article 165 TFEU has then been understood and whether it covers all academic recognition or perhaps a particular subtype thereof. To establish how the respective competences on recognition were ultimately employed it is necessary to examine the use of the competence in the instruments included in this contribution, as well as the recognition type they concern (i.e. the purpose of the instruments).

---

[20] Garben (2011a, pp. 149–150), Schneider (1995, p. 108).

[21] These two paragraphs represented the approach taken in the 1970s for the sectoral professions. At that time, one directive set out minimum training requirements (i.e. harmonised education and training) according to paragraph 2, while another directive set out provisions for recognition according to paragraph 1. See Chapter "The Long History of the Recognition of Qualifications in the EU" of this contribution.

[22] Directives 89/48/EEC and 92/51/EEC.

4 Examining Instruments for Recognition of Qualifications in Light of Theory & Competences

Before examining the instruments to learn about the use of the respective recognition competences and what type of recognition is affected by a particular instrument, it is to be recalled that the following instruments are relevant to the present work (see Table 2):

Table 2 Overview of actors on recognition and their instruments & initiatives

European Union
• Professional Qualifications Directive (PQD)[23]
• Proportionality Test Directive[24]
• European Qualifications Framework for lifelong learning (EQF)[25]
• Europass Decision[26]
• 2020 VET Recommendation[27]
• Automatic Recognition Recommendation[28]
• Micro-credentials Recommendation[29]
• Proposal for a recommendation on a European quality assurance and recognition system in higher education[30]
• Communication on a European degree[31]

(continued)

[23] Directive 2005/36/EC of the European Parliament and of the Council of 7 September 2005 on the recognition of professional qualifications, [2005] OJ L 255/22 *as amended by* Directive 2013/55/EU of the European Parliament and of the Council of 20 November 2013 amending Directive 2005/36/EC on the recognition of professional qualifications and Regulation (EU) No 1024/2012 on administrative cooperation through the Internal Market Information System ('the IMI Regulation'), [2013] OJ L 354/132.

[24] In this contribution, the term "Proportionality Test Directive" is used to refer to Directive (EU) 2018/958 of the European Parliament and of the Council of 28 June 2018 on a proportionality test before adoption of new regulation of professions, [2018] OJ L 173/25.

[25] In this contribution the term "EQF Recommendation" is used to refer to Council Recommendation of 22 May 2017 on the European Qualifications Framework for lifelong learning and repealing the recommendation of the European Parliament and of the Council of 23 April 2008 on the establishment of the European Qualifications Framework for lifelong learning, [2017] OJ C 189/15.

[26] In this contribution the term "Europass Decision" is used to refer to Decision (EU) 2018/646 of the European Parliament and of the Council of 18 April 2018 on a common framework for the provision of better services for skills and qualifications (Europass) and repealing Decision No 2241/2004/EC, [2018] OJ L 112/42.

[27] In this contribution the term "2020 VET Recommendation" is used to refer to Council Recommendation of 24 November 2020 on vocational education and training (VET) for sustainable competitiveness, social fairness and resilience, [2020] OJ C 417/1.

[28] In this contribution the term "Automatic Recognition Recommendation" is used to refer to Council Recommendation of 26 November 2018 on promoting automatic mutual recognition of higher education and upper secondary education and training qualifications and the outcomes of learning periods abroad, [2018] OJ C 444/1.

[29] In this contribution the term "Micro-credentials Recommendation" is used to refer to Council Recommendation of 16 June 2022 on a European approach to micro-credentials for lifelong learning and employability, [2022] OJ C 243/10.

[30] Proposal for a Council Recommendation on a European Quality Assurance and Recognition System in Higher Education, COM(2024) 147 final.

[31] Communication from the Commission to the European Parliament, the Council, the European Economic and Social Committee and the Committee of the Regions—a blueprint for a European degree, COM(2024) 144, p. 3.

Table 2 (continued)

Council of Europe & UNESCO
• Lisbon Recognition Convention[32]
Bologna Process
• The framework of qualifications for the European Higher Education Area (QF-EHEA) • Diploma Supplement • European Credit Transfer and Accumulation System (ECTS)[33] • Standards and guidelines for quality assurance in the EHEA (ESG)
Regional Initiatives
• Benelux Decisions on Mutual Generic Level Recognition[34]

In this section, previous findings on the typology and competences on recognition of qualifications are combined with the instruments above to gain a deeper understanding of the use of the respective competences. Ultimately, this is done by matching the purpose of the instrument or initiative to the relevant competence (if any) on which it was adopted or initiated and the corresponding recognition type.

Starting with the Professional Qualifications Directive (PQD), this instrument allows for the most straightforward categorisation. In fact, the PQD allows for a confirmation of the findings above, namely that it concerns *de jure* professional recognition. Article 1 of the PQD determines that the instrument establishes rules in accordance with which Member States can make access to a regulated profession dependent on recognition of qualifications. Both Directive 2005/36/EC as well as Directive 2013/55/EU (i.e. the two directives which together constitute the PQD) were adopted on the basis Article 53(1) TFEU (i.e. the internal market competence).[35] The same can be said about the Proportionality Test Directive (Directive (EU) 2018/958). The purpose of that Directive is to establish "rules on a common framework for conducting proportionality assessments before introducing new, or amending existing, legislative, regulatory or administrative provisions restricting access to, or the pursuit of, regulated professions".[36] Other than these instruments, Article 53 TFEU has not been used to create other legislation, meaning its use is indeed restricted to *de jure* professional recognition.

[32] In this contribution, the term "Lisbon Recognition Convention" is used to refer to the Convention on the Recognition of Qualifications concerning Higher Education in the European Region, Council of Europe and UNESCO, 11 April 1997, ETS—No. 165.

[33] As taken up in: EHEA, Bologna Process and European Commission, *ECTS Users' Guide* (Publications Office of the European Union, 2015).

[34] Beschikking van het Benelux Comité van Ministers betreffende de automatische wederzijdse generieke niveauerkenning van diploma's hoger onderwijs, M(2015) 3; Beschikking van het Benelux Comité van Ministers tot aanvulling van beschikking M(2015) 3 betreffende de automatische wederzijdse generieke niveauerkenning van diploma's hoger onderwijs, M(2018) 1; Verdrag betreffende de automatische erkenning van diploma's in het hoger onderwijs (14 September 2021).

[35] Both directives furthermore have the supplementary legal bases of Articles 46 and 62 TFEU signifying that the PQD does not only cover establishment but also free movement of workers and services.

[36] Article 1 Proportionality Test Directive.

Moving to the other EU instruments, attention needs to be given first to the European Qualifications Framework for lifelong learning (EQF) and Europass. It follows from the 2018 Europass Decision that its objective is to establish a comprehensive and interoperable framework of tools and information, which focuses both on transnational employment *and* learning mobility.[37] The 2018 Europass Decision states that it aims to meet the needs of all individual end-users such as learners, job seekers, employers, education and training providers, and national authorities.[38] Furthermore, Europass aims at supporting the transparency and understanding of skills acquired in various contexts.[39] These contexts particularly concern formal, non-formal and informal learning and include practical experiences, mobility and volunteering. Therefore, Europass can be considered a transparency tool supporting recognition for any kind of purpose. Indeed, by enhancing transparency, Europass provides for the possibility to tackle challenges following from a lack of familiarity with other Member States' education systems and professions. From this, we may therefore deduce that Europass relates to both professional as well as academic recognition, i.e. Europass concerns all four subtypes of recognition. The same applies to the EQF, which has as its purpose "to improve the transparency, comparability and portability of people's qualifications".[40] According to the Recommendation, qualifications serve a variety of purposes, among others, employment with an employer, to gain access to a regulated profession, and to support evaluations of education and training authorities.[41]

Both the EQF and Europass are of an overarching nature in the sense that they are relevant to all education types and have both been adopted on the basis of Article 165 TFEU on education and 166 on VET. The same legal bases were, however, also employed to adopt the other instruments although their focus on educational types differs. Indeed, the 2020 Recommendation focuses on VET,[42] while the other instruments concern higher education. This particularly applies to the Automatic Recognition Recommendation, proposal for a recommendation on a quality assurance and recognition system in higher education, and communication on a European degree. The Micro-credentials Recommendation is an exception in this context, since it was based on two additional legal bases, namely Article 149 TFEU on employment and Article 292 TFEU. The plans for a European degree also have an exceptional nature. Since these currently constitute a blueprint proposed via communication, no legislative action has been proposed yet, meaning no legal basis was connected to the initiative (yet). Nevertheless, should the plans advance to a legislative stage, it may

[37] Recital 34 Europass Decision.

[38] Recital 26 Europass Decision.

[39] Article 1(1) Europass Decision.

[40] Recital 3 EQF Recommendation.

[41] Recital 1 EQF Recommendation. Recital 7 further supports the finding that the EQF concerns all recognition types since it indicates that key stakeholders are, among others, education and training providers, employers, and bodies involved in the recognition of academic and professional qualifications.

[42] 2020 VET Recommendation.

be presumed that at least Article 165 TFEU would be legal basis, particularly since a European degree contributes to developing a "European dimension in education", encouraging mobility through academic recognition, and promoting cooperation between educational institutions—all objectives set in Article 165 TFEU.

While these instruments were therefore adopted on similar legal bases, more differences arise among the aforementioned instruments when it comes to the recognition types they concern. The Automatic Recognition Recommendation, for example, has the primary objective and key principle to effectuate automatic mutual recognition for further learning.[43] Here, recognition relates to two different situations: on the one hand, the situation where a student has obtained a higher education qualification (or one giving access to higher education) in one Member State, and on the other hand, the situation where outcomes from a learning period abroad must be recognised. Since the recommendation concerns recognition for access to subsequent studies *and* recognition of learning periods means that it concerns academic recognition by both accumulation as well as by substitution.[44]

The 2020 VET Recommendation has a purpose broader than recognition alone. In fact, it seeks to support Member States in implementing a VET policy which ensures that persons are sufficiently equipped to be successful in a changing labour market and society.[45] In relation to recognition of qualifications, this recommendation is primarily important due to its replacement of the previous recommendations on the European Credit System for Vocational Education and Training (ECVET) and European Quality Assurance Reference Network for VET (EQAVET).[46] Since both of these recommendations concerned all recognition types,[47] the same can be concluded

[43] Paragraph 1 Automatic Recognition Recommendation.

[44] Although the Recommendation concerns academic recognition, the fact that it calls for strengthening of the Bologna and Copenhagen Process instruments and initiatives also means that it can—at least indirectly—contribute to improved recognition in the area of the labour market. See Recital 11 of the Automatic Recognition Recommendation.

[45] Point A 2020 VET Recommendation.

[46] Recommendation of the European Parliament and of the Council of 18 June 2009 on the establishment of a European Credit System for Vocational Education and Training (ECVET), [2009] OJ C 155/11 (ECVET Recommendation); Recommendation of the European Parliament and of the Council of 18 June 2009 on the establishment of a European Quality Assurance Reference Framework for Vocational Education and Training, [2009] OJ C 155/1 (EQAVET Recommendation).

[47] ECVET was aimed at facilitating "the transfer, recognition and accumulation of assessed learning outcomes of individuals who are aiming to achieve a qualification". This could occur by allowing experiences from education, work, or life to be used to substitute for part of a qualification, thereby pointing to academic recognition by substitution. However, under ECVET former learners could also benefit from improved transparency and portability of their learning outcomes—something they could benefit from in various contexts such as employment or further learning. This means that although ECVET predominantly concerns academic recognition by substitution, it may be considered as addressing all four types of recognition. See Recital 17 ECVET Recommendation. When it came to EQAVET, this instrument could be said to have served a supporting role in improving recognition. Its objective was to maintain high quality, transparent, and consistent VET to promote mutual trust, mobility of workers and learners, and lifelong learning. By promoting

for the 2020 VET Recommendation. The recommendation is furthermore a prime example of an instrument challenging the typology of recognition. By focusing on accumulating results of flexible learning paths to achieve full qualifications, the recommendation seems to focus on a type of recognition that seems to partially be academic recognition by accumulation (stacking learning experiences) as well as by substitution (replacing parts of a formal qualification with outcomes from non-formal and informal learning).[48] What is more, the 2020 VET Recommendation—similar to the Automatic Recognition Recommendation—calls to maximise implementation of pre-existing instruments related to recognition such as the EQF, ECTS, and Automatic Recognition Recommendation. As far as these instruments concern other recognition types beyond academic recognition, this would mean the 2020 VET Recommendation would also extend to those types of professional recognition.

Continuing with the Micro-credentials Recommendation, this instrument can firstly be considered an extension of the 2020 VET Recommendation in the sense that it elaborates ambitions regarding more lifelong learning and flexible learning paths. In terms of recognition types, the Micro-credentials Recommendation also enhances all types of recognition due to its wide scope. Indeed, micro-credentials are foreseen to complement and enhance education, training, lifelong learning, and employability.[49]

Moving to the proposal for a recommendation on a quality assurance and recognition system in higher education, this initiative can be said to primarily aim for academic recognition. Indeed, the instrument is aimed at enhancing accountability of higher education institutions and enhancing their performance as a way to strengthen trust in higher education qualifications across the EU.[50] Recognition should then benefit from this increase in trust emanating from improved quality assurance processes.[51] Nevertheless, quality assurance is also to have effects beyond the educational sphere alone, since increased trust in qualifications can also spill over into the professional sphere. This would mean that improvements of quality assurance would also benefit trust among employers and competent authorities, i.e. professional recognition also benefits.

---

common standards on the quality of education, trust can be created in foreign qualifications which in turn benefits recognition. We may therefore consider the EQAVET to also supports all four types of recognition, especially since improved quality supports qualification assessors—whether they are educational institutions or providers, employers, or authorities—in recognising qualifications. See Recital 9 EQAVET Recommendation.

[48] See points 5 and 6 2020 VET Recommendation.

[49] See point 4 Micro-credentials Recommendation.

[50] Proposal for a Council Recommendation on a European Quality Assurance and Recognition System in Higher Education, COM(2024) 147 final, pp. 1–2.

[51] Ibid., p. 2. Indeed, the close link between quality assurance, mutual trust, and recognition has been generally accepted, see Towards the European Higher Education Area, Communiqué of the meeting of European Ministers in charge of Higher Education, Prague (2009, p. 122; pp. 339–340); OECD, The Role of National Qualifications Systems in Promoting Lifelong Learning, October 2005, p. 19.

To continue, the blueprint for the European degree also has a direct link to the labour market. Apart from its obvious educational connotation and its support in the achievement of the EEA-2025, increased employability and skills relevance are central to the European degree by increasing the attractiveness of graduates by ensuring they hold highly sought and future proof competencies and skills.[52] Obviously, academic recognition is also enhanced since part of the proposal includes, for example, ambitions to achieve automatic credit recognition and automatic recognition of the level of qualifications.[53] Again we can therefore classify this initiative as supporting all recognition types.

It is therefore clear that most EU action based on the educational competence of Article 165 TFEU supports all types of recognition. While Article 165 therefore explicitly mentions academic recognition, the instruments adopted on the basis of it are broader in scope and venture into the realm of professional recognition. This broadened application of instruments initially aimed at academic recognition seems to be a broader trend, since it is mirrored in instruments adopted by actors beyond the EU. To start with LRC, the Convention clearly concerns both types of academic recognition.[54] However, the LRC covers more than academic recognition alone. In the LRC, the term recognition is defined as "a formal acknowledgement by a competent authority of the value of a foreign educational qualification with a view to access to educational and/or employment activities". The LRC's broader scope furthermore becomes clear from Section VI on "Recognition of higher education qualifications" where Article VI.3 indicates that consequences of recognition under that title can be: access to further higher education, the use of an academic title, or facilitated access to the labour market. The latter two elements of Article VI.3 therefore attest to the LRC also covering professional recognition, a finding further strengthened by Article VI.4 which indicates that assessments of higher education qualifications under the Convention may lead to an advice for (a) general employment purposes, (b) admission into higher education, or (c) advice to any other competent recognition authority. It is hereby clear that the LRC's application is primarily aimed at *de facto* professional recognition. However, the LRC may also indirectly concern regulated professions. This area of overlap concerns the role of ENIC/NARICs.[55] In particular,

---

[52] Communication from the Commission to the European Parliament, the Council, the European Economic and Social Committee and the Committee of the Regions—a blueprint for a European degree, COM(2024) 144 final, pp. 2–3.

[53] For example, see Communication from the Commission to the European Parliament, the Council, the European Economic and Social Committee and the Committee of the Regions—a blueprint for a European degree, COM(2024) 144 final, p. 6.

[54] See the preamble to the Lisbon Recognition Convention which states that people are to benefit from the diversity of education systems in Europe by facilitating the continuation of education or completion of a period of studies in higher education institutions in other countries party to the Convention. We may deduce from this quote that the Lisbon Recognition Convention relates to academic recognition by both accumulation and by substitution. This is further attested to by some of the LRC's sections, e.g. Section IV which concerns "Recognition of qualifications giving access to higher education" and Section V which concerns "Recognition of periods of study".

[55] These cooperate with the national coordinator of the PQD and the competent authorities for *de jure* professional recognition in the EU.

they may establish assessments of higher education qualifications in the context of an advice for general employment purposes or advise competent recognition authorities who take a recognition decision in the context of the PQD.[56]

Next, the Bologna Process consists of several measures contributing to recognition of qualifications. While their aim is again primarily on academic recognition, professional recognition is also affected. First, the Diploma Supplement was described as "a system to aid recognition for academic and professional purposes".[57] This again means that it supports both professional and academic recognition (and their respective subtypes). Second, the QF-EHEA aims to simplify the structure of higher education by connecting national frameworks to ultimately achieve international transparency.[58] The QF-EHEA therefore comprises the three cycle structure the Bologna Process is widely known for. This harmonisation of the structure of higher education makes qualifications more recognisable thus benefiting recognition processes in any context. Third, the ECTS is more limited in scope, as it strives to promote credit mobility and degree mobility.[59] Whereas credit mobility concerns the recognition of credits between institutions in the context of short-term study (i.e. academic recognition by substitution), degree mobility occurs upon completion of a course of study (i.e. academic recognition by accumulation). Therefore, the ECTS only directly affects academic recognition and its two subtypes. Nevertheless, ECTS may also support recognition for professional purposes, though more indirectly, when either employers or authorities consider such credits to acquire additional information on certain components of higher education degrees.[60] Lastly, the role of quality assurance as a driver of mutual trust was already noted previously. Under the Bologna Process, the ESG play a vital role in enhancing recognition through quality assurance by again increasing trust in higher education.[61] By enhancing the mutual acceptance of quality assurance and improving trust, the ESG are able to promote mobility by supporting all four types of recognition.[62]

Finally, the Benelux Decisions on the automatic generic mutual level recognition of higher education degrees, both primarily concern academic recognition.[63]

---

[56] See Revised Recommendation on Criteria and Procedures for the Assessment of Foreign Qualifications (adopted by the Lisbon Recognition Convention Committee at its fifth meeting, Sèvres), 23 June 2010, p. 9; Section II Joint ENIC/NARIC Charter of Activities and Services, Council of Europe and UNESCO, 9 June 2004.

[57] Paris Communiqué—Paris, May 25th 2018: Paris Communiqué—Appendix IV: The Diploma Supplement Template, Paris, May 25th 2018.

[58] Bologna Working Group on Qualifications Frameworks, A Framework for Qualifications of the European Higher Education Area, Copenhagen, 2005, p. 57.

[59] EHEA, Bologna Process and European Commission, *ECTS Users' Guide* (Publications Office of the European Union, 2015), pp. 30 and 34.

[60] Howat, C. et al. (2011, p. 48).

[61] Kelo, M. (2014, p. 149).

[62] Ibid., p. 150.

[63] Gemeenschappelijke memorie van toelichting bij beschikking M(2015) 3 van het Benelux comité van Ministers betreffende de automatische wederzijdse generieke niveauerkenning van diploma's hoger onderwijs; Gemeenschappelijke memorie van toelichting bij beschikking M(2018) 1 van

Both Decisions concern recognition of completed degrees and make no mention of study periods abroad, and therefore concern academic recognition by accumulation. Nevertheless, both Decisions also indicate that they could contribute to the improvement of the cross-border mobility of Benelux graduates helping them to find employment across the Benelux.[64] Both Decisions are furthermore embedded in labour market policy due to their adoption on the basis of Article 8 of the Benelux Recommendation on cross-border labour mobility.[65] This means that an element of professional recognition is also included, although it is limited to *de facto* professional recognition.[66]

The findings discussed in the previous paragraphs are summarised in Table 3. The table shows that most instruments related to recognition contribute to effectuating all types of recognition. In terms of the use of competences, the table confirms the limited use of Article 53 TFEU, which was used only to create instruments on *de jure* professional recognition (i.e. the PQD and Proportionality Test Directive). However, as far as Article 165 TFEU is concerned, we may see that its use has been much wider since most instruments adopted on the basis of that competence cross the professional versus academic recognition divide and concern all recognition types. As mentioned previously, his appears to be a characteristic of instruments aimed at academic recognition primarily since the instruments adopted by non-EU actors reflect the same broadened scope.

The fact that many instruments aimed primarily at academic recognition also affect professional recognition leads to questions regarding the durability and necessity of the dichotomy between professional and academic recognition as represented in the respective Treaty competences on recognition. The legislative reality can therefore be considered a challenge to the typology on recognition. More specifically, a grey area emerges between the two main types of recognition—or perhaps these are rather much more intertwined than they appear at first sight. Indeed, this was

---

het Benelux Comité van Ministers tot aanvulling van beschikking M(2015) 3 betreffende de automatische wederzijdse generieke niveauerkenning van diploma's hoger onderwijs.

[64] Preamble Beschikking van het Benelux Comité van Ministers betreffende de automatische wederzijdse generieke niveauerkenning van diploma's hoger onderwijs, M(2015) 3; Preamble Beschikking van het Benelux Comité van Ministers tot aanvulling van beschikking M(2015) 3 betreffende de automatische wederzijdse generieke niveauerkenning van diploma's hoger onderwijs, M(2018) 1.

[65] Aanbeveling van het Benelux Comité van Ministers inzake grensoverschrijdende arbeidsmobiliteit—M(2014) 17.

[66] The question may be raised whether the Benelux Decisions could also positively affect an assessment under the general system of the PQD. Indeed, an academic diploma may also be necessary as part of a professional qualification required to exercise a regulated profession. Nevertheless, in this case the Benelux Decisions are not applied because the PQD already includes its own requirement for level recognition. This may be seen in Article 13(3) of the directive which states that "the host Member State shall accept the level attested under Article 11 by the home Member State". This means that if the home Member State attests that a diploma is a bachelor, the host Member State must also accept this. Therefore, the Benelux Decisions do not concern *de jure* professional recognition. This is confirmed by the preambles of the Benelux Decisions.

Table 3 Connecting the typology and competences to the instruments on the recognition of qualifications

Instruments	Actors/Context	TFEU competence on recognition (if any)	Recognition types			
			De jure Professional recognition	*De facto* Professional recognition	By accumulation Academic recognition	By substitution Academic recognition
PQD	EU	Art. 53				
Proportionality Test Directive	EU	Art. 53				
Europass	EU	Art. 165				
EQF	EU	Art. 165				
Automatic Recognition Recommendation	EU	Art. 165				
2020 VET Recommendation	EU	Art. 165				
Micro-credentials recommendation	EU	Art. 165				
Proposed Recommendation on a European Quality Assurance and Recognition System in higher education	EU	Art. 165				
Proposed European degree	EU	N/A				
LRC	Council of Europe & UNESCO	N/A				
Diploma Supplement	Bologna Process	N/A				
QF-EHEA	Bologna Process	N/A				
ECTS	Bologna Process	N/A				
ESG	Bologna Process	N/A				
Benelux Decisions	Benelux	N/A				

something previously recognised by scholars specialising in recognition of qualifications. Accordingly, their views on the grey area between professional and academic recognition are explored next.

5 Ambiguities in Recognition: The Grey Area Between Professional & Academic Recognition and Their Corresponding Competences

To start, it may be recalled that recognition consists of the following main- and subtypes (see Table 4):

Although the difference between *de jure* professional recognition and academic recognition by substitution may seem clear, the same cannot be said for *de facto* professional recognition and academic recognition by accumulation,[67] or even *de jure* and *de facto* professional recognition. Consider the increasing numbers of students who commonly (need to) complete internships throughout their studies, PhD researchers who may be considered as students or as employees depending on the country they work in or the contract they have, or individuals who are working to become qualified professionals such as prospective lawyers completing a professional traineeship. The work of Pertek plays a vital role in understanding

[67] Garben (2011a, pp. 136–137).

Table 4 Overview of the typology of the recognition of qualifications

Professional recognition		Academic recognition	
De jure	*De facto*	By accumulation	By substitution
Recognition in case of regulated professions, i.e. professions for which qualification requirements are laid down in legislation	Recognition for any kind of use on the labour market, but may include certain qualification requirements. Generally related to the decision of the employer to hire a person (and therefore recognise their qualifications)	Recognition in case of completion of one course of study and progressing to a next course of study	Recognition in case of exchanges where a student goes abroad or to another institution to pursue studies and uses the courses completed abroad to complete the course of study in the home State

the typology of recognition. Pertek already noted in 1998 that the sharp distinction between academic and professional recognition was hard to reconcile in the context of the Community, especially considering the free movement rights of individuals.[68] Accordingly, he foresaw different situations constituting the grey area between professional and academic recognition types.

The first example entails the situation of persons being affected by the two types of recognition at different stages of their lives.[69] Individuals may choose to exercise their right to freedom of movement to pursue a certain course of studies first and to make professional use of their qualifications later.[70] Individuals may even choose to pursue studies and economic activities at the same time by seeking to obtain a supplementary diploma while being employed in the same host Member State.[71] Admittedly, this concerns less of a situation pertaining to the grey area of recognition types and more of a general argument in favour of streamlined procedures so that recognition at any stage of a person's life may run smoothly in accordance with the same principles.

A clearer example of an area in which the two types of recognition overlap relates to the modernisation of education and training. The boundaries between the two types of recognition are blurred due to the fact that the classic process of acquiring a diploma first and work experience second is no longer the standard since internships and professional training pursued during education are becoming increasingly common.[72] Because a student is then working while in the midst of attaining an academic qualification, this results in the peculiar situation where uncompleted

[68] Pertek (1998, p. 137).

[69] Communication from the Commission on recognition of qualifications for academic and professional purposes, COM(94) 596 final, p. 9.

[70] Ibid.

[71] Pertek (1998, p. 143).

[72] An occurrence already noted by Pertek (1998, p. 142).

academic qualifications are being recognised for professional purposes. That assessment of uncompleted academic qualifications for professional purposes subsequently contributes to the student completing the academic qualifications at hand which may also simultaneously grant access to a profession. Needless to say, the distinction between professional and academic recognition is hard to maintain in situations like these.

However, by far the most important example of overlap between recognition types concerns when academic qualifications are recognised for professional purposes and vice versa. One example here relates to the situation where a decision on recognition of professional qualifications is at stake. Such a decision is heavily dependent on what education and training a person has followed, which is subsequently attested to by a diploma delivered by an educational institution.[73] Therefore, educational qualifications play a crucial role in the assessment aimed at finding out whether professional recognition will be granted. In fact, a purely academic diploma often also constitutes a direct entry qualification for a certain profession.[74] For example, a graduate with a bachelor of science degree is not only able to apply for a master of science graduate programme but is also able to rely on that bachelor's degree to find employment. This therefore means a certain academic qualification can give access to a profession if professional recognition occurs or to further studies if academic recognition by accumulation occurs.

In a similar vein, academic recognition also has effects on professional recognition.[75] According to Pertek, academic recognition anticipates professional recognition in the host Member State, since it is very likely that receiving education and training in another Member State will lead to one wanting to work there as well.[76] According to Pertek, such professional recognition is necessary to advance mobility during the course of studies because the situation of students who studied abroad and who return to their home Member States and are unable to use the acquired qualification in a professional setting will render student mobility unfruitful and counterproductive.[77] Furthermore, other students will be discouraged from making use of their free movement rights during their course of study.

Scenarios constituting the grey area of recognition are not limited to hypothetical situations alone. Indeed, the most prominent example of academic recognition having effects on professional recognition can be seen in the Court of Justice's (CJEU) *Morgenbesser* decision. Christine Morgenbesser was a French national living in Italy who applied to the Bar Council of Genoa to be enrolled in the register of *praticanti*. To support her application, she presented her French *maîtrise en droit*. Her enrolment was denied because her diploma was not issued by an Italian university. To be registered with the Bar Council, Morgenbesser would have had to complete an entire programme of education and training. The Court was asked whether Community law

[73] Ibid., p. 140.

[74] Schneider (1995, p. 108).

[75] Ibid., p. 141.

[76] Ibid., p. 138.

[77] Pertek (1998, p. 139).

precluded Member States from refusing enrolment in the register of *praticanti* on the mere ground that the legal diploma was not issued or confirmed in Italy.[78] Her case could not be assessed under the relevant EU legislation for lawyers[79] because she had not yet completed all the professional qualifications allowing her to perform such an economic activity, nor could she rely on Directive 89/48/EEC because the position of *praticante* was not the same as the regulated profession of *avvocato*.[80] Although the Court did argue that a traineeship is the practical part of training necessary to access the regulated profession of lawyer,[81] it did not consider the traineeship a regulated profession as such since it only constituted a condition of access to a regulated profession.[82] Therefore, Morgenbesser's situation was different from that of professionals exercising a regulated profession because she was not yet a fully qualified professional, a *produit fini*.

Therefore, the Court needed to assess Morgenbesser's case on the basis of the Treaty provisions on free movement of workers and establishment. The position of trainees had already been considered equal to that of a worker, meaning that the provisions on the free movement of workers also applied to that category of professionals.[83] In *Morgenbesser*, the Court reiterated the reasoning developed in the *Vlassopoulou* judgment.[84] In particular, the Court ruled that a diploma rightfully obtained in one Member State was to be regarded as such in all Member States and extended that reasoning to include "all diplomas, certificates and other evidence of formal qualifications as well as to the relevant experience of the person concerned, irrespective of whether they were acquired in a Member State or in a third country".[85] Furthermore, the Court denied the Italian Government's claim that Morgenbesser's case only concerned academic recognition, arguing that "the taking into account of the diploma of the person concerned […] must therefore be carried out in the context of the assessment of the whole of the training, academic and professional which that person is able to demonstrate".[86] Hence, the Court ruled that Member States had to see to which extent the applicant satisfied the conditions for access to the relevant activity thereby focusing on the equivalence of the foreign diploma to national qualifications and the knowledge and qualifications the applicant has in

---

78 Case C-313/01 *Morgenbesser*, ECLI:EU:C:2003:612, para. 33.

79 Directive 98/5/EC of the European Parliament and of the Council of 16 February 1998 to facilitate practice of the profession of lawyer on a permanent basis in a Member State other than that in which the qualification was obtained, [1998] OJ L 77/36.

80 Case C-313/01 *Morgenbesser*, ECLI:EU:C:2003:612, para. 45 and 51–52.

81 Ibid.

82 Case C-101/10 *Pavlov and Famira*, ECLI:EU:C:2011:462, para. 25.

83 In particular, the Court considered that "the essential feature of an employment relationship […] is that for a certain period of time a person performs services for and under the direction of another person in return for which he receives remuneration"; Case C 66/85 *Lawrie-Blum*, ECLI:EU:C:1986:284, para. 17. The worker status of trainee lawyers was confirmed in Case C-3/90 *Bernini*, ECLI:EU:C:1992:89 and Case C-109/04 *Kranemann*, ECLI:EU:C:2005:187.

84 Case C-340/89 *Vlassopoulou*, ECLI:EU:C:1991:193.

85 Case C-313/01 *Morgenbesser*, ECLI:EU:C:2003:612, para. 58.

86 Ibid., para. 63 and 66.

relation to the nature and duration of the studies and training.[87] In the end, the Court ruled that Italy's refusal to grant access to the Genoa Bar Council on the sole ground of Morgenbesser's diploma not being issued or confirmed by an Italian university was precluded by Community law.

The *Morgenbesser* judgment is of crucial importance because the Court applied the *Vlassopoulou* doctrine to a person who was not a fully qualified professional (*produit fini*), which meant that from that point onwards that doctrine also had to be applied to cases concerning purely academic qualifications.[88] The *Morgenbesser* case also meant that EU citizens could henceforth conclude part of their training leading up to a regulated profession in one Member State and continue that training in another Member State.[89] The case can be seen as a prime example of the complexities existing in the classification of professional and academic recognition. With the *Morgenbesser* case the Court essentially pulled the situation of non-fully qualified individuals preparing to exercise a regulated profession into the scope of EU law—and into the realm of professional recognition. Ever since the *Morgenbesser* case, the Court has been confronted with other cases concerning non-fully qualified professionals.[90] However, these judgments have not resulted in a general statement confirming that recognition of all academic degrees for professional purposes is to be considered as professional recognition—and therefore within the scope of EU law. Accordingly, this line of cases can be considered to be the ultimate proof of the grey area between professional and academic recognition. In this context, Garben remarked that the *Morgenbesser* case demonstrated the Court having difficulties demarcating the two types of recognition, thereby also arguing that the Court could have simply pointed out that the case concerned recognition of academic qualifications for professional purposes thus constituting professional recognition.[91]

Reasons can nevertheless be found as to why the Court did not do so. Claessens and Schneider argue that the reason why the Court did not assess the *Morgenbesser* case in the context of Directive 89/48/EEC was not related to the fact that the activities of *praticante* could not be considered as a regulated professional activity. Indeed, the application of Directive 89/48/EEC was precluded because Morgenbesser's qualifications could not be considered as a diploma in light of that directive, as her qualifications did not give her direct access to the training for *avocat* in France.[92] This means that Morgenbesser's qualifications were different from those to which she sought access, thus forcing the Court to deal with the matter outside the explicit

[87] Ibid., para 67–68.

[88] Schneider and Claessens (2005, p. 151).

[89] Schneider and Lubina (2009, p. 139).

[90] Case C-345/08 *Pešla*, ECLI:EU:C:2009:771 and Case C-298/14 *Brouillard*, ECLI:EU:C:2015:652; Case C-166/20 *BB v. Lietuvos Respublikos sveikatos apsaugos ministerija*, ECLI:EU:C:2021:554; Case C-577/20 *A v. Sosiaali- ja terveysalan lupa- ja valvontavirasto*, ECLI:EU:C:2022:467; Case C-634/20 *A v. Sosiaali- ja terveysalan lupa- ja valvontavirasto*, ECLI:EU:C:2022:149.

[91] Garben (2011a, pp. 143–144).

[92] Claessens and Schneider (2011, p. 130).

ambit of the EU legislation on professional recognition.[93] The Court, however, never referred to the specific circumstance of Morgenbesser being unable to access training for *avocat* in France, meaning it proved that the *Morgenbesser* principle is one to be applied generally to all those professionals who are not yet fully qualified to exercise a regulated profession.[94] The question thereby remains whether it would have not made more sense to consider the activities of *praticante* as a regulated profession under Directive 89/48/EEC. Bringing the activities of a trainee lawyer within the ambit of the Directive could lead to advantages regarding the evaluation of qualifications and the imposition of additional measures to mitigate potential shortages of knowledge.[95]

Bringing trainees within the scope of the EU directives on recognition would have certainly benefited legal certainty for these starting professionals. Nevertheless, a general statement confirming all academic degrees recognised for professional purposes could have caused tension with other instruments on recognition adopted outside the EU legal framework and could have touched upon other types of recognition considered subject to the educational competence.[96] Furthermore, the *Morgenbesser* judgment also falls in line with a more general trend in the Court's case law which adopts a restricted approach to the concept of a regulated profession.[97] In particular, this concept is explained restrictively since professional regulation—and the corresponding need for recognition—can act as a barrier to mobility and is therefore to be limited where possible. This discussion also further touches upon the freedom Member States have to decide to how to regulate their professions. It seems that the Court sought to strike a careful balance between ensuring legal protection for non-fully qualified professionals and not encroaching upon the regulatory discretion of Member States. However, since the conclusion in *Morgenbesser* was that non-fully qualified professionals are subject to EU law on freedom of movement, the question does remain whether an expansion of the scope of the EU directives on recognition would not have been the more obvious choice.

While *Morgenbesser* is therefore the prime practical example of a case where academic recognition influences professional recognition, we may also see discussions pertaining to the grey area of recognition types in discussions on the choice of legal basis. While the division and use of competences on internal market (Article 53 TFEU) and education (Article 165 TFEU) may be subject to a clear understanding present-day, this has not always been the case. The CJEU's *Erasmus case* demonstrates that the grey area and discussion on the distinction in two recognition types and corresponding competences also made it into relevant legislation on recognition.

[93] Ibid.

[94] Claessens and Schneider (2011, p. 131).

[95] For the benefits of the inclusion of non-fully qualified professionals in Directive 89/48/EEC see Schneider and Lubina (2009, pp. 144–150). For more on the present situation of non-fully qualified professionals under the PQD, see Chapter "Professional Recognition", Sect. 6 of this research.

[96] See Chapter "Re-Imagining the System for the Recognition of Qualifications in the EU" of this contribution.

[97] See Chapter "Professional Recognition", Sect. 2 of this contribution.

To better understand the background of this dispute it is important to revisit the introduction of education as a competence in the Maastricht Treaty. Already in the 1970s the Court had determined in *Casagrande* that even though competences in the area of education and training were not included in the Treaty, that did not mean that the exercise of Community powers was limited if it affected education and training.[98] The Court therefore opened up to the possibility that Community measures, for which the Community already had a competence, could influence education and training as well.[99] Much of this reasoning is reminiscent of the *Tobacco Advertisement* judgment.[100] Indeed, the Court's reasoning in that case has been employed previously to the field of higher education to convincingly argue for the incorporation of the Bologna Process into the EU legal order.[101] The *Erasmus case* nevertheless reflects the struggle to navigate the achievement of objectives related to education while maintaining a balance with the discretion of Member States and other internal market objectives.

In *Commission v. Council* (*Erasmus*), the Commission brought an action before the Court of Justice to annul the original Erasmus Decision for its adoption on the wrong legal basis.[102] According to the Commission, Article 128 of the EEC Treaty sufficed as a competence for the Erasmus Programme. It may be recalled that the Court had previously confirmed that the conditions of access to vocational training fell within the scope of the Treaty (i.e. Article 128 mentioned above) and higher education was also covered by that concept.[103] By contrast, Article 235 EEC Treaty required unanimity for a measure to be adopted, meaning its inclusion as a legal basis for the Erasmus Decision would have subjected it to more scrutiny by the Member States as opposed to if the Decision had been adopted exclusively on the basis of Article 128, which did not provide for any voting requirements. Unsurprisingly, the Council as well as a number of Member States argued that Article 235 needed to be included next to Article 128 EEC Treaty due to the fact that the subject-matter of the Erasmus Programme exceeded the scope of vocational training.[104] The Court initially agreed with the Commission that Article 128 did allow for the Council to adopt measures imposing obligations on Member States in the area of vocational training.[105] However, the Court also found that Article 235 EEC Treaty was the appropriate supplementary legal basis because the Erasmus Programme not only related to vocational training, but also to research, which was not covered by

---

[98] Case 9/74 *Casagrande*, ECLI:EU:C:1974:74, para. 12.

[99] Käsper and Kerimäe (2012, p. 400).

[100] Case C-376/98 *Germany v. European Parliament and Council*, ECLI:EU:C:2000:544.

[101] Garben (2011b, pp. 192–196).

[102] Case 242/87 *Commission v. Council (Erasmus)*, ECLI:EU:C:1989:217.

[103] Case 293/83 *Gravier*, ECLI:EU:C:1985:69, para. 23–25 and Case 24/86 *Blaizot*, ECLI:EU:C:1988:43, para. 17–20; Case 42/87 *Commission v. Belgium*, ECLI:EU:C:1988:454, para 7–8.

[104] Case 242/87 *Commission v. Council (Erasmus)*, ECLI:EU:C:1989:217, para. 7.

[105] An argument that was not to be invalidated by, among others, the lack of involvement of the European Parliament, lacking requirements as to voting in the Council, and the fact that the Erasmus decision had budgetary implications. Ibid., para. 11–12, 16–18.

Article 128.[106] This particularly concerned exchanges of teaching staff and university administrators foreseen in the programme. Questions can be raised as to the validity of this reasoning which considers these exchanges as part of the Community's research policy. After all, these exchanges were clearly formulated to serve the objective of enhancing student mobility and the development of integrated study programmes—subjects obviously related to education. Accordingly, the *Erasmus* case is exemplary of the Court's caution in not overreaching into the education policies of the Member States.

Despite the *Erasmus* case's importance in revealing the sensitive nature of education policy, it was also important to delineate between professional and academic recognition. One important point in relation to this delineation is the Court's reasoning surrounding Action 3 of the 1987 Decision.[107] The Court also considered whether Article 57 EEC Treaty (current Article 53 TFEU) would possibly have been an appropriate legal basis for the Erasmus Decision, however concluded that the Erasmus decision did not fall under the exclusive scope of application of Article 57 EEC Treaty because recognition itself was not the primary subject-matter of Action 3, as the measures provided there were only designed to "prepare for and encourage the recognition envisaged".[108] This leads to the very plausible assumption that had academic recognition been the subject-matter of the Erasmus programme, it could have fallen under the Article 57 EEC Treaty competence.[109] Therefore, the *Erasmus* case supports the observation that Article 57 EEC Treaty—at some point in time—covered both professional as well as academic recognition.[110]

The lack of clarity in recognition types is therefore reflected not only in the typology itself, but also in EU legislation and CJEU case law. Despite all these overlaps in recognition types, the respective types of recognition developed separately.[111] Nevertheless, attempts have been made to reconcile professional and academic recognition. Soon after the introduction of the education competence in the Maastricht Treaty in 1994, the European Commission issued a Communication to this end. In particular, the Commission identified four fields of action to develop synergies between the two main types of recognition: information provision, creation

[106] Case 242/87 *Commission v. Council (Erasmus)*, ECLI:EU:C:1989:217, para. 37.

[107] That point of Action concerned "Measures to promote mobility through the academic recognition of diplomas and periods of study"; see Action 3, Annex Council Decision of 15 June 1987 adopting the European Community Action Scheme for the Mobility of University Students (ERASMUS), [1987] OJ L 166/20.

[108] Case 242/87 *Commission v. Council (Erasmus)*, ECLI:EU:C:1989:217, para. 20; Garben (2010, p. 192, footnote 21).

[109] Moreover, the fact that the Court mentions that the Erasmus Decision did not fall under the *exclusive* scope of application of Article 57 implies that the Erasmus Decision did partly fall under the Article 57 recognition competence. This means that, at the time of the *Erasmus* judgment, Article 57 may have been held to cover both professional as well as academic recognition. See: Garben (2010, pp. 192–193, footnote 21), Minor (1992, p. 16).

[110] Garben (2010, pp. 192–193, footnote 21).

[111] See Chapter "The Long History of the Recognition of Qualifications in the EU" of this contribution.

of academic and professional networks, joint adaptation of courses, and evaluation of quality.[112] The Commission indicated that academic recognition had developed through bilateral and multilateral agreements and mobility programmes while professional recognition was organised through directives.[113] However, more importantly, the Commission acknowledged that academic and professional recognition had been neither planned nor undertaken as a coherent whole and that this was due to action on academic recognition being undertaken much later than that on professional recognition[114]—all observations very much confirmed in this contribution.

The Communication nevertheless also expressed the approach to professional and academic recognition that became fundamental to how the present-day instruments are set up. In particular, the Commission wrote that both academic recognition as well as *de jure* professional recognition stemmed from legislation, since mobility here was governed by regulations on curricula or the right to exercise professions.[115] *De facto* professional recognition was thereby considered to be of a different nature. In particular, the Commission indicated that *de facto* professional recognition rather required growing social awareness constituting a sociological phenomenon which, though possibly subject to action, could not be legally imposed.[116] This statement is heavily reliant on the idea that *de facto* professional recognition merely depends on a decision of an employer but is otherwise free from (formal) regulation. This may be considered an overly narrow interpretation of *de facto* professional recognition since examples can be found of ways to include non- or semi-binding provisions related to qualifications for non-regulated professions that constitute barriers to mobility.[117]

In fact, the main issue regarding the distinction between professional and academic recognition is in the current understanding of the competences. In particular,where Article 53 TFEU is considered a *de jure* professional recognition competence while Article 165 is the competence for the residual recognition types. This over-extensive reading of Article 165 TFEU paired with the restricted application of Article 53 TFEU gives rise to potential issues in the realm of *de facto* professional recognition. While this type of recognition has been pulled into the realm of Article 165 TFEU, it also remains subject to national law since the shared nature of the internal market competence means areas where the EU has not initiated action remain with the Member States. However, *de facto* professional recognition is also subject to the

[112] Communication from the Commission on recognition of qualifications for academic and professional purposes, COM(94) 596 final, pp. 2–3.

[113] Ibid., p. 4.

[114] Ibid., pp. 4 and 7.

[115] Ibid., p. 8.

[116] Ibid., p. 8.

[117] For example, in the Netherlands the profession of nurse with a specialisation in intensive care (N.B. not a specialised nurse, but a different specialisation) is not a regulated profession. Nevertheless, quality standards maintained in care require these intensive care nurses to have a certain degree issued by a Dutch provider of healthcare education and training. No procedure for recognition of foreign qualifications is foreseen since no formal regulation exists, yet the existence of this quality standard leads to uncertainty among employers who are unsure if they can hire intensive care nurses with formal qualifications without going against the quality standard; see Kortese (2018).

right of free movement in the Treaties. In particular, Articles 45, 49, and 56 TFEU ensure that EU citizens in non-regulated professions may go to another Member State in the context of employment activities. Accordingly, Member States must refrain from adopting "any measure which could jeopardize the attainment of the objectives" of the Treaty and all national measures "liable to hamper or to render less attractive the exercise […] of fundamental freedoms guaranteed by the Treaty" are precluded by the Treaty unless they are sufficiently justified.[118] Due to the fact that national qualification requirements could hinder other Member State nationals from exercising their fundamental freedoms, in particular, when no account is taken of "the knowledge and qualifications already acquired by the person concerned in another Member State", Member States must take all diplomas, certificates and other evidence of qualifications acquired by a citizen into consideration.[119] This means that, apart from being subject to national law, *de facto* professional recognition is also subject to more general EU internal market law on freedom of movement.

Application of more general EU law on free movement mainly occurs in the realm of *de facto* professional recognition when academic qualifications are recognised for labour market purposes.[120] Here, the *Kraus* case is of importance. In this case, the Court of Justice was asked to rule on the compatibility with EU law of authorisation procedures allowing professionals to use their foreign academic titles originating from other Member States in Germany. The Court considered that although an academic title was generally not a requirement for access to a profession, having such a title nevertheless did amount to an advantage on the labour market proving additional professional qualification and fitness for a particular post.[121] In some cases, it could even be required to pursue a career. Nevertheless, the procedure for authorisation to use an academic title was not necessary for Kraus to exercise his profession (i.e. he did not need authorisation of his English LL.M. to access a profession). An unsatisfying part of the *Kraus* case is therefore that the CJEU did not confirm whether a requirement regarding authorisation of an academic title would have constituted *de jure* professional recognition.[122] Nevertheless, it did attempt to assess Kraus's situation under Directive 89/48/EEC (which did not apply due to the shorter duration of Kraus's studies) and Directive 92/51/EEC (which did not apply yet). Ultimately, the Court concluded that the authorisation procedure was permitted, though under strict

---

[118] See Case 71/76 *Thieffry*, ECLI:EU:C:1977:65, para. 16; Case 222/86 *Heylens*, ECLI:EU:C:1987:442, para. 12; Case C-340/89 *Vlassopoulou*, ECLI:EU:C:1991:193, para. 14; Case C-19/92 *Kraus*, ECLI:EU:C:1993:125, para. 32. See also Case C-55/94 *Gebhard*, ECLI:EU:C:1995:411, para. 37; Case C-424/97 *Haim II*, ECLI:EU:C:2000:357, para. 57; Case C-285/01 *Burbaud*, ECLI:EU:C:2003:432, para. 95; Case C-575/11 *Nasiopoulos*, ECLI:EU:C:2013:430, para. 21.

[119] Case C-340/89 *Vlassopoulou*, ECLI:EU:C:1991:193, para. 15–16.

[120] One of the examples constituting the grey area between professional and academic recognition described earlier in this section.

[121] Case C-19/92 *Kraus*, ECLI:EU:C:1993:125, para. 18 and 19. See also Case C-153/02 *Neri*, ECLI:EU:C:2003:614, para. 42.

[122] Ibid., para. 20.

conditions.[123] According to the Court, Community law did govern the authorisation procedures because they facilitated access to a profession.[124] However, there was no specific legislation governing the topic of the use of academic titles.[125] The absence of harmonisation regarding the use of such titles allowed Member States to establish rules on this topic.[126]

The case is nevertheless indicative of the interaction between *de jure* and *de facto* professional recognition, and even academic recognition by accumulation. Indeed, it follows from the *Kraus* case that whereas the lack of EU measures on a certain topic cannot lead to a situation where citizens are denied the practical benefit of the freedoms guaranteed by the Treaties,[127] Member States are free to undertake action in areas in which the EU has not. Or phrased differently: since no EU legislation was applicable to the case it was held to be within the discretion of the Member States although they had to adhere to general rules on free movement in the context of the internal market.[128] It is for this reason that the EU's inaction in the area of *de facto* professional recognition allows Member States to maintain additional procedures for recognition in relation to the non-regulated part of the labour market. The freedom of Member States then provides them with the opportunity to develop their own procedures. It can even enable use of other legislative instruments such as the LRC to be used in the area of *de facto* professional recognition. Because Member States have this freedom, they may use concepts normally employed in the field of academic recognition in the area of *de facto* professional recognition. In this context, the EU's legislative inaction in the area of *de facto* professional recognition has ensured that *de facto* professional recognition is pulled further into the realm of education and subject to a fragmented legal landscape. This is particularly visible when creating an overview of the different recognition types, competences, and how they were employed by adding the instruments discussed in this contribution. Figure 1 reflects this development.

While *Kraus* is the main example containing the EU's approach to the existence of additional procedures that do not concern *de jure* professional recognition, other examples may be found. From these cases, we may see a trend emerge where the Court seeks to balance the autonomy of Member States with EU free movement law. In particular, we may perceive the progressive development of case law guiding Member States in relation to what they can and cannot ask of professionals in the context of *de facto* professional recognition. For example, *Thieffry* established that Member States may maintain procedures to establish either the academic effect or the civil effect (i.e.

---

[123] The Court set a number of conditions for authorisation procedures to be considered in line with EU Law. First, they could only be imposed to verify that a degree was properly obtained. Second, the authorisation procedure had to be easy to access and not require excessive fees. Third, decisions had to be open to judicial proceedings. Fourth, penalties imposed had to be proportionate to the offence committed. See Case C-19/92 *Kraus*, ECLI:EU:C:1993:125, para. 38–41.

[124] Ibid., para. 23.

[125] Ibid., para. 24.

[126] Ibid., para. 27 and 34.

[127] Ibid., para. 30.

[128] See Article 2(2) TFEU.

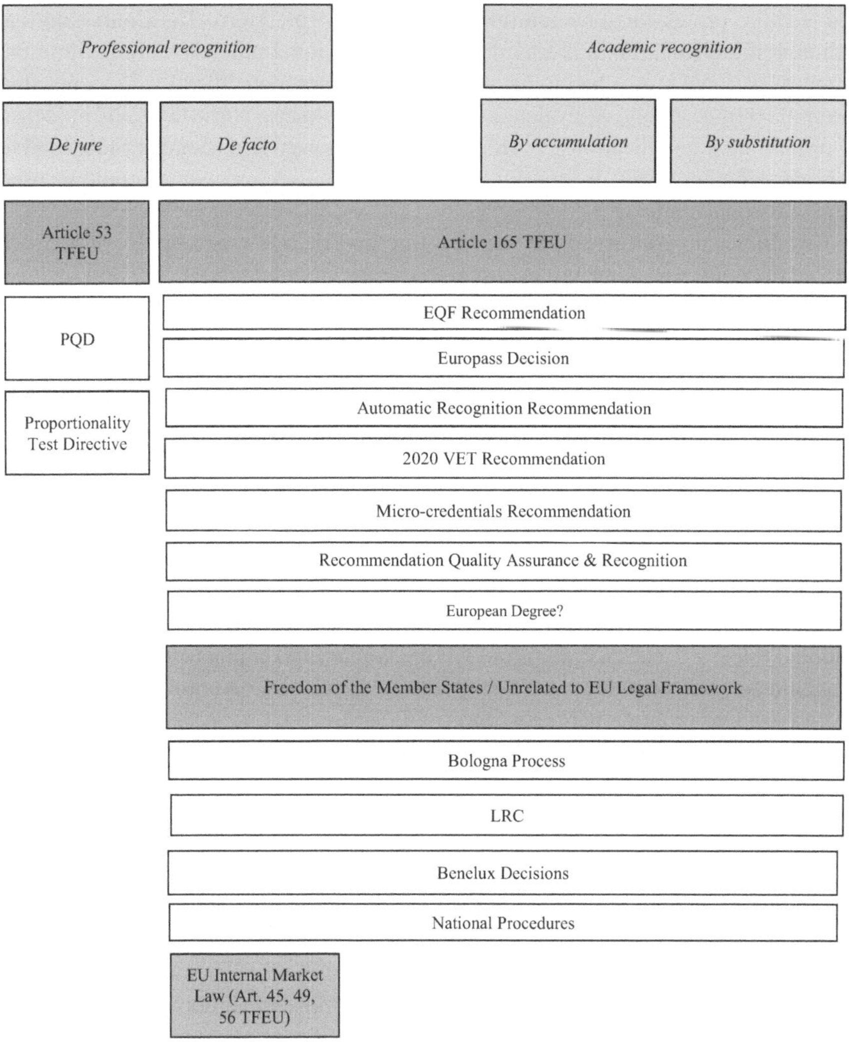

Fig. 1 Illustrating the over-extensive use of Article 165 TFEU and legal disparity on de facto professional recognition and academic recognition in the European System for the Recognition of Qualifications

enabling professional use) of qualifications.[129] In this case, the individual concerned had undergone a procedure to confirm the equivalence of his foreign degree to the corresponding French degree (i.e. an academic recognition procedure). However, that equivalence was subsequently not considered to suffice for a professional recognition (i.e. he could not use the result of the academic equivalence procedure to immediately

[129] Case 71/76 *Thieffry*, ECLI:EU:C:1977:65, para. 22.

also acquire professional recognition to access the profession). The Court held that although the distinction in academic versus professional procedures fell within the ambit of national law, it had to be considered whether a qualification recognised in the context of academic equivalence recognition could also constitute valid evidence of professional qualifications.[130] Hence, *Thieffry* showed that Member States had to consider whether results from prior academic recognition procedures could be used in professional contexts.

Aranitis again concerned the use of a foreign title. He was a holder of a Greek degree in geology seeking authorisation to use the German title of *Diplom-Geologe*. The Court confirmed that the profession could not be considered regulated since there was no regulation governing access to that profession.[131] Nevertheless, the Court did determine that, in practice, only those holding the title of *Diplom-Geologe* were hired, but concluded that this still did not render the profession regulated.[132] This meant that the predecessors of the PQD could not be applied in such cases. The Court therefore ruled that in light of the principle of non-discrimination on the basis of nationality it should be possible for persons with foreign degrees to work in another Member State. And this required them to "take into consideration the diplomas, certificates and other evidence of qualifications which the person concerned has acquired in order to exercise the same profession in another Member States by making a comparison between the specialized knowledge and qualifications required by the national rules".[133] The case therefore left the labour market practices in the Member States intact, but extended the *Vlassopoulou* formula to non-regulated professions (i.e. to *de facto* professional recognition).[134]

In the later *Fernández de Bobadilla* case the Court again reflected on the regulated status of a profession for which access was subject to a procedure for academic recognition. The Court there reiterated its prior reasoning from *Aranitis* to the extent that EU law allowed employers to require candidates to prove their suitability for the position through their qualifications, which had to be in line with the fundamental freedoms (given effect to through the *Vlassopoulou* formula).[135] In *Morgenbesser*, the Court established that both academic and civil equivalence procedures could be relevant for enrolment at another Member State's Bar.[136] However, the Court went on to rule that it was not necessary for the competent authority to examine the *academic* equivalence in the case of a non-fully qualified professional seeking access to a *professional* traineeship.[137] While academic equivalences constitute thorough procedures confirming the similarity of academic degrees, recognition of professional qualifications focuses more on the general suitability of a person to carry out a certain

[130] Ibid., para. 25.

[131] Case C-164/94, *Aranitis*, ECLI:EU:C:1996:23, para. 20.

[132] Ibid., para. 22–23.

[133] Ibid., para. 31.

[134] Ibid., para. 32.

[135] Case C-234/97 *Fernández de Bobadilla*, ECLI:EU:C:1999:367, para. 11 and 28–36.

[136] Case C-313/01 *Morgenbesser*, ECLI:EU:C:2003:612, para. 64.

[137] Ibid., para. 65.

profession. Therefore, in the case of Morgenbesser, the *Vlassopoulou* principle had to be applied to determine whether her qualifications were suitable.[138]

Such reasoning appeared to open the way for a more restricted approach to academic equivalence procedures for professional purposes. In *Brouillard* the Court ruled on the case of a person who had applied for the competition to be recruited as a legal secretary at the Belgian *Cour de cassation* with a vocational master's degree in law, economics, and management from France. While he also applied for academic equivalence, the result of that procedure was not yet known when his application was considered inadmissible. However, some parts of his degree as well as professional experience gained could potentially be relevant, although it was unclear whether these were considered in his application. The Court determined that although boards competent to select candidates for a profession can rely on academic equivalence procedures to determine whether foreign qualifications are equivalent to the national ones required, they are obliged to assess all evidence of qualifications in the context of such procedures (i.e. not solely a diploma).[139] In accordance with *Brouillard*, prior procedures for the recognition of academic qualifications may also contribute to professional recognition.[140]

Beyond the case law of the Court, examples of such national procedures challenging recognition types can be seen when taking a closer look at procedures to determine the academic equivalence of foreign qualifications. These procedures are sometimes also described as academic recognitions or equivalences and can be considered to assimilate the foreign qualification to a national one (as opposed to recognition under the PQD where the qualification will still be foreign though considered similar enough to allow access to the profession). In these procedures, the diploma in principle forms the object of these procedures (again, as opposed to the PQD where work experience and other evidence of qualifications are also considered for suitability to exercise the profession). Such procedures are often not mandatory as such but can contribute to improved chances on the labour market (similar to the situation in *Kraus*) since they attest that a foreign diploma is effectively the same as a national diploma. Occasionally, such procedures are relevant for employment in the public service. Alternatively, these procedures can even be relevant to persons exercising regulated professions, as they can provide a back-up in case recognition under the (national transposition) of the PQD is not possible.

Focusing on the Benelux region, we may see some EU Member States in which procedures from the academic sphere may be relevant to the professional one. In the

---

[138] Ibid., para. 66–72.

[139] Case C-298/14 *Brouillard*, ECLI:EU:C:2015:652, para. 60 and 67.

[140] While the case of *Brouillard* concerned a non-regulated profession (i.e. *de facto* professional recognition), the Court has been more decisive in the case of regulated professions. In previous case law, it indicated that if recognition is to take place in accordance with the PQD, additional academic recognition/equivalence procedures are prohibited. See Case C-286/06 *Commission v. Spain*, ECLI:EU:C:2008:586, para. 76–82; Case C-234/97 *Fernández de Bobadilla*, ECLI:EU:C:1999:367, para. 27; Case C-141/04 *Peros*, ECLI:EU:C:2005:472, para. 35.

Flemish Community, for example, we may perceive two types of equivalence procedures: full equivalence and level equivalence.[141] While the former primarily relates to content, the latter only relates to the level of the degree thereby demonstrating why the Benelux Decisions on the automatic mutual generic level recognition of higher education degrees also concern *de facto* professional recognition. Because of these Decisions holders of a higher education degree issued in the Benelux do not need to undergo such level equivalence procedures, as the level of higher education degrees has been declared equivalent.[142] Similar procedures can be found in the French and German-Speaking Communities in Belgium.[143] In the Netherlands, it is possible to request a credential evaluation which is an explanation of a foreign degree in the context of the Dutch education system (i.e. not an equivalent to a Dutch degree).[144] However, for some academic titles, equivalence needs to be established if the person wants to carry the corresponding Dutch title.[145] Lastly, in Luxembourg holders of a secondary and higher education diploma can obtain an academic recognition to carry an academic title.[146]

Combining these findings from a selection of Member States with the case law above, supports the statement that academic recognition procedures are permitted for non-regulated professions (i.e. *de facto* professional recognition) as long as the results thereof are considered for professional use and all evidence of qualifications is considered during these procedures. In this context, the question may be raised whether it would not be easier to expand the concept of a regulated profession to also cover those professions for which any qualification requirement is set.[147] A more expansive reading of that concept would ensure maximum use of the PQD's safeguards.

[141] Article 1(1)(7) Besluit van de Vlaamse Regering betreffende de voorwaarden en de procedure tot erkenning van buitenlandse studiebewijzen uitgereikt in het hoger onderwijs, BS 18 juli 2013.

[142] Gemeenschappelijke memorie van toelichting bij beschikking M(2015) 3 van het Benelux Comité van Ministers betreffende de automatische wederzijdse generieke niveauerkenning van diploma's hoger onderwijs, p. 2.

[143] Arrête du Gouvernement de la Communauté française déterminant les conditions et la procédure d'octroi de l'équivalence des titres, diplômes et certificats d'études supérieures délivrés à l'étranger, MB 16 septembre 2016; Arrête royal déterminant les conditions et la procédure d'octroi de l'équivalence des diplômes et certificats d'études étrangers, MB 5 auguste 1971; Circulaire 8171 du 30 juin 2021—Equivalence de titres'études primaires et secondaires étrangers; Gesetz vom 19. März 1971 über die Gleichwertigkeit ausländischer Diplôme und Zeugnisse; Königlicher Erlass vom 20. Juli 1971 zur Festlegung der Bedingungen und des Verfahrens zwecks Zuerkennung der Gleichwertigkeit ausländischer Diplome und Zeugnisse.

[144] Article 7.4.7 Wet educatie en beroepsonderwijs.

[145] Article 7.23 and 7.23a Wet op het hoger onderwijs en wetenschappelijk onderzoek.

[146] Title V Chapter 4 Loi du 28 octobre 2016 relative à la reconnaissance des qualifications professionnelles; Chapter II Règlement grand-ducal du 17 février 2017 relatif à la reconnaissance des qualifications professionnelles.

[147] Indeed, the definition of a regulated profession is a matter of EU law, meaning that any legislative, regulatory or administrative provision laying down a requirement related to the qualification (of which having a certain title is one) should be considered regulated. See the case law of the Court of Justice in Case C-234/97 *Fernández de Bobadilla*, ECLI:EU:C:1999:367, para. 14; Case C-586/08 *Rubino*, ECLI:EU:C:2009:801, para. 23; Case C-372/09 and C-373/09 *Peñarroja Fa*, ECLI:EU:C:2011:156, para. 27; Case C-285/01 *Burbaud*, ECLI:EU:C:2003/432, para. 43.

However, such a reading likely encounters objections in terms of creating unnecessary market access restrictions and would run contrary to ambitions to diminish professional regulation.[148] At the same time, the question must also be raised whether the doctrine deduced from the CJEU's case law above is sufficiently known in practice among individuals, employers, professional bodies, and authorities, or whether they would benefit from some information, guidance or other action to enhance the familiarity this case law and its effects in practice.

6 Conclusion

Over the course of this chapter, the typology of the recognition of qualifications was explained in-depth. In accordance with this typology, two main types and four subtypes of recognition were identified. The two main types of recognition are structured along the two main purposes persons may have to use certain qualifications in another country, namely for work (i.e. professional recognition) and study (i.e. academic recognition). Both types of recognition each have two subtypes. Professional recognition consists of *de facto* and *de jure* recognition, representing the distinction between professions for which qualification requirements are set by law (i.e. they are regulated) and those that are not. For academic recognition, a distinction is made between temporary attendance at an educational institution in another Member State (e.g. in the context of an exchange) and the situation where persons are enrolled for a full course of study in another Member State. These two subtypes of recognition are labelled academic recognition by substitution and academic recognition by accumulation respectively.

Although the distinction between professional and academic recognition logically reflects the realities of needing recognition for work or study, this chapter also showed that the distinction in recognition types can be challenged. This is of importance since the development of instruments on recognition has followed the distinction between work (professional recognition) and study (academic recognition), due to the pairing of these respective types of recognition with separate competences: one shared on internal market and the other supporting on education. In turn, this distinction enabled the current pluriform legal and policy landscape to arise.

However, this chapter also showed that the use of competences does not follow the strict delineation between professional and academic recognition types. Indeed, existing instruments can affect recognition types secondary to those they were primarily created for. It has thereby become clear that this particularly gives rise to tension in the area of *de facto* professional recognition where instruments adopted by the EU on the basis of its academic recognition competence of Article 165 TFEU intersect with more general free movement law, as well as instruments by the Council of Europe & UNESCO and adopted in the context of the Bologna Process, as well

[148] See Chapter "Introduction", Sect. 4 and Chapter Professional Recognition", Sect. 2.1.1 of this contribution.

as national law. While this chapter has shown that the legislative inaction on *de facto* professional recognition on behalf of the EU was originally a conscious choice, the question may be raised whether this stance should be maintained—especially in light of the CJEU's case law discussed above. In light of these findings, attention should be turned to the question whether the system for recognition of qualifications resulting from the instruments contributing to or effectuating recognition is comprehensive and can ensure smooth recognition at all stages of life in line with common European principles. This question is particularly pertinent for reasons related to legal certainty of individuals undergoing recognition as well as authorities and employers taking decisions on qualifications. What is more, it is necessary to reconsider the system in light of the future ambitions for the internal market and European Education Area affecting recognition which revolve around enhancing automatic recognition and flexibility as well as reducing excessive regulation.[149]

However, before questions such as these can be addressed, it is necessary to better understand the instruments for recognition. In this chapter, examination of the instruments was limited to the purpose of these instruments to determine the recognition types concerned and competence relied on (if any). Naturally, each instrument has different characteristics in terms of extent to which it is (or is not) legally binding, who it is directed at (individuals and/or authorities and employers vs. Member States), and how it achieves or contributes to achieving recognition. Accordingly, Chapters "Professional Recognition" and "Academic Recognition" are dedicated to exploring the instruments in-depth before Chapter "Re-Imagining the System for the Recognition of Qualifications in the EU" examines the extent to which the system for recognition is comprehensive and future-proof.

References

Bergan S (2009) Academic recognition: status and challenges. Assess Educ Principles Policy Pract 16:39–53

Claessens S, Schneider H (2011) Legal education and free movement of lawyers in the EU. In: Heringa AW, Akkermans B (eds) Educating European lawyers. Intersentia, Antwerp, pp 121–156

Dalichow F (1992) Academic Recognition in the EC. In: J. Pertek (ed.), General Recognition of Diplomas and Free Movement of Professionals, European Institute of Public Administration, p. 91-98.

Garben S (2010) The Bologna process: From a European law perspective. Eur Law J 16:186–210

Garben S (2011a) On recognition of qualifications for academic and professional purposes. Tilburg Law Review 16:127–156

Garben S (2011b) EU higher education law: the Bologna process and harmonization by stealth. Kluwer Law International, Alphen aan den Rijn

Howat C, Ulicna D, Harris P, GHK, DTI (2011) Revised final report — Study evaluating the Professional Qualifications Directive against recent educational reforms in EU Member States. DG Internal Market and Services - European Commission

Käsper K, Kerimäe T (2012) Access to higher education in the EU: evolving case law of the CJEU. Eur J Law Reform 14:399–413

[149] See Chapter "Introduction", Sect. 4.

Kelo M (2014) Quality assurance as an element of international recognition. In: Bergan S, Blomqvist C (eds) The Lisbon Recognition Convention at 15: making fair recognition a reality. Council of Europe Publishing, Strasbourg, pp 145–156

Kortese L (2018) De grensoverschrijdende mobiliteit van gespecialiseerde verpleegkundigen IC—Nederland/België. Institute for Transnational and Euregional Cross Border Cooperation and Mobility, Maastricht

Minor J (1992) Introductory lecture on the directive of 21 December 1988. In: Pertek J (ed) General recognition of diplomas and free movement of professionals. European Institute of Public Administration, Maastricht, pp 3–16

Pertek J (1998) Une dynamique de la reconnaissance des diplômes à des fins professionnelles et à des fins académiques: réalisations et nouvelles réflexions. In: Pertek J (ed) La reconnaissance des qualifications dans un espace européen des formations et des professions. Bruylant, Bruxelles, pp 119–204

Rauhvargers A (2004) Improving the recognition of qualifications in the framework of the Bologna process. Eur J Educ 39:331–347

Rauhvargers A (2009) Recognition and qualifications frameworks. Assess Educ Principles Policy Pract 16:111–125

Schneider H (1995) Die Anerkennung von Diplomen in der Europäischen Gemeinschaft. MAKLU Uitgevers, Antwerpen–Apeldoorn

Schneider H, Claessens S (2005) The recognition of diplomas and the free movement of professionals in the European Union. In: Schneider H (ed) Migration, integration and citizenship: a challenge for Europe's future—Volume I. Forum Maastricht, Maastricht, pp 123–166

Schneider H, Lubina K (2009) Freizügigkeit von Juristen in der Europäischen Gemeinschaft: Der Fall Lubina und seine Folgen für deutsch-niederländische Juristen. In: De Groot R, Janssen A (eds) Festschrift anlässlich des sechzigjährigen Bestehens der deutsch-niederländischen Juristenkonferenz. LIT Verlag, Berlin, pp 125–157

West A, Barham E (2009) Student mobility, qualifications and academic recognition in the EU. Assess Educ Principles Policy Pract 16:25–37

Under the Looking Glass: Instruments for Recognition of Qualifications in the EU

Professional Recognition

1 Introduction

Previous chapters have shown that action on recognition can be retraced to the early days of European cooperation. Indeed, the first legal basis from the Rome Treaty marked the beginning of a long and complex process through which the recognition of professional qualifications as it stands today was developed. The recognition of professional qualifications is inextricably linked with the freedoms of establishment and workers, as well as the freedom to provide services, freedoms which were developed at the European level via the Court of Justice's case law and through legislative developments. These legislative developments culminated in Directive 2005/36/EC which itself was modernised in 2013—together referred to as the Professional Qualifications Directive (PQD).[1] In 2018, the last branch was added to the PQD with the introduction of the Proportionality Test Directive (2018/958). This chapter discusses the system for professional recognition as it presently stands through three main topics, namely the scope of the directive, the different systems for recognition, and the crucial difference between recognition and access reflected in the directive. Finally, attention is also given to case law by the CJEU which constitutes a "fallback system" for cases not covered by the directive.

[1] In this research, the term "Professional Qualifications Directive" is used to refer to Directive 2005/36/EC of the European Parliament and of the Council of 7 September 2005 on the recognition of professional qualifications, [2005] OJ L 255/22 *as amended by* Directive 2013/55/EU of the European Parliament and of the Council of 20 November 2013 amending Directive 2005/36/EC on the recognition of professional qualifications and Regulation (EU) No 1024/2012 on administrative cooperation through the Internal Market Information System ('the IMI Regulation'), [2013] OJ L 354/132. The consolidated version of the Professional Qualifications Directive can be accessed at: https://eur-lex.europa.eu/legal-content/EN/TXT/?uri=CELEX%3A02005L0036-20251029.

L. S.J. Kortese, *Effectuating Free Movement in the EU through Recognition of Qualifications*, https://doi.org/10.1007/978-3-032-21335-8_4

2 The Scope of Application of the Professional Qualifications Directive

A first important point to give attention to is the scope of the PQD. According to Article 2(1), the instrument is applicable "to all nationals of a Member State wishing to pursue a regulated profession in a Member State…". Three elements are of particular importance in the context of the Directive's scope: the term "regulated profession", whether a professional falls within the scope of application of another instrument on recognition, and the fact that it is primarily applicable to EU citizens.

2.1 Defining the Term Regulated Profession

When looking at the term "regulated profession", it can be said to take up a central place in the PQD. According to Article 3(1)(a) of the PQD the term covers:

> a professional activity or group of professional activities, access to which, the pursuit of which, or one of the modes of pursuit of which is subject, directly or indirectly, by virtue of legislative, regulatory or administrative provisions to the possession of specific professional qualifications; in particular, the use of a professional title limited by legislative, regulatory or administrative provisions to holders of a given professional qualification shall constitute a mode of pursuit.

Through its case law, the Court of Justice confirmed that the definition of a regulated profession is a matter of EU law.[2] Therefore, a profession is to be considered regulated if a Member State lays down qualification requirements in laws, regulations or administrative provisions. The definition also means that the PQD applies where a Member State makes access to or pursuit of a professional activity dependent on the possession of specific professional qualifications.[3] The phrases "professional activity" or "group of professional activities" are used to cover different types of regulation. For example, this definition encompasses both monopolies of activity (also called licensing or reserved activities) and protected titles (also called certification).[4] Whereas monopolies of activity entail that professional qualifications are required by law to carry out a certain activity, a protected title entails that activities

---

[2] Case C-234/97 *Fernández de Bobadilla*, ECLI:EU:C:1999:367, para. 14; Case C-285/01 *Burbaud*, ECLI:EU:C:2003:432, para. 43; Case C-586/08 *Rubino*, ECLI:EU:C:2009:801, para. 23; Case C-372/09 and C-373/09 *Peñarroja Fa*, ECLI:EU:C:2011:156, para. 27.

[3] Article 1 Professional Qualifications Directive.

[4] See for example Case C-164/94, *Aranitis*, ECLI:EU:C:1996:23, para. 7. Here, the Court indicated that Directive 89/48/EEC was to apply in the first place to regulation via monopolies and that it also extended to regulation via a protected title. In another case, the Court briefly touched upon the question to which extent a regulated economic activity could also be considered a regulated profession, considering that the regulation of professions in the construction sector could even be considered as part of the regulation of the construction sector as an economic activity; Case C-458/08 *Commission v. Portugal*, ECLI:EU:C:2010:692, para. 90–99.

are open for all to carry out, but only those who fulfil legal requirements can carry the professional title.[5]

Considering the fact that the PQD's scope encompasses different types of regulation, the core criterion to define the regulated status of a profession is the presence of legislative, regulatory or administrative provisions reserving the exercise of a professional activity to those fulfilling certain requirements.[6] Such existence of legislative, regulatory or administrative provisions constitutes direct regulation. The CJEU has, however, also discussed the concept of indirect regulation in the *Aranitis* case. In particular, the Court argued that the regulated status of a profession depends on the legal situation in the host Member State and does not depend on conditions on the labour market.[7] In *Aranitis* this meant that the profession of geologist was not to be regarded as indirectly regulated because only people who held the title and diploma of *Diplom-Geologe* were hired by employers in Germany. Therefore, if a situation arises on the labour market where only people with a specific qualification can work in a certain profession, but where this is not laid down in any law, regulation or administrative provision, a profession is considered non-regulated. Despite this clear verdict, the *Aranitis* case does leave open questions regarding the distinction between the concepts of direct and indirect regulation. As of yet, the latter concept appears to concern only regulation through collective agreements. In *Fernández de Bobadilla*, the Court considered that collective agreements could include conditions of access to employment, thereby constituting laws, regulations or administrative provisions.[8] Collective agreements, although not constituting legislation at first instance, can therefore be regarded as such if they govern the right to take up or pursue a profession in a general way and are the result of a single administrative policy maintained at national level.[9]

Beyond this opening for collective agreements, the Court has proven to maintain a strict interpretation of the term regulated profession. Other disputes pertaining to the meaning of the term regulated profession did not lead to an extension of that concept. For example, the Court did not consider professions for which access depended on the successful completion of a selection procedure to be regulated.[10] The existence of a legally established register of expert court translators was also not considered to constitute a regulated profession since the purpose of that legislation was to facilitate

---

[5] Minor (1992, pp. 5–6).

[6] Case C-164/94, *Aranitis*, ECLI:EU:C:1996:23, para. 19.

[7] Ibid., para. 23.

[8] Case C-234/97 *Fernández de Bobadilla*, ECLI:EU:C:1999:367, para. 18–20.

[9] Ibid., para. 20 and 22. The required criterion of governing the right to take up a profession in a general way must, however, not be underestimated. In the case of Fernández de Bobadilla the Court considered that the collective agreement at stake only governed the relations between an employer (here, the Prado Museum) and the employees (here, Fernández de Bobadilla). In the present case, the Court ultimately left this decision to the Spanish court but did make it clear that a confirmation of the regulated status of the profession in Spain would also mean application of Directives 89/48/EEC and 82/51/EEC. See also paragraphs 23–27 of the aforementioned case.

[10] Case C-586/08 *Rubino*, ECLI:EU:C:2009:801; Case C-298/14 *Brouillard*, ECLI:EU:C:2015:652.

recourse to the services of professionals and not to lay down rules governing qualifications.[11] The connection between qualification requirements and the objective of legislation as a determining factor for the regulated status of a profession was later confirmed.[12] In particular, if a qualification is meant to prepare candidates for a broad range of professions (instead of one particular profession), it will not be considered as regulated.[13]

The case law mentioned above indicates that the Court not only maintains a strict interpretation of the term regulated profession, but that it has actually limited the scope of application of that term by arguing that even the presence of legal provisions having effects on qualifications could not lead to a profession being considered as regulated. The reasoning behind this is economic in nature: a more limited scope of the PQD is in support of free movement since the barrier of recognition is taken away. However, a stricter interpretation of the term regulated profession is regrettable in terms of legal certainty, since limitation of the scope of application of the PQD prevents EU citizens from being able to benefit from its safeguards.

2.1.1 Assessing the Need for Regulation

In this context, the European Commission proposed an exercise as part of the 2013 modernisation aimed at examining the motivation behind certain rules regulating professions.[14] This exercise was rooted in Article 59 PQD which, on the one hand, consisted of a transparency exercise and, on the other hand, of a mutual evaluation exercise.[15] While the transparency part of the exercise mostly consisted of Member States notifying the Commission of which professions were regulated to update the Regulated Professions Database,[16] the mutual evaluation exercise is much more interesting in light of the discussion regarding which professions are considered regulated and therefore subject to the PQD. The mutual evaluation exercise was meant to increase understanding as to *why* professions are regulated and to encourage Member States to compare regulatory approaches.[17] Through this exercise, Member

[11] Case C-372/09 and C-373/09 *Peñarroja Fa*, ECLI:EU:C:2011:156, para. 30. In fact, even the existence of titles connected to those expert translators did not alter the Court's reasoning on the unregulated status of these translators (see para. 31 of the aforementioned case).

[12] Case C-298/14 *Brouillard*, ECLI:EU:C:2015:652; Case C-729/17 *Commission v. Greece*, ECLI:EU:C:2019:534.

[13] Case C-298/14 *Brouillard*, ECLI:EU:C:2015:652, para. 38; Opinion of Advocate General Sharpston in Case C-298/14 *Brouillard* [2015], ECLI:EU:C:2015:408, para. 54.

[14] Proposal for a Directive of the European Parliament and of the Council amending Directive 2005/36/EC on the recognition of professional qualifications and Regulation on administrative cooperation through the Internal Market Information System, COM(2011) 883 final, p. 3.

[15] See respectively Article 59(1)(2) and Article 59(3–9) Professional Qualifications Directive.

[16] This database contains an overview of all professions regulated in the EU and their corresponding authorities.

[17] European Commission, Evaluating national regulations on access to professions—frequently asked questions, MEMO/13/839, p. 1.

States essentially conducted a proportionality assessment related to the regulation of their professions examining whether requirements restricting access to professions were non-discriminatory, justified by overriding reasons in the general interest, and proportionate.[18] The exercise was superseded by two further initiatives: a Guidance on reform needs for Member States for regulation in professional services along with a proposal for a new directive on a proportionality test—ultimately leading to Directive 2018/958.[19]

The Guidance was based on what the Commission coined the "restrictiveness indicator" which provided for different groups of restrictions that were assessed for a certain profession in all Member States.[20] After this assessment, the Commission would issue recommendations to support Member States in creating regulations that were conducive to growth, innovation and the creation of jobs.[21] In particular, the restrictiveness indicator covered the Member State's regulatory approaches (e.g. reserved activities and title protection), qualification requirements (e.g. years of education and training), other entry requirements (e.g. registration with a professional body), and exercise requirements (e.g. shareholding requirements).[22] The Commission noted that the restrictiveness indicator would not reveal non-regulatory barriers or the role of specific laws or mechanisms protecting consumers and public interest objectives.[23] Therefore, the indicator was accompanied by a qualitative assessment and analysis providing additional information to accurately depict reality.[24]

Next, Directive 2018/958 contains the framework to conduct proportionality tests and consolidates the Court's case law in cases such as *Kraus* and *Gebhard*.[25] As the text above shows, the mutual evaluation exercise was essentially an exercise regarding the proportionality of national professional regulation. However, this exercise showed the Commission that Member States experienced difficulties whilst carrying out the assessments, pointing to an underlying problem relating to how

---

[18] Article 59(3)(a–c) Professional Qualifications Directive. The mutual evaluation exercise was pursued following a three-step plan proposed by the Commission examining regulations for various clusters of professions. See Communication from the Commission to the European Parliament, the Council and the European Economic and Social Committee on Evaluating national regulations on access to professions, COM(2013) 676 final, pp. 9–11.

[19] Directive (EU) 2018/958 of the European Parliament and of the Council of 28 June 2018 on a proportionality test before adoption of new regulation on professions, [2018] OJ L 173/25.

[20] The analysis was conducted for architects, civil engineers, accountants, lawyers, patent agents, real estate agents, and tourist guides. See European Commission, Communication from the Commission to the European Parliament, the Council, the European Economic and Social Committee and the Committee of the Regions on reform recommendations for regulation in professional services, COM(2016) 820 final, pp. 8–29.

[21] European Commission, Communication from the Commission to the European Parliament, the Council, the European Economic and Social Committee and the Committee of the Regions on reform recommendations for regulation in professional services, COM(2016) 820 final, p. 3.

[22] Ibid., p. 8.

[23] Ibid., p. 9.

[24] Ibid.

[25] Ibid., p. 4 and 13; Case C-19/92 *Kraus,* ECLI:EU:C:1993:125; Case C-55/94 *Gebhard,* ECLI:EU:C:1995:411.

the need for regulation and its effects were evaluated.[26] It had turned out that the Member States interpreted the proportionality test of Article 59(3) of the PQD incorrectly during the mutual evaluation exercise.[27] What the proportionality test essentially implies is that the Member States have to do an *ex ante* assessment of new or amending laws, regulations, and administrative provisions where they: (1) evaluate the possible discriminatory nature of the provision, (2) evaluate the applicable public interest grounds for justification, and (3) take into account a range of factors to decide whether additional regulation is necessary.[28] Directive 2018/958 applies to any new or existing law, regulation or administrative provision restricting access to a regulated profession (or its (modes of) pursuit) which falls within the scope of the PQD.[29] When Member States assess proportionality, they must explain why the new or amended measure complies with the principle of proportionality and must put forward qualitative and quantitative evidence to substantiate that finding.[30] For transparency purposes, the proportionality assessment results are to be communicated in the Regulated Professions Database.[31]

During the adoption phase of the Proportionality Test Directive, criticism was voiced from different perspectives. The European Economic and Social Committee (EESC), for example, identified subsidiarity concerns since a negative result of the proportionality test would make it very difficult for national legislators to continue with the proposed regulation which would affect their regulatory freedom.[32] The European Parliament furthermore considered the Proportionality Test Directive to be very heavily based on the assumption that regulation is a barrier to competition, a potentially misleading idea leading the Parliament to plead in favour of smart regulation as opposed to no regulation.[33] The call for smart regulation had already been made previously by the European Parliament in the context of its resolution on the Commission Guidance.[34] Indeed, although not the purpose of the mutual evaluation exercise nor Proportionality Test Directive, deregulation may be a side effect of these activities. In the case of the recognition of qualifications, a diminution of laws stipulating requirements of qualifications and of governmental interference could result in the situation where individuals no longer have to go through recognition procedures,

---

[26] Proposal for a Directive of the European Parliament and of the Council on a proportionality test before adoption of new regulation of professions, COM(2016) 822 final, p. 3.

[27] Recital 5 Directive (EU) 2018/958.

[28] Articles 5–7 Directive (EU) 2018/958.

[29] Article 2(1) Directive (EU) 2018/958.

[30] Article 4(3)(4) Directive (EU) 2018/958.

[31] Article 11(1) Directive (EU) 2018/958.

[32] Opinion of the European Economic and Social Committee on (b) Proposal for a Directive of the European Parliament and of the Council on a proportionality test before adoption of new regulation of professions, [2017] OJ C 288/43.

[33] Working document on the proposal for a directive of the European Parliament and of the Council on a proportionality test before adoption of new regulation of professions, Committee on the Internal Market and Consumer Protection (Rapporteur: Adreas Schwab), DT\1125181EN, p. 2.

[34] European Parliament resolution of 18 January 2018 on the implementation of Directive 2005/36/EC as regards regulation and the need for reform in professional services (2017/2073(INI)).

thus taking away this potential impediment to mobility. However, a diminution of regulation can indeed lead concerns such as those voiced by the European Parliament to materialise. While the Commission has expressly stated that deregulation is not the subject of the mutual evaluation exercise,[35] tackling overregulation may nonetheless lead to a removal of regulation, non-regulation or to different forms of regulation. Despite the beneficial effects associated with such alterations in regulation from an economic perspective, attention should be paid that such alternative forms of regulation do not raise non-regulatory barriers.

The Commission had already noted previously that other means of protection such as approval procedures, compliance with technical and safety standards, and inspection mechanisms should be evaluated as safeguards whereby regulation on access to a profession by means of a specific qualification would only be allowed if such safeguards proved insufficient.[36] Alternative forms of regulation would therefore also be accepted. Regarding professional regulation, the presence of laws or regulations setting qualification requirements is the strictest. A careful reading of the Commission's proposal for the Proportionality Test Directive suggests that this specific type of regulation was especially targeted in the context of the mutual evaluation exercise. Under this type of regulation, also known as licensing, reserved activities or a monopoly of activity, only those individuals able to demonstrate the specified level of competence can obtain a licence that would allow them to carry out tasks covered by regulation.[37] Examples of this type of regulation are often seen in the medical professions, such as with doctors or nurses.

Alternative types of regulation may include certification schemes or non-governmental accreditation schemes. In the case of certification, a qualification requirement is not necessarily linked to a profession as such,[38] meaning that there is no legal restriction as to who may carry out a profession but professionals may apply to be certified and/or to be able to carry a legally protected title.[39] This means that anyone may carry out activities belonging to the profession. However, only a designated group may use a certain title after obtaining recognition by a competent authority. The third type of regulation is the least binding of the three. Accreditation schemes are usually maintained by professional bodies or industry associations and are not connected to legally protected titles or functions.[40] Whereas licensing

---

[35] Proposal for a Directive of the European Parliament and of the Council on a proportionality test before adoption of new regulation of professions, COM(2016) 822 final, p. 2.

[36] Communication from the Commission to the European Parliament, the Council and the European Economic and Social Committee on Evaluating national regulations on access to professions, COM(2013) 676 final, p.7.

[37] Koumenta and Pagliero (2016, p. 9).

[38] Communication from the Commission to the European Parliament, the Council and the European Economic and Social Committee on Evaluating national regulations on access to professions, COM(2013) 676 final, p. 12.

[39] Koumenta and Pagliero (2016, p. 9).

[40] Ibid.

and certification include the presence of laws, regulations and administrative provisions, non-governmental accreditation schemes do not, meaning they are considered formally as unregulated and fall outside the PQD's scope of application. An example of this type of regulation can be seen in the Netherlands as regards the profession of psychologist (*basispsycholoog*). The profession itself is unregulated, as there are no laws or regulations laying down qualification requirements, nor is there a protected title. This means that anyone may decide to call himself or herself a psychologist and receive patients. However, those who have a bachelor's and a master's degree in psychology may apply for a registration with the *Nederlands Instituut van Psychologen* (Dutch Association of Psychologists—NIP).[41]

Existing research on the impacts of regulation on the economy and the labour market has long been heavily dominated by US studies.[42] Whereas American economists often indicated the negative effects of regulation,[43] economists in the EU have only more recently been able to gather and access relevant data allowing them to start estimating the economic effects of EU professional regulation.[44] In general, the research conducted thus far, nonetheless, appeared to also favour a diminution of regulation, or perhaps rather, a shift to different types of regulation. In a study commissioned by the Commission, Koumenta and Pagliero found that scaling back on regulation in the form of licensing had beneficial effects on the EU's economy and its citizens. For example, they found that licensing led to higher wages which were not necessarily linked to increased worker productivity, that the stock of foreign-born workers is significantly lower among licensed workers, and that licensing was not always associated with the acquisition of skills.[45] In conclusion to their research, they called for increased attention to be paid to certification and accreditation as alternatives to licensing.[46]

While professional regulation can indeed contain protectionism masked by a system of safeguards, careful consideration of alternative means of regulation is nonetheless necessary.[47] The Commission already indicated that accreditation schemes in particular could be seriously detrimental to professionals. Although their purpose is to improve transparency, the quality and functioning of these schemes themselves should be actively monitored to prevent professional associations from assuming too dominant positions thereby isolating migrating EU professionals from

---

[41] Nederlands Instituut van Psychologen, 'NIP-registraties', https://www.psynip.nl/registraties/nip-registraties/.

[42] Adamis-Császár et al. (2019, p. 27).

[43] See Koumenta and Pagliero (2016, p. 6) and the sources cited.

[44] European Commission, Communication from the Commission to the European Parliament, the Council, the European Economic and Social Committee and the Committee of the Regions on reform recommendations for regulation in professional services, COM(2016) 820 final, p. 6; Koumenta and Pagliero (2016, pp. 6–7).

[45] Koumenta and Pagliero (2016, pp. 129–131).

[46] Ibid., p. 131.

[47] Adamo and Binder (2018, pp. 55–56).

the labour market.[48] However, if insufficient monitoring occurs, migrating EU professionals may fall victim to non-regulatory barriers. Not only is this problematic due to such barriers being irreconcilable with the EU's fundamental freedoms, but this situation is furthermore problematic in terms of legal certainty and effective remedies. The application of the PQD hinges on the term regulated profession, which in turn revolves around the presence of legislative, regulatory or administrative provisions. This means that only that regulation which can be categorised as licensing/reserved activities/monopoly of activity or certification/protected title is subject to the PQD's procedural safeguards—leaving those covered by accreditation schemes outside the PQD's scope.

While some recognition has been given to this issue,[49] it is unclear what follow-up has been or will be given to prevent this situation from materialising. While attention may be diverted to the Proportionality Test Directive to prevent issues in this respect, that instrument rather focuses on preventing excessive regulation from being adopted and is therefore aimed at preventing Member States from instituting regulatory barriers (instead of private actors instituting non-regulatory barriers). Nevertheless, the main focus as of yet appears to be aimed at ensuring the effects of the transparency and mutual evaluation exercise are maximised and the functioning of the Proportionality Test Directive optimised, an exercise proving challenging. In this context, a 2020 Commission report showed challenges existed among the Member States to follow-up on the reporting requirements of that exercise and an improvement of the situation only followed after infringement actions by the Commission.[50] The first evaluation of the Proportionality Test Directive reflected similar challenges. Though late transposition challenged full evaluation of the directive, the Commission reported late transpositions, failures to subject all rules to the proportionality

[48] Communication from the Commission to the European Parliament, the Council and the European Economic and Social Committee on Evaluating national regulations on access to professions, COM(2013) 676 final, p. 13.

[49] The Commission already warned about the detrimental effects of malfunctioning accreditation schemes in its 2013 Communication. The topic again resurfaced in the Guidance in which the Commission noted that restrictions could also exist in Member States not regulating a profession. Furthermore, the Commission already indicated that the restrictiveness indicator maintained in the Guidance did not (yet) reveal non-regulatory barriers and was therefore accompanied by a qualitative assessment providing additional relevant information. See Communication from the Commission to the European Parliament, the Council and the European Economic and Social Committee on Evaluating national regulations on access to professions, COM(2013) 676 final, p. 13; European Commission, Communication from the Commission to the European Parliament, the Council, the European Economic and Social Committee and the Committee of the Regions on reform recommendations for regulation in professional services, COM(2016) 820 final, pp. 5 and 9.

[50] Report from the Commission to the European Parliament, the Council, the European Economic and Social Committee and the Committee of the Regions on the implementation of certain new elements introduced by Directive 2013/55/EU of the European Parliament and of the Council of 20 November 2013 amending Directive 2005/36/EC on the recognition of professional qualifications and Regulation (EU) No 1024/2012 on administrative cooperation through the Internal Market Information System ('the IMI Regulation'), COM(2020) 191 final, pp. 22–25.

test requirements, and failures to accurately transpose the assessment criteria for the test.[51]

2.2 Specific Professions & Their Exclusion from the PQD's Scope

Although the scope of application of the PQD is tremendously wide whereby the instrument covers a great number of professions, it does not cover every regulated profession in existence. Indeed, in accordance with Article 2(3) where "other specific arrangements directly related to the recognition of professional qualifications are established in a separate instrument of Community law, the corresponding provisions of this Directive shall not apply". Several categories of professionals have specific pieces of legislation, namely sailors and seafarers,[52] statutory auditors,[53] insurance intermediaries,[54] transport operators,[55] professions handling toxic products,[56] lawyers,[57] and commercial agents.[58] Apart from these professions, the PQD also does not apply to notaries who are appointed by an official government act.[59]

---

[51] Report from the Commission to the European Parliament and the Council on the implementation of Directive (EU) 2018/958 of the European Parliament and of the Council of 28 June 2018 on a proportionality test before adoption of new regulation of professions, COM(2024) 544 final, p. 3.

[52] Directive 2008/106/EC of the European Parliament and of the Council of 19.

November 2008 on the minimum level of training of seafarers (recast), [2008] OJ L 323/33 as amended by Directive 2012/35/EU of the European Parliament and of the Council of 21 November 2012 amending Directive 2008/106/EC on the minimum level of training of seafarers, [2012] OJ L 343/78.

[53] Directive 2006/43/EC of the European Parliament and of the Council of 17 May 2006 on statutory audits of annual accounts and consolidated accounts, amending Council Directives 78/660/EEC and 83/349/EEC and repealing Council Directive 84/254/EEC, [2006] OJ L 157/87.

[54] Directive 2002/92/EC of the European Parliament and of the Council of 9 December 2002 on insurance mediation, [2003] OJ L 9/3.

[55] Regulation (EC) No 1071/2009 of the European Parliament and of the Council of 21 October 2009 establishing common rules concerning the conditions to be complied with to pursue the occupation of road transport operator and repealing Council Directive 96/26/EC, [2009] OJ L 300/51.

[56] Council Directive of 4 June 1974 laying down detailed provisions concerning transitional measures relating to activities, trade in and distribution of toxic products and activities entailing the professional use of such products including activities of intermediaries (74/556/EEC), [1974] OJ L 307/1; Council Directive 74/557/EEC of 4 June 1974 on the attainment of freedom of establishment and freedom to provide services in respect of activities of self- employed persons and of intermediaries engaging in the trade and distribution of toxic products, [1974] OJ L 307/5.

[57] Council Directive 77/249/EEC of 22 March 1977 to facilitate the effective exercise by lawyers of freedom to provide services, [1977] OJ L 78/17; Directive 98/5/EC of the European Parliament and of the Council of 16 February 1998 to facilitate practice of the profession of lawyer on a permanent basis in a Member State other than that in which the qualification was obtained, [1998] OJ L 77/36.

[58] Council Directive 86/653/EEC of 18 December 1986 on the coordination of the laws of the Member States relating to self-employed commercial agents, [1986] OJ L 382/17.

[59] Article 2(4) Professional Qualifications Directive.

In 2011 the Court of Justice ruled against nationality requirements for notaries.[60] These were maintained previously because notaries were considered to exercise of official authority (see Article 51 TFEU).[61] Whereas the Commission proposed to include notaries in the PQD in the run up to the 2013 modernisation, the European Parliament's opposition led to the maintenance of the status quo meaning notaries continue to be excluded from the PQD's scope.[62]

Lawyers occupy a special position in this respect. Despite the profession being subject to its own specific legislation on the recognition of qualifications and access to the profession, the PQD may still be applied.[63] Indeed, there are three modalities of the free movement of lawyers representing the ways in which lawyers may exercise their profession outside their home Member State: lawyers may want to occasionally provide services, they may want to establish themselves permanently in another Member State *without* becoming a part of the legal profession of that state, or they may want to establish themselves and become *fully integrated* in the host Member State's legal profession.[64] Only in the case of the last option is the PQD applicable to lawyers.

2.3 In or Out? Recognition of Professional Qualifications from Third Countries and of Third Country Nationals

The PQD mainly provides rules for EU citizens who have acquired their professional qualifications in another Member State of the Union. In the past, qualifications held by those who are not a national of an EU Member State fell outside the scope of EU law, meaning the freedom of movement or any directive effectuating that freedom did not apply to those individuals.[65] Nevertheless, the situation is not so black and white anymore. In particular, there is a need to distinguish the situations EU citizens with third country qualifications and third country nationals looking to exercise a regulated profession in the EU.

[60] See Case C-47/08 *Commission v. Belgium*, ECLI:EU:C:2011:334; Case C-50/08 *Commission v. France*, ECLI:EU:C:2011:335; Case C-51/08 *Commission v. Luxembourg*, ECLI:EU:C:2011:336; Case C-53/08 *Commission v. Austria*, ECLI:EU:C:2011:338; Case C-54/08 *Commission v. Germany*, ECLI:EU:C:2011:339; Case C-61/08 *Commission v. Greece*, ECLI:EU:C:2011:340.

[61] Claessens (2014, p. 7).

[62] Ibid., p. 7.

[63] Case C-359/09 *Ebert*, ECLI:EU:C:2011:44.

[64] Claessens (2008, p. 4).

[65] See Case C-147/91 *Ferrer Laderer*, ECLI:EU:C:1992:278.

2.3.1 EU Citizens with Third Country Qualifications

Even though the PQD is an instrument that relates first and foremost to qualifications obtained by EU citizens within the EU, the Directive nonetheless provides some insight into how non-EU qualifications held by EU citizens are recognised. Article 2(2) of the PQD allows Member States to recognise professional qualifications from third countries in line with national law when access is sought to a regulated profession. While it appears that this group is therefore subject exclusively to national law, this is not entirely correct. First, an EU law component will always be present for EU citizens who have qualified as doctor, nurse, dentist, veterinarian, midwife, pharmacist or architect outside the EU. For these professions, extensive harmonisation of the education and training leading up to individuals to being qualified has occurred at EU level,[66] meaning that the professional qualifications held by anyone looking to exercise one of the professions mentioned above always need to fulfil the harmonised standards of education and training (called minimum training conditions) set at EU level.[67]

However, the fulfilment of the minimum training conditions is not the sole European law component in recognition procedures of EU citizens with third country qualifications since they may also be subject to the PQD if three other conditions are fulfilled.[68] First, the EU citizen needs to have obtained recognition of his or her third country qualifications in one of the Member States under national law. Second, the individual concerned must have exercised the profession for three years in the Member State of first recognition. Third, the Member State which has first recognised the third country professional qualifications must certify that recognition has taken place and that the holder has three years' professional experience in that Member State. Fulfilment of these conditions means that the non-EU qualifications held by EU citizens can be considered as evidence of formal qualifications under the PQD. These provisions concern a departure from the previous legal practice where a prior recognition of third country qualifications did not have effects for a subsequent recognition.[69] The abovementioned conditions have become common practice since the *Hocsman* judgment where the Court ruled that prior experience and qualifications

---

[66] See Sect. 3.2.1 of this chapter.

[67] Article 2(2) Professional Qualifications Directive.

[68] Article 3(3) Professional Qualifications Directive.

[69] In *Tawil-Albertini*, the Court was asked to rule on whether Directive 78/686/EEC (on dentists) did not apply to third country qualifications recognised by a first Member State. In this case, Belgium had recognised the Lebanese diploma held by Tawil-Albertini. However, France refused to grant recognition arguing that recognition in Belgium could not serve as a basis for the application of Directive 78/686/EEC. The Court argued that the Directive only governed relations between Member States, meaning that they were free to authorise holders of third country qualifications to work in their territory, but more importantly, that prior recognition by one Member State did not bind the other Member States. This judgment was confirmed in the *Haim I* case where the Court confirmed that prior recognition did not automatically exempt holders of third country qualifications from training periods required in a second Member State. Case C-154/93 *Tawil-Albertini*, ECLI:EU:C:1994:51, para. 12–13 and Case C-319/92 *Haim I*, ECLI:EU:C:1994:47, para. 19–22.

obtained in the EU had to be considered when assessing third country qualifications in a second Member State.[70]

Apart from prior recognitions playing a role in a subsequent recognition, another EU law component can be identified in the recognition of third country qualifications held by EU citizens, although more of an indirect nature. The discussion of the case law above shows that qualifications held by EU citizens who have been outside the EU for their studies or work are first recognised under national law upon their return in the Union. However, the PQD does not preclude Member States from applying their laws that transpose the directive's provisions in the national legal framework to this situation. Member States are thus free to decide what national legislation to apply to these EU citizens.

2.3.2 Third Country Nationals

When it comes to the recognition of the professional qualifications of third country nationals (hereinafter: TCNs), it is necessary to distinguish a further two scenarios. First of all, TCNs may come to the EU in the context of one of the legal immigration directives. The second category of TCNs may come to an EU Member State and apply for a residence permit under national law. Concerning recognition, the situation of this second category of TCNs is relatively straightforward. Their professional qualifications will be recognised under national law as there is no EU law component governing their situation. Indeed, the PQD states that it "does not create an obstacle to the possibility of Member States recognising, in accordance with their rules, the professional qualifications acquired outside the territory of the European Union by third country nationals".[71] Nevertheless, even when such qualifications from third countries are recognised under national law, Member States must again respect the minimum training conditions set for the professions of doctor, nurse, dentist, veterinarian, midwife, pharmacist or architect. Additionally, as in the case of non-EU qualifications of EU citizens, the PQD does not preclude Member States from applying their national laws implementing the directive to TCNs whose situation is not governed by European law—although in many cases they may have separate procedures.

The situation is more complex for those TCNs who want to access the EU in the context of the legal immigration directives. Those directives contain clauses ensuring that beneficiaries must be treated equally to EU citizens as regards the recognition of

---

[70] Case C-238/98 *Hocsman*, ECLI:EU:C:2000:440; Recital 6 Directive 2001/19/EC of the European Parliament and of the Council of 14 May 2001 amending Council Directives 89/48/EEC and 92/51/EEC on the general system for the recognition of professional qualifications and Council Directives 77/452/EEC, 77/453/EEC, 78/686/EEC, 78/687/EEC, 78/1026/EEC, 78/1027/EEC, 80/154/EEC, 80/155/EEC, 85/384/EEC, 85/432/EEC, 85/433/EEC and 93/16/EEC concerning the professions of nurse responsible for general care, dental practitioner, veterinary surgeon, midwife, architect, pharmacist and doctor, [2001] OJ L 206/1.

[71] Recital 10 Professional Qualifications Directive.

their qualifications. The following categories of TCNs benefit from such equal treatment: long-term residents,[72] TCN family members of EU citizens,[73] researchers,[74] Blue Card holders,[75] refugees,[76] TCNs falling under the Single Permit Directive,[77] and Intra-corporate Transferees.[78] Assuming that TCNs are treated equally to EU citizens regarding the recognition of their professional qualifications leads to the situation where they would fall within the scope of application of the PQD if they have EU professional qualifications obtained in a Member State other than the State where they have migrated to under one of the directives mentioned above. Where they possess a third country qualification, they would fall under national law just like EU citizens with third country qualifications. While this situation regarding the professional qualifications held by TCNs still follows directly from the applicable legislation, change may be on the horizon. In 2023, the Commission introduced a recommendation to better align recognition processes for TCNs with practices applicable to EU citizens.[79] In relation to the PQD, the recommendation indeed encourages Member States to align their national recognition processes for TCNs

[72] Article 11(1)(c) Council Directive 2003/109/EC of 25 November 2003 concerning the status of third-country nationals who are long-term residents, [2004] OJ L 16/44.

[73] Article 24(1) Directive 2004/38/EC of the European Parliament and of the Council of 29 April 2004 on the right of citizens of the Union and their family members to move and reside freely within the territory of the Member States amending Regulation (EEC) No 1612/68 and repealing Directives 64/221/EEC, 68/360/EEC, 72/194/EEC, 73/148/EEC, 75/35/EEC, 90/364/EEC, 90/365/EEC and 93/96/EEC, [2004] OJ L 158/77.

[74] Article 22 Directive (EU) 2016/801 of the European Parliament and of the Council of 11 May 2016 on the conditions of entry and residence of third-country nationals for the purposes of research, studies, training, voluntary service, pupil exchange schemes or educational projects and au pairing (recast), [2016] OJ L 132/21.

[75] Article 16(1)(d) Directive (EU) 2021/1883 of the European Parliament and of the Council of 20 October 2021 on the conditions of entry and residence of third-country nationals for the purpose of highly qualified employment, and repealing Council Directive 2009/50/EC, [2021] OJ L 382/1.

[76] Article 28 Directive 2011/95/EU of the European Parliament and of the Council of 13 December 2011 on standards for the qualifications of third-country nationals or stateless persons as beneficiaries of international protection, for a uniform status for refugees or for persons eligible for subsidiary protection and for the content of protection granted, [2011] OJ L 337/9. The Qualification Directive is updated by Regulation (EU) 2024/1347 which will enter into force by July 2026. Article 30 of the new Qualification Regulation contains provisions regarding access to procedures for recognition of qualifications. For more on the changes instituted in the regulation see Kortese (2025).

[77] Article 12(1)(d) Directive 2011/98/EU of the European Parliament and of the Council of 13 December 2011 on a single application procedure for a single permit for third-country nationals to reside and work in the territory of a Member State and on a common set of rights for third-country workers legally residing in a Member State, [2011] OJ L 343/1. The Single Permit Directive is updated by Directive (EU) 2024/1233 which will enter into force by May 2026. Article 12 of the recast Single Permit Directive still contains the provisions on equal treatment.

[78] Article 18(1)(b) Directive 2014/66/EU of the European Parliament and of the Council of 15 May 2014 on the conditions of entry and residence of third-country nationals in the framework of an intra-corporate transfer, [2014] OJ L 157/1.

[79] Such approach was also previously suggested by Vankova (2020, p. 248).

with those of the PQD.[80] While such recommendation does not (yet) carry legal force, it has been described as a "minor revolution in respect of the treatment of third-country nationals in EU and Member State law".[81] Indeed, the introduction of this recommendation can be considered the beginning of a more integrated approach to recognising qualifications held by TCN.[82]

3 Routes to Recognition: The Different Regimes Under the PQD

The PQD can be considered a multilevel roadmap for recognition in the context of accessing a regulated profession in another EU Member State. To begin with, a distinction is made between service provision and establishment. Those individuals seeking to exercise their profession temporarily and occasionally in the territory of a Member State other than the one in which they are qualified are subject to a different regime than those professionals seeking to permanently establish themselves elsewhere.

3.1 Service Provision

Contrary to the regime for establishment, the regime for service provision can be considered lighter. In fact, these professionals do not need recognition of their qualifications. They may only be obliged to make a declaration on their insurance or other protection of personal liability before the first service provision.[83] This means that the service provider remains established in their home Member State and will move from there to another Member State temporarily and occasionally to exercise the profession.[84] This principle entails that Member States are not allowed to require service providers to undergo recognition procedures or fulfil the same requirements as maintained in the case of establishment.[85] Furthermore, it is important to stress

[80] Commission Recommendation of 15 November 2023 on the recognition of third-country nationals, C(2023) 7700 final.

[81] McCormack-George (2025, p. 156).

[82] A further change may be underway since at the time of conclusion of this manuscript, the Commission had just launched consultations for an upcoming Skills Portability Initiative bringing together efforts on digitalisation, increased transparency, and improved recognition procedures in relation to skills and qualifications. This initiative also included plans to simplify recognition procedures for third-country nationals. The adoption of the Skills Portability Initiative was planned for Q3 of 2026.

[83] Article 7(1) Professional Qualifications Directive.

[84] Article 5(1)(a)(2) Professional Qualifications Directive.

[85] Case C-458/08 *Commission v. Portugal*, ECLI:EU:C:2010:692.

that the service provider needs to physically move from one Member State to another to trigger the application of the regime for service provision under the PQD.[86]

Article 7 of the PQD can be considered the heart of the regime for service provision since it provides the preconditions to be fulfilled before the first service provision. In particular, a service provider needs to provide documentation such as a proof of nationality and an attestation indicating that he or she is legally established in another Member State and that there are no prohibitions on carrying out the profession in that state.[87] Should a professional come from a Member State where the profession is unregulated, he or she must submit proof of having exercised the profession for at least one year during the previous 10 years.[88] An exception applies to professionals in the security sector, healthcare professionals, and those concerned with the education of minors who must all provide evidence of their having no criminal convictions.[89] Regarding healthcare professionals, it should also be noted that such professions also need to present a declaration on language knowledge.[90]

While service provision does not imply a full recognition procedure, Member States have the possibility to check the professional qualifications of service providers whose activities have public health or safety implications. However, Member States' competent authorities are prevented from going too far since prior checks are only allowed where "the purpose of the check is to avoid serious damage to the health or safety of the service recipient due to a lack of professional qualifications of the service provider and where the check does not go beyond what is necessary for that purpose".[91] In such a case, competent authorities must inform a professional of a decision not to check qualifications or of the result of the check. However, Article 7(4)(b)(i) PQD allows authorities to impose an aptitude test when there is a substantial difference between the qualifications of the professional and the qualifications required in the host Member State—and that difference is so large as to be harmful to public health or safety and cannot be compensated by the professional's experience or knowledge, skills and competences acquired through lifelong learning. Despite its possible limitation to free movement, this procedure is designed to be quick. Even if such a test is imposed, the professional must be able to start providing the service *within* one month of the decision to impose an aptitude test. Accordingly, if the competent authority fails to produce a decision within two months, the professional is allowed to provide the service.[92] While authorities therefore do not extensively examine qualifications, documentation is essential to verify the professional's aptitude and credibility. The qualification check plays one role in this process. However, competent authorities have the possibility to request additional information *in the event of justified doubts* and—if they decide to check the qualifications—request

[86] Case C-342/14 *X-Steuerberatungsgesellschaft*, ECLI:EU:C:2015:827, para. 35.

[87] Article 7(2)(a)(b) Professional Qualifications Directive.

[88] Article 5(1)(b) and 7(1)(d) Professional Qualifications Directive.

[89] Article 7(1)(e) Professional Qualifications Directive.

[90] Article 7(1)(f) Professional Qualifications Directive.

[91] Article 7(4) Professional Qualifications Directive.

[92] Article 7(4) paragraph 5 Professional Qualifications Directive.

further information on the training followed by the professional in order to be able to assess substantial differences.[93]

Once the initial declaration is made and a potential check of the qualifications has taken place, the service provider can exercise the profession on the entire territory of a Member State.[94] While providing services, they are subject to the professional rules of the host Member State.[95] Nevertheless, the regime for service provision is again lighter since service providers are exempt from having to fulfil requirements related to authorisation/registration/membership of a professional organisation or body[96] as well as registrations with public social security bodies when settling accounts with insurers.[97]

3.2 *Establishment*

While service provision consists of the temporary and occasional exercise of a profession in another Member State, establishment concerns the long-term or permanent exercise of a profession in another Member State. In this case—and unlike service provision—recognition is an *absolute precondition* to accessing a regulated profession. The PQD provides for two overarching systems for recognition in the case of establishment: a general system and a system for automatic recognition. The general system operates on the basis of the principle of mutual recognition and provides a general framework for recognition which most regulated professions are subject to. By contrast, in the case of automatic recognition certain agreements have been made at EU level for certain professions regarding the qualifications one needs to exercise those professions.

3.2.1 Automatic Recognition Under the PQD

Whereas the PQD includes one system for which is formally named the system for automatic recognition, it does comprise a total of three systems which enable expedited recognition through previously agreed standards. These can be found in the

[93] Article 8(1) Professional Qualifications Directive.

[94] In particular, this prevents Member States with a federal structure from restricting the activities of the service provider to a specific area. Although Member States may require additional information if (a) the profession is regulated differently in various parts of the Member State, (b) that regulation is applicable to all nationals of that Member State, (c) the differences in regulation are justified by public health or safety considerations, and (d) the Member State has no other means of obtaining such information (such as via the documents service providers need to provide in addition to the prior declaration); see Article 7(2a) Professional Qualifications Directive.

[95] Article 5(3) Professional Qualifications Directive.

[96] As an alternative, *pro forma* memberships or temporary registration with such organisations or bodies can be required. See Article 6(a) Professional Qualifications Directive.

[97] Article 6(a)(b) Professional Qualifications Directive.

Directive under the denominations recognition of professional experience, recognition on the basis of coordination of minimum training conditions, and automatic recognition on the basis of common training principles. Contrary to what the terminology supposes, automatic recognition under the PQD is not automatic in the sense of it being immediate and without procedures. Instead, professionals do need to apply for recognition in every Member State—although the provisions on automatic recognition speed up this process and mean in-depth examinations of the content of qualifications are not necessary.

Recognition of Professional Experience

The system for the recognition of professional experience contains the remnants of the very first EU legal instruments on professional recognition. The origins of this system can be traced to the transitional directives adopted in the 1960s that had been consolidated in Directive 1999/42/EC. Under this system for recognition of professional experience professionals working in crafts, commerce, and industry are able to obtain (automatic) recognition if they have exercised their profession for a specific number of years in a particular capacity.

This system for recognition is made operational through Articles 16–19 of the PQD. In particular, Member States must recognise the previous pursuit of certain professional activities in other Member States where the pursuit of those activities depends on the "possession of general, commercial or professional knowledge and aptitudes".[98] This knowledge and aptitude subsequently follows from the interaction of Articles 17 through 19 and Annex IV of the Directive. Annex IV of the PQD subsequently includes three lists of activities in crafts, commerce, and industry. Each of the Articles 17 through 19 corresponds to the activities laid down in one of the lists. These Articles themselves define different capacities in which a professional should have exercised the activities in the corresponding list paired with a specific number of years' experience. The PQD acknowledges four capacities in which one must have exercised the activities of Annex IV, namely (1) in a self-employed capacity, (2) as a manager of an undertaking, (3) in an executive position, and (4) on an employed basis. Depending on the particular situation, professionals qualifying for automatic recognition of their professional experience need between two and six consecutive years of professional experience. This means that someone who, for example, wishes to pursue activities regarding the manufacture of textiles in another Member State where the pursuit of such activities depends on specific knowledge and aptitudes, is allowed to do so when he or she has already pursued the activities for six consecutive years on a self-employed basis or as a manager of an undertaking in the home Member State.[99]

---

[98] Article 16 Professional Qualifications Directive.

[99] Article 17(1)(a) Professional Qualifications Directive.

Recognition on the Basis of Coordination of Minimum Training Conditions

The system for recognition on the basis of coordination of minimum training conditions constitutes the second part of the system for automatic recognition, functioning alongside the system for professional recognition. The system is the most intricate and complex part of the Directive, containing the legacy of the sectoral directives adopted in the 1970s and 1980s for the professions of doctor, nurse, dentist, veterinarian, midwife, pharmacist, and architect.[100] This approach entailed a combination of harmonised education and training *together with* a list of diplomas awarded according to that coordinated education and training. The structure established via the sectoral approach is maintained in the PQD today since Title III Chapter III starts with Articles 21 through 23a which stipulate conditions for automatic recognition while the harmonised education and training (i.e. minimum training conditions) and lists of diplomas fulfilling those standards are found in Articles 24 through 49 and Annex V respectively.

Article 21 of the PQD can be considered the essential Article of the system for recognition on the basis of coordination of minimum training conditions as it establishes the principle of automatic recognition and conditions surrounding it. According to the principle of automatic recognition, each Member State recognises evidence of formal qualifications satisfying the minimum training conditions established for the designated professions.[101] This applies to all Member State nationals who have obtained a qualification included in the PQD Annexes in a Member State other than that of which they are a national.[102] Therefore, qualifications obtained in the home Member State have the same effect in the host Member State as qualifications issued by the latter state. However, automatic recognition ultimately depends on fulfilment of three conditions: (1) the minimum training conditions of Articles 24 through 49 must be fulfilled for a certain profession and the evidence of qualifications must be documented on the list in Annex V, (2) the evidence must be issued by a competent authority, and (3) the evidence may need to be supplemented by a certificate. Once these conditions are fulfilled, recognition is automatic and unconditional.[103]

---

[100] Minimum training conditions were nevertheless established for the professions of doctors, nurses, dentists, veterinarians, midwives, and pharmacists—and not for architects. No minimum training conditions were adopted for them because there were large differences in educational requirements and the Member States were unable to reach an agreement. Instead, the first directive for architects (Directive 85/384/EEC) provided for qualitative and quantitative criteria to be fulfilled before recognition could be granted. See Schoenmaekers (2010, pp. 86–88).

[101] Article 21(1) Professional Qualifications Directive; Case C-365/13 *Ordre des architectes*, ECLI:EU:C:2014:280, para. 23.

[102] In *Broekmeulen*, the Court ruled that the then sectoral directive for the recognition of doctor qualifications applied to all Member State nationals. Broekmeulen was a Dutch citizen who trained as a doctor in Belgium but wanted to exercise his profession as a general practitioner in the Netherlands. His request for registration with the competent authority was refused because Dutch legislation only allowed other Member State nationals—not Dutch nationals trained in another Member State—to register as general practitioners after having obtained recognition under Directives 75/362/EEC and 75/363/EEC. See Case 246/80 *Broekmeulen*, ECLI:EU:C:1981:218, para. 18–20.

[103] Case C-110/01 *Tennah-Durez*, ECLI:EU:C:2003:357, para. 30.

By contrast, if a diploma is not explicitly mentioned in the PQD's Annexes, it cannot be recognised under the system for automatic recognition. Therefore, the correctness and topicality of the PQD Annexes must be guaranteed by the Member States in order to ensure that professionals exercising one of the sectoral professions can benefit from automatic recognition.[104]

It is clear that the minimum training conditions play a central role in the functioning of this system for automatic recognition. What is important to mention is the exclusionary nature of these minimum training conditions. In particular, Member States are prohibited from demanding fulfilment of additional requirements.[105] And not only that, the existence of minimum training conditions also signifies that Member States are not allowed to create qualifications that depart from the minimum training conditions (i.e. they may not maintain training that does not fulfil the conditions).[106] While its role in achieving recognition may be clear, the automatic and unconditional nature of the system for automatic recognition can lead to contrary situations at the national level. In *Ordine degli Ingegneri di Verona e Provincia*, the Court was confronted with a question on reverse discrimination occurring with civil engineers in Italy. When such professionals were trained in Italy, they were not allowed to take part in civil construction projects that had an artistic character or that were concerned with restoring culturally important structures. However, civil engineers trained in other Member States could obtain automatic recognition on the basis of Directive 85/384 meaning that they could take part in artistic or culturally important architectural projects in Italy. Considering the fact that the Court had already held that the EU law principle of equal treatment could not be invoked in a purely internal situation, the national judge asked whether Italy could require foreign-trained civil engineers to undergo a specific examination as to their qualifications.[107] This examination would then mitigate the reverse discrimination because it could prevent Italy from having to admit other Member State nationals to that part of the architecture profession to which it restricted access for its own nationals. However, the Court did not allow this reiterating that additional tests would infringe Directive 85/384 and that inclusion of a diploma on the list of the directive meant that access to activities relating to buildings of artistic importance could therefore not be refused.[108]

In *Preindl*, the Court confirmed the automatic and unconditional nature of the system for automatic recognition indicating its automatic and unconditional nature may even lead to the situation where a host Member State must accept a qualification obtained according to PQD compliant training which it itself prohibits. Hannes Preindl trained as a surgeon and dentist simultaneously in Austria whereby some examinations were taken into account for the acquisition of both qualifications. He

---

[104] Case C-447/93 *Dreessen*, ECLI:EU:C:1994:321.

[105] Case C-365/13 *Ordre des architectes*, ECLI:EU:C:2014:280, para. 25; Case 246/80 *Broekmeulen*, ECLI:EU:C:1981:218, para. 26.

[106] Case C-110/01 *Tennah-Durez*, ECLI:EU:C:2003:357, para. 54.

[107] Case C-111/12 *Ordine degli Ingegneri di Verona e Provincia*, ECLI:EU:C:2013:100, para. 22 and 31.

[108] Ibid., para. 43–44 and 51.

first requested recognition of his dentist qualifications in Italy, after which he also requested recognition for his qualification as a surgeon. Although the first request was granted, the second was denied since Italy does not permit students to be enrolled in more than one training course. The Court ultimately ruled that recognition of both the qualifications as dentist and surgeon are subject to automatic and unconditional recognition, meaning that Member States must accept the equivalence of qualifications covered by the PQD.[109] More specifically, the Court argued that the PQD permits part-time training and that there is no provision in the PQD prohibiting simultaneous enrolment.[110] Therefore, a host Member State may be forced to accept training that was followed in another Member State in a way that it does not foresee itself.

Despite these cases, the obligation not to depart from the minimum training conditions is not applicable to *all* education and training for the sectoral professions. In a case brought before the CJEU, the French *Conseil national de l'ordre des médecins* sought annulment of a decision from the French Ministry of Higher Education and Research and the French Ministry for Social Affairs and Health. The contested decision established a specialised training course in oral surgery open to graduates of both basic medical training as well as basic dental training. In particular, the *Conseil* argued that the course was in violation of the PQD and its minimum training conditions and created a new profession open for doctors and dentists. The Court, however, did not follow the reasoning of the *Conseil* arguing that if a Member State creates a specialised training course not corresponding to the titles in the PQD's Annexes, that specialisation is not a course within the meaning of Articles 25 and 35 of the PQD.[111] However, the Court also argued that the PQD does preclude persons from working as doctors or dentists if they have not completed basic medical or dental training in line with the PQD's minimum training requirements of Articles 24 and 34.[112] With this case, the Court essentially specified that the minimum training conditions had to be adhered to for basic medical and dental training, but that Member States are allowed to create specialised subsequent training courses that do not qualify for automatic recognition.[113]

Recognition on the Basis of Common Training Principles

Common training principles were one of the introductions of Directive 2013/55/EU[114] and consist of common training *frameworks* and common training *tests* found

[109] Case C-675/17 *Preindl*, EU:C2018:990, para. 31.

[110] Ibid., para. 29–30. The judgment from the Court of Justice of the EU was taken over by the national judge. See Consiglio di Stato, 30 maggio 2019, n. 4118, in *Reg. Prov. Coll.*, 2019.

[111] Case C-492/12 *Conseil national de l'ordre des médecins*, ECLI:EU:C:2013:576, para. 38.

[112] Ibid., para. 40–41.

[113] And will subsequently be subject to the PQD's general system. See Sect. 3.2.2 below.

[114] These came to replace the common platforms previously provided under Directive 2005/36/EC. Initially, common platforms were introduced as a means to achieve harmonisation of compensation

in Articles 49a and 49b of the PQD respectively. While a common training framework is "a common set of minimum knowledge, skills and competences necessary for the pursuit of a specific profession",[115] a common training test is "a standardised aptitude test available across participating Member States and reserved to holders of a particular professional qualification".[116] While these descriptions may not seem very telling at first, common training principles are a new means to achieve automatic recognition since, in essence, they are a way to extend automatic recognition to professions for which it is not yet available (i.e. professions falling under the general system).

Common training principles are proposed by EU or national level professional organisations, or competent authorities coming from at least one-third of the Member States.[117] Once accepted, however, the principles become applicable to all EU Member States.[118] The one-third Member States minimum is therefore only required for the introduction of the principle and is not maintained in its later functioning. This particularity explains why both Articles 49a and 49b include an exemption clause allowing a Member State not to participate in that common training principle.[119] While this general application may cause some to question the feasibility of the common training principles, a common training test has been adopted for ski instructors, thereby providing for automatic recognition for that profession. The common training test does not replace any national regulation nor does it impose additional EU-level legislation. Instead, ski instructors with relevant qualifications can take a test, the successful completion of which results in automatic recognition.[120]

---

measures. They were meant to be established by professional associations which would decide on a set of criteria, the fulfilment of which would attest to "a sufficient level of competence for the pursuit of a given profession". However, no common platforms were ever adopted and they were thus replaced by their successors: common training principles; Proposal for a Directive of the European Parliament and of the Council on the recognition of professional qualifications, COM(2002) 119 final, p. 8; Proposal for a Directive of the European Parliament and of the Council amending Directive 2005/36/EC on the recognition of professional qualifications and Regulation on administrative cooperation through the Internal Market Information System, COM(2011) 883 final, p. 10; European Commission, Evaluation of the Professional Qualifications Directive (Directive 2005/36/EC), Brussels 5 July 2011, p. 39.

[115] Article 49a(1) Professional Qualifications Directive.

[116] Article 49b(1) Professional Qualifications Directive.

[117] Article 49a(3) and Article 49b(3) Professional Qualifications Directive.

[118] This may be inferred from Article 49a(5) and Article 49b(5) which show that Member States may be exempted from the obligation of organising a common training principle. This exemption means that, as a rule, Member States are obliged to apply the common training principle once it is accepted.

[119] Article 49a(5) and Article 49b(5) Professional Qualifications Directive.

[120] Report from the Commission to the European Parliament, the Council, the European Economic and Social Committee and the Committee of the Regions on the implementation of certain new elements introduced by Directive 2013/55/EU of the European Parliament and of the Council of 20 November 2013 amending Directive 2005/36/EC on the recognition of professional qualifications and Regulation (EU) No 1024/2012 on administrative cooperation through the Internal Market Information System ('the IMI Regulation'), COM(2020) 191 final, p. 12.

The run-up to the introduction of the test for ski instructors nevertheless shows the degree of consensus that must already exist for a common training principle to be accepted.[121] In the case of ski instructors this led to Commission Delegated Regulation 2019/907 being adopted in June 2019 thus establishing the test for ski instructors. Article 2(2) of the Commission Delegated Regulation shows that the common training test consists of a "test certifying technical ability of ski instructors and a test certifying safety-related competences of ski instructors". Annex II subsequently establishes the rules for the organisation of these tests. The rules relate to, among others, the persons admitted to the test, the jury able to decide whether a person has passed the test, and what the ski course should look like. Annex I of the Commission Delegated Regulation then lists all national qualifications with which individuals are able to qualify for the common training test. In line with Article 6 of the Commission Delegated Regulation, a person can be exempted from certain parts of the common training test.

While the adoption of the first common training test must be considered a success, the preparation necessary to create the test also leads to questions regarding to which extent common training principles may be adopted also for other professions. Following the 2020 evaluation of parts of Directive 2013/55/EU, the Commission indicated that a variety of professional organisations had expressed interest in common training principles, although varying reasons were given for which the initial interests were not followed up ranging from not meeting the required threshold of Member States to fears of extending regulation at national level thus negatively impacting mobility.[122] Furthermore, case studies were undertaken by the Commission to examine the possible adoption of common training principles though these did not result in the adoption of a common training framework nor test.[123] In relation

[121] The common training test originates from a 2012 pilot project through which a professional card (N.B. not the *European* Professional Card) for ski instructors was established via a Memorandum of Understanding (MoU). From that project, it became apparent that certain standardised tests were required for automatic recognition of ski instructor qualifications among the participating nine Member States. Since the MoU establishing the professional card was only applicable for a limited period of time, efforts were undertaken to establish a common training test to achieve automatic recognition for ski instructors. Apart from these activities, the introduction of the test was preceded by an extensive mapping study was conducted by the European Commission in 2015 through which the qualifications for ski instructors in 32 countries were examined. See Recital 3 Commission Delegated Regulation (EU) 2019/907 of 14 March 2019 establishing a Common Training Test for ski instructors under Article 49b of Directive 2005/36/EC of the European Parliament and of the Council on the recognition of the professional qualifications, [2019] OJ L 145/7; European Commission (2015) Mapping of professional qualifications and relevant training for the profession of ski instructor in the EU-28, EEA and Switzerland—Final Report.

[122] Report from the Commission to the European Parliament, the Council, the European Economic and Social Committee and the Committee of the Regions on the implementation of certain new elements introduced by Directive 2013/55/EU of the European Parliament and of the Council of 20 November 2013 amending Directive 2005/36/EC on the recognition of professional qualifications and Regulation (EU) No 1024/2012 on administrative cooperation through the Internal Market Information System ('the IMI Regulation'), COM(2020) 191 final, p. 12.

[123] Taking engineers as example, a project was commissioned by the European Commission to examine the possibility for common training principles for these professionals. An extensive

to common training frameworks, it can be considered that Member States are reluctant to give up some of their discretion under the general system and thus their power to make individual assessments as to qualifications—thus indicating low levels of mutual trust in other Member States' qualification systems.[124] While the case of ski instructors shows the importance of such mutual trust, it also shows the importance of pre-existing cooperation and good will among stakeholders concerned.

3.2.2 The General System

While the previous sections focused on different configurations of automatic recognition under the PQD, most professionals will in practice be subject to the general system. The effectiveness of that system is vital considering that there are more than 6000 regulated professions in the EU Member States (i.e. only a limited number of professios is subject to automatic recognition).[125] The general system is also the part of the PQD that operates on the basis of the principle of mutual recognition. Translated from the free movement of goods[126] to the field of diplomas the principle entails that qualifications should be recognised, unless there are substantial differences between the qualifications held by a person and those required in the host Member State. Unsurprisingly, the space provided by the principle of mutual recognition to balance free movement of individuals with the interests of Member States is where discussions arise—and accordingly what makes the general system the most disputed part of the PQD. Of course, issues on recognition under the general system originate from different education and training systems across Member States. A 2019 report conducted at the request of the European Parliament's Employment and Social Affairs Committee found that "the main obstacles to the effective recognition of qualifications in the general system as opposed to the automatic system are precisely those differences in education and training requirements and also national recognition practices across the EU, some of which are more fragmented and/or less transparent than others".[127]

mapping and consultation took place. In the final project report, the team reported on some of the complexities experienced. In particular, the team noted that, at times, the allocation of the competences of national authorities were not only complex, but also unclear. Furthermore, the team concluded that the process was not strictly intellectual, but also political in nature due to the fact that automatic recognition touches upon the foundation of national systems. The team furthermore reported that stakeholders often expressed the desire to continue carrying out individual assessments in the host Member State, indicating low levels of mutual trust in the other Member States' training systems thereby affirming that stakeholders partly felt that their national systems would be endangered by a common training framework that was not in full compliance with their national system. See ECEC (2017) Common Training Principles for Engineers (491/PP/GRO/IMA/15/5123); ECEC (2017) CTF for Civil Engineers—Recommendations of ECEC Project Team.

[124] See the previous footnote.

[125] European Commission, 'Regulated Professions Database', https://ec.europa.eu/growth/tools-databases/regprof/home.

[126] See Case 120/78 *Rewe-Zentral AG (Cassis de Dijon)*, ECLI:EU:C:1979:42.

[127] Adamis-Csásár et al. (2019, p. 71).

Differences in education and training give way to discussions on recognition in different ways. Whereas many discussions centre on whether there are substantial differences meaning compensation measures can be imposed, other issues have arisen in the past before the CJEU where competent authorities considered individuals were trying to circumvent national education and training by obtaining qualifications in other Member States and relying on EU law to again gain access to the profession in their home Member State. The Court has been very clear in these instances: "the fact that the national of a Member State has chosen to acquire a professional qualification in a Member State other than that in which he resides in order to benefit there from more favourable legislation is not, in itself [...] sufficient ground to conclude that there is an abuse of rights".[128] EU citizens can therefore exercise their right of free movement to make use of a qualification structure more beneficial than that provided by their home Member State—and continue to rely on the PQD's general system.

That being said, the general system is the widest of the PQD's systems in scope. Not only does it cover a residual category of professions not covered by automatic recognition, but it can also cover persons whose profession does qualify for automatic recognition but whose specific qualifications do not fulfil the necessary requirements for automatic recognition[129] as well as those who have obtained their qualifications in a third country.[130] The PQD even covers those whose profession is not regulated in their home Member State and who move to a Member State that does regulate the same profession.[131] Once it is clear that the general system applies, a qualification assessment begins with the classification of the qualification into one of the five levels described in Article 11 of the PQD. Attestations of competence, certificates, and diplomas make up the five levels of qualifications that are accepted for assessment under the general system. With Directive 2013/55/EU, a new level of qualification

[128] Cases C-58/13 and C-59/13 *Torresi*, ECLI:EU:C:2014:2088, para. 50. See also Case C-118/09 *Koller*, ECLI:EU:C:2010:805.

[129] In this case, there need to be "specific and exceptional reasons" for which they do not satisfy the requirements for automatic recognition. The Court of Justice of the EU specified in *Angerer* that application of the general system to sectoral professions (normally subject to automatic recognition) depends on two cumulative criteria: (1) the professional does not hold the qualifications for automatic recognition and (2) there are specific and exceptional reasons. Such reasons refer to the circumstances causing the professional not to have the right qualifications for automatic recognition, but cannot mean that an applicant is seeking access to a profession other than the one for which he or she is qualified in the home Member State; Case C-477/13 *Angerer*, ECLI:EU:C:2015:239.

[130] Article 10 Professional Qualifications Directive. Also see Sect. 2.3 of this chapter for more on the recognition of third country qualifications and the qualifications held by third country nationals.

[131] In that case, recognition can still be granted if the professional has pursued the profession one year (full or part-time) in the 10 years prior to the move. When Member State competent authorities are assessing this one-year pursuit of the profession, they must ensure that professional activities "consisted of the continuous and regular pursuit of a range of professional activities which characterise the profession concerned in the Member State of origin". However, there is no need for the professional concerned to have focused wholly and exclusively on the full range of activities part of the profession concerned, as this would be an overly restrictive interpretation of the PQD. See Article 13(2) Professional Qualifications Directive; Case C-424/09 *Toki*, ECLI:EU:C:2011:210.

was introduced in Article 11(c)(ii),[132] but more importantly the Directive created convergence with the Bologna Process.[133] Indeed, Article 11(d) came to refer to Bachelor's degrees and Article 11(e) to Master's degrees, whereby ECTS credits were also included in the PQD for these cycles because of their widespread use in European higher education institutions.[134] Equally important, the 2013 modernisation also required Member States to henceforth recognise the level of the qualification attested to by the home Member State.[135]

After categorisation into one of the five levels of Article 11, competent authorities evaluate the qualifications in more detail. This brings us to Article 13 and the heart of the general system with the principle of mutual recognition found in paragraph 1 of that Article.[136] This principle applied to the field of recognition of qualifications embodies a "presumption of recognition" which entails that Member States have a duty to recognise qualifications.[137] This presumption is far-reaching, especially since recognition can only be refused in one instance, namely in the event of a four-level difference if a person holds a qualification classified under Article 11(a) while the profession in the host Member State requires a qualification classified under Article 11(e) of the PQD.[138] The limitation of refusal grounds was solidified

[132] This was mostly done to ensure it was no longer necessary to keep track of training with a special structure in one of the PQD's Annexes (former Annex II), meaning the Commission no longer has to adopt implementing regulations to update the Annex; See article 1(52) Directive 2013/55/EU.

[133] The Bologna Process is the non-EU intergovernmental cooperation of European states in the area of higher education that resulted in some of the most radical changes in European higher education. Among others, it introduced a three-cycle structure for higher education (bachelor's, master's, and doctorate) and a system of ECTS credits. The Bologna Process is discussed more extensively in Chapter "Academic Recognition" of this contribution.

[134] Recitals 11 and 17 Directive 2013/55/EU. The inclusion of these levels resolved issues with the recognition of the Bologna Process's different levels. While countries party to the process agreed on the general cycle names bachelor, master, and doctorate, they did not establish a fixed number of credits, instead they agreed on *ranges*. This means that countries participating in the Process may decide how many ECTS they allot to a certain degree. For example, master's degrees in the Netherlands typically consist of 60 ECTS credits (one year), while master's degrees in Belgium usually consist of 120 ECTS credits (two years). Differences in the way countries interpret the three-cycle structure instituted by the Bologna Process were found to limit convergence in the context of the PQD and prevent the Bologna Process from supporting recognition under the PQD; Howat et al. (2011, pp. 33, 37 and 57).

[135] Article 13(3) Professional Qualifications Directive.

[136] Article 13(1) Professional Qualifications Directive reads as follows: "If access to or pursuit of a regulated profession in a host Member State is contingent upon possession of specific professional qualifications, the competent authority of that Member State shall permit applicants to access and pursue that profession, under the same conditions as apply to its nationals, if they possess an attestation of competence or evidence of formal qualifications referred to in Article 11, required by another Member State in order to gain access to and pursue that profession on its territory."

[137] See Article 13(1) Professional Qualifications Directive.

[138] This means that individuals whose qualifications are based on professional experience who are seeking access to a profession for which a master's degree is required are the only category of professionals who may still face refusals based on qualification level. Article 13(4) Professional Qualifications Directive; Proposal for a Directive of the European Parliament and of the Council amending Directive 2005/36/EC on the recognition of professional qualifications and Regulation

through Directive 2013/55/EU. Prior to the 2013 modernisation of the PQD, level played a more important role in a qualification assessment conducted by authorities.[139] However, the change was introduced since a 2011 study found that the level differences were barely used to exclude individuals from the scope of application of the general system.[140] In its proposal for Directive 2013/55/EU, the Commission indicated that the qualification levels of Article 11 should henceforth only be used as a benchmarking tool and may no longer be a basis for excluding professionals from the scope of the Directive.[141]

This means that a qualification assessment is focused primarily on the content of the qualifications submitted. However, even when focusing solely on content we can see the presuming nature of the principle of mutual recognition at work. In relation to assessments regarding the content of qualifications, the Court has ruled that diplomas under the general system are not recognised on the basis of the intrinsic value of the education and training to which they attest, but because those diplomas give the right to take up a regulated profession in a host Member State.[142] That right is therefore connected to the qualification as an "end-product", rather than its various parts, which enables exercise of the profession. This strong presumption that underlies the principle of mutual recognition necessitates considerable levels of trust in other Member States' qualifications. According to Cambien, mutual trust and mutual recognition must be distinguished from one another in the context of the internal market, even though the two are strongly related notions.[143] He rightly considers mutual trust to be a prerequisite for a properly functioning system based on mutual recognition and for successful internal market harmonisation.[144] Indeed, a host Member State will mutually recognise qualifications on the basis of trust in the education system and in the profession of the home Member State. In a way, mutual trust may be considered the foundation and mutual recognition the consequence to follow from that trust. However, to simply designate mutual recognition as a consequence of mutual trust would not do justice to the principle, since—at least in the area of the recognition of qualifications—the presuming part of the principle requires host Member States to accept qualifications originating from other Member

---

on administrative cooperation through the Internal Market Information System, COM(2011) 883 final, p. 8.

[139] Under Directive 2005/36/EC, competent authorities could always refuse recognition if the home Member State's qualification was more than one level lower than the one required in the host Member State. Only one instance of a two-level difference was explicitly permitted under Directive 2005/36/EC; See Article 13(1)(b)(3) Directive 2005/36/EC.

[140] Howat et al. (2011, p. 158).

[141] Proposal for a Directive of the European Parliament and of the Council amending Directive 2005/36/EC on the recognition of professional qualifications and Regulation on administrative cooperation through the Internal Market Information System, COM(2011) 883 final, p. 8.

[142] Case C-102/02 *Beuttenmüller*, ECLI:EU:C:2004:264.

[143] Cambien (2017, p. 99).

[144] Ibid., p. 114.

States. Mutual recognition therefore operationalises the obligation of Member States to recognise qualifications.[145]

While this seems to tip the balancing act embodied in the principle of mutual recognition very much in favour of the individual rather than the Member States, the balance is again restored since the principle also allows Member States to derogate from recognition as a final result of a qualification assessment. This is especially the case when the host Member State considers that the home Member State's qualifications are insufficiently similar to its own, i.e. in case of substantial differences. In that case, the Member State may make recognition conditional. Therefore, the principle of mutual recognition has been described as being semi-automatic in the context of the PQD,[146] thereby allowing for what Hoogenboom aptly describes as a "middle way" by balancing integration and diversity concerns with harmonisation and mutual recognition of values and standards.[147] Mutual recognition under the PQD therefore consists of two elements: a presumption of recognition and compensation measures to mitigate substantial differences.

Indeed, as part of the balancing act in and representing the interests of Member States, the PQD provides for compensation measures which may be imposed if knowledge gaps are identified. The imposition of compensation measures means recognition becomes conditional upon completion of those measures. However, compensation measures are permissive, meaning that Member States are not required to impose such measures.[148] In fact, when Member States decide not to impose such measures, recognition may in some way be considered automatic.[149] The presumption of recognition paired with the optional nature of the compensation measures means that these measures may only be applied in exceptional cases—something important to stress since compensation measures dilute the principle of mutual recognition.[150] They are, nonetheless, inevitable considering the complexity and multiplicity of regulated professions and education and training falling under the PQD.[151]

The PQD provides for two types of compensation measures[152]: (1) an adaptation period of a maximum of three years, or (2) an aptitude test.[153] Such compensation

---

[145] Hoogenboom (2014, p. 250).

[146] See for example Blitz (1999, p. 316); Peixoto (2001, p. 43).

[147] Hoogenboom (2014, pp. 238 and 251).

[148] Report to the European Parliament and the Council on the state of application of the general system for the recognition of higher education diplomas—Made in accordance with Article 13 of Directive 89/48/EEC, COM(96) 46 final, p. 7.

[149] Parkins (1992, pp. 42–43).

[150] Schneider (1995, pp. 193).

[151] Ibid.

[152] In principle, applicants have a right to choose between the two according to Article 14(2) of the PQD although this right is not absolute. Member States may decide to impose either one of the compensation measures depending on the fulfilment of the conditions in Article 14(3) of the directive.

[153] Although the latter are much less common. In fact, in the run-up to the 2013 modernisation the Commission found that the frequency, availability and cost of the compensation measures were an

measures may be imposed in one of two scenarios. First, in the event that there are substantial differences between the home and host Member State qualifications. Second, Adaptation periods or aptitude tests may also be imposed if substantial differences are paired with the profession in the home Member State comprising fewer professional activities than those of the profession in the host Member State. The term "substantially different matters"[154] is thereby employed to avoid an arbitrary use of compensation measures and Member States must confirm the existence of such substantial differences before imposing compensation measures. Nevertheless, competent authorities are allowed ample discretion in determining the presence of substantial differences. In fact, there is only one element of the definition preventing Member States' competent authorities from having a *carte blanche* in this respect. substantial differences may only be found in those areas of the profession that are *essential* for its exercise.

The concept of substantial differences has nevertheless been subject to simplification. In the first place, Directive 2013/55/EU ensured that the focus in assessing substantial differences was shifted from duration to content.[155] Additionally, competent authorities are also required to look beyond mere knowledge and must also assess the *skills and competences* of the applicant.[156] In line with the principle of proportionality, the competent authority is therefore required to first ascertain whether all knowledge, skills, and competences acquired through experience or lifelong learning (and formally validated) within or outside the EU can or cannot cover the substantial differences—before imposing compensation measures.[157]

As remarked previously in this section, the general system is the most disputed part of the PQD. Accordingly, cases have also been presented before the CJEU on substantial differences and the imposition of compensation measures. For example, in *Vandorou* the Court was faced with a national authority which imposed compensation measures without taking into account certain practical experience of the persons

issue. In particular, the low frequency of aptitude tests (sometimes not even yearly) caused some professionals to have to wait a long time before being able to take the test. Directive 2013/55/EU therefore obliges Member States to organise aptitude tests within six months after deciding on imposing such a measure on the applicant; Article 14(7) Professional Qualifications Directive; European Commission, Evaluation of the Professional Qualifications Directive (Directive 2005/36/EC), Brussels 5 July 2011, p. 31.

[154] Article 14(4) Professional Qualifications Directive contains the definition of these substantial differences and reads: *"[...]'substantially different matters' means matters in respect of which knowledge, skills and competences acquired are essential for pursuing the profession and with regard to which the training received by the migrant shows significant differences in terms of content from the training required by the host Member State."*

[155] According to the Commission, the duration of training was not particularly relevant because differences in the duration of training could, for example, be explained by variations in the organisation of education systems that could not systematically be considered substantial; European Commission, Evaluation of the Professional Qualifications Directive (Directive 2005/36/EC), Brussels 5 July 2011, p. 30.

[156] Article 14(4) Professional Qualifications Directive.

[157] Article 4(5) Professional Qualifications Directive.

concerned. In that case, their experience could not be considered as practical experience under the Directive since it was obtained *prior* to the formal pursuit of the regulated profession (e.g. in employment in a profession other than the regulated one to which access was sought).[158] The Court considered that, in light of the principle of proportionality, the fundamental freedoms would be unjustifiably hindered if not all practical experience was taken into account.[159] Therefore Member State competent authorities were obliged, on the basis of current Articles 45 and 49 TFEU,[160] to take into account all knowledge, qualifications, and experience held by applicants, and had to determine which value to attach to that experience in light of the profession in the host Member State.[161]

Discussions on the theme of proportionality were continued in a case on intermediaries. Greece demanded documentation that was unnecessary to proportionately evaluate the content of the training completed by the applicants.[162] What is more, the Greek legislation was also held to be contrary to the PQD because it allowed for the imposition of compensation measures without a prior evaluation for substantial differences and required intermediaries to have taken part in at least three procedures before equivalence could be established.[163] While this case is an example of a Member State exceeding its margin of discretion under the general system, such practices are not uncommon. In particular, there has long been a tendency to reverse the principle of mutual recognition and the exceptional nature of compensation measures.[164] Indeed, in the run-up to the 2013 modernisation the Commission also found that the margin of discretion awarded to competent authorities at

[158] Cases C-422/09, C-425/09 and C-426/09 *Vandorou, Giankoulis and Askoxilakis*, ECLI:EU:C:2010:732, para. 64. In a different, though related case, the Court was asked to rule about a person's work experience in relation to remuneration. The case again showed that not all experience was to be taken into account. When Adelheid Krah wanted to work as a senior lecturer/postdoc at the University of Vienna, the University's policy prescribed that only four years previous experience could be taken into account. She initiated a complaint procedure against this arguing that she was subject to a different (and higher) remuneration scale if all her work experience was taken into account. According to the Court, the rule at hand could be considered an obstacle to free movement. However, a distinction was to be made between the work experience acquired abroad that was similar to that of senior lecturer/postdoc and that work experience which was different. The Court argued that only the former had to be taken into account because not doing so could constitute an impediment to free movement; Case C-703/17 *Krah*, ECLI:EU:C:2019:850.

[159] Cases C-422/09, C-425/09 and C-426/09 *Vandorou, Giankoulis and Askoxilakis*, ECLI:EU:C:2010:732, para. 65, 66 and 69.

[160] The Treaty provisions on free movement of workers and establishment have come to form what can be described as a "fallback system" that works as an alternative to provide procedural safeguards under EU law for those with qualifications (or parts of qualifications) that are outside the scope of relevant EU directives on recognition. The existence of this fallback system is discussed more extensively in Sect. 6 of this chapter.

[161] Cases C-422/09, C-425/09 and C-426/09 *Vandorou, Giankoulis and Askoxilakis*, ECLI:EU:C:2010:732, para. 66 and 69.

[162] Meaning requirements were assessed that did not follow from the PQD. See Case C-729/17 *Commission v. Greece*, ECLI:EU:C:2019:534, para. 96.

[163] Ibid., para. 98–100.

[164] Pertek (1992, p. 100).

times resulted in compensation measures being disproportionate, imposed arbitrarily or insufficiently justified.[165] Issues regarding legal certainty were also found since some applicants did not receive a clear decision containing a justification regarding the reason for which compensation measures were imposed.[166] Such issues led to the introduction of Article 14(6) of the PQD requiring that applicants are provided with information on the level of the professional qualification required in the host Member State and that held by the applicant as well as information of the substantial differences and the reason for which they cannot be compensated with existing qualifications.[167] The specification of the duty to motivate decisions to impose compensation measures is welcome in principle, although the case of the intermediaries above shows that excesses of discretion by competent authorities may still occur even after the introduction of Article 14(6).[168] In any case, the Member States' obligation to justify decisions to impose compensation measures introduced by that provision is a welcome addition, if not to ensure compliance by the Member States from the outset, then to form the basis for its enforcement before a court of law.

4 Digital Tools Under the Professional Qualifications Directive

Any discussion on recognition of qualifications in the twenty-first century cannot be without reference to digital tools. Such tools are essential to facilitate administrative cooperation and potentially expedite recognition as such.

4.1 The Internal Market Information System

The Internal Market Information System (IMI system) was developed to support administrative cooperation.[169] The origins of the IMI system date back to the 2004 enlargement. The system was introduced to overcome obstacles to administrative

[165] European Commission, Evaluation of the Professional Qualifications Directive (Directive 2005/36/EC), Brussels 5 July 2011, p. 30.

[166] Commission Staff Working Paper—Impact Assessment: Accompanying the document Proposal for a Directive of the European Parliament and of the Council amending Directive 2005/36/EC on the recognition of professional qualifications and Regulation on administrative cooperation through the Internal Market Information System, SEC(2011) 1558 final—Part II, p. 15.

[167] See Proposal for a Directive of the European Parliament and of the Council amending Directive 2005/36/EC on the recognition of professional qualifications and Regulation on administrative cooperation through the Internal Market Information System, COM(2011) 883 final, p. 8.

[168] The transposition date of Directive 2013/55/EU that introduced the provision was on 18 January 2016.

[169] European Commission, Evaluation of the Professional Qualifications Directive (Directive 2005/36/EC), Brussels 5 July 2011, p. 11.

cooperation such as finding the right contact person, language barriers, and differences in administrative cultures.[170] Initially, the system was introduced specifically for the Services Directive and the PQD.[171] However, it currently also extends to other internal market areas such as cross-border healthcare, the Internal Market Problem Solving Network (SOLVIT), and the Posted Worker's Directive.[172]

The IMI system is managed by the Commission and provides a secure online application allowing authorities at different levels and in different Member States to communicate with each other.[173] The system's main objectives are[174]: (1) to support competent authorities in finding the right authority in another Member State, (2) to help overcome language barriers by providing pre-translated texts, and (3) to provide for a tracking mechanism so authorities can follow the progress of their request. In the run-up to Directive 2013/55/EU stakeholders expressed their support for a mandatory use of the system under the PQD.[175] The system has since come to play an important role in facilitating cooperation and communication under the PQD, especially since the European Professional Card and the Alert Mechanism operate through it.[176]

[170] Communication from the Commission to the European Parliament, the Council, the European Economic and Social Committee and the Committee of the Regions—Better governance of the Single Market through greater administrative cooperation: A strategy for expanding and developing the Internal Market Information System ('IMI'), COM(2011) 75 final, p. 3–4.

[171] Recital 4 Commission Decision of 12 December 2007 concerning the implementation of the Internal Market Information System (IMI) as regards the protection of personal data, [2008] OJ L 13/18; European Commission, Evaluation of the Professional Qualifications Directive (Directive 2005/36/EC), Brussels 5 July 2011, p. 76.

[172] Article 3 in conjunction with the Annex Regulation (EU) No 1024/2012 of the European Parliament and of the Council of 25 October 2012 on administrative cooperation through the Internal Market Information System and repealing Commission Decision 2008/49/EC ('the IMI Regulation'), [2012] OJ L 316/1.

[173] Lottini (2014, p. 110).

[174] Communication from the Commission to the European Parliament, the Council, the European Economic and Social Committee and the Committee of the Regions—Better governance of the Single Market through greater administrative cooperation: A strategy for expanding and developing the Internal Market Information System ('IMI'), COM(2011) 75 final, p. 4.

[175] Green Paper: Modernising the Professional Qualifications Directive, COM(2011) 367 final, p. 13; Article 56(2a) Professional Qualifications Directive.

[176] Articles 4a through 4e, Article 56a Professional Qualifications Directive. Furthermore, the significance of the IMI System may continue to grow. In 2023, the Commission adopted an implementing decision for a pilot project to implement other elements of administrative cooperation under the PQD and the Proportionality Test Directive in the IMI System. See Commission Implementing Decision (EU) 2023/423 of 24 February 2023 on a pilot project to implement the administrative cooperation provisions relating to regulated professions set out in Directive 2005/36/EC and (EU) 2018/958 of the European Parliament and of the Council by means of the Internal Market Information System and to integrate the database of regulated professions into that system, [2023] OJ L 61/62.

4.2 The European Professional Card

Whereas the European Professional Card (EPC) can be hailed as one of the main modernisations instituted by Directive 2013/55/EU, the idea of a professional card was not entirely new.[177] Previous attempts at professional cards were nevertheless unsuccessful, one of the reasons being that previous initiatives for professional cards hinged on the involvement of professional organisations. Concerns related to commercial and public interest conflicts led to the desire to develop a professional card that would be issued by competent authorities, rather than professional organisations.[178] Furthermore, previous attempts at professional cards were unsuccessful since they did not confer any rights to professionals.[179]

Consequently, there was a need to adapt the basic idea underlying the card which ultimately led to the European Professional Card (EPC), an instrument foreseen "to facilitate and accelerate the recognition procedure while at the same time making it more transparent".[180] Contrary to what its name may suggest, the EPC is not an actual card. Instead, it is an *electronic certificate* attesting to the fact that the professional fulfils all conditions for recognition in relation to service provision or establishment under the PQD.[181] Benefits of an electronic certificate over a physical card relate to countering concerns of fraud as well as making adequate use of available modern technologies. Indeed, an electronic certificate does away with the need to compile hardcopy dossiers, facilitates the validation process, and can generally lead to a less time-intensive recognition process.

Despite the EPC's suitability for this digital age, the instrument has several caveats since the acquisition of an EPC is dependent on two conditions: (1) the professional concerned has submitted an application for a card, and (2) the card is available because the Commission has adopted an implementing act for a certain profession.[182] Starting with the latter, EPCs are not available for all professions subject to the PQD. Instead,

[177] Directive 2005/36/EC already mentioned the introduction of such cards at the level of professional associations or organisations to facilitate the mobility of professionals by speeding up information exchanges. The professional cards that were foreseen under Directive 2005/36/EC were explained as enabling the monitoring of the career of professionals who establish themselves in various Member States and would contain information on, among others, qualifications, the professional's establishment, and the details of the relevant competent authority. However, only two of these professional card projects were initiated According to the Commission, initiatives were undertaken under Recital 32 for health professionals as well as engineers. Additionally, the Commission makes mention of two stand-alone initiatives for lawyers and mountain guides. See Recital 32 Directive 2005/36/EC; European Commission, Evaluation of the Professional Qualifications Directive (Directive 2005/36/EC), Brussels 5 July 2011, p. 80.

[178] European Commission, Evaluation of the Professional Qualifications Directive (Directive 2005/36/EC), Brussels 5 July 2011, p. 79.

[179] Ibid., p. 81.

[180] Proposal for a Directive of the European Parliament and of the Council amending Directive 2005/36/EC on the recognition of professional qualifications and Regulation on administrative cooperation through the Internal Market Information System, COM(2011) 883 final, p. 7.

[181] Article 3(1)(k) Professional Qualifications Directive.

[182] Article 4a(1) Professional Qualifications Directive.

the Commission can only make the EPC available for a certain profession when three conditions are fulfilled: (1) there is significant mobility or potential thereto, (2) stakeholders have expressed their interest in the EPC, and (3) the profession itself or the education and training leading up to the exercise of a profession are regulated in a significant number of Member States.[183]

When the Commission was preparing the EPC, it conducted a thorough consultation leading to the identification of seven professions for which the EPC could first become available.[184] When it came to two of the professions (doctor and engineer), the EPC did not gain sufficient support.[185] However, for the other five professions identified all the EPC criteria were fulfilled and Commission Implementing Regulation (EU) 2015/983 was adopted, which made the EPC available for general care nurses, pharmacists, physiotherapists, mountain guides, and real estate agents.[186] Professionals pursuing these professions may accordingly *choose* to apply for the EPC or to make use of the regular recognition procedures under the PQD.[187] However, should they opt for the use of the EPC and the card is issued, the competent authorities must ensure that they benefit from all the rights contained in Articles 4b to 4e.[188] These rights are primarily related to procedural aspects and data protection.

The procedure for the application for an EPC is laid down in Article 4b of the modernised PQD. Professionals apply for an EPC by registering in the IMI system where a dedicated file is created.[189] Authorities subsequently have a duty to acknowledge the receipt of the application within one week of submission—and to inform the applicant of any missing documentation to be provided. Home Member State authorities play a particularly important role in the EPC application. They (1) issue any supporting certificate required under the PQD, (2) verify whether a professional is legally established in their Member State, (3) confirm the validity and authenticity of the documentation, and (4) request an applicant to provide certified copies in case of justified doubts.[190] The home Member State plays an important role, not only in

[183] Article 4a(7)(a–c) Professional Qualifications Directive.

[184] Commission Staff Working Document accompanying the document Commission's Implementing Regulation (EU) No 2015/983 on the procedure for issuance of the European Professional Card and the alert mechanism pursuant to Directive 2005/36/EC of the European Parliament and of the Council, SWD(2015) 123 final, p. 3.

[185] In the case of doctors, the general sentiment among stakeholders regarding the EPC for that profession seemed to be fairly positive although two large organisations appeared to have been in favour of introducing the EPC for doctors at a later stage. Regarding engineers, the stakeholders consulted generally questioned the added value of the EPC; Commission Staff Working Document accompanying the document Commission's Implementing Regulation (EU) No 2015/983 on the procedure for issuance of the European Professional Card and the alert mechanism pursuant to Directive 2005/36/EC of the European Parliament and of the Council, SWD(2015) 123 final, pp. 5–6 and 12–13.

[186] Annex I Commission Implementing Regulation (EU) 2015/983.

[187] Article 4a(2) Professional Qualifications Directive.

[188] Article 4a(3) Professional Qualifications Directive.

[189] Article 4b(1) Professional Qualifications Directive.

[190] Article 4b(3) Professional Qualifications Directive.

processing the EPC application, but also in issuing the card. In fact, the involvement of the home Member State authority is what helps to facilitate and accelerate recognition procedures.[191]

The PQD subsequently provides for two different EPC procedures depending on the duration of the exercise of professional activities and the type of profession exercised. Consequently, the Directive distinguishes (1) professionals who want to *establish* themselves in the host Member State and those who want to provide services in a *profession having public health and safety implications* from (2) all other professionals seeking to provide services in another Member State on a temporary and occasional basis.[192] The other main difference between these two procedures relates to the Member State issuing the EPC. In the case of professionals looking to provide services *without* public health and safety implications (EPC option 2), the home Member State both processes the application *and* grants the card.[193] The home Member State authority must issue the EPC within three weeks of submission of a completed IMI file. Once an EPC is issued, it must be transmitted to the host Member State's competent authority and the applicant must be informed. In the case of service provision, the EPC doubles as the declaration service providers may have to provide under the regular procedure in Article 7(1) PQD.[194] Service providers therefore have several rights under this EPC procedure, most notably designated time periods, a right not to provide additional declarations, and a right of appeal under national law against the decision of the home Member State competent authority or the lack of a decision.[195] Lastly, Article 4c(4) of the PQD states that service provision EPC's remain valid in the entire territory of the Member States concerned for as long as the EPC holder has a right to practise his or her profession on the basis of the IMI file.

The other EPC procedure (EPC option 1 above) is aimed at professionals who want to establish themselves in another Member States or for those who want to provide services but exercise a profession having public health and safety implications. In this case, the authority in the home Member State will take all the preparatory steps relating to the EPC while the card will be issued by the host Member State authority.[196] In this case, the home Member State's authority has one month to verify the authenticity and validity of the documents provided.[197] Article 4d subsequently introduces a further distinction in two categories of professionals reflective of other parts of the PQD: (1) professionals qualifying for automatic recognition are distinguished from (2) those who either qualify for general system recognition or seek to provide services in a profession with public health and safety implications. In the

[191] Proposal for a Directive of the European Parliament and of the Council amending Directive 2005/36/EC on the recognition of professional qualifications and Regulation on administrative cooperation through the Internal Market Information System, COM(2011) 883 final, p. 7.

[192] Article 4a(4)(5) Professional Qualifications Directive.

[193] Article 4a(4) and 4c Professional Qualifications Directive.

[194] Article 4a(4) and Article 4c(1) Professional Qualifications Directive.

[195] Article 4c(2) Professional Qualifications Directive.

[196] Article 4a(5) Professional Qualifications Directive.

[197] Article 4d(1) Professional Qualifications Directive.

case of automatic recognition, the host Member State's competent authority must decide on the EPC within one month.[198] In the case of general system recognition or service provision in a profession with public health and safety implications, the host Member State's competent authority has two months to decide to either issue the EPC or to impose compensation measures.[199] Should justified doubts arise in either of the two scenarios, extra information can be requested and must be supplied by the home Member State authorities within two weeks. The role of the home Member State authority is important here: if it does *not* adhere to this period, the host Member State can refuse the EPC.[200]

One important benefit of the EPC in respect to regular procedures relates to time periods. Host Member States are urged to take a decision on the EPC application within the respective one or two-month period provided by Article 4d. Should they fail to comply with these time limits, Article 4d(5) provides that the EPC will be considered issued. The EPC is even transmitted automatically to the professional concerned when no timely decision is taken. The time periods may nonetheless be extended twice by a two-week period, thereby amounting to a maximum period of two to three months. Extensions should be explained accordingly and the second two-week extension may only be applied when "strictly necessary, in particular for reasons relating to public health or safety of the service recipients". Should a professional disagree with a decision taken by the host Member State, or a lack of a decision, he or she again has a right to appeal under national law.[201]

Finally, the EPC also includes rules on data protection.[202] These rules are essential to balancing two of the most important interests related to recognition: the protection of consumers and patients and, the mobility of professionals. These rules particularly concern the information to be included in the IMI file, possible prohibitions or restrictions the professional faces which prevent him or her from exercising the profession, and the conditions under which individuals, authorities, and other parties[203] may request to view the information in the IMI file.[204]

While it is therefore clear that the EPC provides several safeguards and rights to migrating EU professionals, the most important right when migrating to another Member State for work has not been transferred—namely the right of access. In the case of establishment, the EPC does *not* constitute an automatic right to access a profession if there are other requirements needing to be fulfilled before being able

[198] Article 4d(2) Professional Qualifications Directive.

[199] Article 4d(3) Professional Qualifications Directive.

[200] Article 4d(4) Professional Qualifications Directive.

[201] Article 4d(7) Professional Qualifications Directive.

[202] Consisting of a right to request (1) rectification of incorrect or incomplete data, or (2) deletion or blocking of his or her IMI file; see Article 4e(5) Professional Qualifications Directive.

[203] Access to the IMI file is in principle limited to the competent authorities, although certain parties (e.g. employers, professional organisations, and even patients) may gain insight into the file by being allowed to verify the authenticity and validity of an EPC; Article 22 Commission Implementing Regulation (EU) 2015/983.

[204] Article 4e Professional Qualifications Directive.

to gain access.[205] This means that when a professional wants to establish him- or herself in another Member State and is in possession of an EPC, he or she has fulfilled the requirement for recognition. It does *not*, however, mean that they may start exercising their profession. This applies especially for those requesting an EPC for the purpose of establishment. For these professionals, the EPC only expedites their recognition process and ensures that it takes place electronically. In this context, the innovative character of the EPC is perhaps tempered further since the 2013 modernisation also introduced a provision requiring Member States to ensure that (regular) recognition procedures can take place electronically.[206] The added value of the EPC for professionals falling under the establishment regime is therefore limited to shortened time periods and quicker validation. This reinforces the idea that the EPC is more of a "workflow" that does not modify the material recognition rules.[207]

On a more optimistic note, the EPC *does* entail a right of access in the case of service provision even if the professional exercises a profession with public health or safety implications. This is explained by the fact that the regime for service provision is less strict.[208] However, the key distinction as to why the EPC does allow service providers to immediately start exercising their profession and prohibits those seeking to establish themselves elsewhere may be explained by the difference between the two regimes: service providers remain established in their home Member State. Presumably, their presence in the host Member State is "less noticeable", or perhaps rather "less intrusive", than that of professionals looking to establish themselves in another Member State.

Ten years after its first introduction, the EPC is still limited to the original five professions for which it was made available initially. Evidence can be found that, though considered to have added value,[209] the use of the EPC was still relatively limited in comparison to the traditional recognition procedures.[210] While the EPC has been subject to several technical improvements,[211] the question can be raised whether the tool would not benefit from expanding its use to also cover a right of access to be granted for all professionals for whom the card is available.

---

[205] Article 4a(5) second paragraph Professional Qualifications Directive. See also Sect. 5 of this chapter.

[206] Article 57a Professional Qualifications Directive.

[207] Berthoud (2016, p. 355).

[208] See Article 5(1) Professional Qualifications Directive and Sect. 3.1 above.

[209] Commission staff working document: Assessment of stakeholders' experience with the European Professional Card and the Alert Mechanism procedures, SWD(2018) 90 final, p. 46.

[210] See, for example, Adamis-Csásár et al. (2019, p. 37), Schneider and Kortese (2019, p. 11).

[211] Commission Staff Working Document: Assessment of stakeholders' experience with the European Professional Card and the Alert Mechanism procedures, SWD(2018) 90 final, pp. 42–45.

4.3 The Alert Mechanism

Professional regulation is often primarily aimed at protecting service recipients from malpractice.[212] The underlying reasoning is that the imposition of minimum quality standards may lead to increased welfare in the event that consumers cannot examine the quality of professionals due to the existence of information asymmetries.[213] This way, regulation serves public interest which is central to the alert mechanism introduced by Directive 2013/55/EU. An alert mechanism was previously introduced in the context of the Services Directive (2006/123/EC) where competent authorities would warn each other "of serious specific acts or circumstances relating to a service activity that could cause serious damage to the health or safety of persons or to the environment".[214] The Services Directive alert mechanism therefore already applied to those professions covered by that directive (i.e. mainly crafts professions). Nevertheless, the Commission found there to be broad support for an alert mechanism that extended beyond the Services Directive.[215] Under the PQD, competent authorities are obliged to inform authorities in all other Member States about professionals who are prohibited, temporarily or permanently, from exercising their profession or who have used falsified documents during their recognition requests.[216] In terms of scope, the alert mechanism primarily covers most professions subject to automatic recognition[217] as well as professionals exercising professions with patient safety implications and involving minors.[218]

Like the EPC, the alert mechanism also functions by means of the IMI system.[219] The mechanism is accompanied by a Commission Implementing Regulation which sets out specific provisions on the designation of competent authorities and how they handle alerts.[220] When Member States' competent authorities have been appointed to handle alerts, they must adhere to certain procedural obligations. In the event that

---

[212] Koumenta and Pagliero (2016, p. 116).

[213] Ibid., pp. 116–117.

[214] Article 32(1) Directive 2006/123/EC of the European Parliament and of the Council of 12 December 2006 on services in the internal market, [2006] OJ L 376/36.

[215] European Commission, Evaluation of the Professional Qualifications Directive (Directive 2005/36/EC), Brussels 5 July 2011, p. 78.

[216] Article 56a(1) Professional Qualifications Directive; European Commission, Modernisation of the Professional Qualifications Directive—frequently asked questions, MEMO/13/867, p. 5.

[217] Article 56a(1)(a-j) Professional Qualifications Directive. Interestingly enough though, the only profession subject to the regime for automatic recognition on the basis of minimum training conditions *not* included in the alert mechanism is that of architect.

[218] Article 56a(1)(k)(l) Professional Qualifications Directive.

[219] Article 56a(2) Professional Qualifications Directive.

[220] Not all national authorities competent to deal with any matter related to the recognition of professional qualifications are involved in the operation of the alert mechanism. In keeping with data protection considerations, only those authorities that are directly affected by an alert are granted access to the alert mechanism. Furthermore, Member States have to appoint specific authorities that will be competent to handle outgoing and incoming alerts, as well as one or several coordinating competent authorities that have the task of ensuring that alerts are assigned to the appropriate competent authorities. Those authorities tasked with handling alerts send and withdraw alerts,

they issue an alert, they must do so within three days from the date when the decision restricting or prohibiting the pursuit of the professional activity was adopted.[221] Apart from reporting instances where professionals have been restricted from exercising their profession, Member State competent authorities must also issue alerts when professionals have been found to use falsified evidence of their professional qualifications during recognition procedures.[222]

Article 56a PQD and the Commission Implementing Regulation show that two interests are at stake. On the one hand, and as shown above, competent authorities have an obligation to warn each other about professionals' restrictions on carrying out a profession, thereby protecting consumers and patients. On the other hand, safeguards are provided for professionals against whom an alert has been issued. These safeguards mainly relate to data protection[223] and to the professionals' right of appeal[224] against a potentially wrongful issuance of an alert. Both these aspects can be seen clearly when examining the time periods related to the alert mechanism. Competent authorities handling alerts not only have an obligation to issue an alert within three days after which a decision restricting access to professional activities was adopted, but also have a similar obligation to inform other competent authorities of the expiration of a prohibition or restriction without delay.[225] The rules on time periods are strongly related to data protection. Indeed, alerts may only be processed within IMI as long as they are valid.[226] If not, i.e. when they have been revoked or have expired, they must be closed and all related personal data deleted within three days.[227]

Challenges related to the alert mechanism have to do with high numbers of alerts and differences in national disciplinary and professional rules.[228] Indeed, the alert mechanism does not harmonise national sanctions (which are the subject of an

correct information and modify alerts, and close and delete alerts. Article 56a(8) Professional Qualifications Directive; Recital 11, Article 23 and Article 27(a–d) Commission Implementing Regulation (EU) 2015/983.

[221] Article 56a(2) Professional Qualifications Directive.

[222] Article 56a(3) Professional Qualifications Directive.

[223] For example, when sending alerts, the information taken up in them is restricted to the identity of the professional, the profession concerned, information about the national authority or court adopting the decision on restriction or prohibition, the scope of the restriction/prohibition, and the period during which it applies; Article 56a(2(a-e) Professional Qualifications Directive.

[224] Professionals must be informed that an alert has been issued against them and professionals must have possibilities for appeal against alert decisions or to call for their rectification. In addition, professionals must be able to access remedies in the event that any damage has been caused by false alerts; Article 56a(6) Professional Qualifications Directive.

[225] Article 56a(5) Professional Qualifications Directive.

[226] Article 56a(7) Professional Qualifications Directive; Article 28(1)(3) Commission Implementing Regulation (EU) 2015/983.

[227] Article 56a(7) Professional Qualifications Directive; Article 28(2)(4)(5) Commission Implementing Regulation (EU) 2015/983.

[228] Commission Staff Working Document: Assessment of stakeholders' experience with the European Professional Card and the Alert Mechanism procedures, SWD(2018) 90 final, pp. 39–40 and p. 46.

alert) and national disciplinary, professional and criminal systems.[229] For example, it may occur that a professional organisation is responsible for imposing disciplinary measures, meaning such measures are not imposed by an authority or court as—something required to trigger the alert mechanism.[230]

5 Recognition vs. Access: An Overlooked Distinction

One distinction that often goes overlooked that is essential in understanding both recognition of qualifications and the pursuit of a profession in another Member State concerns the difference between recognition of qualifications and access to the profession. Regulation of a profession usually entails the situation where legally defined requirements or rules exist that govern both conditions of access to a profession or conditions concerning the exercise of a profession.[231] This means that recognition may only be one step to be fulfilled in order to gain access to a profession. Earlier in this chapter, the case law of the CJEU in, among others, *Heylens* and *Vlassopoulou* was already discussed to explain that Member States are free to determine which qualification requirements to maintain, i.e. how to regulate a profession.[232] In light of the present discussion it should therefore be noted that this applies more broadly than solely to qualification requirements necessitating recognition. For example, Member States may decide to impose criminal penalties when a person has neglected to obtain recognition before taking up professional activities.[233] The fact that EU law provides for freedom of movement does not mean that such conditions are automatically in violation of the fundamental freedoms since public interest consideration may justify restrictions, if proportionate.[234]

In terms of legislation, those exercising a regulated profession are of course primarily subject to the PQD. However, when it comes to other matters beyond qualifications—and that are not taken up in the PQD—the Services Directive may be of relevance.[235] According to Article 3(1)(d) of the Services Directive, the PQD has precedence over the former instrument in case of potential conflicts between provisions the two directives. Conflicts are nevertheless unlikely, as the Services Directive is complementary to the PQD. Whereas the PQD concerns recognition with the objective of access to a regulated profession, the Services Directive concerns the quality

[229] Ibid., p. 20.

[230] See Article 56a(1) Professional Qualifications Directive.

[231] Koumenta and Pagliero (2016, pp. 8–9).

[232] Case 222/86 *Heylens*, ECLI:EU:C:1987:442, para. 10; Case C-340/89 *Vlassopoulou*, ECLI:EU:C:1991:193, para. 9.

[233] Case C-104/91 *Borrell*, ECLI:EU:C:1992:202, para. 19.

[234] See for example Cases C-330/90 and C-331/90 *Brea and Palacios*, ECLI:EU:C:1992:39, para. 15.

[235] Directive 2006/123/EC of the European Parliament and of the Council of 12 December 2006 on services in the internal market, [2006] OJ L 376/36.

of services by focusing on the prohibition of national measures restricting establishment and free movement.[236] Examples of topics relating to the quality of services concern professional liability insurance, commercial communications, multidisciplinary activities, and administrative simplification.[237] Furthermore, complementarity is enhanced since administrative cooperation takes place via the IMI system for both the PQD and the Services Directive.[238]

Beyond legislative instruments, we can also turn to the CJEU's case law for more guidance on how additional requirements beyond those relating to qualifications should be considered. In principle, the regulatory freedom of Member States does not go so far as to allow regulations that unequivocally restrict the freedom of movement. For example, the Court ruled in *Klopp* that a requirement demanding a lawyer to only have offices in one Member State was contrary to the Treaty Articles on freedom of establishment.[239] In *Konstantinides,* the Court considered that a requirement concerning predetermined medical fees to be charged by doctors would not be covered by the PQD, but could instead be considered a restriction liable to hinder the freedom to provide services.[240] In *Payroll Data Services* the Court considered that a national provision requiring small undertakings to entrust the preparation and printing of payslips to a data-processing centre staffed exclusively by persons registered with a specific professional organisation was contrary to the freedom of establishment.[241] In *Vanderborght*, the Court subsequently ruled that a general and absolute prohibition of any advertisement of dental services—even if it was maintained in light of public health considerations—was contrary to Article 56 TFEU.[242]

While restrictions to free movement are therefore in principle prohibited, the doctrine surrounding public interest justifications also means Member States have opportunities to justify restrictions. The conclusion that certain requirements are in violation of the freedom of movement can only be reached after an exercise where free movement rights are balanced with the interests at stake (i.e. proportionate). An interesting case in this context is *Federspiel.* Ms Federspiel was an Italian citizen that received a bursary from the Province of Bolzano in Italy to complete medical training at the University of Innsbruck in Austria. Upon completion of her studies, she took up residence and employment in Austria where she was working for over a decade when she was requested to provide evidence of her having practised as a doctor in Bolzano. Upon indicating that she had not exercised the profession there, she was ordered to repay 70% of the bursary amount received for her studies in Austria plus interest. At the time, the receipt of the bursary was dependent on a five-year practice within ten years in Bolzano upon completion of studies. Federspiel had signed a declaration indicating her awareness of this fact. While the Court did consider there

[236] Schoenmaekers (2010, p. 154).

[237] Recital 31 Directive 2006/123/EC.

[238] Barnard (2008, pp. 347–348).

[239] Case 107/83 *Klopp*, ECLI:EU:C:1984:270, para. 17–18.

[240] Case C-475/11 *Konstantinides*, ECLI:EU:C:2013:542, para. 49.

[241] Case C-79/01 *Payroll Data Services*, ECLI:EU:C:2002:592.

[242] Case C-339/15 *Vanderborght*, ECLI:EU:C:2017:335.

to be a restriction on the free movement of workers and freedom of establishment,[243] it found the restriction to be justified. In particular, the rule was held to protect public health by helping to meet the demand for specialist doctors in Bolzano therefore meeting the overall objective of guaranteeing sufficient and permanent access to high quality medical services and also contributing to the cost efficiency of such services.[244] Moreover, doctors only had to work in Bolzano if a specialist doctor position was available at the right moment and when there appeared to be no suitable alternative measure to recruit sufficient doctors who were also capable of practising in both official languages of Bolzano (i.e. German and Italian)—attributing to the proportionality of the measure.[245]

Cases such as these show that while different types of professional regulation may constitute restrictions to free movement, they may be justified. Ultimately, an assessment is necessary to balance the regulatory freedom of Member States with the free movement rights held by individuals. Returning to the discussion on recognition of qualifications, this line of case law also shows that qualification requirements are distinct from other requirements connected to the exercise of a profession. Indeed, it also means that recognition can be merely one step in the process of accessing a profession in another Member State. While the PQD in principle concerns recognition of qualifications, some of its provisions also concern access. This particularly applies for the provisions of Title IV on "Detailed rules for pursuing the profession" which contains rules on, among others, language knowledge, use of academic titles, and recognition of professional traineeships. Furthermore, the PQD's provisions on partial access also concern the discussion on recognition vs. access.

5.1 Partial Access

Through case law, the Court established the *principle of partial access*. This principle enables professionals whose profession covers different activities in the home and host Member States to exercise the part of the profession for which they are qualified in a host Member State. It is important to first remark that partial access leads to the

[243] Case C-419/16 *Federspiel*, ECLI:EU:C:2017:997, para. 37.

[244] Ibid., para. 46.

[245] Ibid., para. 47–49.

exercise of the profession and is therefore different than partial recognition.[246] The principle of partial access was developed through the *Colegio* case.

In *Colegio*, a civil engineer had obtained a qualification specialising in hydraulics in Italy. The Spanish Ministry of Development had recognised his professional qualifications which granted him full access to the profession of civil engineer in Spain. However, the *Colegio de Ingenieros* objected to this arguing that the profession and education of a civil engineer in Spain and that of a civil engineer specialised in hydraulics in Italy were fundamentally different. This dispute led the national judge to refer the matter to the Court, essentially asking whether national authorities were allowed to grant access to part of the profession. Considering that the primary objective of the legislation on the recognition of qualifications is to facilitate the use of a qualification in other Member States and ultimately to strengthen the right of European nationals to use their professional experience in other Member States,[247] allowing professionals access to parts of the profession in the host Member State was considered in line with EU law. In particular, partial access was to be granted if a professional was obliged to follow an entire course of study, as this would most likely discourage the professional from making use of his or her right of free movement.[248] With this judgment, the Court not only confirmed partial access but also developed conditions for it which been taken up in the PQD with the 2013 modernisation.

Indeed, Article 4f of the PQD lays down the criteria for partial access. To benefit from partial access, the professional should (1) be fully qualified to exercise the profession in the home Member State, (2) the differences between the professional activity in the home Member State and the profession in the host Member State need to be so large as to require a full additional programme of education and training, and (3) the professional activity must be objectively separated from the other activities that constitute the profession in the host Member State. When granted, the profession must be exercised under the professional title of the *home* Member State and is paired

---

[246] Partial recognition may be understood as the conditional acceptance of qualifications and training paired with the fulfilment of additional requirements before recognition is granted. The origins of partial recognition can again be retraced to the *Vlassopoulou* judgment where the Court argued that Member States must carry out a comparative assessment of the professional's qualifications and those of the host Member State. However, the Court also added that if the foreign qualifications correspond only partially, "the host Member State is entitled to require the person concerned to show that he has acquired the knowledge and qualifications which are lacking". Article 14 of the PQD subsequently stipulates that if there is actually a lack of knowledge and qualifications amounting to substantial differences, Member States may impose compensation measures. In the case law following the *Vlassopoulou* judgment, the Court confirmed the possibility for authorities to grant partial recognition and went even further in stating that such partial recognition may not just be notional, thereby specifying that compensation measures must be tailored to fit the knowledge which the applicant lacks. See Blitz, (1999, p. 312); Case C-340/89 *Vlassopoulou*, ECLI:EU:C:1991:193, para. 19; Case C-330/03 *Colegio de Ingenieros de Caminos, Canales y Puertos*, ECLI:EU:C:2006:45, para. 18 and 25; Case C-345/08 *Peśla*, ECLI:EU:C:2009:771, para. 58.

[247] Case C-330/03 *Colegio de Ingenieros de Caminos, Canales y Puertos*, ECLI:EU:C:2006:45, para. 23.

[248] Ibid., para. 35.

with an obligation for professionals to share the scope of their activities with service recipients.[249]

Some may wonder whether partial access will not be detrimental to consumer and health protection. Such concerns played a central role in *Nasiopoulos*. This case revolved around a Greek citizen who had obtained his qualification as a medical masseur-hydrotherapist in Germany, but who was refused access to the profession of physiotherapist in Greece because the profession of medical masseur-hydrotherapist was not regulated in Germany and because the two qualifications were held to differ in level. The Court was asked to rule on the question whether Article 49 TFEU precludes national legislation preventing partial access to the profession of physiotherapist. The Court considered that although it is necessary to be vigilant, sufficient protection could be achieved through less restrictive means than a total exclusion of partial access.[250] Nevertheless, in the case the Court did imply that partial access would be precluded for *medical* professions as opposed to the *paramedical* profession at stake in the case.[251] This line of reasoning has made its way into the PQD. Article 4f(6) PQD states that partial access does not apply to those professionals benefiting from automatic recognition (i.a. medical professions such as doctors and nurses). The non-applicability of partial access to automatic recognition professions was confirmed in *Reynaud*. In that case, the Court was asked to rule on the exercise of the profession of Clinical Dental Technician in Malta. Although partial access does not feature prominently in this judgment, Advocate General Mengozzi argued that professions for which automatic recognition is available may only be accessed fully since the conditions of training have been harmonised in the PQD.[252]

Further concerns expressed in relation to partial access concern confusion and potential fragmentation of markets.[253] Although confusion is countered by the presence of strict rules on the use of titles, fragmentation can indeed occur, as professions may—in individual cases—be divided into several professional activities belonging to the profession. Nevertheless, such concerns should be limited by the fact that partial access is applied on a case-by-case basis.[254] Furthermore, partial access in the PQD is paired with a justification system since Article 4f(2) prescribes that partial access may be rejected if justified by overriding reasons of general interests and that rejection is proportionate. It could be argued even further that the principle of partial access as it stands now is insufficiently suitable to facilitate mobility, meaning its effects remain

---

[249] See Article 4f(2)(5) Professional Qualifications Directive.

[250] Case C-575/11 *Nasiopoulos*, ECLI:EU:C:2013:430, para. 25.

[251] In particular, medical masseur-hydrotherapists' services were considered to merely constitute the "implementation of a therapy prescribed to the patient not by that masseur but by a doctor"; Ibid., para. 28-29.

[252] Opinion of Advocate General Mengozzi in Case C-125/16 *Reynaud*, ECLI:EU:C:2017:707, para. 17.

[253] Commission Staff Working Paper—Impact Assessment: Accompanying document to the Proposal for a Directive of the European Parliament and of the Council amending Directive 2005/36/EC on the recognition of professional qualifications and Regulation on administrative cooperation through the Internal Market Information System, SEC(2011) 1558 final—Part I, p. 14.

[254] Article 4f(1) Professional Qualifications Directive.

limited—also in respect to the concerns voiced above. The 2019 Report conducted at the request of the European Parliament's Employment and Social Affairs Committee found that partial access has been applied in very few cases and attributed this to a lack of awareness of the construct and the difficulty of objectively separating activities of a profession.[255] Indeed, the precondition that demands the professional activity in the home Member State to differ considerably from the profession in the host Member State—so much as to require a full programme of education and training—severely restricts possibilities for application of partial access.[256]

More flexible provisions on partial access, especially relating to the criterion above, would allow for the principle to truly facilitate mobility. As mentioned above, concerns related to confusion are prevented by the strict rules on which title one is allowed to carry set by the PQD and by the precondition requiring that the professional concerned is qualified in his or her home Member State. In keeping with the principle of mutual trust, Member States must rest assured that the quality of the other Member States' qualifications is sufficient. Although it is true that a more flexible interpretation of the principle of partial access could lead to fragmentation of professions, the principle would still be applied on a case-by-case basis and allow justified and proportionate refusals of partial access under Article 4f(2) PQD, meaning the actual fragmentation of a profession should remain limited.

To conclude, a positive development in this respect comes from the Commission's 2020 evaluation of Directive 2013/55/EU. Apparently, the Commission has insisted partial access to be applied *ex officio*, meaning competent authorities should either immediately assess the possibility of partial access where relevant or clearly inform applicants of this possibility.[257] According to the Commission, such provision was necessary since most individuals undergoing procedures are likely unaware of the possibility of partial access.

5.2 *Language Requirements*

By now it is abundantly clear that Member States remain free to determine how to regulate certain professions (and to require evidence thereof) because the conditions of access to professions are not harmonised at EU level. While Member States can make the pursuit of professional activities dependent on certain rules, these measures should be justified and proportionate if they are liable to hinder the exercise of

255 Adamis-Csásár et al. (2019, p. 43).

256 See Kortese (2022, pp. 117–133).

257 Report from the Commission to the European Parliament, the Council, the European Economic and Social Committee and the Committee of the Regions on the implementation of certain new elements introduced by Directive 2013/55/EU of the European Parliament and of the Council of 20 November 2013 amending Directive 2005/36/EC on the recognition of professional qualifications and Regulation (EU) No 1024/2012 on administrative cooperation through the Internal Market Information System ('the IMI Regulation'), COM(2020) 191 final, p. 15.

the fundamental freedoms.[258] In the past, language requirements were considered restrictions to free movement. In *Groener*, for example, the Court ruled that the Gaelic language requirement maintained at Irish schools could be used to express national identity and culture and that the important role education had in this expression was such as to justify the language requirement which was found to be "corresponding to the knowledge required by reason of the nature of the post to be filled".[259] In *Angonese* the Court determined that the requirement of one specific language qualification was contrary to the free movement provisions.[260] *Haim II* showed that, in the case of healthcare professionals, the reliability of a practitioner being able to communicate both with patients and with the administrative authorities and professional bodies concerned was to be viewed as an overriding reason of general interest thus allowing the language requirement.[261]

Nevertheless, cases such as these precede the provisions on language requirements in the PQD. At present, Article 53 of the PQD allows Member States to ensure that professionals have adequate language knowledge to carry out their profession. In particular, provisions on language knowledge were first included in the PQD to tackle protectionism by preventing Member States from using language tests to fend off foreign professionals from their national labour markets.[262] However, the other main reason for provisions on language knowledge is of course related to the protection of consumers and patients. Article 53, therefore, prescribes that foreign professionals must have a level of language knowledge necessary to carry out the profession and confirms that controls of language knowledge may only take place *after* recognition has been granted or *after* issuance of an EPC (i.e. it is not part of the recognition process).[263] Language controls must furthermore be proportionate, restricted to the knowledge of one language and may only be examined for professions with patient safety implications. Controls for other professions may only be imposed when there are serious and concrete doubts about the professional's proficiency in a language. This seems indicative of *ad hoc* examinations regarding language knowledge instead of blanket language requirements, thus leading to the question whether the PQD permits a general language requirement maintained nationally for certain professions.

In terms of level of language knowledge, it is, however, clear that no requirements are made in the PQD. Furthermore, it is important to emphasise that Article 53 PQD relates only to establishment. For service provision, Article 7(2)(f) PQD prescribes that assessing knowledge of a language is either allowed *before* the first service

---

[258] Case C-55/94 *Gebhard*, ECLI:EU:C:1995:411, para. 37.

[259] Case C-379/87 *Groener*, ECLI:EU:C:1989:599, para. 18–21.

[260] Furthermore, the Court determined that Member States' competent authorities must accept all evidence attesting to the language knowledge of the applicant when testing the language knowledge of the individual concerned. See C-281/98 *Angonese*, ECLI:EU:C:2000:296.

[261] Case C-424/97 *Haim II*, ECLI:EU:C:2000:357, para. 59.

[262] European Commission, Evaluation of the Professional Qualifications Directive (Directive 2005/36/EC), Brussels 5 July 2011, p. 70.

[263] This is of course the general rule. If a person is applying for a profession in which knowledge of the language is essential as part of that profession (e.g. a speech and language therapist) then language knowledge can be part of the assessment of the qualifications in the context of recognition.

provision in another Member State or when there is a *material change* in the situation previously attested to. In this context, knowledge of a language may only be assessed for those professions having patient safety implications.

5.3 Use of Academic & Professional Titles

Discussions concerning the use of either academic or professional titles have been subject to cases before the CJEU. In *Kraus*, for example, a German citizen objected to needing prior authorisation for him to be able to use the academic title his foreign diploma awarded him in his home State of Germany. Although concerning an internal situation (i.e. a German citizen in Germany),[264] the Court held that Kraus's situation fell within the scope of the Treaties: the fact that the qualification was obtained in another Member State brought a European dimension to the case preventing it from concerning a wholly internal situation.[265] The Court again confirmed that Member States remained competent to establish detailed rules governing the use of academic titles because there was no specific harmonisation concerning the type of diploma such as was awarded to Kraus.[266] Still, the fact that such harmonising legislation had not yet been adopted did not allow Member States to deny individuals the practical benefit of the fundamental freedoms guaranteed by the Treaty.[267] The Court therefore for the first time in *Kraus* applied a justification plus proportionality test[268] that was later generalised in *Gebhard* and would become a standard approach to dealing with restrictions to free movement.[269]

Different from *Kraus*, however, *Gebhard* concerned the use of a professional title. Gebhard was a German national who lived and practised law in Milan who opened an office to practise law under the Italian title of *avvocato*. He was sanctioned for using that title in contravention of national law. The *Gebhard* case can be considered a seminal case in multiple aspects. First, due to its distinction between the concepts

[264] A situation must be considered as purely internal when a person has a certain Member State's nationality, has obtained his or her qualifications in that Member State, and works in that same Member State. The Court of Justice of the EU argued that, in such case, there is no connection with any situation envisaged by EU free movement law meaning that it cannot be applied, nor can the PQD; See Cases C-225/95, C-226/95 and C-227/95 *Kapasakalis, Skiathitis, and Kougiankas*, ECLI:EU:C:1998:332.

[265] Case C-19/92 *Kraus*, ECLI:EU:C:1993:125, para. 23–24.

[266] Ibid., para. 27.

[267] Ibid., para. 30.

[268] In particular, the justification of the prior authorisation necessary for use of the academic title could only take place to: (1) verify whether the title was properly awarded by a competent authority; (2) the procedure had to be easily accessible and not overly expensive; (3) the procedure for verifying academic titles had to be in conformity with Community law regarding the effective protection of fundamental rights (in particular access to judicial proceedings); and (4) the penalties imposed on offenders had to be proportionate; Ibid, para. 38–41.

[269] Claessens (2008, p. 21).

of services and establishment.[270] Second, because of its generalisation of the *Kraus* justification test. The Court particularly noted that although carrying out a profession could be made conditional on provisions laid down by national law,[271] Member States did have to comply with the case law from *Kraus* and *Vlassopoulou*. Therefore, national legislation setting conditions for the exercise of a profession had to be applied in a non-discriminatory manner, had to be justified by imperative requirements in the general interest, had to be suitable for attaining the pursued objective, and needed to be proportionate.[272] Finally, Member States had to take into account the knowledge and qualifications the professional had already acquired elsewhere when applying their national legislation.[273] While the use of titles has therefore been harmonised in the PQD since the cases of *Kraus* and *Gebhard*, these cases remain of importance for the development of the justification test that continues to be used when examining national requirements needing to be fulfilled to exercise professions.

Nevertheless, these cases again preceded the PQD, which now contains provisions on the use of both professional as well as academic titles. Regarding *professional* titles, the standard rule is that the professional will use the title of the host Member State after recognition.[274] Exceptions here occur in the case of partial access and in the case of service provision, when the home Member State title is to be used.[275] However, the *professional* title is to be distinguished from *academic* titles. While the former attest to a person's capacity to pursue a certain profession, the latter attest to the completion of certain education. Under Article 54 PQD beneficiaries of the Directive should be able to use the academic title from their home Member States when exercising a profession in a host Member State.[276] However, to prevent confusion among service recipients the host Member State may require additions in terms of the institution where the title was obtained or may require an alternative appropriate format.

5.4 Traineeships

The inclusion of provisions on recognition of traineeships in the PQD took place with Directive 2013/55/EU.[277] The preamble of Directive 2013/55/EU confirms that

---

[270] Case C-55/94 *Gebhard*, ECLI:EU:C:1995:411, para. 25–27.

[271] Ibid., para. 35.

[272] Ibid., para. 37; Case C-19/92 *Kraus*, ECLI:EU:C:1993:125.

[273] Ibid., para. 38; Case C-340/89 *Vlassopoulou*, ECLI:EU:C:1991:193.

[274] See Article 52(1) Professional Qualifications Directive.

[275] Articles 4f(5) and 7(3) Professional Qualifications Directive.

[276] Meaning requests for authorization to use certain academic titles obtained in other Member States (as was the case in *Kraus*) are not required anymore.

[277] Proposal for a Directive of the European Parliament and of the Council amending Directive 2005/36/EC on the recognition of professional qualifications and Regulation on administrative cooperation through the Internal Market Information System, COM(2011) 883 final, p. 5.

the recognition of professional traineeships was introduced into the PQD to facilitate the mobility of young graduates active in regulated professions.[278] Under Article 3(1)(j) of Directive 2013/55/EU, a professional traineeship is described as "a period of professional practice carried out under supervision provided it constitutes a condition for access to a regulated profession, and which can take place either during or after completion of an education leading to a diploma". Article 55a(1) of the PQD subsequently prescribes that Member States, in which a professional traineeship is required for accessing a profession, must recognise professional traineeships carried out in other Member States—and even in third countries. Therefore, Article 55a is only applicable to individuals who go abroad for a traineeship and return to their home Member State (i.e. the Member State where they received education and training) which requires a professional traineeship for them to gain access to a profession.

The inclusion of the recognition of professional traineeships may be reminiscent of the *Morgenbesser* case.[279] Christine Morgenbesser had obtained a diploma in law in France but sought access to the professional traineeship to become a lawyer in Italy. The Court ruled that, although Morgenbesser was not yet fully qualified as a lawyer, this did not prevent Italy from having to assess her qualifications and professional experience.[280] However, it is important to emphasise that the present formulation of Article 55a PQD in fact does *not* codify the *Morgenbesser* doctrine. Indeed, the recognition of professional traineeships under Article 55a PQD has effect only towards the home Member State, meaning that any obligation placed on the host Member State under the *Morgenbesser* ruling for host Member States to consider all qualifications of non-fully qualified professionals remains effective only through case law. This means that non-fully qualified professionals still have to rely on the *Vlassopoulou* principle because the PQD does not apply to them.[281] This is regrettable in terms of legal certainty for (mostly early career) professionals. The inclusion of non-fully qualified professionals through codification of the *Morgenbesser* principle would ensure that the principle of mutual recognition would also apply them, meaning recognition is presumed and compensation measures may only be imposed in exceptional cases.[282]

Some indications may be found that broader recognition of traineeships was at some point considered for inclusion under the PQD. More specifically, in the impact assessment accompanying the proposal for Directive 2013/55/EU, the Commission had considered different policy options for non-fully qualified professionals. Under one of the options, the Commission considered that the scope of the PQD was to

---

[278] Recital 27 Directive 2013/55/EU.

[279] The case was discussed extensively in Chapter "Challenging Convention: Theory, Competences & The Grey Area of Recognition" of this contribution.

[280] Case C-313/01 *Morgenbesser*, ECLI:EU:C:2003:612. The *Morgenbesser* ruling was later elaborated on by the Court in, among others, Case C-345/08 *Pešla*, ECLI:EU:C:2009:771 and Case C-298/14 *Brouillard*, ECLI:EU:C:2015:652. See Sect. 6 of this chapter for more on these cases.

[281] See also Claessens (2014, pp. 6–7).

[282] Schneider and Lubina (2009, pp. 147–148).

be extended to include non-fully qualified professionals by allowing such applications to be assessed under the general system—and combined with recognition of traineeships conducted abroad upon return to the home Member State. While this was indicated as the preferred option, the current version of the PQD shows only the latter option was ultimately implemented.[283] Therefore, under the current version of the PQD, access to a traineeship in another Member State thus remains within the realm of the *Morgenbesser* ruling, which is unfortunate considering that non-fully qualified professionals seeking access to professional traineeships will remain subject to the different interpretations given to the *Morgenbesser* ruling at national level.[284] In a broader sense, this category of professionals remains subject to what may be described as the "fallback system" created through the Court's case law and originating from the *Vlassopoulou* doctrine discussed below. As of yet, it is regrettable that the *Morgenbesser* principle has gone uncodified and the original policy option unadopted, seeing as it would have been able to provide a level of legal certainty that is generally lacking for non-fully qualified professionals.

[283] Proposal for a Directive of the European Parliament and of the Council amending Directive 2005/36/EC on the recognition of professional qualifications and Regulation on administrative cooperation through the Internal Market Information System, COM(2011) 883 final, p. 16 and 20; Commission Staff Working Paper—Impact Assessment: Accompanying the document Proposal for a Directive of the European Parliament and of the Council amending Directive 2005/36/EC on the recognition of professional qualifications and Regulation on administrative cooperation through the Internal Market Information System, SEC(2011) 1558 final—Part II, pp. 44–45.

[284] Claessens (2014, p. 7). Indeed, in the *Lubina* case, the *Orberlandesgericht Düsseldorf* had to rule on academic qualifications to be used for the purpose of accessing the *Referendariat* (i.e. the professional traineeship to qualify as a lawyer in Germany). Lubina possessed, among others, a Dutch diploma in law with *civiel effect* thereby granting her access to the professional traineeship to become qualified as a lawyer in the Netherlands. However, such access was not directly granted in Germany. At first, her application for access to the *Referendariat* was refused. The *Oberlandesgericht* argued that the position of trainee did not fall under the free movement rights of the EU Treaties. Furthermore, the *Oberlandesgericht* argued that access could not be granted because Lubina did not pass the First State Examination (*Ersten Deutschen Staatsexamen*). The case was brought before the *Verwaltungsgericht Düsseldorf* who ruled that the *Oberlandesgericht* had to reconsider the case in light of the relevant case law of the Court of Justice of the EU. The CJEU had already ruled in *Bernini* and in *Kranemann* that the position of trainee was equal to that of a worker, meaning that the free movement provisions of the Treaty applied in the case. Interestingly, the *Oberlandesgericht* went on to consider the profession of *Referendar* as a regulated profession (something which was explicitly denied by the Court of Justice in *Morgenbesser*). This categorisation of the profession of trainee as a regulated profession would have meant that the general system was applicable in this situation. Nevertheless, a separate assessment was maintained and additional courses were imposed as a precondition for her to access the *Referendariat*; Schneider and Lubina (2009, pp. 144–147).

6 Beyond the Professional Qualifications Directive: The CJEU's "Fallback System"

Throughout this chapter and in Chapter "Challenging Convention: Theory, Competences & The Grey Area of Recognition" the *Vlassopoulou* case was already discussed. It may be recalled that the case led the CJEU to conclude that all diplomas, certificates and other evidence of formal qualifications had to be taken into account when examining professional qualifications.[285] Having now discussed the PQD and its procedures and safeguards this requirement may not sound as important. However, with the *Vlassopoulou* doctrine the CJEU has created what can be described as a "fallback system" which applies to those who are not subject to the PQD. This particularly covers those whose situation is outside the Directive's scope and means they still derive rights regarding recognition on the basis of EU law (i.e. the Treaty provisions on free movement).

The doctrine is firmly rooted in CJEU case law on recognition dating back to the 1970s. In the earliest of days when there were no directives on recognition of professional qualifications yet, the Court already confirmed that not recognising previously obtained qualifications from other Member States was contrary to EU law.[286] In particular, Member States had to reconcile qualification requirements with free movement by maintaining procedures which would enable "national authorities to assure themselves, on an objective basis, that the foreign diploma certifies that its holder has knowledge and qualifications which are, if not identical, at least equivalent to those certified by the national diploma".[287] Furthermore, the status of access to employment as a fundamental right was held to necessitate a right to a judicial remedy to effectively protect that right.[288]

Against this background, the *Vlassopoulou* doctrine was developed. To recall, the case concerned a Greek lawyer with a degree in German law who was denied access to practise as a lawyer in Germany for not having the relevant qualifications—even when she was already practising law in Germany under the responsibility of one of her colleagues. While at the time of this case a directive on recognition had been adopted,[289] it could not be applied to the case since the implementation period had not yet passed.[290] The Court was therefore forced to examine the case on the basis of (what is today) Article 49 TFEU. In the judgment, the Court considered that in the

[285] Case C-340/89 *Vlassopoulou*, ECLI:EU:C:1991:193.

[286] In *Thieffry* this was particularly the case since an academic degree had been declared equivalent to the relevant national degree and a supplementary professional certificate was obtained after an examination in the host Member State to accompany the academic degree; see Case 71/76 *Thieffry*, ECLI:EU:C:1977:65. See also Case 222/86 *Heylens*, ECLI:EU:C:1987:442.

[287] Case 222/86 *Heylens*, ECLI:EU:C:1987:442, para. 13.

[288] Ibid, para. 14–16.

[289] Most notably Directive 89/48/EEC containing the precursor of the present-day PQD's general system.

[290] Opinion of Advocate General Van Gerven in Case C-340/89 *Vlassopoulou*, ECLI:EU:C:1991:426, para. 3.

event that Member States were obliged to "make a comparison between the specialized knowledge and abilities certified by those diplomas and the knowledge and qualifications required by the national rules".[291] This with the objective of ensuring that the host Member State could assure itself that the holder of the qualifications has knowledge which is at least equivalent to that certified by a national diploma.[292] More specifically, a comparative exercise was to be carried out between the home and host Member State diplomas to consider objective differences.[293] In the case of sufficient correspondence between the home and host Member State qualifications recognition would have to follow. However, in the case of only a partial overlap the host Member State could require the person concerned to show that the missing knowledge and qualifications were in fact acquired.[294] Not only knowledge obtained during education and training had to be considered in this respect, but also practical experience—and all of this in the context of a procedure that would protect the right to an effective remedy.[295]

The *Vlassopoulou* doctrine was soon extended to persons who were looking to access a regulated profession and sought recognition of their qualifications from outside the EU.[296] In this context, the adoption of directives on recognition did not immediately render the *Vlassopoulou* doctrine obsolete.[297] In fact, the doctrine was also used to supplement relevant directives on recognition.[298] Furthermore, the scope of the *Vlassopoulou* doctrine has widened beyond covering only those who want to exercise a regulated profession but are outside the scope of the PQD. In the *Fernández de Bobadilla* and *Aranitis* cases, the Court also pointed to the use of the *Vlassopoulou* doctrine if a profession was not considered formally regulated.[299] The Court also confirmed that, if no procedure for recognition was laid down at the national level, the *Vlassopoulou* doctrine was to be applied by the relevant hiring body to determine the equivalence of the qualifications at hand. These cases therefore attest to the general nature of the *Vlassopoulou* doctrine as a fallback system and general Treaty-based procedure for recognition of qualifications.

Case law since that time has confirmed the application of the *Vlassopoulou* doctrine to new situations and concretised its application. Initially, the application of the *Vlassopoulou* doctrine to these cases was developed in the *Morgenbesser* case. To recall, Morgenbesser had applied to the Bar Council of Genoa to be enrolled in the

---

[291] Case C-340/89 *Vlassopoulou*, ECLI:EU:C:1991:193, para. 16.

[292] Ibid., para. 17.

[293] Ibid., para. 18.

[294] Ibid.., para. 19.

[295] Ibid.., para. 20–22.

[296] Case C-319/92 *Haim I*, ECLI:EU:C:1994:47; Case C-238/98 *Hocsman*, ECLI:EU:C:2000:440.

[297] Case C-238/98 *Hocsman*, ECLI:EU:C:2000:440, para. 31–34.

[298] See Cases C-422/09, C-425/09 and C-426/09 *Vandorou, Giankoulis and Askoxilakis*, ECLI:EU:C:2010:732; Case C-31/00 *Conseil National de l'Ordre des Architectes v. Dreessen*, ECLI:EU:C:2002:35; Case C-285/01 *Burbaud*, ECLI:EU:C:2003:432.

[299] See Case C-234/97 *Fernández de Bobadilla*, ECLI:EU:C:1999:367, para. 28 and 31–33; Case C-164/94, *Aranitis*, ECLI:EU:C:1996:23, para. 30–32. See also Case C-586/08 *Rubino*, ECLI:EU:C:2009:801.

register of *praticanti* with her French *maîtrise en droit*. Her enrolment was denied because her diploma was not issued by an Italian university and her registration made conditional upon completion of an entire programme of education and training. In Morgenbesser's case, neither the directive on lawyers[300] nor the more general Directive 89/48/EEC could be applied.[301] Morgenbesser's status as a non-fully qualified professional therefore left her outside the scope of the relevant directives. Regarding the formulation of the *Vlassopoulou* doctrine, the Court did not add much to its previous formulation. Indeed, all qualifications and experience again had to be taken into account to make a comparison between the qualifications held by the applicant and those required by the national rules.[302] Furthermore, all evidence of qualifications and experience had to be taken into account whether acquired within the EU or outside it, an obligation which would not cease to exist if directives on recognition would exist.[303] The need to determine whether the qualifications were at least equivalent to those required in the host Member State was still central to the assessment—and if the comparison of qualifications would show only a partial overlap the host Member State should require the applicant to prove to have acquired the lacking knowledge and qualifications.[304] Part of the case to emphasise here is that while an application of the *Vlassopoulou* doctrine does require an assessment of the qualifications, it does not require recognition to be automatic.[305]

Furthermore, the Court confirmed in *Morgenbesser* that the application of the *Vlassopoulou* doctrine was distinctly different from examinations regarding the academic equivalence of diplomas—and constituted a broader, more general assessment, of an academic degree placed in the context of the whole of training (academic and professional) the applicant could demonstrate.[306] Nevertheless, *Morgenbesser* did not lead to a general statement that all academic qualifications recognised for professional purposes constituted professional recognition.[307] Some scholars argue that the Court could have simply pointed out that *Morgenbesser* constituted professional recognition with this recognition of academic qualifications for professional

[300] Directive 98/5/EC of the European Parliament and of the Council of 16 February 1998 to facilitate practice of the profession of lawyer on a permanent basis in a Member State other than that in which the qualification was obtained, [1998] OJ L 77/36.

[301] This was particularly the case since Morgenbesser had not yet completed all the professional qualifications allowing her to perform economic activities as a lawyer and because the position of *praticante* was not the same as the regulated profession of *avvocato*. Instead, the position of trainee lawyer was considered a condition to access the profession of lawyer—i.e. it is one of the additional steps that need to be fulfilled next to having the relevant qualifications. See Case C-313/01 *Morgenbesser*, ECLI:EU:C:2003:612, para. 45 and 51–54 and Case C-101/10 *Pavlov and Famira*, ECLI:EU:C:2011:462, para. 25.

[302] Case C-313/01 *Morgenbesser*, ECLI:EU:C:2003:612, para. 57.

[303] Ibid., para. 58.

[304] Ibid., para. 68–71.

[305] Ibid., para. 44.

[306] Ibid., para. 66.

[307] See Chapter "Challenging Convention: Theory, Competences & The Grey Area of Recognition", Sect. 5 of this contribution.

purposes.[308] This would have allowed a broader range of cases to be pulled into the realm of Article 53 TFEU, i.e. all instances of academic qualifications recognised for professional purposes would be subject to that legal basis. *Morgenbesser* is still to be considered a welcome addition to the CJEU's case law since it does extend EU internal market law to non-fully qualified professionals—and could perhaps in the future lead to an inclusion of provisions on their qualifications in the PQD.[309] As of yet, however, *Morgenbesser* and the applicable *Vlassopoulou* doctrine behind it remain a separate category subject to the CJEU's case law based on the Treaty provisions on freedom of movement.[310]

While *Morgenbesser* solidified the use of the *Vlassopoulou* doctrine for cases outside the scope of the PQD, subsequent case law continued to develop the fallback system. In *Peśla* the Court was again confronted with a person who had a degree in law, but which did not constitute the qualification to enter the legal profession. *Peśla* particularly argued that—in the comparative exercise conducted as part of the *Vlassopoulou* doctrine—the home Member State qualifications should be leading (and not those of the host Member State) since the difference of legal systems would mean freedom of movement for lawyers would be ineffective.[311] Furthermore, the case revolved around the question whether host Member States are obliged to lower their qualification requirements to accommodate those with qualifications from other Member States.[312] The Court rejected both of these claims. As a starting point, qualifications of applicants have to be examined in light of the required qualifications of the *host* Member State.[313] Furthermore, according to the Court free movement was already facilitated sufficiently by Member States having to take into account qualifications obtained previously, i.e. it is not necessary for them to lower their national requirements to facilitate those with qualifications from other Member States.[314]

---

308 Garben (2011, p. 144). However, the fact that Morgenbesser's qualifications could not be considered as a diploma in light of Directive 89/48/EEC could have been an important reason to prevent the Court from considering the case an instance of professional recognition. It may be recalled that because Morgenbesser's qualifications did not give her direct access to the training for *avocat* in France. This means that Morgenbesser's qualifications were different from those to which she sought access, thus forcing the Court to deal with the matter outside the explicit ambit of the EU legislation on professional recognition. See Claessens and Schneider (2011, p. 130); Case C-313/01 *Morgenbesser*, ECLI:EU:C:2003:612, para. 54.

309 See Sect. 5.4 of this chapter.

310 A related note in this respect related to *Morgenbesser* is that while the Court considered the case based on (present-day) Articles 45 and 49 TFEU, it also pointed to the possibility of an extra option coming from other Treaty provisions such as (present-day) Articles 18, 26, and 165 TFEU. Whereas such a second fall-back option has not been explored, it would have been interesting to see what effects could be given especially to provisions such as Article 18 TFEU on EU citizenship and Article 165 TFEU on education in the EU. Case C-313/01 *Morgenbesser*, ECLI:EU:C:2003:612, para. 32 and 56.

311 Case C-345/08 *Peśla*, ECLI:EU:C:2009:771, para. 42.

312 Ibid., para. 49 and further.

313 Ibid., para. 44–46.

314 Ibid., para. 50 and 53–54.

While these initial responses of the Court may seem to tip the scales in favour of the Member States, the Court did also elaborate the *Vlassopoulou* doctrine in favour of mobile professionals in the *Peśla* case. To start, the Court confirmed that while Member States are not obliged under EU law to relax their national requirements, they are always free to do so.[315] Furthermore, the "taking into account" of previous qualifications should result in partial recognition thereof, which should not be merely notional. This means that in *Peśla*, the Court confirmed that the result of the comparative examination initially developed in *Vlassopoulou* should have consequences in the recognition procedure. Worded differently, the Court in *Peśla* confirmed that in the case of partial overlaps of qualifications found in the *Vlassopoulou* comparative assessment, partial recognition should lead to tailored measures to compensate for the knowledge found to be lacking.[316]

In *Brouillard* the Court subsequently clarified the relationship between the *Vlassopoulou* doctrine and equivalence (academic recognition) procedures as well as the evidence of qualifications needing to be examined in such contexts.[317] Equivalence procedures exist at national level and comprise more detailed comparisons to determine whether a foreign qualification can be considered equivalent to the corresponding national one. However, in the context of these procedures equivalence carries different weight than it does in the context of the *Vlassopoulou* doctrine since a higher degree of similarity is often required before an equivalence procedure can successfully be completed. As is by now abundantly clear, the *Vlassopoulou* doctrine necessitates an exercise in which the home and host state qualifications are compared. In *Brouillard*, this appeared not to have been the case. The case concerned a person who had applied for the competition to be recruited as a legal secretary at the Belgian *Cour de cassation* with a French vocational master's degree in law, economics, and management. While he also applied for academic equivalence of his degree, the result of that procedure was not yet known when his application was considered inadmissible. Furthermore, it was unclear whether some relevant parts of his degree as well as professional experience were taken into account during the procedure. The Court resolved the case on the basis of the Treaty provisions since the PQD could not be applied because the case concerned a non-regulated profession.[318] In particular, the Court ruled that while academic equivalence procedures could be used to determine the suitability of foreign qualifications for the exercise of a non-regulated profession, parties assessing those qualifications are obliged to assess *all* evidence of qualifications in line with the *Vlassopoulou* doctrine.[319]

Development of the *Vlassopoulou* doctrine has therefore strongly been shaped around the qualifications of those who were either not fully qualified, or those whose academic qualifications had to be recognized for professional purposes. *BB* is a recent case on the latter topic as well as a further example of the aberrations that can occur

---

315 Ibid., para. 56–57.

316 Ibid., para. 58–61.

317 Case C-298/14 *Brouillard*, ECLI:EU:C:2015:652.

318 Ibid., para. 35–45.

319 Ibid., para. 60 and 67.

in recognition procedures. The case concerned a pharmacist with complete academic qualifications from the UK, but incomplete professional qualifications. Accordingly, when she returned to Lithuania BB was issued a certificate recognizing the equivalence of her UK degree to an equivalent Lithuanian master's degree in pharmacy studies. However, since this only constituted an academic equivalence and not a professional recognition, further practical training had to be completed in Lithuania since that was not completed in the UK. However, upon completion of that training professional recognition was again rejected for reasons of not having completed professional qualifications in an EU Member State—despite clearly having pursued education and training in two EU Member States. The main issue in the case stemmed from the fact that BB had not completed the full professional qualification (4 years pharmacists study and 12 months practical training) in one Member State, but had instead completed the 4 years study plus six months practical training in the UK and another six months in Lithuania.

It may be recalled that pharmacists are one of the professions for which automatic recognition is available under the PQD. However, since BB had not completed all training in one Member State that route was closed off to her. The first question posed to the CJEU therefore became whether she could instead rely on the PQD's general system. The Court—perhaps surprisingly—answered that question in the negative. According to the Court, the PQD is meant to facilitate access to other Member States' labour markets for those who already have access to carry out a regulated profession in their home Member State (i.e. the Member State of qualification).[320] Since BB had not completed the required practical training in the UK she could not be considered fully qualified in the UK meaning she did not have access to the profession of pharmacist in the home Member State. Since the PQD could not be applied, BB also became subject to the CJEU's fallback system based on Articles 45 and 49 TFEU.[321] In *BB*, the Court formulated an important addendum to the *Vlassopoulou* doctrine: the system for recognition of qualifications as formulated on the basis of Article 53 TFEU is aimed at facilitating recognition—and not to make it more difficult—meaning Member States still have to comply with their Treaty obligations to recognize qualifications in cases of persons not covered by the PQD.[322] The Court proceeded to reiterate the *Vlassopoulou* doctrine but more clearly applied the PQD's language to cases covered by the fallback system. Whereas in the past the Court predominantly spoke of partial correspondence of qualifications, in *BB* it adopted the PQD's terminology of substantial differences. Accordingly, if the comparative examination conducted in the context of the *Vlassopoulou* doctrine

[320] Case C-166/20 *BB v. Lietuvos Respublikos sveikatos apsaugos ministerija,* ECLI:EU:C:2021:554, para. 25–28.

[321] Interestingly, the Court was also asked to examine whether Article 15 of the Charter on the right to seek employment and to work was relevant in the context of the case. According to the Court, Article 52(2) Charter rights recognized by the Charter had to be exercised under the conditions set in the EU Treaties. Since the interpretation of Art. 15(2) Charter already corresponded with Articles 45 and 49 TFEU, there was no need to rely further on the Charter provisions. See Case C-166/20 *BB v. Lietuvos Respublikos sveikatos apsaugos ministerija,* ECLI:EU:C:2021:554, para. 32–33.

[322] Ibid., para 36 and 38.

revealed substantial differences, the authorities could set compensatory measures to remedy differences.[323]

A similar situation occurred in the case of *A*. She had trained as a psychotherapist in Finland. However, the training she followed was organized by an educational institution based in the UK (together with Finnish partners). She was therefore in the peculiar situation that she still had to obtain recognition since her degree was considered as being obtained in another Member State. Nevertheless, the Court ultimately considered the PQD not to be applicable since she had not pursued the profession for one year.[324] This was required pursuant to Article 13(2) PQD since the profession of psychotherapist was not regulated in the UK while it was in Finland. This meant that her case needed to be examined in light of the fallback system of articles 45 and 49 TFEU.[325] While the Court reiterated its previous case law,[326] it also specified what evidence authorities could use during the recognition procedure. According to the Court, the examination procedure (part of the *Vlassopoulou* doctrine) presupposes mutual trust among Member States regarding the evidence that is issued.[327] This means that host Member State authorities must in principle consider documents from other Member States authentic.[328] However, in the event that serious doubts arise an obligation arises on the issuing authority (i.e. the one in the home Member State) in light of the principle of sincere cooperation. In particular, that authority should re-examine the issue of the diploma and possibly withdraw it if there is evidence that a particular level of knowledge is not obtained.[329] Correspondingly, if there is a manifest lack of authenticity of the diploma[330] the host Member State is not required under EU law to overlook the situation—especially since Member States still have the right to take measures restricting free movement to prevent their national vocational training requirements from being evaded.[331]

The last in the line of cases on the fallback system concerns a doctor who had the relevant degree in medicine from the UK, but not the accompanying certificate required under the Annexes of the PQD to benefit from automatic recognition. The general system also could not be applied since the doctor in the case also could not access the regulated profession of doctor in the UK, thus making them subject to

---

[323] Case C-166/20 *BB v. Lietuvos Respublikos sveikatos apsaugos ministerija*, ECLI:EU:C:2021:554, para. 41.

[324] Case C-577/20 *A v. Sosiaali- ja terveysalan lupa- ja valvontavirasto*, ECLI:EU:C:2022:467, para. 35.

[325] Ibid., para. 36.

[326] Ibid., paras. 40–44, 47.

[327] Ibid., para. 48.

[328] Ibid., para. 52.

[329] Ibid., para. 49–50, 53.

[330] Particularly when it is clear "that the actual content of the training provided differs considerably from the content of the training courses as evidenced by the relevant diploma"; see Ibid., para. 56.

[331] In particular, the Court considers that the protection of public health (as at stake in the case with psychotherapists) is an overriding reason in the general interest that can justify restrictions to free movement, if proportionate. See ibid, para. 53–55.

the fallback system of Articles 45 and 49 TFEU.[332] While the Court reiterated its reference to compensatory measures made in *BB* before, it also repeated its case law in *Vandorou* in which it had previously prescribed that compensatory measures must always be proportionate.[333] Accordingly, national legislation making no distinction in terms of compensation measures (i.e. does not tailor them to the lacking knowledge of the individual concerned) does not adhere to the *Vlassopoulou* doctrine, nor the proportionality principle.[334] This case therefore reinforces the Court's prior case law in *Peśla* which had already established that partial recognition should lead to tailored measures to compensate lacking knowledge.[335] Furthermore, the case also again streamlines the use of terminology within the fallback system with that of the PQD.

In conclusion, the line of cases discussed above has ensured that the doctrine originally developed in *Vlassopoulou* has been fully developed into a fallback system covering all professionals not covered by the PQD. Accordingly, the Court has determined a clear obligation to recognize qualifications within this fallback system and can therefore be said to have reinforced the principle of mutual recognition observed in the PQD.[336] The development of this line of case law is furthermore interesting for its scope, which extends beyond the PQD to cover non-fully qualified professionals and may even cover non-regulated professions. Finally, the growing convergence in terminology between the fallback system and PQD is another interesting and welcome development.

7 Conclusion

The present chapter has extensively discussed EU law on professional recognition. The PQD thereby takes a central role. Providing various routes to recognition, the Directive effectuates the principle of mutual recognition in relation to qualifications for regulated professions. Recent years have seen the addition of new technologies such as the EPC and alert mechanism, as well as a transparency exercise aimed to tackle ineffective forms of regulation. Regarding this latter point, attention should be given to developing a better understanding of what is to be understood by smart or effective regulation. The situation to be avoided is one where formal regulation is removed but no safeguards are provided for individuals thus potentially submitting them to non-regulatory barriers. Another complexity of the directive concerns

---

[332] Case C-634/20 *A v. Sosiaali- ja terveysalan lupa- ja valvontavirasto*, ECLI:EU:C:2022:149, para. 38, 41–44.

[333] Ibid., para. 45. See also Cases C-422/09, C-425/09 and C-426/09 *Vandorou, Giankoulis and Askoxilakis*, ECLI:EU:C:2010:732.

[334] Case C-634/20 A v. Sosiaali- ja terveysalan lupa- ja valvontavirasto, ECLI:EU:C:2022:149, para. 47.

[335] Ibid., para. 58–61.

[336] It may be recalled that the PQD carries a presumption of recognition meaning that possibilities to refuse are limited. See Sect. 3.2.2 of this chapter.

its focus on recognition while also covering some aspects related to access to the profession. Matters to be improved here concern the conferral of a right of access in the context of the EPC procedure and facilitation of the principle of partial access. In particular, the criterion requiring a full programme of education and training to be imposed severely inhibits the application of partial access. Relaxation—or even removal—of this criterion and a stronger focus on proportionality can increase the principle's scope of application while allowing Member States to protect their fundamental interests.

Furthermore, this chapter has also shown that the CJEU's case law which most notably affected non-fully qualified professionals has come to form a fully-fledged fallback system alternative to the PQD. Recent case law also shows the Court approximated the terminology applied in the system to more strongly align with the PQD. However, the question can be raised whether there is a general awareness of the existence of this fallback system and its relevance to both regulated and non-regulated professions.

Historically, updates to the system for recognition of professional qualifications have quite quickly succeeded one another.[337] The examination of the PQD and CJEU case law related to professional qualifications above raises questions regarding the future of the instrument. In 2020, the elements of the PQD modernized by Directive 2013/55/EU were evaluated by the European Commission.[338] Equally the Proportionality Test Directive was subject to a first evaluation in 2024.[339] In that same year, the PQD was subject to an extensive examination by the European Court of Auditors which identified a variety of challenges ranging from limited use of the systems for recognition of the PQD to differences between Member states regarding procedural matters and limited use of innovative tools instituted by Directive 2013/55/EU.[340] The PQD was furthermore also examined in the context of the Commission's regulatory fitness and performance programme (REFIT). Suggestions developed in that context related to extending the EPC to other professions, extending the implementation of common training principles, clarifying the situation for non-fully qualified professionals (described as mixed professional and academic qualifications which should also be able to benefit from recognition under the PQD), and updating the restrictiveness indicator (which can be said to connect to the concern on non-regulatory barriers

[337] See Chapter "The Long History of the Recognition of Qualifications in the EU" for the historical development of the recognition of (professional) qualifications in the EU.

[338] Report from the Commission to the European Parliament, the Council, the European Economic and Social Committee and the Committee of the Regions on the implementation of certain new elements introduced by Directive 2013/55/EU of the European Parliament and of the Council of 20 November 2013 amending Directive 2005/36/EC on the recognition of professional qualifications and Regulation (EU) No 1024/2012 on administrative cooperation through the Internal Market Information System ('the IMI Regulation'), COM(2020) 191 final.

[339] Report from the Commission to the European Parliament and the Council on the implementation of Directive (EU) 2018/958 of the European Parliament and of the Council of 28 June 2018 on a proportionality test before adoption of new regulation of professions, COM(2024) 544 final, p. 3.

[340] European Court of Auditors (2024) The recognition of professional qualifications in the EU: An essential mechanism, but used sparsely and inconsistently, Special Report 10.

since the indicator is said to focus too much on regulation governing access to professions and insufficient attention to practical barriers).[341] Based on Article 60(2) PQD, the Commission is furthermore required to publish a report on the implementation of the directive every five years starting 2019. Indeed, work appears underway regarding the next evaluation report.[342] In light of all these reporting activities it will be interesting to see how the instrument will continue to develop itself and which suggested amendments may be in store to improve recognition of professional qualifications in the EU.

References

Adamis-Csásár K, De Keyser L, Fries-Tersch E et al (2019) Labour mobility and recognition in the regulated professions. European Parliament—Committee on Employment and Social Affairs, Luxembourg.

Adamo S, Binder T (2018) Union citizens and the recognition of professional qualifications: where do we go from here? In: De Vries S et al (eds) EU citizens' economic rights in action: re-thinking legal and factual barriers in the internal market. Edward Elgar, Cheltenham, pp 37–59

Barnard C (2008) Unravelling the Services Directive. Common Mark Law Rev 45:323–394

Berthoud F (2016) La reconnaissance des qualifications professionnelles: Union européenne et Suisse—Union européenne, Schultess Médias Juridiques SA, Zurich

Blitz B (1999) Professional mobility and the mutual recognition of qualifications in the European Union: two institutional approaches'. Comp Educ Rev 43:311–331

Cambien N (2017) Mutual recognition and mutual trust in the internal market. Eur Pap 2:93–115

Claessens S (2008) Free movement of lawyers in the European Union. Wolf Legal Publishers, Nijmegen

Claessens S (2014) Modernisering van de Richtlijn erkenning beroepskwalificaties'. SEW 1:2–11

Claessens S, Schneider H (2011) Legal education and free movement of lawyers in the EU. In: Heringa AW, Akkermans B (eds) Educating European lawyers. Intersentia, Antwerp, pp 121–156

Garben S (2011) On recognition of qualifications for academic and professional purposes. Tilburg Law Rev 16:127–156

Hoogenboom A (2014) Origin and meaning of mutual recognition as foundational principle in the European integration process. Eur Tidskr 17:237–265

Howat C, Ulicna D, Harris P, GHK, DTI (2011) Revised final report — Study evaluating the Professional Qualifications Directive against recent educational reforms in EU Member States. DG Internal Market and Services - European Commission

Koumenta M, Pagliero M (2016) Measuring prevalence and labour market impacts of occupational regulation in the EU. European Commission, Brussels

[341] Fit for Future Platform Opinion (2023), Fostering professional mobility in the Single Market.

[342] See, for example, European Commission, Minutes Meeting of the Group of Coordinators for the recognition of professional qualifications, 20 June 2024. The document indicates publication of the evaluation report was planned for 2025. At the time of completion of this manuscript (December 2025), the report had not yet been published. At the time of conclusion of this manuscript the Commission had nevertheless just initiated its activities for the development of the Skills Portability Initiative. That initiative is focused on various matters related to qualifications including digitalisation, increased transparency, and improved recognition procedures. The adoption of the Skills Portability Initiative is planned for Q3 of 2026.

Kortese L (2022) The evolution of the principle of partial access under the professional qualifications directive: pitfalls and possibilities. In: Schoenmaekers S, Melin P (eds) The art of moving borders: Liber Amicorum Hildegard Schneider. Eleven, The Hague, pp 117–133

Kortese L (2025) Erkenning van kwalificaties van derdelanders: Asiel- & Migratiepact, Blauwe Kaart Richtlijn en aanbeveling van Commissie. A&MR 10:455–460

Lottini M (2014) An instrument of intensified informal mutual assistance: the Internal Market Information System (IMI) and the protection of personal data. Eur Public Law 20:107–125

McCormack-George D (2025) Recognition of professional qualifications of third-country nationals in the European Union: A Comment. Eur Labour Law J 16:146–156

Minor J (1992) Introductory lecture on the Directive of 21 December 1988. In: Pertek J (ed) General recognition of diplomas and free movement of professionals. European Institute of Public Administration, Maastricht, pp 3–156

Parkins N (1992) Directive 89/48/EEC: progress towards implementation. In: Pertek J (ed) General recognition of diplomas and free movement of professionals. European Institute of Public Administration, Maastricht, pp 37–54

Peixoto J (2001) Migration and policies in the European Union: highly skilled mobility, free movement of labour and recognition of diplomas. Int Migr 39:33–61

Pertek J (1992) A few comments on the implementation of the system and on the prospects. In: Pertek J (ed) General recognition of diplomas and free movement of professionals. European Institute of Public Administration, Maastricht, pp 99–104

Schneider H (1995) Die Anerkennung von Diplomen in der Europäischen Gemeinschaft. MAKLU Uitgevers, Antwerpen

Schoenmaekers S (2010) The regulation of architects in Belgium and the Netherlands. Datawyse / Universitaire Pers Maastricht, Maastricht

Schneider H, Kortese L (2019) B-solutions "roadmap and factsheet for the recognition of qualifications for highly demanded professions"—step 3: approach and findings. ITEM, Maastricht

Schneider H, Lubina K (2009) Freizügigkeit von Juristen in der Europäischen Gemeinschaft: Der Fall Lubina und seine Folgen für deutsch-niederländische Juristen. In: De Groot R, Janssen A (eds) Festschrift anlässlich des sechzigjährigen Bestehens der Deutsch-Niederländischen Juristenkonferenz. LIT Verlag, Berlin, pp 125–157

Vankova Z (2020) Circular migration and the rights of migrant workers in Central and Eastern Europe: the EU promise of a triple win solution. Springer, Cham

Academic Recognition

1 Introduction

While the realm of professional recognition was explored in Chapter "Professional Recognition", this chapter moves the focus to discussing academic recognition. Different from professional recognition which is governed primarily by the EU through the Professional Qualifications Directive and CJEU's case law, the area of academic recognition is characterised by a multitude of actors having adopted some binding but mostly non-binding legislation and instruments. Apart from the EU, action in this area has primarily been taken in the context of the Council of Europe and the Bologna Process. Furthermore, smaller configurations of Member States such as the Benelux have also adopted initiatives to advance action taken in the context of the Bologna Process. This chapter accordingly focuses on exploring the main initiatives on academic recognition in the EU. The chapter will first analyse the Bologna Process due to its great influence on higher education and the structure thereof. The Bologna Process contributed to academic recognition through its three-cycle structure taken up in the Qualifications Framework for the European Higher Education Area (QF-EHEA), the European Credit Transfer System (ECTS), diploma supplement, and cooperation on quality assurance. Furthermore, provisions on recognition were provided in the context of the Bologna Process through the incorporation of the Lisbon Recognition Convention, which is discussed next. Though a legal instrument in its own right, it has a strong connection to the Bologna Process due to it being the Process' only legally binding text. Attention is subsequently given to EU action on academic recognition. Action in the EU for a long time mirrored action taken in the context of the Bologna Process, notably in the form of the Copenhagen Process. Nevertheless, recent years have seen a significant departure from the status quo, with ambitions being raised for the EU to become a frontrunner of the Bologna Process by adopting new instruments on topics such as automatic recognition and micro-credentials. Finally, some attention is given to the case law of the CJEU on

L. S.J. Kortese, *Effectuating Free Movement in the EU through Recognition of Qualifications*, https://doi.org/10.1007/978-3-032-21335-8_5

education. This section will show that education is strongly connected to other areas of law such as free movement and EU citizenship.

2 The Bologna Process: An Umbrella for Extensive Action

The origins of the Bologna Process lie outside the EU framework. Earlier in this research, the unique nature of the Bologna Process was already discussed.[1] Despite being initiated by EU Member States, the Bologna Process itself is located outside the realm of the EU's legal framework. Indeed, a total of 49 countries are a party to the Bologna Process thereby comprising the EU Member States.[2] Progress in the Process is achieved via Ministerial Conferences at which Communiqués are adopted.[3] The Bologna Process is perhaps best known for its large-scale harmonisation in the structure of higher education thereby facilitating recognition by providing a common structure for higher education degrees. At the time when the Bologna Process was first adopted, EU Member States were wary of EU action on education, fearing it would move from diversity to a harmonisation approach.[4] However, the Bologna Process signified a complete change from any previous suspicions since the Member States adopted a convergence approach and undertook their cooperation in a way that is intergovernmental, thereby initially removing the EU from the picture.[5] Even if the European Commission is currently a part of the Bologna Process,[6] the creation of the Process by some EU Member States has been considered a re-nationalisation of higher education cooperation by some.[7] In this context, the Bologna Process is to be considered remarkable considering its non-binding nature, its far-reaching effects, and its location outside the EU legal framework. According to Ravinet, the States that are party to the Bologna Process are increasingly bound by the Process despite its intergovernmental nature due to its follow-up structures.[8]

Through time, the Bologna Process has evolved into a fully-fledged European Higher Education Area (EHEA) covering many topics ranging far beyond the reach of the present contribution. While its *modus operandi* continues to be characterised as intergovernmental (and thereby legally non-binding) cooperation, some dedicated action within the EHEA has been subject to legally binding follow-up. Indeed, the incorporation of the Lisbon Recognition Convention (LRC) into the EHEA and follow-up initiatives such as the Benelux Decisions on automatic recognition mean

[1] See Chapter "The Long History of the Recognition of Qualifications in the EU" of this contribution.

[2] EHEA, 'Full Members', http://www.ehea.info/pid34250/members.html.

[3] For more information on the content of these documents, see Chapter "The Long History of the Recognition of Qualifications in the EU".

[4] Wächter (2004, p. 271).

[5] Ibid.

[6] The European Commission is a full member of the Bologna Process.

[7] Verbruggen (2003, p. 204).

[8] Ravinet (2008, p. 361).

legal follow-up has been given to Bologna Process initiatives. In relation to recognition of qualifications particularly, some key elements of the Bologna Process continue to be effectuated through non-legally binding instruments. Apart from procedural provisions on recognition (which for the Bologna Process are laid down in the LRC), these concern instruments such as qualifications frameworks, credit systems, common documentation formats, and quality assurance. These elements of the Bologna Process are explored in the following sections.

2.1 The European Higher Education Area's Qualifications Framework: The Three-Cycle Degree System and ECTS

When the Bologna Process was first introduced, the European Ministers for Education already spoke of the creation of a multiple cycle degree system.[9] At the Berlin Ministerial Conference, Ministers encouraged the countries party to the Bologna Process "to elaborate a framework of comparable and compatible qualifications for their higher education systems, which should seek to describe qualifications in terms of workload, level, learning outcomes, competences and profile" and undertook to elaborate "an overarching framework of qualifications for the European Higher Education Area".[10] The proposed framework, comprising three cycles, generic descriptors, and credit ranges, was proposed through the 2003 Berlin Communiqué and adopted in 2005 at the Bergen Ministerial Conference where Ministers also committed to elaborate national qualifications frameworks that were compatible with the EHEA qualifications framework.[11] The qualifications framework, laying down the Bologna Process's three-cycle system is the spearhead of the initiative as well as its most far-reaching and straightforward feature.[12] The role of the qualifications framework has since been solidified through subsequent communiqués and by its implementation being monitored.[13]

[9] Sorbonne Joint Declaration on harmonisation of the architecture of the European higher education system, Paris 25 May 1998; Bologna Declaration of 19 June 1999—Joint declaration of the European Ministers of Education.

[10] Realising the European Higher Education Area, Communiqué of the Conference of Ministers responsible for Higher Education in Berlin on 19 September 2003.

[11] Ibid.; The European Higher Education Area—Achieving the Goals, Communiqué of the Conference of European Ministers Responsible for higher Education, Bergen 19–20 May 2005.

[12] Garben (2011b, p. 23).

[13] See for example: Tirana EHEA Ministerial Conference, 29–30 May 2024 (Tirana Communiqué); Bologna Process Stocktaking—Report from a working group appointed by the Bologna Follow-up Group to the Conference of European Ministers Responsible for Higher Education, Bergen 19–20 May 2005; Bologna Process Stocktaking Report 2007—Report from a working group appointed by the Bologna Follow-up Group to the Ministerial Conference in London, May 2007; Bologna Process Stocktaking Report 2009—Report from working groups appointed by the Bologna Follow-up Group to the Ministerial Conference in Leuven/Louvain-La-Neuve, 28–29 April 2009; European Commission, Eurydice, Eurostat, Eurostudent, The European Higher Education Area in 2012: Bologna Process Implementation Report; European Commission, EACEA, Eurydice, The European

The framework of qualifications for the European Higher Education Area (QF-EHEA) is essentially a two-page document providing qualitative and quantitative guidelines for the degrees contained in the three-cycle degree system.[14] The qualitative guidelines are learning outcomes students must have achieved after conclusion of a cycle of higher education.[15] The generic outcomes of a qualification (i.e. the learning outcomes common to all holders of a certain qualification) can be expressed in a qualification descriptor.[16] In the Bologna Process, such descriptors are also known as the "Dublin Descriptors".[17] These were developed in the context of the Joint Quality Initiative. Each of the level descriptors contains five components: knowledge and understanding, applying knowledge and understanding, making judgments, communication, and lifelong learning skills.[18] The descriptors were developed to be applied in a general manner thus identifying the nature of the whole qualification.[19] They are not prescriptive nor exhaustive meaning that additional elements and outcomes may be added at the national level. An example of one of the Dublin Descriptors for the second cycle (i.e. a master's degree) entails that a student must "have demonstrated knowledge and understanding that is founded upon and extends and/or enhances that typically associated with the first cycle, and that provides a basis or opportunity for originality in developing and/or applying ideas, often within a research context". Additionally, a student must have obtained between 60 to 120 ECTS credits.

As the description of the second cycle above shows, the Bologna Process establishes ranges for credits and general descriptions of learning outcomes. The reason for the Bologna Process not establishing a defined number of credits or more specific learning outcome descriptions lies in the fact that the QF-EHEA is a meta-framework. This means that national frameworks are developed within the context of the QF-EHEA which, among others, "stipulates the outline and boundary of national qualifications frameworks, and is a device, which helps to provide clearer understanding of how the various qualifications made within the European Higher Education Area are related to each other and articulate with each other".[20] At the heart of the QF-EHEA is transparency which is achieved by simplifying the structure of higher education across countries and by linking national frameworks together. However, it does not provide for a single framework to be copied by participating countries.

Higher Education Area in 2015: Bologna Process Implementation Report; European Commission, EACEA, Eurydice, The European Higher Education Area in 2018: Bologna Process Implementation Report.

[14] Terry (2008, p. 31).

[15] EHEA, The framework of qualifications for the European Higher Education Area.

[16] Bologna Working Group on Qualifications Frameworks, A Framework for Qualifications of the European Higher Education Area, Copenhagen, 2005, p. 63.

[17] Ibid., p. 101.

[18] Joint Quality Initiative, Shared 'Dublin' descriptors for Short Cycle, First Cycle, Second Cycle and Third Cycle Awards, 18 October 2004.

[19] Bologna Working Group on Qualifications Frameworks, A Framework for Qualifications of the European Higher Education Area, Copenhagen, 2005, p. 65.

[20] Ibid., p. 58.

As far as credits are concerned, these make up the quantitative guidelines of the QF-EHEA. The credits are counted according to the European Credit Transfer System (ECTS) which is laid down in the ECTS Users' Guide.[21] As the Dublin Descriptors above have shown, the QF-EHEA establishes credit ranges for higher education (particularly the short cycle as well as the first and second cycles of higher education). The ECTS is one of the core elements associated with the Bologna Process. Nevertheless, unlike the Bologna Process, its roots lie within the context of the EU's action on Erasmus. In 1987, EU Member States adopted a decision by which the Erasmus scheme was established.[22] The Erasmus Decision also included an action line on academic recognition which specified that the Community would cooperate with the Member States on "measures to promote the European Community Course Credit Transfer System (ECTS) on an experimental and voluntary basis in order to provide a means by which students undergoing or having completed higher education and training may receive credit for such training carried out at universities in other Member States". In 1998, the System was first mentioned in the context of the Sorbonne Declaration and in 1999 the Ministers for Education of the countries participating in the Bologna Process included as one of the primary objectives of the cooperation the "establishment of a system of credits—such as in the ECTS—as a proper means of promoting the most widespread student mobility".[23]

Since that time, the ECTS has become one of the key features of the Bologna Process and the European Higher Education Area.[24] In particular, the ECTS provides for the possibility to measure and compare learning achievements whereby credits are a way of expressing the volume of learning based on the attainment of certain learning outcomes and workload.[25] Where learning outcomes are "statements of what the individual knows, understands and is able to do on completion of a learning process", workload is defined as "an estimation of the time the individual typically needs to complete all learning activities such as lectures, seminars, projects, [...] required to achieve the defined learning outcomes in formal learning environments".[26] According to the ECTS Users' Guide, 60 ECTS credits are allocated to a full-time academic year.[27]

---

[21] EHEA, Bologna Process and European Commission, *ECTS Users' Guide* (Publications Office of the European Union, 2015). As of the time of writing of this contribution the ECTS Users' Guide was under revision (foreseen for 2027 when the next ministerial conference was to take place).

[22] Council Decision of 15 June 1987 adopting the European Community Action Scheme for the Mobility of University Students (ERASMUS), [1987] OJ L 166/20.

[23] Sorbonne Joint Declaration on harmonisation of the architecture of the European higher education system, Paris 25 May 1998; Bologna Declaration of 19 June 1999—Joint declaration of the European Ministers of Education.

[24] EHEA, Bologna Process and European Commission, *ECTS Users' Guide* (Publications Office of the European Union, 2015), p. 14.

[25] Bologna Working Group on Qualifications Frameworks, A Framework for Qualifications of the European Higher Education Area, Copenhagen, 2005, p. 44.

[26] EHEA, Bologna Process and European Commission, *ECTS Users' Guide* (Publications Office of the European Union, 2015), p. 10.

[27] Ibid.

Accordingly, the ECTS may be useful for both academic recognition *by accumulation* as well as *by substitution*. Depending on the situation, the ECTS is employed differently. Under the ECTS, academic recognition by substitution is labelled as "credit mobility", whereas academic recognition by accumulation is called "degree mobility".[28] In both cases, the ultimate objective of the ECTS is recognition of credits which is defined as "the process through which an institution certifies that learning outcomes achieved and assessed in another institution satisfy the requirements of one of the programmes they offer".[29] For credit mobility (academic recognition by substitution) to take place, the ECTS provides for a number of supporting documents such as course catalogues, learning agreements, record transcripts, and traineeship certificates to ensure that the credits obtained in a host country may actually count for the achievement of the diploma in the home country.[30] In the case of degree mobility (academic recognition by accumulation), recognition depends on the provisions of the Lisbon Recognition Convention as there is no agreement between the host and the home State's higher education institution.

In the case of degree mobility, individuals may be faced with a difficulty related to the ECTS. It was mentioned earlier that the QF-EHEA is a meta-framework meaning it extends over national qualifications frameworks and does not prescribe one single format to be adopted by the countries of the EHEA. As far as the ECTS is concerned, this means that there is no fixed number of credits associated with a certain cycle of the Bologna Process's degree system. Instead, there are credit ranges. The ECTS credit ranges can be cause for difficulties at the national level. Whereas Member State A may maintain 60 ECTS for a master's degree, Member State B may maintain 120 ECTS for a master's degree. A graduate from Member State A could then face difficulties and even not be recognised in Member State B due to not having completed a two-year master's degree comprising 120 ECTS. Part of the issue has to do with the fact that recognition of the level of higher education degrees under the Bologna Process is not yet automatic all throughout the EHEA. Indeed, whereas the Bologna Process increases the transparency of qualifications by providing a common structure of higher education, its function as a meta-framework providing general descriptors and credit ranges prevents it from providing participating countries with one common format to be recognised automatically. Therefore, individuals and competent authorities may still be faced with difficulties related to credit ranges. According to the ECTS Users' Guide, differences in the number of ECTS credits should not be the primary factor when evaluating qualifications, as the learning outcomes achieved by the individual should be the main factor to be taken into account.[31] The ECTS Users' Guide makes further reference to the LRC, according to which a flexible attitude should be adopted towards differences in content, profile, workload, quality and

[28] Ibid., pp. 30–31 and 34.

[29] Ibid., p. 30.

[30] Ibid., p. 34.

[31] EHEA, Bologna Process and European Commission, *ECTS Users' Guide* (Publications Office of the European Union, 2015), p. 30.

learning outcomes.[32] Only where the existing differences are substantial may full recognition be refused.[33] According to the ECTS Users' Guide, differences must be understood as substantial only where they "prevent the applicant from succeeding in the desired activity such as further study, research activities or employment".[34] However, the ECTS User's Guide also expresses a clear guidance where the number of ECTS is subsidiary to the content pursued in a degree.[35]

Despite the focus on content expressed through the ECTS, issues related to differences in credit ranges will not be definitively resolved unless agreements are effectuated to accept differences in credit ranges. Here, the discussion is to be turned to the question how to automate recognition of credits and ultimately the level of higher education degrees in the QF-EHEA. Earlier in this contribution it was already made clear that there are several initiatives for automatic recognition at the European and regional levels. The Bologna Process initiated action in this respect. Indeed, the Ministers of the participating countries pledged to cooperate to achieve automatic recognition and instituted a Pathfinder Group on Automatic Recognition to this end in the Bucharest Communiqué.[36] The subsequent Yerevan Communiqué indicated that automatic recognition was a goal to be achieved by 2020.[37] Indeed, the achievement of automatic recognition can be considered to have become one of the main Bologna Process objectives regarding recognition since it was reiterated in the most recent Paris, Rome, and Tirana Communiqués.[38] Apart from these calls, automatic recognition of the level of higher education degrees as established in the QF-EHEA was already achieved in certain European regions such as the Benelux (explored below). Since 2018 automatic recognition is also pursued in the EU context by way of recommendation.[39]

2.1.1 Effectuating Automatic Recognition in the Benelux Region

While the Bologna Process and EHEA set the general framework with the QF-EHEA, other initiatives have automated the recognition of the three-cycle structure and ECTS

---

[32] Revised Recommendation on Criteria and Procedures for the Assessment of Foreign Qualifications (adopted by the Lisbon Recognition Convention Committee at its fifth meeting, Sèvres, 23 June 2010).

[33] N.B. Partial recognition should still be considered; Paragraph 37 Revised Recommendation on Criteria and Procedures for the Assessment of Foreign Qualifications (adopted by the Lisbon Recognition Convention Committee at its fifth meeting, Sèvres, 23 June 2010).

[34] EHEA, Bologna Process and European Commission, *ECTS Users' Guide* (Publications Office of the European Union, 2015), p. 32.

[35] Ibid., p. 30.

[36] Making the Most of Our Potential: Consolidating the European Higher Education Area, Bucharest Communiqué, 26–27 April 2012.

[37] Yerevan Communiqué, 14–15 May 2015; Paris Communiqué—Paris, May 25th 2018.

[38] Rome Ministerial Communiqué, 19 November 2020; Tirana EHEA Ministerial Conference, 29-30 May 2024 (Tirana Communiqué).

[39] The Automatic Recognition Recommendation is discussed in Sect. 4.3.1 of this Chapter.

part of that framework. One prominent example concerns the Benelux with its Decisions on the automatic mutual generic level recognition of higher education degrees in the Benelux. The first Decision was adopted in May 2015 and was supplemented by a new Decision in January 2018. In 2021 the Benelux even entered into a Treaty together with the Baltic States on automatic recognition.[40]

Starting with the Benelux Decisions, both the 2015 and the 2018 Decisions are binding on the Benelux countries and came to arch over existing initiatives in the Benelux region. In particular, these included the pre-existing mutual automatic recognition of bachelor's and master's degrees between the Netherlands and Flanders, the automatic recognition among the three Belgian Communities, and the Luxembourg level recognitions.[41] Indeed, the initiative has ensured that the level of higher education degrees could no longer be disputed in the Benelux countries. This means that issues related to differences in durations of higher education programmes and ECTS as described above were resolved. Automatic level recognition was achieved by declaring that all bachelor's and master's degrees issued are recognised automatically and without any formalities. Nevertheless, in order to render recognition automatic two criteria are maintained.[42] First, the minimum quality of the bachelor's and master's programmes must be guaranteed by recognition from a competent authority in the area of higher education and must be accredited by a quality assurance organisation adhering to the Bologna Process's Standards and Guidelines for Quality Assurance in the EHEA (ESG). Second, the diploma must be issued and recognised at national level in accordance with national laws and regulations. At the same time, these criteria are also maintained for the automatic mutual generic level recognition of associate's degrees[43] and doctorates, the two other types of higher

[40] Treaty on the Automatic Recognition of Higher Education Qualifications, Brussel 14 September 2021.

[41] Beschikking van het Benelux Comité van Ministers betreffende de automatische wederzijdse generieke niveauerkenning van diploma's hoger onderwijs, M(2015) 3.

[42] Article 3(1)(a) Beschikking van het Benelux Comité van Ministers betreffende de automatische wederzijdse generieke niveauerkenning van diploma's hoger onderwijs, M(2015) 3.

[43] The relation of the associate's degree to the Bologna Process' three cycle structure may not be as apparent as the doctorate. Associate's degrees are placed between Vocational Education and Training (VET) and higher education and are scaled at level 5 of the EQF, as opposed to the Bologna Process's other cycles that are scaled at EQF levels 6 (bachelor's), 7 (master's), and 8 (doctorate). These degrees enable the holder to either pursue further studies at higher education level or enter the labour market. The associate's degrees, while not part of the original three-cycle structure, were originally proposed in the 2003 Berlin Communiqué and elaborated by the Joint Quality Initiative which established the Dublin Descriptors. In the context of the Bologna Process, these short cycles constitute about 120 ECTS credits and may be either linked to or included in the first cycle of higher education (i.e. the bachelor's degree). See: Joint Quality Initiative, Shared 'Dublin' descriptors for Short Cycle, First Cycle, Second Cycle and Third Cycle Awards, 18 October 2004; Bologna Working Group on Qualifications Frameworks, A Framework for Qualifications of the European Higher Education Area, Copenhagen, 2005, p. 72.

education degrees existing under the Bologna Process and subject to the second Decision on automatic level recognition adopted in 2018.[44]

Therefore, automatic recognition of the level now extends to all higher education degrees in the Benelux. Although the extension of the principle of automatic mutual generic level recognition to encompass all types of higher education provided in the Benelux region is a logical next step following the introduction of the 2015 Decision, it does raise the question whether non-recognition of the level of associate's degrees and doctorates really did occur that frequently in practice. The issue that can arise with bachelor's and master's degrees related to ECTS credit ranges is not applicable to doctorates, as they are not measured in terms of such credits. Assumedly, difficulties regarding the recognition of doctorate degrees could have arisen from the fact that doctorate regulations may differ per higher education institution (even per faculty) and are highly individualised. By contrast, the associate's degree consists of 120 ECTS credits. As no credit ranges appear to be maintained for associate's degrees, non-recognition pertaining to these ranges appears to also be less likely. Nevertheless, the term"associate's degree" is not always used to describe the short-cycle higher education degrees introduced under the Bologna Process. Part of the added value of the Benelux Decision for associate's degrees therefore lies in the identification of those national degrees that are considered to belong to the category of associate's degrees in the Benelux countries.[45]

Another line of question can be posed in relation to the scope of both Decisions which concern *academic* recognition of level, and not the content of academic qualifications nor to carrying professional titles or professional recognition in the context of the EU Professional Qualifications Directive.[46] In fact, the Decisions do not even pertain to the specification such as 'of arts' or 'of sciences' added to bachelor's and master's degrees. Despite this limitation in scope of application, the Decisions mention the improvement of the intra-Benelux cross-border mobility of Benelux graduates as well as finding employment in another Benelux country as a positive effect. Moreover, both instruments were adopted in the context of the Benelux Recommendation on cross-border *labour* mobility.[47] Article 8 of that Recommendation specifically mentions the commitment of national authorities to realise automatic generic mutual level recognition of higher education degrees within the Benelux. The

---

[44] Beschikking van het Benelux Comité van Ministers tot aanvulling van beschikking M(2015) 3 betreffende de automatische wederzijdse generieke niveauerkenning van diploma's hoger onderwijs, M(2018) 1.

[45] This means that ever since the 2018 Decision was introduced, the Dutch associate's degree, Luxembourg *brevet de technician supérieur* and *diplôme d'études supérieures générales*, as well as the Belgian degrees *diploma/graad van gegradueerde* and *brevet d'enseignement supérieur* have all been declared to be EQF level 5 short-cycle higher education degrees within the Benelux.

[46] Gemeenschappelijke memorie van toelichting bij beschikking M(2015) 3 van het Benelux comité van Ministers betreffende de automatische wederzijdse generieke niveauerkenning van diploma's hoger onderwijs; Gemeenschappelijke memorie van toelichting bij beschikking M(2018) 1 van het Benelux Comité van Ministers tot aanvulling van beschikking M(2015) 3 betreffende de automatische wederzijdse generieke niveauerkenning van diploma's hoger onderwijs.

[47] Aanbeveling van het Benelux Comité van Ministers inzake grensoverschrijdende arbeidsmobiliteit—M(2014) 17.

objectives of that same Recommendation are to improve cross-border employment by strengthening administrative cooperation, clarifying the roles and relations of the employment authorities, and determining administrative organisation of cooperation on cross-border employment.[48] Despite both of the Decision's limited scope in the area of academic recognition, these instruments are clearly embedded in labour market policy.

This embeddedness of the Benelux Decisions in labour market policy seems to again point to the overlap in recognition types occurring especially between *de facto* professional recognition and academic recognition by accumulation.[49] It may be recalled that while the EU is the main actor in the area of professional recognition, it has not adopted any legislation on recognition of non-regulated professions (*de facto* professional recognition). However, even if the EU has not taken any legislative action for non-regulated professions, its Member States have. In the Benelux-Germany region, this may result in procedures which professionals exercising non-regulated professions can rely on to demonstrate to their potential employer how their foreign qualifications hold up against the equivalent national ones. These procedures may be known by different names such as academic recognitions or equivalences and can, for example, be found in Belgium, where these procedures may be useful (and sometimes even necessary) for employment purposes.[50] In Belgium, a further distinction is made between specific recognition of equivalence which relates to assessments as to the content of qualifications, and recognition of equivalence in level. The latter procedure is where the Benelux Decisions mainly advance mobility. Because all higher education degrees in the Benelux countries must now all be recognised as equal, the recognition of equivalence in level is no longer necessary for holders of higher education degrees obtained in the Benelux.

To conclude, with these Decisions, the Benelux countries have managed to codify a core aspect of the QF-EHEA thus automating the recognition of the level of the degrees developed in the context of that framework. While concerns can be expressed at the fact that such automatic level recognition or an agreement thereto has not been reached at the level of all Bologna Process countries, the Benelux Decisions are to be considered a laudable initiative to increase legal certainty of holders of higher education degrees and improve their mobility. The Benelux moreover seems to have fully

[48] Article 2 Aanbeveling van het Benelux Comité van Ministers inzake grensoverschrijdende arbeidsmobiliteit—M(2014) 17.

[49] See Chapter "Challenging Convention: Theory, Competences & The Grey Area of Recognition", Sect. 5 of this contribution.

[50] See Article 1(1)(7) Besluit van de Vlaamse Regering betreffende de voorwaarden en de procedure tot erkenning van buitenlandse studiebewijzen uitgereikt in het hoger onderwijs, BS 18 juli 2013; Arrête du Gouvernement de la Communauté française déterminant les conditions et la procédure d'octroi de l'équivalence des titres, diplômes et certificats d'études supérieures délivrés à l'étranger, MB 16 septembre 2016; Arrête royal déterminant les conditions et la procédure d'octroi de l'équivalence des diplômes et certificats d'études étrangers, MB 5 auguste 1971; Circulaire 8171 du 30 juin 2021—Equivalence de titres'études primaires et secondaires étrangers; Gesetz vom 19. März 1971 über die Gleichwertigkeit ausländischer Diplôme und Zeugnisse; Königlicher Erlass vom 20. Juli 1971 zur Festlegung der Bedingungen und des Verfahrens zwecks Zuerkennung der Gleichwertigkeit ausländischer Diplome und Zeugnisse.

embraced its frontrunner role on automatic level recognition: in 2021, the Benelux countries expanded the reach of automatic mutual level recognition by concluding a Treaty with the Baltic States.[51] While much of the Treaty mirrors the content of the prior intra-Benelux Decisions on automatic level recognition, one provision is worth emphasising. Under Article 13 of the Benelux-Baltic States Treaty all States having ratified the LRC and who are members of the EHEA are able to accede to the present Treaty if they have adequate quality assurance systems, have implemented the QF-EHEA, and referenced their national qualifications framework to the European Qualifications Framework for lifelong learning. Through this provision the Benelux-Baltic States Treaty on automatic recognition provides an important opportunity to codify the essence of the QF-EHEA and thereby enhance legal certainty for and improve the mobility of graduates all across Europe.

2.2 *Enhanced Transparency Through Common Documentation—The Diploma Supplement*

The Diploma Supplement is another important feature of the Bologna Process and EHEA enhancing transparency of qualifications, thus contributing to their recognition. As is the case for the degree system and ECTS, the Diploma Supplement is one of the Bologna Process's core elements first proposed by the European Ministers for Education through the 1999 Bologna Declaration. However, the Diploma Supplement was initially proposed in the context of the LRC. Indeed, Article IX.3 LRC indicates that the Diploma Supplement is to be promoted by the Parties to the Convention. Accordingly, the Diploma Supplement may be considered a prime example of the convergence among the realms of the Bologna Process, Lisbon Recognition Convention and European Union, as the supplement itself was developed jointly by the European Commission, Council of Europe, and UNESCO in 1999.[52]

In the context of the Bologna Process, the objective of the Diploma Supplement was to contribute to the creation of a system of easily readable and comparable degrees.[53] The core of the Supplement is to promote the transparency of higher education qualifications by explaining the content and form of higher education qualifications in an internationally understandable manner.[54] The widespread use of the Diploma Supplement has been promoted on several occasions. In 2005 for example, a pledge was made to ensure that the Diploma Supplement would be given

[51] Treaty on the Automatic Recognition of Higher Education Qualifications, Brussel 14 September 2021.

[52] Bergan et al. (2000), p. 15.

[53] Bologna Declaration of 19 June 1999—Joint declaration of the European Ministers of Education.

[54] Council of Europe and UNESCO, Explanatory Report to the Convention on the Recognition of Qualifications concerning Higher Education in the European Region, 11 April 1997, ETS—No. 165, p. 23.

to all students graduating from 2005 onwards.[55] In the 2018 Paris Communiqué, the Ministers approved a proposal for a revised Diploma Supplement to be incorporated in the same manner in the frameworks of the LRC and Europass, thus signifying further convergence between EU and non-EU initiatives. For now, suffice it to say that the renewed document establishes what information is to be included by higher education institutions in the Diploma Supplement and in what order the information is to be presented.[56] The Diploma Supplement provides information on, among others, the name of the qualification, the institution at which it was obtained, the level of the qualification, learning outcomes, information on access to further studies or to a regulated profession, and information on the national higher education system. According to the revised template, the Diploma Supplement is based on a number of founding principles. One of these principles relates to the fact that the Diploma Supplement is "a system to aid recognition for academic and professional purposes", thus indicating that the increased transparency resulting from the Diploma Supplement may support access not only to further studies but also to the labour market.[57]

2.3 *The Bologna Process's Cooperation on Quality Assurance*

The final element of the Bologna Process to be discussed in this contribution relates to quality assurance. Cooperation on quality assurance was one of the original Bologna objectives (together with the three-cycle system, ECTS, and Diploma Supplement).[58] The EHEA countries have been promoting European cooperation in quality assurance to develop comparable criteria and methodologies. The first step in this process was set at the Bergen Ministerial Conference in 2005 when the first set of quality assurance standards and guidelines was announced which was later developed by the European Association for Quality Assurance in Higher Education (ENQA) in cooperation with the European University Association (EUA), the European Association of Institutions in Higher Education (EURASHE) and the National Unions of Students in Europe (ESIB).[59]

---

[55] Realising the European Higher Education Area, Communiqué of the Conference of Ministers responsible for Higher Education in Berlin on 19 September 2003.

[56] Paris Communiqué—Paris, May 25th 2018; Paris Communiqué—Appendix IV: The Diploma Supplement Template, Paris, May 25th 2018.

[57] Ibid.

[58] Bologna Declaration of 19 June 1999—Joint declaration of the European Ministers of Education.

[59] Realising the European Higher Education Area, Communiqué of the Conference of Ministers responsible for Higher Education in Berlin on 19 September 2003; The European Higher Education Area—Achieving the Goals, Communiqué of the Conference of European Ministers Responsible for Higher Education, Bergen 19–20 May 2005; ENQA, Standards and Guidelines for Quality Assurance in the European Higher Education Area, Helsinki 2005.

The 2005 Standards and Guidelines for Quality Assurance in the European Higher Education Area (ESG) were designed to be applicable to all higher education institutions and quality assurance agencies in Europe.[60] Besides developing standards and guidelines, ENQA, EUA, EURASHE and ESIB (together the E4 organisations), suggested the creation of a register of recognised external quality assurance agencies operating in higher education within Europe.[61] The European Register of Quality Assurance Agencies (EQAR) was subsequently established in 2008 as the first (and so far only) legal entity within the context of the Bologna Process.[62] EQAR and the ESG play an important role in enhancing recognition through quality assurance. Recognition benefits from trust in the similarity of qualifications awarded abroad and increased trust in higher education is one of the main tasks of quality assurance.[63] The EQAR supports the creation of trust on quality assurance decisions by, among others, providing a list of quality assurance agencies deemed trustworthy that may subsequently be relied on by higher education institutions ultimately responsible to recognise qualifications of students.[64]

The ESG were revised in 2015.[65] The revision of the ESG mainly took into account developments in higher education in Europe since its adoption. For example, the scope of the 2015 ESG was clarified. In particular, it was specified that the ESG also applied to cross-border and transnational higher education, e-learning and higher education not provided in the context of a programme leading to a formal degree.[66] Despite such changes, the revision of the ESG left the previous structure intact. The standards and guidelines are divided into three (complementary) parts: internal quality assurance, external quality assurance, and quality assurance agencies.[67] Each of these parts contains a number of standards paired with guidelines which are to be considered together. Whereas the standards establish practices for higher education quality assurance that have been agreed and are thus prescriptive, guidelines elaborate on the importance of the standards and set out good practices for their implementation. For example, when looking at internal quality assurance of higher education institutions, one set of standards and guidelines relates to student-centred

[60] ENQA, Standards and Guidelines for Quality Assurance in the European Higher Education Area, Helsinki 2005, p. 11.

[61] Ibid., p. 27.

[62] ENQA, Mapping the Implementation and Application of the ESG (Map-ESG Project)—Final report of the project Steering Group, ENQA 2011, p. 9.

[63] Kelo (2014, p. 149).

[64] Ibid., p. 150.

[65] The revision followed on the 2011 mapping of the implementation and application of the ESG and was deemed necessary to improve their clarity, applicability and usefulness. The revision of the ESG was endorsed in the 2012 Bucharest Communiqué. See: ENQA, Mapping the Implementation and Application of the ESG (Map-ESG Project)—Final report of the project Steering Group, ENQA 2011, p. 24 and ENQA et al., Standards and Guidelines for Quality Assurance in the European Higher Education Area (ESG), Brussels 2015.

[66] Equip, Comparative analysis of the ESG 2015 and ESG 2005, 2016, p. 1.

[67] ENQA et al., Standards and Guidelines for Quality Assurance in the European Higher Education Area (ESG), Brussels 2015, p. 9.

learning, teaching and assessment. For this topic, the standard reads: "Institutions should ensure that the programmes are delivered in a way that encourages students to take an active role in creating the learning process, and that the assessment of students reflects this approach".[68] The corresponding guidelines indicate that implementation of student-centred learning and teaching, among others, uses a variety of pedagogical methods, promotes mutual respect within the learner-teacher relationship, and has appropriate procedures to handle students' complaints.

3 The Lisbon Recognition Convention

The Convention on the Recognition of Qualifications concerning Higher Education in the European Region, also known as the Lisbon Recognition Convention (LRC), was adopted by the Council of Europe and UNESCO in 1997.[69] The instrument is to be considered the main document on academic recognition in the European region. The LRC was introduced following major changes that had taken place in higher education.[70] These drastic changes meant that the previous Conventions adopted between the 1950s and 1960s were out-of-date. As the Convention's preamble shows, the LRC consolidated a number of earlier Conventions and has been said to be a "replacement Convention",[71] the idea being that ultimately all previous Conventions adopted between the 1950s through the early 1990s would be replaced.[72]

The LRC builds on and arches over previous Conventions. Whereas in the period of the 1950s through early 1990s instruments related to specific topics such as admission to universities, equivalence of periods of university study, and recognition of university qualifications,[73] the LRC includes provisions on all of these subjects in its Sections IV through VI. However, the LRC consists of provisions other than

---

[68] Ibid., p. 12.

[69] Convention on the Recognition of Qualifications concerning Higher Education in the European Region, Council of Europe and UNESCO, 11 April 1997, ETS—No. 165. The Convention is referred to as the Lisbon Recognition Convention or LRC.

[70] Zgaga (2014, p. 22).

[71] Previous Conventions can however continue to apply between signatories to the LRC in their relations with other States who are Party to those Conventions but not to the LRC. See: Council of Europe and UNESCO, Explanatory Report to the Convention on the Recognition of Qualifications concerning Higher Education in the European Region, 11 April 1997, ETS—No. 165, p. 25 and Article XI.4(1)(a) Lisbon Recognition Convention.

[72] Council of Europe and UNESCO, Explanatory Report to the Convention on the Recognition of Qualifications concerning Higher Education in the European Region, 11 April 1997, ETS—No. 165, p. 25.

[73] In particular, the LRC now arches over the following conventions: European Convention on the Equivalence of Diplomas leading to Admission to Universities, 11 December 1953, ETS—No. 15; European Convention on the Equivalence of Periods of University Study, 15 December 1956, ETC—No. 21; European Convention on the Academic Recognition of University Qualifications, 14 December 1959, ETS—No. 32; Convention on the Recognition of Studies, Diplomas and Degrees concerning Higher Education in the States belonging to the Europe Region, Paris 21 December 1979;

those consolidating the earlier Conventions. For example, the LRC introduced a new provision on the recognition of qualifications held by refugees and displaced persons (Section VII). In sum, the LRC consists of 11 sections aimed at realising mobility through recognition. The preamble to the LRC confirms that its main aim is for individuals to benefit from the diversity of education systems by facilitating the efforts of individuals to pursue studies in higher education in other countries. Moreover, the LRC points out that recognition of "studies, certificates, diplomas and degrees" obtained in other countries of the European region is an important measure for the promotion of academic mobility among the States party to the LRC.[74]

3.1 The LRC: International or European Law? Explaining the LRC from an EU Law Perspective

By now it is clear that the LRC does not originate from the EU legal order. Indeed, the Convention's scope on the European region includes not only the EU with its 27 Member States, but a total of 56 Parties.[75] In fact, the Convention may be said to have expanded its reach well beyond the European region, as States such as New Zealand, Canada, and Tajikistan have either signed and/or ratified the Convention. This global application of the LRC attests to the international law nature of the Convention—even though its primary focus is on the European region.[76] The question may therefore be posed how the EU Member States were able to become involved in such a Convention on recognition in 1997 long after the start of European cooperation. In the TFEU, Article 351 ensures that agreements concluded between Member States and third countries before 1 January 1958 (or before a Member State's accession to the EU) are not affected by the EU Treaties. This provision therefore upholds pre-existing international agreements. However, considering the introduction of the LRC in 1997, this provision does not appear to be applicable.[77]

How should the LRC be understood then in light of the EU legal order? In particular, it is necessary to examine what consequence the international law status of the LRC has in relation to the EU legal order. To start, all Council of Europe conventions

European Convention on the General Equivalence of Periods of University Study, 6 November 1990, ETS—No. 138.

[74] Preamble Lisbon Recognition Convention.

[75] See Council of Europe, 'Chart of signatures and ratifications of Treaty 165', https://www.coe.int/en/web/conventions/full-list/-/conventions/treaty/165/signatures?p_auth=t2Zxa3nR.

[76] Benoît-Rohmer and Klebes (2005, p. 13).

[77] While one of the conventions replaced by the LRC did precede European cooperation, the other three conventions it replaced did not. See European Convention on the Equivalence of Periods of University Study, 15 December 1956, ETS—No. 21; European Convention on the Academic Recognition of University Qualifications, 14 December 1959, ETS—No. 32; Convention on the Recognition of Studies, Diplomas and Degrees concerning Higher Education in the States belonging to the Europe Region, Paris 21 December 1979; European Convention on the General Equivalence of Periods of University Study, 6 November 1990, ETS—No. 138.

are considered international treaties within the meaning of the Vienna Convention on the Law of Treaties.[78] We may furthermore find confirmation of the international law status of instruments originating from the Council of Europe in EU law. For example, Article 220 TFEU prescribes that the EU is to establish appropriate forms of cooperation with particular international organisations, one of which is the Council of Europe. Indeed, the Council of Europe has a special status in the EU Treaties. To this effect, Article 165(3) TFEU indicates that "the Union and the Member States shall foster cooperation with third countries and the competent international organisations in the field of education and sport, in particular the Council of Europe".[79] In the 2007 Memorandum of Understanding (MoU) concluded between the Council of Europe and the EU both parties pledged to cooperate by exchanging views on their activities and implementing common strategies and programmes for particular areas.[80] Education constitutes one of these areas of shared interest. The Council of Europe and the EU cooperate to build a knowledge-based society and democratic culture in Europe. They also support the Bologna Process, education networks, and student exchanges at all levels while enhancing synergies and avoiding duplication of efforts.[81] It is clear that, within the context of the Bologna Process, the Council of Europe is primarily responsible for recognition of qualifications through the LRC. By contrast, the EU's role was considered to consist primarily of providing financial support through the Erasmus programme.[82]

Interestingly, the LRC is a Council of Europe convention to which the EU Member States are Parties—not the EU. Therefore, we may ask what consequences this has when qualifications of EU citizens are in need of recognition. Such a situation occurred in *Commission v. Austria*. In this case, Austria was found to maintain qualification requirements for access to higher education for persons originating from other Member States that resulted in a heavier burden for them than its own nationals. In particular, students had to prove that their qualification gave access to the subsequent course of study in the state of qualification. For students from other Member States, this meant that they essentially had to fulfil access criteria in both the state of qualification and in Austria. According to the Court, access to education (thereby including academic recognition) was subject to EU law, meaning that the principle of non-discrimination was to be respected. Maintaining criteria that weighed more heavily on other Member State nationals was considered discriminatory which could only be allowed if justified and proportionate.[83] Austria attempted to justify the differential treatment by indicating, among others, that its national law was consistent with the LRC. The Court here confirmed the consequences of

---

[78] Benoît-Rohmer and Klebes (2005, pp. 11 and 13).

[79] In fact, a similar clause on cooperation exists in regard to cooperation on culture and is laid down in Article 167(3) TFEU.

[80] Memorandum of Understanding between the Council of Europe and the European Union, May 2007 Strasbourg, p. 3.

[81] Ibid., pp. 3 and 6.

[82] Juncker (2006, p. 15).

[83] Case C-147/03 *Commission v. Austria*, ECLI:EU:C:2005:427, para. 46–48.

Article 351 TFEU mentioned above. In particular, rights and obligations arising from agreements concluded pre-accession may generally be maintained although possible incompatibilities with Treaty provisions must be remedied.[84] However, in case of later agreements, such obligations may be upheld only in relation to third countries but not in intra-community relations.[85]

In general, international agreements concluded by Member States become part of the national legal orders of the Member States. This also means that—as part of national law—these international agreements would have to yield to norms of EU law.[86] Indeed, it followed from *Commission v. Austria* that recognition of academic qualifications is covered by EU law since it constitutes a condition of access to education. However, while this does mean the principle of non-discrimination applies when holders of academic qualifications seek access to education in other Member States, i.e. they must be treated equally, this does not result in detailed rights to recognition of their academic qualifications. The continued application of the LRC is therefore likely explained by the limited competence in the area of education and prohibition of harmonisation contained in Article 165(4) TFEU which mean that, to date, the LRC is the only instrument that provides procedural requirements for academic recognition procedures in relation to higher education. Furthermore, the special cooperation with the Council of Europe as attested by Articles 165(3) and 220 TFEU also appears to sustain the application of the LRC in EU Member States' legal orders.

The point of this discussion is not to challenge the existence of the Convention. Rather, it is to ultimately arrive at a situation where the system for recognition in the EU can be said to uphold important principles such as legal certainty by providing consistent procedural safeguards applicable across the EU. The LRC can be said to provide such safeguards since it establishes rights and obligations for individuals and parties recognising qualifications. However, from an EU law perspective the protection associated with these rights and duties is limited by the LRC's status outside the EU legal order and lack of involvement of the CJEU in protecting these rights. An interesting avenue to explore in this respect would be whether the EU could become party to the LRC.[87] The LRC itself opens the possibility for EU accession in Article XI.3(3) of the Convention. In particular, the EU's accession to the LRC is made conditional upon an explicit request by the Member States, something which does not appear to have happened yet.[88] On the side of the EU, it is able to conclude

[84] Ibid., para. 72.

[85] Ibid., para. 73. See also Rosas (2011, pp. 1317–1320).

[86] Rosas (2011, p. 1314).

[87] The EU is already part to some Council of Europe Treaties. See: Council of Europe, 'Treaty list for a specific State: European Union', https://www.coe.int/en/web/conventions/by-non-member-states-of-the-coe-or-the-european-union?module=treaties-full-list-signature&CodePays=1&CodeSignatureEnum=&DateStatus=07-24-2025&CodeMatieres=.

[88] Although here too some ambiguity exists. At the side of the Council of Europe, the LRC is mentioned as one of the Conventions on the Treaty list for the EU, paired with its general adoption date and general date on its entry into force. However, on the list of signatories to the LRC the EU is mentioned under the category "International Organisations" followed

international agreements that bind its institutions and its Member States. This means that if the EU enters into an international agreement, that agreement becomes an integral part of the EU legal order thus binding Member States following Article 216(2) TFEU.

Of course, such integration into the EU legal order is paired with certain consequences. In terms of hierarchy, an international agreement acceded to by the EU would rank below primary EU law and above secondary legislation.[89] Furthermore, such international agreements could produce direct effect, as long as the provisions of the agreement are clear, precise, and unconditional.[90] Accession would therefore have as its main effect to ensure that provisions of the LRC could be pulled into the scope of the EU legal order thereby including observance by the CJEU.[91] While perhaps the potential positioning of the LRC between primary and secondary legislation may result in a somewhat peculiar relationship to other legislation on recognition of qualifications (most notably the Professional Qualifications Directive),[92] the possibility of direct effect and involvement of the CJEU can be considered positive to support the uniform interpretation and application of the LRC across the Member States. Nevertheless, as of yet there appears to be no evidence supporting a possible accession of the EU to the LRC. This means the Convention remains outside the scope of EU law. Despite this status, the Convention remains essential for the recognition of academic qualifications in the EU. The following sections explore the provisions of the Convention in-depth.

3.2 From Principles to Practice: The LRC's Subsidiary Texts, Committee, and Networks

A notable aspect of the LRC is that it is rather general in nature since it lays down key principles on which recognition should be based.[93] One such principle is that States may maintain more favourable provisions on recognition and possibility to

by an "a" for accession. However, no date is included to indicate when such accession would have occurred. See: Council of Europe, 'Chart of signatures and ratifications of Treaty 165', https://www.coe.int/en/web/conventions/by-non-member-states-of-the-coe-or-the-european-union?module=signatures-by-treaty&treatynum=165. In relation to the EU, a search of its main legislative database Eur-lex yielded no results confirming the EU's possible accession to the LRC.

[89] Mohay (2017, p. 157).

[90] Grimonprez (2020, pp. 191–192).

[91] As such, Council of Europe legislation is to be considered "exogenic" to the EU legal order and outside the scope of law for which the CJEU ensures observance. This changes upon accession of the EU to a Council of Europe instrument which would become part of the EU legal order. See Grimonprez (2020, p. 184).

[92] For more on the relationship between the LRC and Professional Qualifications Directive see Chapter "Re-Imagining the System for the Recognition of Qualifications in the EU" of this contribution.

[93] De Bruin (2014, p. 211).

maintain existing agreements containing such favourable provisions or adopt new ones.[94] Particular mention is made here of future or existing agreements in the context of the EU, the Nordic Council, and the Commonwealth.[95] Apart from such general provisions, additional instructions and guidance are elaborated in the subsidiary texts to the Convention.[96] These contribute to the implementation of the LRC and must be read in parallel with the Convention. The LRC implementation process is supervised, promoted and facilitated by a Committee, consisting of one representative of each Party, as well as the European Network of National Information Centres on academic mobility and recognition (the ENIC Network).[97] The Committee is tasked with supervising the implementation of the Convention and has the competence to adopt recommendations, declarations, protocols and models of good practice.[98] Over the course of time, several subsidiary texts have been adopted by the Committee. Existing documents are recommendations on the qualifications held by refugees, the recognition of joint degrees, the use of qualifications frameworks in the recognition of foreign qualifications, and criteria and procedures for the assessment of foreign qualifications. Moreover, statements and codes of good practice have been adopted by that same Committee.

Next to the Committee, the ENIC Network is also of crucial importance to implement the LRC. That Network was created by the Council of Europe and UNESCO in 1994 by a merger of two organisations, the NEIC Network of the Council of Europe and the NIB Network of UNESCO.[99] Furthermore, the ENIC Network already had a pre-existing counterpart in the European Community. That network was created by the European Commission in 1984 and was named the National Academic Recognition Information Centres (NARIC Network).[100] Even if the EU and the Council of Europe and UNESCO had their separate networks with different purposes, the two networks decided to work together from 2004 onwards under the auspices of the LRC, an agreement that was solidified in their Charter of Activities and Services.[101] This means that in the EU, the EEA, and Turkey organisations may be considered ENICs and NARICs *at the same time*. Outside the EU, EEA, and Turkey, one may only find ENICs.[102] In line with the LRC, the national role of ENIC is to facilitate access to authoritative and accurate information on the higher education system and

---

[94] Article II.3 Lisbon Recognition Convention.

[95] Council of Europe and UNESCO, Explanatory Report to the Convention on the Recognition of Qualifications concerning Higher Education in the European Region, 11 April 1997, ETS—No. 165, p. 11.

[96] De Bruin (2014, p. 21 1).

[97] Article X.1 and Article X.2(1) Lisbon Recognition Convention.

[98] Article X.2(5) Lisbon Recognition Convention.

[99] Article X.1(b) Lisbon Recognition Convention; Council of Europe and UNESCO, Explanatory Report to the Convention on the Recognition of Qualifications concerning Higher Education in the European Region, 11 April 1997, ETS—No. 165, p. 24.

[100] Zgaga (2014, p. 2 3).

[101] Terry (2008, p. 12); Joint ENIC/NARIC Charter of Activities and Services, Council of Europe and UNESCO, 9 June 2004.

[102] Bergan (2009a, p. 43).

qualifications of the country in which it is located, facilitate access to information on the higher education systems and qualifications of the other Parties, and give advice or information on recognition matters and assessment of qualifications, in accordance with national laws and regulations.[103] It is therefore clear that the ENICs play an essential role in providing the right information to credential evaluators and other parties, as they are often faced with the complexity of an abundance of information that is not per se authoritative, adequate or relevant. Apart from these duties related to the provision of information, ENICs may also be granted a competence under national law enabling them to make recognition decisions.[104]

3.3 Core Definitions of the LRC

Essential to the LRC is the concept of "higher education". This is defined as any type of course of study or training at postsecondary level which is recognised by the relevant authorities of a Party as belonging to its higher education system. The LRC therefore requires a diploma to be recognised nationally in order to benefit from recognition. If a diploma is not considered part of the national higher education system, it cannot be recognised under the LRC. In some countries where accreditation or recognition at central level is not necessary for an institution to offer higher education courses, this criterion may be decisive in whether or not a qualification can be recognised. This can especially form issues for graduates of private institutions who have not been recognised as part of the national higher education system.[105]

---

[103] Article IX.2(2) Lisbon Recognition Convention.

[104] Council of Europe and UNESCO, Explanatory Report to the Convention on the Recognition of Qualifications concerning Higher Education in the European Region, 11 April 1997, ETS—No. 165, p. 22.

[105] For example, up until the adoption of the 2011 Bundesgesetz über die Förderung der Hochschulen und die Koordination im schweizerischen Hochschulbereich (Hochschulförderung- und -koordinationsgesetz, HFKG)—or Higher Education Act (HEdA) in English—Switzerland did not require higher education institutions to obtain prior authorisation in order to offer higher education courses, organise examinations, or issue private degrees. These private institutions were nevertheless not considered to be a part of the country's public higher education sector. In terms of the labour market, "Swiss tradition has been to allow clients or the labour market itself to decide whether a private institution offers education quality rather than to leave this decision up to the State". If an individual decided to go abroad with his or her private degree, it would be "up to the national authorities in the host country" to decide whether to recognise the degree issued by a private institution. However, if the host country decided that a qualification had to be issued by a recognised/accredited/authorised higher education institution, holders of a degree from a private university may have come up empty handed due to the lack of a check as to the quality of their higher education institution. See: Federal Department of Home Affairs FDHA—State Secretariat for Education and Research SER, Validity of degrees issued by private institutions in Switzerland—Office circular, at: https://www.eda.admin.ch/content/dam/countries/countries-content/china/en/100930_SER_Office_circular_en.pdf. Another example of possible issues faced by holders of diplomas from private institutions under EU law can be seen in the *Panagiotopoulou* case. In this case, the Court of First Instance ruled that there is no EU legislation on how to interpret degrees issued by private

How then does the LRC define a qualification? The LRC distinguishes two types of qualifications: higher education qualifications and qualifications giving access to higher education. Whereas the former can be "any degree, diploma or other certificate issued by a competent authority attesting the successful completion of a higher education programme", the latter refer to "any diploma or other certificate issued by a competent authority attesting the successful completion of an education programme and giving the holder of the qualification the right to be considered for admission to higher education". Admission must subsequently be distinguished from access. The latter term is to be understood as the right of an individual to apply for higher education.[106] Admission occurs afterwards and entails that an applicant who has been deemed qualified is actually allowed to pursue higher education studies.[107]

Next, competent authorities under the LRC are those in charge of recognition (i.e. bodies making binding decisions on foreign qualifications). Competent authorities tasked with recognising foreign qualifications may either be central authorities or, in federal states, decentralised authorities. Either way, these authorities are bound by the provisions of the LRC and must take necessary measures to ensure transposition of the Convention.[108] Countries that are Party to the LRC may also delegate the competence to make recognition decisions to higher education institutions, in which case the text of the Convention must be transmitted to the institutions involved and the State must do everything possible "to encourage the favourable consideration and application of its provisions".[109] It is important, however, to note that competent recognition authorities may be distinguished from other authorities competent for

institutions in light of the EU institutions' recruitment procedures. The Court considered that the selection board for the competition at stake had to consider whether Ms Panagiotopoulou had produced a diploma certifying university studies under Greek law. Considering that Greek law did not consider the diploma issued by a private institution as a higher education degree, the selection board also did not have to consider the degree as being of that level. The fact that Panagiotopoulou had obtained recognition of her Greek degree in the UK did not change this, since Member States were considered free to confer greater effects on foreign qualifications than those recognised by the law in which they were awarded. However, any such effect was to remain restricted to the Member State recognising the qualifications (i.e. prior recognitions are not transferrable across Member States). The Court thereby ruled that there was no obligation for Member States to have procedures for the validation of diplomas from private institutes. In paragraph 58, it argued that"it is within the powers of the Member States in the matter of the organization of education to define the status of private educational institutes operating on their territory and to determine whether the qualifications awarded by those institutes may be given official recognition". See Case T-16/90 Panagiotopoulou, EU:T:1992:11. The Court later, however, ruled in *Neri* that an impossibility for any examination, and ultimately recognition, of degrees issued by private institutions was not proportionate to the objective put forward by the Italian government to ensure high standards of university education. See Case C-153/02 Neri, ECLI:EU:C:2003:614, para. 46–52.

[106] Article I Lisbon Recognition Convention.

[107] Article I Lisbon Recognition Convention. In a sense, a parallel could be drawn to recognition under the Professional Qualifications Directive where recognition is to be distinguished from access to the profession. However, different in the realm of academic recognition is that access is actually the possibility to apply while admission means the actual possibility to pursue studies.

[108] Article II.1(1) Lisbon Recognition Convention.

[109] Article II.1(2) Lisbon Recognition Convention.

other parts of higher education.[110] In a similar vein, the definition of competent recognition authority under the LRC already shows that different parties such as higher education institutions can be designated as competent authorities.

The final essential definition of the LRC of course concerns the term recognition. This is taken to entail "a formal acknowledgement by a competent authority of the value of a foreign educational qualification with a view to access to educational and/or employment activities".[111] The additional focus on employment activities is surprising considering that the LRC's preamble only makes mention of academic mobility and recognition to facilitate such mobility. The mention of recognition to access employment activities is indicative of an overlap between the EU instruments on professional recognition and non-EU instruments on academic recognition—while also showing that the LRC's application is not just restricted to the realm of academic recognition.

3.4 The LRC's Procedural Safeguards & Transparency Requirements

Section III of the Lisbon Recognition Convention contains its basic principles aimed at ensuring that procedures for the recognition of higher education degrees operate smoothly. In Section III, individuals applying for recognition are granted assurance of their right to an assessment of their qualifications. Equally, the principle of non-discrimination,[112] entailing that no other circumstance other than the qualifications of the individual concerned may be considered during the recognition procedure, can be found in this part of the LRC.[113] Apart from a duty to provide information on the structure of their education systems, Parties to the LRC are also obliged to ensure that the procedures for recognition are transparent, coherent and reliable.[114] However, not just the procedures for recognition must be transparent. An important element facilitating recognition processes which is encouraged by the LRC relates to the transparency of qualifications and to the quality and status of higher education institutions and programmes in the countries party to the LRC. Provisions related to such aspects may be found in Sections VIII and IX of the LRC.

---

[110] Council of Europe and UNESCO, Explanatory Report to the Convention on the Recognition of Qualifications concerning Higher Education in the European Region, 11 April 1997, ETS—No. 165, p. 7.

[111] Article I Lisbon Recognition Convention.

[112] N.B. the concept of non-discrimination is broader than the non-discrimination on the basis of nationality seen under EU free movement law. Non-discrimination in the LRC relates to gender, race, colour, disability, language, religion, political or other opinion, national, ethnic or social origin, association with a national minority, property, birth or other status, or any other grounds.

[113] Article III.1(2) Lisbon Recognition Convention.

[114] Articles III.4 and III.2 Lisbon Recognition Convention.

First, transparency of qualifications is essential in order to ensure that recognition procedures operate smoothly. To this end, the LRC supports the use of transparent descriptions of higher education qualifications,[115] such as the European Credit Transfer System (ECTS).[116] Transparency may equally be promoted through the use of the Diploma Supplement,[117] which explains the contents and form of the qualifications.[118] Whereas the Diploma Supplement was first proposed in the context of the LRC, the format for the document currently continues to be updated in the EU by a cooperation of the Council of Europe, UNESCO and the European Commission.[119] Another way of promoting transparency is through qualifications frameworks (e.g. National Qualifications Frameworks and/or overarching qualifications frameworks such as the QF-EHEA and the European Qualifications Framework for lifelong learning).[120]

As to transparency in relation to the status and quality of higher education institutions and programmes, countries Party to the LRC must ensure that adequate information is available stating whether or not a higher education institution or programme belongs to its national higher education system.[121] It is important for competent authorities recognising qualifications of individuals to know about the quality and status of an institution or programme as part of higher education in another country Party to the Convention in order to determine whether recognition of a qualification should be granted.[122] This aspect may be taken to relate particularly to quality assurance. In fact, when Parties to the LRC have a quality assurance system in place, competent authorities of the host country must take these structures and the results of quality assurance assessments into account when evaluating qualifications.[123] Exceptionally, recognition authorities do not need to investigate the quality of a qualification

[115] Article IX.1 Lisbon Recognition Convention.

[116] Council of Europe and UNESCO, Explanatory Report to the Convention on the Recognition of Qualifications concerning Higher Education in the European Region, 11 April 1997, ETS—No. 165, p. 22.

[117] See Sects. 2.2 and 4.1.1 of this chapter.

[118] Council of Europe and UNESCO, Explanatory Report to the Convention on the Recognition of Qualifications concerning Higher Education in the European Region, 11 April 1997, ETS—No. 165, p. 23.

[119] Article 5(2) Decision (EU) 2018/646 of the European Parliament and of the Council of 18 April 2018 on a common framework for the provision of better services for skills and qualifications (Europass) and repealing Decision No 2241/2004/EC, [2018] OJ L 112/42.

[120] Recommendation on the use of Qualifications Frameworks in the Recognition of Foreign Qualifications, the Committee of the Convention on the Recognition of Qualifications concerning Higher Education in the European Region, 19 June 2013, p. 5.

[121] Article VII.1 and VII.2 Lisbon Recognition Convention.

[122] Council of Europe and UNESCO, Explanatory Report to the Convention on the Recognition of Qualifications concerning Higher Education in the European Region, 11 April 1997, ETS—No. 165, pp. 20–21.

[123] Paragraph 31 Revised Recommendation on Criteria and Procedures for the Assessment of Foreign Qualifications (adopted by the Lisbon Recognition Convention Committee at its fifth meeting, Sèvres, 23 June 2010).

if it is placed in a self-certified or referenced National Qualifications Framework, due to there being an assumption that the qualification is quality assured in such a case.[124]

Taking into account the quality of higher education institutions and programmes is particularly relevant in light of the diversification of higher education which has led to the existence of many higher education institutions and programmes, some of which are privately run and financed.[125] In the case of such institutions, the explanatory report particularly notes that a lack of information on whether or not such an institution belongs to the national higher education system permits an authority in another country taking part in the LRC to withhold recognition. However, private institutions are not the only type of higher education institutions that are located outside the "regular" national education system. In fact, the diversification of higher education has led to an increase in higher education institutions established via transnational arrangements and to a rise in joint degrees. To this end, two subsidiary texts to the LRC specify how authorities should verify the quality of qualifications issued in the context of such arrangements: a Code of Good Practice in the Provision of Transnational Education and a Recommendation on the Recognition of Joint Degrees.[126] If the transnational education or joint degree does not comply with these texts, recognition would normally not be granted.[127] In order to provide adequate information on the status and quality of their higher education institutions and programmes and thus to facilitate assessments by other countries' competent authorities, Parties to the LRC must also maintain overviews of different types of higher education institutions belonging to their higher education system, a list of recognised institutions belonging to their higher education system, a description of higher education programmes, and a list of educational institutions located outside the country's territory but which are considered part of its higher education system.[128]

Turning away from the topic of transparency and refocussing on procedural requirements, one aspect that is of key importance in recognition procedures relates to the duration of such procedures. In this context, Article III.5 of the Lisbon Recognition Convention states that "decisions on recognition shall be made within a reasonable time limit specified beforehand by the competent authority and calculated from

[124] Recommendation on the use of Qualifications Frameworks in the Recognition of Foreign Qualifications, the Committee of the Convention on the Recognition of Qualifications concerning Higher Education in the European Region, 19 June 2013, p. 6.

[125] Council of Europe and UNESCO, Explanatory Report to the Convention on the Recognition of Qualifications concerning Higher Education in the European Region, 11 April 1997, ETS—No. 165, pp. 20–21.

[126] Paragraph 30 Revised Recommendation on Criteria and Procedures for the Assessment of Foreign Qualifications (adopted by the Lisbon Recognition Convention Committee at its fifth meeting, Sèvres, 23 June 2010).

[127] Explanatory Memorandum—Revised Recommendation on Criteria and Procedures for the Assessment of Foreign Qualifications (adopted by the Lisbon Recognition Convention Committee at its fifth meeting, Sèvres, 23 June 2010), p. 24; Explanatory memorandum—Revised Recommendation on the Recognition of Joint Degrees Adopted by the Committee of the Convention on the Recognition of Qualifications concerning Higher Education in the European Region on 29 February 2016 at its seventh meeting in Paris, France, p. 9.

[128] Article VIII.2 Lisbon Recognition Convention.

the time all necessary information in the case has been provided". Therefore, timely transmission of information is important considering the fact that the procedure can only start when "all necessary information" has been received.[129] No further specifications are made in the LRC as to which documents may be required. Instead, applicants must provide "adequate information", in good faith.[130] However, the Recommendation on Criteria and Procedures for the Assessment of Foreign Qualifications does specify that applicants should be provided with standardised information on the documentation required.

In some cases, an applicant may need to provide additional information on his or her qualifications. The higher education institutions that have issued a qualification have an obligation to provide further information to the applicant, institution or competent authority of the Member State in which recognition is sought.[131] There are nonetheless limits to what higher education institutions must do to satisfy such requests for information.[132] Examples of documentation to be provided by higher education institutions are transcripts of the relevant parts of the institution's records, information on courses taken, and information on grades that were obtained.[133]

Although under Article III.5 authorities have the obligation to specify the time limit before the recognition procedure is initiated, there is no fixed time limit set by the LRC. The explanatory report to the LRC recalls that the maximum time period for recognition procedures under the EU's Professional Qualifications Directive is four months, but does not enforce this time limit. That four-month limit is nevertheless reiterated in the Recommendation on Criteria and Procedures for the Assessment of Foreign Qualifications which specifies that "applications should be processed as promptly as possible, and the time of processing should not exceed four months". Importantly, "uncomplicated cases should, as a rule, be evaluated faster".[134]

Assuming that a national authority has set a time limit and has failed to take a timely decision, or in the event that the authority has taken a negative decision as to recognition, applicants must have the right to make an appeal according to Article III.5 of the Convention. How these appeals are organised is subject to the national

---

[129] The same is maintained under the Professional Qualifications Directive. According to Article 51(2) of the PQD, the time periods only start once the complete file has been submitted.

[130] Article III.3(2) Lisbon Recognition Convention.

[131] Article III.3(3) Lisbon Recognition Convention.

[132] This is especially the case if the qualifications concerned have been obtained a very long time ago, when the information needed can be found easily through other sources that are well known, or when the information requested cannot be accessed without extensive searches of archives; see Council of Europe and UNESCO, Explanatory Report to the Convention on the Recognition of Qualifications concerning Higher Education in the European Region, 11 April 1997, ETS—No. 165, p. 13.

[133] Ibid.

[134] Explanatory Memorandum—Revised Recommendation on Criteria and Procedures for the Assessment of Foreign Qualifications (adopted by the Lisbon Recognition Convention Committee at its fifth meeting, Sèvres, 23 June 2010), p. 15.

law of the country concerned and may therefore differ.[135] Applicants should be made aware of the possibilities to appeal early on in the procedure and must be made aware of formal aspects such as deadlines.[136]

If an individual is confronted with a refusal of his or her request for recognition, the Parties to the LRC have a duty to motivate their refusals of recognition.[137] This is in line with the responsibility of competent recognition authorities to demonstrate that an applicant does not fulfil the relevant requirements.[138] Furthermore, information must be provided of the "possible measures the applicant may take in order to obtain recognition at a later stage".[139] The explanatory report to the LRC subsequently confirms that in cases of refusals, applicants may need to undergo additional education, examinations or other measures.[140] The competent authority subsequently has the obligation to inform the applicant about the possibilities to make up for knowledge gaps.

Time limits, possibilities for appeals, motivated rejections, and possibilities to make up for knowledge that is lacking are some essential practical matters related to the recognition of one's qualifications. However, this list of practical recognition essentials is not entirely complete without specifications of the fees to be paid and provisions on possible translation of documents. Although the LRC itself does not provide indications as to these aspects, the Recommendation on Procedures and Criteria for the Assessment of Foreign Qualifications does. On the topic of procedural fees, the Recommendation specifies that authorities should consider providing assessments "as a public service free of charge'. Should this prove not to be feasible, "fees should be kept as low as possible and should not be so high as to constitute a barrier to the assessment of foreign qualifications". When deciding on the amount of the fees, authorities should take due account of the financial situation of applicants.[141]

Regarding translations, the Recommendation specifies that translation requirements should be "carefully weighed and clearly specified, especially as concerns the need for authorised translations by sworn translators". Indeed, costs for such authorised translations may cause the total costs of recognition procedures to rise

---

[135] Council of Europe and UNESCO, Explanatory Report to the Convention on the Recognition of Qualifications concerning Higher Education in the European Region, 11 April 1997, ETS—No. 165, pp. 13–14.

[136] Explanatory Memorandum—Revised Recommendation on Criteria and Procedures for the Assessment of Foreign Qualifications (adopted by the Lisbon Recognition Convention Committee at its fifth meeting, Sèvres, 23 June 2010), p. 14.

[137] Article III.5 Lisbon Recognition Convention.

[138] Article III.3(5) Lisbon Recognition Convention.

[139] Article III.5 Lisbon Recognition Convention.

[140] Council of Europe and UNESCO, Explanatory Report to the Convention on the Recognition of Qualifications concerning Higher Education in the European Region, 11 April 1997, ETS—No. 165, p. 14.

[141] Paragraph 22 Revised Recommendation on Criteria and Procedures for the Assessment of Foreign Qualifications (adopted by the Lisbon Recognition Convention Committee at its fifth meeting, Sèvres, 23 June 2010).

substantially. Use of transparency documents such as the Diploma Supplement is encouraged in order to reduce the need for translation of documents.[142]

3.5 The Body of the Lisbon Recognition Convention: Recognition in Different Situations

While the LRC consists of a total of 11 sections, four of these can be considered the "operational core" of the Convention,[143] as they include the provisions for recognition of various higher education qualifications. At its core, the LRC functions on the basis of a principle much resembling that of mutual recognition in the EU context,[144] namely qualifications giving the holder access to higher education in one Party should give the holder the same rights in the other Parties.[145] The LRC's second main principle is what Rauhvargers calls the "principle of substantial differences", a principle that is similar in both the LRC and the EU's Professional Qualifications Directive.[146] The principle implies a comparison of a foreign qualification with the prototype qualification in the host country.[147]

Emphasis should be placed on how higher education qualifications are assessed in the context of the LRC. The term "substantial differences" takes the diversity of higher education into account by recognising that there will usually be differences between corresponding qualifications.[148] Nevertheless, differences alone do not provide sufficient ground for non-recognition.[149] In order to establish when differences are *substantial*, additional information is provided in the Recommendation on Criteria and Procedures for the Assessment of Foreign Qualifications. One of the general principles of that document is the flexible application of international and national legal frameworks regulating recognition of higher education qualifications. If recognition as requested by the applicant cannot be granted, authorities

---

[142] Paragraph 23 Revised Recommendation on Criteria and Procedures for the Assessment of Foreign Qualifications (adopted by the Lisbon Recognition Convention Committee at its fifth meeting, Sèvres, 23 June 2010).

[143] Bergan and Rauhvargers (2005, p. 12).

[144] Case 120/78 *Rewe-Zentral AG (Cassis de Dijon)*, ECLI:EU:C:1979:42; Case C-340/89 *Vlassopoulou*, ECLI:EU:C:1991:193.

[145] Council of Europe and UNESCO, Explanatory Report to the Convention on the Recognition of Qualifications concerning Higher Education in the European Region, 11 April 1997, ETS—No. 165, p. 14.

[146] Rauhvargers (2009, p. 112).

[147] Ibid.

[148] Bergan (2009b, p. 17).

[149] Ibid.

should consider alternative means for recognition or partial recognition.[150] Moreover, if an applicant possesses certain qualifications which grant him or her certain formal rights, authorities in the host country should strive to grant applicants similar formal rights in the host country based on the qualification of the applicant.[151]

The Recommendation furthermore establishes assessment criteria that have been drawn up to increase the consistency and transparency of the procedures.[152] Paragraphs 18 and 34 of the Recommendation particularly promote consistency by encouraging competent recognition authorities to draw up inventories of "typical recognition cases" and by having past practice serve as a guide. When assessing higher education qualifications qualitative criteria must prevail over quantitative criteria. This means that aspects of a qualification related to length of study must be restricted and the assessment's main focus must be on "the quality of applicants' learning outcomes and qualifications".[153] Accordingly, authorities are encouraged to maintain flexible attitudes, as qualifications may be at the same level but differ in terms of content, workload, and learning outcomes. Substantial differences may then be found in relation to the learning outcomes of the applicant's qualification, the access to further activities (e.g. study, research, and employment) rendered possible by the applicant's qualification, key elements of the programme completed by the applicant, and the quality of the applicant's programme and/or institution of choice.[154]

Whereas the previous paragraphs have examined the general provisions on these principles, within the LRC these are concretised in Articles IV.1, IV.3, V.1 and VI.1. The principles are documented in four different Articles because of the multiple topics the LRC covers: recognition of qualifications giving access to higher education, recognition of periods of study, and recognition of higher education qualifications. Details on these different situations are discussed below.

---

[150] Paragraph 8 Revised Recommendation on Criteria and Procedures for the Assessment of Foreign Qualifications (adopted by the Lisbon Recognition Convention Committee at its fifth meeting, Sèvres, 23 June 2010).

[151] Paragraph 38 Revised Recommendation on Criteria and Procedures for the Assessment of Foreign Qualifications (adopted by the Lisbon Recognition Convention Committee at its fifth meeting, Sèvres, 23 June 2010).

[152] Paragraphs 10 and 11 Revised Recommendation on Criteria and Procedures for the Assessment of Foreign Qualifications (adopted by the Lisbon Recognition Convention Committee at its fifth meeting, Sèvres, 23 June 2010).

[153] Explanatory Memorandum—Revised Recommendation on Criteria and Procedures for the Assessment of Foreign Qualifications (adopted by the Lisbon Recognition Convention Committee at its fifth meeting, Sèvres, 23 June 2010), p. 14.

[154] Paragraph 37 Revised Recommendation on Criteria and Procedures for the Assessment of Foreign Qualifications (adopted by the Lisbon Recognition Convention Committee at its fifth meeting, Sèvres, 23 June 2010).

3.5.1 Recognition of Qualifications Giving Access to Higher Education

Under Section IV of the LRC, those who possess a qualification granting them access to higher education in one signatory State, may gain access in the other States party to the LRC unless a substantial difference can be shown between the qualifications the individual possesses and those which are required in the host Member State. Section IV relates particularly to the general requirements for access to higher education.[155] The term "general requirements" here must be understood as concerning the content of primary and secondary education. Here we again find the prioritisation of content over aspects such as duration, as the LRC explanatory report encourages those examining qualifications to consider the merits of the individual qualifications in question without having recourse to an automatic comparison of the length of study required to obtain the qualification.

Apart from secondary education qualifications, the Convention also allows for non-traditional qualifications (e.g. prior learning or work experience) to be recognised and therefore to give access to higher education if a State party to the Convention enables such access.[156] Moreover, some degrees do not originate from national education systems and are considered international access qualifications instead (e.g. the International Baccalaureate). Provisions on the topic of international access qualifications can be found in a Recommendation (i.e. a subsidiary text to the LRC).[157]

When it is clear that a qualification may be recognised in the context of the LRC, admission to higher education may still depend on aspects other than the suitability of the applicant's qualifications. For example, a prospective student may be required to have a qualification in a specific field in order to access a certain course of study or may have to take an examination before being able to access higher education. According to Article IV.4, Parties to the LRC are allowed to demand such additional specific requirements equally from holders of qualifications from the other Parties. As to examinations, Article IV.5 specifies that Parties to the LRC may require individuals to have taken such an examination before their migration if that examination is required for general access to higher education. Alternatively, Parties to the LRC may provide for alternative means for the fulfilment of this requirement. Nevertheless, even if an applicant possesses a qualification giving access to higher education, is specialised in the required field, and has taken the necessary examinations, admission may still be restricted in the sense of a *numerus clausus* or language requirements.[158]

---

155 Article IV.1 Lisbon Recognition Convention.

156 Article IV.8 Lisbon Recognition Convention.

157 Recommendation on International Access Qualifications Adopted by the Intergovernmental Committee of the Lisbon Recognition Convention in Vilnius on June 16, 1999.

158 Article IV.6 and IV.7 Lisbon Recognition Convention.

3.5.2 Recognition of Periods of Study

Recalling the typology of the recognition of qualifications, academic recognition may serve two purposes: access to a full education programme or temporary access to certain courses part of an education programme that a student follows abroad instead of in the home country. The latter of the two was described as academic recognition *by substitution*. Most of the LRC pertains to cumulative academic recognition. However, Section V on the recognition of periods of study illustrates that the LRC also provides for academic recognition by substitution.

Indeed, periods of study that are completed within the framework of a higher education programme in another State that is a Party to the LRC and which are needed for the completion of higher education also follow the general principle: they should be recognised unless there are substantial differences.[159] In the context of the recognition of periods of study, substantial differences particularly relate to discrepancies in the courses taken abroad in relation to the courses that normally form part of the full education programme in the home country. Moreover, Article V.3 specifically ensures that recognition is facilitated when two higher education institutions (or competent authorities) in different countries that are a Party to the LRC have concluded an agreement or when the higher education institution in the host country has issued a certificate attesting successful completion of the period of study.

3.5.3 Recognition of Higher Education Qualifications

Section VI ensures that higher education qualifications are recognised unless substantial differences can be shown between the qualifications of the applicant and those required in the host country.[160] Considering the LRC's primary aim to realise academic recognition, one may be tempted to assume that Section VI of the LRC relates exclusively to academic recognition by accumulation. However, this may prove to be an incorrect assumption. According to Article VI.3, recognition under Section VI can be said to have the primary goal of ensuring one's access to further higher education studies, including relevant examinations and/or preparation for doctorates. However, Section VI has a secondary purpose in realising the use of an academic title and even a tertiary purpose, namely facilitating access to the labour market.

Whereas the secondary purpose of Section VI may initially seem to relate exclusively to academic recognition, there is an overlap with the world of professional recognition. Even though the use of academic titles was traditionally considered academic recognition, it may also be considered *de facto* professional recognition.[161] This was made particularly clear in the *Kraus* case from the Court of Justice of the

[159] Article V.1 Lisbon Recognition Convention.

[160] Article VI.1 Lisbon Recognition Convention.

[161] Garben (2011a, p. 138).

EU (CJEU), where the individual concerned was unable to use the title of his foreign degree in Germany, since this had to be authorised. Although the Court concluded that Member States were allowed to maintain prior authorisation procedures to ascertain whether a foreign title was properly awarded, it made some interesting considerations in relation to the use of academic titles on the labour market. First, it noted that an academic title may be a prerequisite for access to certain professions.[162] Second, having a certain academic title could be beneficial for the individual concerned in light of the amount of remuneration to be acquired.[163] Lastly, having an academic title could support establishment in another Member State.[164] The *Kraus* case therefore shows that recognition of a higher education qualification for the use of an academic title can be both academic as well as professional recognition.

However, the LRC's objective of recognising completed higher education qualifications is even more indicative of the instrument's overlapping purpose in realising both academic as well as professional recognition. From a theoretical perspective, the combination of the two types of recognition in one instrument seems logical. After obtaining a bachelor's degree, one may decide to either access the labour market with that degree or use the same degree to access master's studies. After completion of a master's degree, the same situation occurs: access may be sought either to doctoral studies or to the labour market. In that sense, the LRC is well-adapted to reality. Nevertheless, the LRC's provisions on the recognition of higher education qualifications and access to the labour market may venture into the realm of professional recognition, an area which is in principle governed by EU law. Although the Union has been quite active on *de jure* professional recognition with the Professional Qualifications Directive, it has not made use of its Article 53 TFEU competence to take action to the benefit of *de facto* professional recognition. Nevertheless, in the context of the EU the interrelationship between the PQD and LRC can be considered in light of the *lex specialis* principle, meaning that the PQD takes precedence in the case of regulated professions. Nevertheless, an area of overlap may arise between the LRC and *de facto* professional recognition.[165]

Notwithstanding the fact that the scope of the LRC appears to be limited to *de facto* professional recognition, an opening exists enabling the LRC to also play a role in *de jure* professional recognition. Article VI.4 states that assessments of higher education qualifications may take the form of advice for general employment purposes, advice to educational institutions for admission, and advice to any other competent recognition authority. In the terms of the LRC, an assessment is "the written appraisal or evaluation of an individual's foreign qualifications by a competent body". Depending on the result of that assessment, recognition may be

---

[162] Case C-19/92 Kraus, ECLI:EU:C:1993:125, para. 20,

[163] Ibid., para. 21.

[164] Ibid., para. 22.

[165] Ibid., p. 21. This potential area of overlap between the LRC and EU law is discussed further in Chapter "Re-Imagining the System for the Recognition of Qualifications in the EU", Sect. 2 of this contribution.

granted by a competent recognition authority.[166] Nevertheless, an assessment may also result in advice to a competent recognition authority taking the decision or a statement addressed to individuals, institutions, potential employers or others.[167] Whereas higher education institutions may be responsible for both the assessment and the recognition of higher education qualifications, this may be different in terms of the labour market—and especially for EU Member States. ENICs and NARICs, which in the EU Member States are the same organisation, play an important role in all types of recognition (i.e. academic recognition, *de jure* and *de facto* professional recognition).[168] In particular, the ENIC/NARICs may have a competence on professional recognition and will cooperate with the national coordinator *and* the competent authorities for *de jure* professional recognition in the EU.[169] This means that, in EU Member States, ENIC/NARICs have the following roles: (1) giving advice, issuing statements or even granting *de facto* professional recognition; and (2) advising competent recognition authorities which finally take a recognition decision (i.e. the ENIC/NARIC will assess the qualifications and advise the authority on whether or not to recognise a qualification).

3.5.4 Recognition of Qualifications Held by Refugees, Displaced Persons and Persons in a Refugee-Like Situation

Recognition of the qualifications held by refugees, displaced persons and persons in a refugee-like situation may be considered as having a completely different character from "regular" recognition procedures since evidence of qualifications may often not be present. In order to encourage the recognition of the qualifications held by refugees, Article VII of the LRC indicates that parties shall take feasible and reasonable steps to develop procedures to assess whether refugees fulfil requirements to access higher education or employment—even where qualifications cannot be proven through documentary evidence. This Article commits Parties to the LRC to adopt flexible attitudes when recognising qualifications of refugees.[170] The explanatory report explains that Parties to the LRC may, for example, decide to grant a provisional

---

[166] It may be recalled that a competent recognition authority is 'a body officially charged with making binding decisions on the recognition of foreign qualifications'; Article I Lisbon Recognition Convention.

[167] Paragraph 11 Revised Recommendation on Criteria and Procedures for the Assessment of Foreign Qualifications (adopted by the Lisbon Recognition Convention Committee at its fifth meeting, Sèvres, 23 June 2010).

[168] Preamble Joint ENIC/NARIC Charter of Activities and Services, Council of Europe and UNESCO, 9 June 2004.

[169] Section II Joint ENIC/NARIC Charter of Activities and Services, Council of Europe and UNESCO, 9 June 2004.

[170] Council of Europe and UNESCO, Explanatory Report to the Convention on the Recognition of Qualifications concerning Higher Education in the European Region, 11 April 1997, ETS—No. 165, p. 20.

recognition on the basis of a sworn statement or may provide for special examinations to allow refugees to prove that they do possess a certain level of knowledge.

Article VII of the LRC may have been first adopted in the context of the conflicts in former Yugoslavia in the 1990s, but its relevance became all the more important in Europe after 2015.[171] The refugee crisis involved massive displacement of populations and refugees who were trying to reach Europe and led to a sharp increase in the number of refugees, displaced persons and persons in a refugee-like situation which prompted the Committee of the LRC to adopt a statement.[172] In it, the Committee invited the Parties to the LRC to fully implement Article VII by implementing procedures for the recognition of refugee qualifications before the end of 2018 and furthermore invited the LRC Committee's Bureau to develop a Recommendation. That Recommendation was adopted in November 2017 and provides for principles to be implemented by the LRC Parties at the national level.[173] The Recommendation's central principle is the entitlement of refugees to have their qualifications or periods of study assessed when applying for admission to a study programme or for the purpose of seeking employment. However, it is important to note that the more flexible procedures for recognition may only be applied to those refugees whose qualifications are inadequately documented. If this is the case, assessments must be provided at no or at low cost, must be transparent and must be communicated to refugees as soon as possible after their arrival in a country. By contrast, if there is full documentation of a refugee's qualifications, he or she is entitled to a "regular" assessment under the LRC.[174]

Another important aspect of the Recommendation entails the cooperation and mutual trust between recognition authorities of the Parties to the LRC. Refugees may arrive in one country where they commence a recognition procedure only to move to another country or be forced to move elsewhere. In this case, there is no need for them to initiate the recognition process anew, as authorities are encouraged to make use of the information gathered by the competent authority in the first country so as to not waste resources.[175] Parties to the Convention may furthermore

---

[171] Explanatory memorandum to the Recommendation on the Recognition of Qualifications Held by Refugees, Displaced Persons and Persons in a Refugee-like Situation, Council of Europe and UNESCO, 14 November 2017, DGII/EDU/HE (2017) 3 rev.

[172] Statement of the Committee of the Convention on the Recognition of Qualifications concerning Higher Education in the European Region on the recognition of the qualifications held by refugees, displaced persons and persons in a refugee-like situation, February 2016.

[173] Recommendation on the Recognition of Qualifications Held by Refugees, Displaced Persons and Persons in a Refugee-like Situation, Council of Europe and UNESCO, 14 November 2017, DGII/EDU/HE (2017) 3 rev.

[174] General consideration 3 Recommendation on the Recognition of Qualifications Held by Refugees, Displaced Persons and Persons in a Refugee-like Situation, Council of Europe and UNESCO, 14 November 2017, DGII/EDU/HE (2017) 3 rev.

[175] Nevertheless, this reasoning does not apply to regulated professions; Explanatory memorandum to the Recommendation on the Recognition of Qualifications Held by Refugees, Displaced Persons and Persons in a Refugee-like Situation, Council of Europe and UNESCO, 14 November 2017, DGII/EDU/HE (2017) 3 rev, p. 12.

create a background document, meaning an authoritative description recording the qualifications the applicant may have obtained with all the available documents.[176]

4 EU Action on (Academic) Recognition

So far, this chapter has focused on recognition-related instruments of non-EU actors. It has thereby been established previously that the possibility for their activity originates from the supporting competence held by the EU on academic recognition in the context of its broader education competence (Art. 165 TFEU). However, the existence and activity of actors beyond the EU does not mean that the EU itself is not active. In fact, it may be argued that the EU is becoming increasingly active on academic recognition and education and making use of Article 165 TFEU as a legal basis. Early action on academic recognition started in the 1970s and has evolved into the creation of a fully-fledged European Education Area which was to be completed by 2025 (EEA-2025). Contrary to the EHEA connected to the Bologna Process, the EEA-2025 is very much embedded in the EU legal framework. Interestingly, the advent of the EEA-2025 also marks a change in approach regarding education in the EU—and especially action related to recognition of qualifications. Whereas the EU initially mirrored action taken in the Bologna Process for vocational education and training (VET), the EEA-2025 seems to have increased the level of ambition—at least for some types of education.

For a long time, EU action on education and academic recognition took place under the umbrella of the Copenhagen Process. The Copenhagen Process was initiated by a Resolution on enhanced European cooperation in the area of Vocational Education and Training (VET) and situated within the EU framework.[177] The Copenhagen Process had a similar means of achieving progress as seen in the Bologna Process since it was kicked off by a Declaration and based on voluntary cooperation.[178] Advances in the Copenhagen Process were also made through Communiqués. However, different from the Bologna Process, the Copenhagen Process concerns

[176] Several initiatives for the creation of such a document had already been implemented at the time of the adoption of the Recommendation. See Explanatory memorandum to the Recommendation on the Recognition of Qualifications Held by Refugees, Displaced Persons and Persons in a Refugee-like Situation, Council of Europe and UNESCO, 14 November 2017, DGII/EDU/HE (2017) 3 rev, pp. 15–16.

[177] Council Resolution of 19 December 2002 on the promotion of enhanced European cooperation in vocational education and training, [2003] OJ C 13/2.

[178] Declaration of the European Ministers of Vocational Education and Training, and the European Commission, convened in Copenhagen on 29 and 30 November 2002, on enhanced European cooperation in vocational education and training—"The Copenhagen Declaration", p. 2.

VET.[179] While this gives the impression that VET excludes higher education qualifications, EU education law traditionally maintains a broad understanding of VET, i.e. higher education qualifications are included in this concept. This interpretation stems from the case law by the CJEU in the landmark case *Gravier*. In that case, the Court indicated that vocational training was to be understood as comprising: any type of education which prepared individuals for a qualification for a particular profession, trade or employment; or any type of education which provided the necessary training and skills for a profession, trade or employment.[180] The Court later confirmed in *Blaizot* that university studies also constituted VET.[181] Following this definition, an overlap could be perceived between the Bologna and Copenhagen Processes meaning instruments adopted in the context of the Copenhagen Process could also be relevant to higher education simultaneously subject to the Bologna Process.

Another difference between the two processes concerns instruments. Unlike the Bologna Process, the Copenhagen Process included a number of EU legal instruments from its inception. Similar to the Bologna Process, the Copenhagen Process included instruments on common documentation formats (Europass),[182] a qualifications framework (EQF),[183] another credit system (ECVET),[184] and an instrument on quality assurance (EQAVET).[185] Out of these initiatives, the Europass Decision is the only legally binding instrument. However, much like the Bologna Process, the soft law status of these instruments does not necessarily reflect the level of bindingness of these instruments. Terpan argues that EU soft law is both binding and non-binding since soft law can have legal relevance because these norms can be used in court to interpret another rule while simultaneously being non-binding.[186] In particular, the binding or non-binding nature of a rule depends on the combination of obligation and enforcement.[187] Indeed, as is the case for the Bologna Process, monitoring tools and

---

179 The 2002 Barcelona European Council called for an initiative similar to the Bologna Process, but instead focused on VET qualifications; Presidency Conclusions Barcelona European Council, 15 and 16 March 2002.

180 Case 293/83 *Gravier*, ECLI:EU:C:1985:69, para. 30.

181 Case 24/86 *Blaizot*, ECLI:EU:C:1988:43, para. 17-20.

182 Decision (EU) 2018/646 of the European Parliament and of the Council of 18 April 2018 on a common framework for the provision of better services for skills and qualifications (Europass) and repealing Decision No 2241/2004/EC, [2018] OJ L 112/42.

183 Council Recommendation of 22 May 2017 on the European Qualifications Framework for lifelong learning and repealing the recommendation of the European Parliament and of the Council of 23 April 2008 on the establishment of the European Qualifications Framework for lifelong learning, [2017] OJ C 189/15.

184 Recommendation of the European Parliament and of the Council of 18 June 2009 on the establishment of a European Credit System for Vocational Education and Training (ECVET), [2009] OJ C 155/11.

185 Recommendation of the European Parliament and of the Council of 18 June 2009 on the establishment of a European Quality Assurance Reference Framework for Vocational Education and Training, [2009] OJ C 155/1.

186 Terpan (2015, pp. 71–72).

187 Ibid., pp. 72–74.

follow-up mechanisms can lead EU action on education to be more committal than one would expect based on the initiative's intergovernmental and voluntary nature. In the EU context, this is especially the case since progress on education is often achieved following the Open Method of Coordination (OMC), which constitutes an intergovernmental way of working central to the area of education and embedded in the Education and Training 2010 and 2020 Work programmes.[188]

The OMC continues to be the main *modus operandi* in the context of the EEA-2025, something that becomes apparent from the Commission's 2020 Communication on the EEA-2025 where a call was made for an enabling framework which was to strengthen flexible cooperation methods (i.a. through targets and indicators) as well as synergies with other initiatives such as the Bologna and Copenhagen Processes, and the European Research Area. This framework was to also form the basis of a fully-fledged governance framework for the EEA-2025, but would initially operate on the basis of the methods previously maintained in the Education and Training 2020 Work Programme.[189] The call for this framework was followed up in 2021 with Council Resolutions which reiterated the importance of the OMC.[190] This concretisation of the EEA-2025 was strongly rooted in the need for post-pandemic recovery and sought to build on the previous decades of cooperation on education in the EU. The EEA-2025 is developed along various dimensions including: quality of education, green & digital transitions, teachers & trainers, lifelong learning, and higher education.[191] The latter point is particularly relevant since some of the most important actions on recognition are on higher education. Measures proposed concern the creation of a European Degree, a genuine European-level quality assurance system, strengthening existing action on automatic mutual recognition, and using Europass' digital tools to facilitate recognition. In this context, it can also be observed that the EU is striving to speed up and deepen cooperation undertaken in the Bologna Process. The 2020 Commission Communication on the EEA-2025 indicates EU higher education systems should aim for[192]:

> Automatic recognition of qualifications and study periods abroad for the purpose of further learning, quality assurance of joint transnational activities and the recognition and portability of short courses leading to micro-credentials. This would allow Member States to go deeper and faster in their cooperation, as compared to what they are able to do now in the context

[188] Kortese (2024).

[189] Communication from the Commission to the European Parliament, the Council, the European Economic and Social Committee and the Committee of the Regions on achieving the European Education Area by 2025, COM(2020) 625 final, pp. 25–27.

[190] Council Resolution on a strategic framework for European cooperation in education and training towards the European Education Area and beyond (2021–2030), [2021] OJ C 66/1.

[191] Communication from the Commission to the European Parliament, the Council, the European Economic and Social Committee and the Committee of the Regions on achieving the European Education Area by 2025, COM(2020) 625 final, p. 5; Council Resolution on a strategic framework for European cooperation in education and training towards the European Education Area and beyond (2021–2030), [2021] OJ C 66/1.

[192] Communication from the Commission to the European Parliament, the Council, the European Economic and Social Committee and the Committee of the Regions on achieving the European Education Area by 2025, COM(2020) 625 final, p. 11.

> of the Bologna process. The European Education Area can act as a motor for the Bologna process, inspiring and supporting other member countries of the European Higher Education Area to benefit from a similar path.

The focus of these recognition-related measures in the area of higher education is cause for two observations. First, the frontrunner role that the EU is envisioning in the context of the Bologna Process can be considered a reclaiming of cooperation on higher education in the EU context in a sense.[193] Second, higher education being subject to extra measures on recognition is especially interesting considering the reach of the Copenhagen Process which focused on VET, thereby including higher education. As far as the EEA-2025 is concerned, it is focused on education in a broad sense and covers all education from early childhood education and care to higher education, VET, and adult learning. Meanwhile the abovementioned initiatives are aimed at higher education.[194] Higher education being subject to additional actions on recognition can be considered a sign of the bond between VET and higher education being severed thus leading to questions whether this is the end to the Court's case law in cases like *Gravier* and *Blaizot*. At the same time, the Copenhagen Process has not ceased to exist. In fact, that process suggests a growing area of overlap and blurred boundaries between VET and higher education and the importance of VET programmes at EQF levels 5–8 (constituting the higher education cycles of the QF-EHEA).[195]

In this context, some of the instruments supporting recognition originally introduced in the Copenhagen Process still appear relevant for both VET and higher education. This particularly applies for the European Qualifications Framework for lifelong learning (EQF) and Europass. Apart from those instruments, different types of education (VET or higher education) appear to now follow a different trajectory, thereby comprising different instruments. The present section discusses some of the most important initiatives on academic recognition initiated on the basis of Article 165 TFEU and in the context of the EEA-2025. Apart from the EQF and Europass, which apply to all types of education, this section discusses the Automatic Recognition Recommendation, the Commission's initiative for a higher education quality assurance system at EU level, the blueprint for the European Degree, the 2020 VET Recommendation which came to replace ECVET and EQAVET, and the Micro-credentials Recommendation.

---

[193] It has previously been argued that the Bologna Process could be considered a re-nationalisation of higher education. See for example: Verbruggen (2003, p. 204).

[194] This development can furthermore be seen in: Communication from the Commission to the European Parliament, the Council, the European Economic and Social Committee and the Committee of the Regions on a European strategy for universities, COM(2022) 16 final; Council Recommendation of 5 April 2022 on building bridges for effective European higher education cooperation, [2022] OJ C 160/01.

[195] Osnabrück Declaration on vocational education and training as an enabler of recovery and just transitions to digital and green economies, endorsed on 30 November 2020, p. 5.

4.1 Overarching Initiatives

4.1.1 Europass: Promoting Transparency Through Common Documentation

The first Europass Decision was adopted in 2004 and is to be considered a direct response to the calls made by the European Council in Lisbon in 2000, which explicitly requested increased transparency of qualifications.[196] Moreover, the Decision answered the call made by the EU VET ministers in the Copenhagen Declaration to increase transparency of VET by integrating existing initiatives such as the European CV and diploma supplements in one framework.[197] With transparency as its main objective, it is nevertheless important to remark that the Europass Decision does not effectuate recognition. Instead, increased transparency may contribute to recognition and further improve understanding and appreciation of qualifications and competences on the labour market.[198] With this, Europass relates to the whole spectrum of recognition (i.e. *de jure* and *de facto* professional recognition, as well as academic recognition by accumulation and by substitution).

The objective to create a single Community framework for transparency was central to the Europass initiative. It was to particularly be achieved via the creation of a portfolio of documents which citizens could use on a voluntary basis.[199] This newly developed framework came to arch over five existing tools for transparency which were managed separately before the introduction of the first Europass Decision in 2004.[200] Ultimately, these instruments were placed under the umbrella of Europass at the initiative of the Commission and included: the Europass CV, Europass-Mobility, Diploma Supplement, Language Portfolio, and Certificate Supplement.[201] Whereas the Europass CV allows citizens to present their qualifications and competences,[202] Europass-Mobility is a personal document recording a learning pathway achieved by an individual in another Member State.[203] These documents both stemmed from

[196] Lisbon European Council—23 and 24 March 2000—Presidency Conclusions.

[197] Declaration of the European Ministers of Vocational Education and Training, and the European Commission, convened in Copenhagen on 29 and 30 November 2002, on enhanced European cooperation in vocational education and training—"The Copenhagen Declaration", p. 2.

[198] Proposal for a Decision of the European Parliament and of the Council on a single framework for the transparency of qualifications and competences (Europass), COM(2003) 796 final, p. 4.

[199] Article 1 Decision No 2241/2004/EC of the European Parliament and of the Council of 15 December 2004 on a single Community framework for the transparency of qualifications and competences (Europass), [2004] OJ L 390/6.

[200] These instruments particularly concerned the European CV format, Diploma Supplement, Europass-Training, Certificate Supplements, and Language Portfolios; Proposal for a Decision of the European Parliament and of the Council on a single framework for the transparency of qualifications and competences (Europass), COM(2003) 796 final, p. 7.

[201] Articles 5 through 9 Decision No 2241/2004.

[202] Article 5 and Annex III Decision No 2241/2004.

[203] Annex III Decision No 2241/2004.

initiatives adopted within the Community framework.[204] The same cannot be said for some of the other documents falling under the Europass framework. The first of these documents is the Diploma Supplement (DS), which is granted to higher education graduates and provides information on their achievements.[205] This document was proposed in the context of the LRC and its format had previously been developed by the Council of Europe and UNESCO in cooperation with the European Commission.[206] The DS has its VET equivalent in the Certificate Supplement (CS).[207] Different from the DS, the CS was proposed in the EU context within the framework of a cooperation between the European Commission and Cedefop.[208] In contrast with the DS, the CS is not a personal document, meaning that it is connected to the certificate and not to the certificate holder.[209] The main advantage of this approach is that it simplifies the issuance of supplements where the qualifications are very diverse, as is the case for VET.[210] Last but not least, the final document falling under the auspices of the Europass framework is the Language Portfolio. This instrument was also developed by the Council of Europe and allows citizens to present their language skills.[211] In particular, the Portfolio helps learners reflect on their learning objectives and documents an individual's language proficiency allowing them to inform others in a way that is internationally comparable.[212]

Europass was first implemented through a cooperation of especially established National Europass Centres (NECs)[213] and the European Commission.[214] Part of the implementation involved the creation of an online information system allowing citizens to complete the Europass documents in an electronic form which they could then download or print.[215] Europass in this format stayed in place until 2016 when the Commission issued the New Skills Agenda for Europe to, among others, make skills and qualifications more visible and comparable.[216] To achieve the objectives

---

[204] Commission Recommendation of 11 March 2002 on a common European format for curricula vitae (CVs), [2002] OJ L 79/66; Council Decision of 21 December 1998 on the promotion of European pathways in work-linked training, including apprenticeship, [1999] OJ L 17/45.

[205] Article 7 Decision No 2241/2004.

[206] Article IX.3 Lisbon Recognition Convention; Recital 4 Decision 2241/2004.

[207] Article 9 Decision 2241/2004.

[208] Deane (2005, p. 284).

[209] Annex VI Decision No 2241/2004.

[210] Deane (2005, p. 289). It may be recalled that VET has not undergone a widespread structural harmonisation as was the case for higher education, meaning qualifications are more varied than in the case of higher education.

[211] Recital 4 and Article 8 Decision 2241/2004.

[212] Annex V Decision No 2241/2004.

[213] Article 11 Decision 2241/2004.

[214] Article 12 Decision 2241/2004.

[215] Article 10 io. Annex VII Decision 2241/2004.

[216] Communication from the Commission to the European Parliament, the Council, the European Economic and Social Committee and the Committee of the Regions, A New Skills Agenda for Europe: Working together to strengthen human capital, employability and competitiveness, COM(2016) 381 final, p. 3.

of the New Skills agenda, some of instruments under the Copenhagen Process were to be updated, including the Europass framework. Europass was to be revised to achieve better service provision for skills and qualifications.[217] The proposal that followed confirmed that the proposed amendment of the Europass framework sought to "modernise EU tools and services and to ensure that they reflect the changing needs of all potential users from the labour market and education and training sectors; are always updated to technological developments, new forms of sharing information and of the collaborative economy; and capable of supporting individuals in their multiple life transitions of learning-work".[218] This objective was to be achieved through a two-tiered approach consisting of a first layer through which Europass would become a European-wide platform moving Europass from a document-based initiative to a service-based platform, and a second layer which consists of on-the-ground outreach services.[219]

Therefore, under the new Europass Decision the existing Europass internet-based information system was replaced by an online platform.[220] Article 3(2) of the Decision shows that the Europass platform includes much more information than just the pre-existing document templates, as it includes information on, among others, learning opportunities, qualifications frameworks/systems, opportunities for the validation of non-formal and informal learning, and recognition practices and legislation in the EU and in third countries. In terms of scope, the new Decision applies to all skills and qualifications acquired in formal, non-formal and informal educational settings, practical (work) experience, mobility and volunteering.[221] Interestingly, the 2018 Europass Decision gives more attention to third-country nationals and skills and qualifications obtained in third countries. Whereas the 2004 Decision only mentioned that third-country nationals resident in the EU had to also be able to benefit from the Europass system, the 2018 Decision considers "the needs of third country nationals arriving or residing in the Union to support their integration".[222]

To continue with the transition from a document-based framework to web-based tools, the purpose of those tools is mainly listed in the Decision—as opposed to what they look like.[223] Although the CV and the Diploma and Certificate Supplements still appear in this shift to an online platform,[224] other previous documents are not included. The preamble recognises the achievements attained by the five Europass documents, but soon shifts to the use of the term tools. In particular, new tools are

[217] Ibid., p. 18.

[218] Proposal for a Decision of the European Parliament and of the Council on a common framework for the provision of better services for skills and qualifications (Europass) and repealing Decision No 2241/2004, COM(2016) 625 final, p. 2.

[219] Ibid., pp. 2–3.

[220] Recital 37 and Article 12(2) Decision (EU) 2018/646 of the European Parliament and of the Council of 18 April 2018 on a common framework for the provision of better services for skills and qualifications (Europass) and repealing Decision No 2241/2004/EC, [2018] OJ L 112/42.

[221] Article 1 Decision (EU) 2018/646.

[222] Recital 26 Decision (EU) 2018/646.

[223] See Article 3 Decision (EU) 2018/646.

[224] Article 3(a)(a)(d) Decision (EU) 2018/646.

available which may facilitate the presentation of skills and qualifications through online and digital formats and individuals should be able to use these and self-assess their skills and qualifications.[225] The proposal to the Decision seems to indicate that the former Europass documents will still be a part of the Europass online platform, but will be supplemented by existing online information tools.[226] Therefore, the new Europass framework (i.e. online platform) is set to bring together existing tools such as the Learning Opportunities and Qualifications in Europe Portal, the EU Skills Panorama, and the ESCO portal.

4.1.2 The European Qualifications Framework for Lifelong Learning

Another one of the instruments proposed in the Copenhagen Process concerns the European Qualifications Framework for lifelong learning. In 2004, the VET Ministers called for an open and flexible European qualifications framework, founded on transparency and mutual trust which would provide a common reference to facilitate recognition of all levels of qualifications.[227] After subsequent calls in important policy documents,[228] the European Qualifications Framework for lifelong learning (EQF) was proposed in 2006[229] and subsequently adopted in 2008.[230] The objective of the EQF was to "create a common reference framework which should serve as a translation device between different qualifications systems and their levels, whether for general and higher education or for vocational education and training".[231] Despite its adoption on the basis of the EU's education and vocational training

[225] Recital 22 Decision (EU) 2018/646.

[226] Proposal for a Decision of the European Parliament and of the Council on a common framework for the provision of better services for skills and qualifications (Europass) and repealing Decision No 2241/2004, COM(2016) 625 final, p. 3.

[227] Maastricht Communiqué on the Future Priorities of Enhanced European Cooperation in Vocational Education and Training (VET)—14 December 2004), p. 4.

[228] "Education & Training 2010": The Success of the Lisbon Strategy hinges on urgent Reforms—Joint interim report of the Council and the Commission on the implementation of the detailed work programme on the follow-up of the objectives of education and training systems in Europe, Council document 6905/04; Modernising Education and Training: A Vital Contribution to Prosperity and Social Cohesion in Europe—2006 joint interim report of the Council and of the Commission on progress under the 'Education & Training 2010' work programme, [2006] OJ C 79/1; Council resolution of 27 June 2002 on lifelong learning, [2002] OJ C 163/1; European Council Brussels 22 and 23 March 2005—Presidency conclusions, p. 11; Brussels European Council 23/24 March 2006—Presidency conclusions, p. 6.

[229] Proposal for a Recommendation for the European Parliament and of the Council on the establishment of the European Qualifications Framework for lifelong learning, COM(2006) 479 final.

[230] Recital 12–13 Recommendation of the European Parliament and of the Council of 23 April 2008 on the establishment of a European Qualifications Framework for lifelong learning, [2008] OJ C 111/1 (hereinafter: 2008 EQF Recommendation).

[231] Recital 12 2008 EQF Recommendation.

competences,[232] the inclusion of the instrument in the Lisbon strategic goals and the corresponding high political relevance of the Recommendation compelled Member States to contribute to the realisation of the European and national qualifications frameworks.[233]

The EQF itself consists of eight reference levels defined by a set of descriptors indicating the learning outcomes relevant to the qualifications concerned. Through these eight levels, the EQF covers every qualification from the most basic to the most advanced.[234] Classifications of levels are based on learning outcomes, which are "statements of what a learner knows, understands and is able to do on completion of a learning process, which are defined in terms of knowledge, skills and competence".[235] Furthermore, Member States must be able to demonstrate the link between national levels and EQF levels.[236] Accordingly, Member States had to develop national qualifications frameworks (NQFs) in parallel to the EQF. Core to connecting NQFs to the EQF is the process of referencing which requires national qualifications to be referenced those of the EQF. This process is based on existing *levels* of qualifications in the Member States, meaning it is not about referencing specific individual qualifications.[237] Furthermore, NQFs and the EQF are of a fundamentally different nature. The EQF can be considered as a 'meta-framework', entailing that implementation is carried out on a voluntary basis and its development is dependent on the mutual trust and willingness of Member States to cooperate.[238] Mutual trust and a willingness to cooperate were embedded in the 2008 EQF Recommendation since Member States were asked to relate their national qualifications frameworks to the EQF through a referencing process. Additionally, the Member States were recommended to include a reference to EQF levels in all new qualifications certificates, diplomas, and Europass documents.[239]

As the above shows, the EQF covers any type of qualification originating from both higher education as well as VET. Section 2 of this chapter already showed that the countries taking part in the Bologna Process have also developed a qualifications framework. This means that, at least in the EU Member States, there are two meta-frameworks for qualifications: the EQF and the Qualifications Framework of the European Higher Education Area (QF-EHEA). Compatibility between the EQF and QF-EHEA was nevertheless ensured by having the top four levels of the EQF (levels 5–8) relate to the QF-EHEA cycles (short-cycle higher education, bachelor's, master's, and doctorate).[240]

---

[232] Articles 149(4) and 150(4) EC Treaty, current Articles 165 and 166 TFEU.

[233] Bouder (2008, p. 116).

[234] Rauhvargers (2009, p. 116).

[235] Annex I, point f 2008 EQF Recommendation.

[236] Ibid.

[237] Devaux et al. (2013, p. 12).

[238] Bohlinger (2012, p. 284).

[239] 2008 EQF Recommendation, para. 3.

[240] Overall, the objective of the EQF was to 'create a common reference framework which should serve as a translation device between different qualifications systems and their levels, whether for

In 2016, the Commission issued a proposal to update the EQF. According to the Commission, the 2008 EQF Recommendation was reaching its full implementation but its main objectives of transparency, comparability and portability of qualifications were not fully achieved due to limitations in the Recommendation itself.[241] In particular, the Commission found that nine challenges needed to be met through the updated Recommendation.[242] One of these challenges related to the fact that not all countries referenced their entire qualifications system to the EQF, despite the EQF's overarching character. This meant that national qualifications frameworks could be restricted to qualifications obtained after formal or informal learning and excluded private, non-formal and international qualifications from the NQF, i.e. holders of these qualifications could not benefit from increased transparency. Participating States were accordingly recommended to complete the referencing process in accordance with the eight levels of the EQF (which remained unchanged in the 2017 update) and by using the reference criteria established in Annex III of the Recommendation.[243] This Annex was introduced in 2017 and is the result of the Commission and Member States agreeing to the creation of a minimum set of information describing learning outcomes, quality assurance, and credits connected to qualifications.[244] This Annex sought to resolve another challenge of the former EQF Recommendation, namely the fact that substantial variations existed among the Member States regarding the description of the content of similar qualifications. Indeed, the Annex provides Member States with certain guidelines to be followed in the referencing process. Examples of the guidelines included are the need for a clear and demonstrable link between qualifications levels in the NQFs and the levels in the EQF and the need for the referencing procedures to be transparent.

Annex IV on quality assurance was also reviewed in the 2017 EQF Recommendation. These principles must also always be taken into account in the referencing process.[245] An update was needed since the 2008 EQF recommendation excluded quality assurance principles for qualifications from general education, qualifications

general and higher education or for vocational education and training'; see recitals 9 and 12 2008 EQF Recommendation.

[241] Proposal for a Council Recommendation on the European Qualifications Framework for lifelong learning and repealing the Recommendation of the European Parliament and of the Council of 23 April 2008 on the establishment of the European Qualifications Framework for lifelong learning, COM(2016) 383 final, p. 3.

[242] Ibid, pp. 3–4.

[243] Paragraph 1 Council Recommendation of 22 May 2017 on the European Qualifications Framework for lifelong learning and repealing the recommendation of the European Parliament and of the Council of 23 April 2008 on the establishment of the European Qualifications Framework for lifelong learning, [2017] OJ C 189/15 (hereinafter: 2017 EQF Recommendation).

[244] Proposal for a Council Recommendation on the European Qualifications Framework for lifelong learning and repealing the Recommendation of the European Parliament and of the Council of 23 April 2008 on the establishment of the European Qualifications Framework for lifelong learning, COM(2016) 383 final, pp. 3–4.

[245] Paragraph 1 and 2 2017 EQF Recommendation.

from non-formal, informal and private sectors, as well as those obtained internationally.[246] This inclusion of other types of education aligns seamlessly with the recommendation to reference all types of qualifications. In fact, the update of the EQF can be considered to largely have been an exercise in expansion of the qualification types covered.

However, the EQF has not only been expanded in terms of qualifications, but also in terms of definitions. A change in definition concerns the term learning outcomes in relation to the eight EQF levels. Whereas they were previously defined in terms of knowledge, skills and competences,[247] these outcomes are now defined in terms of knowledge, skills and responsibility and autonomy.[248] The last two terms are again described as "the ability of the learner to apply knowledge and skills autonomously and with responsibility".[249] Nevertheless, the term "competence" was also maintained in the 2017 EQF Recommendation meaning "the proven ability to use knowledge, skills and personal, social and/or methodological abilities, in work or study situations and in professional and personal development".[250] This change introduced with the 2017 EQF Recommendation is meant to correct an inconsistency of the 2008 EQF Recommendation where competences were defined as responsibility and autonomy, something which was considerably more restricted than the overarching definition of competence as is widely used in European education and training.[251]

As the adjustment of the terminologies above shows, establishing coherence with other EU and national policies is of importance for the continued development of the EQF.[252] The 2017 EQF Recommendation therefore also sought for a better connection with credit transfer and accumulation systems (such as ECTS). The Commission noted in its proposal that no common arrangement existed for such credit accumulation and transfer systems making it more difficult for individuals to move between learning settings and thereby inhibiting flexible learning paths.[253] According to the 2017 EQF Recommendation, these links had to be promoted following common principles on the use of credit systems for the promotion of flexible learning pathways,

---

[246] Proposal for a Council Recommendation on the European Qualifications Framework for lifelong learning and repealing the Recommendation of the European Parliament and of the Council of 23 April 2008 on the establishment of the European Qualifications Framework for lifelong learning, COM(2016) 383 final, p. 4.

[247] Annex I, point f 2008 EQF Recommendation.

[248] Annex I point e 2017 EQF Recommendation.

[249] Annex I point h 2017 EQF Recommendation.

[250] Annex I point i 2017 EQF Recommendation.

[251] Proposal for a Council Recommendation on the European Qualifications Framework for lifelong learning and repealing the Recommendation of the European Parliament and of the council of 23 April 2008 on the establishment of the European Qualifications Framework for lifelong learning, COM(2016) 383 final, p. 4.

[252] Recital 25 2017 EQF Recommendation.

[253] Proposal for a Council Recommendation on the European Qualifications Framework for lifelong learning and repealing the Recommendation of the European Parliament and of the council of 23 April 2008 on the establishment of the European Qualifications Framework for lifelong learning, COM(2016) 383 final, p. 4.

the facilitated transfer of learning outcomes through credit systems, and ensuring credit systems are underpinned by quality assurance.[254]

Apart from coherence with EU and national policies on credit transfer systems, a link is also established with the Professional Qualifications Directive. Although the 2017 EQF Recommendation maintains the principle of the 2008 EQF Recommendation that reference to EQF levels must not affect labour market access in the case of regulated professions (to which the Directive applies), EQF levels may come to play a role when common training frameworks are developed under that Directive. It may be recalled from Chapter "Professional Recognition" that such frameworks are a way of introducing automatic recognition for professions which currently fall under the PQD's general system. The introduction of such a framework will occur via a Commission delegated act and will be based on the EQF's levels.[255]

4.2 Academic Recognition & VET in the EU

While the EQF and Europass have since become staple instruments to enhance the transparency of qualifications within the EU, recent years have seen quite some changes to previous transparency instruments. Whereas these were previously located under the umbrella of the Copenhagen Process—and therefore mimicked the Bologna Process—a more distinct approach has since been adopted. While the EU is aiming to accelerate work done in the EHEA/Bologna Process for higher education, its approach on VET has come to place more emphasis on innovation in the sense of internationalisation and the twin transitions, and on flexibility in terms of learning paths and qualifications. This latter aspect is particularly relevant for recognition and has been elaborated via the 2020 VET Recommendation. In the context of this recommendation, we see the consolidation and further development of pre-existing instruments such as principles of the European Credit System for Vocational Education and Training (ECVET) and European Quality Assurance Reference Framework for Vocational Education and Training (EQAVET). Simultaneously, flexibility of learning pathways is encouraged through the development of a European approach to micro-credentials.[256]

---

[254] Paragraph 4 and Annex V 2017 EQF Recommendation.

[255] Article 49a(1)(d)(4) Directive 2005/36/EC of the European Parliament and of the Council of 7 September 2005 on the recognition of professional qualifications, [2005] OJ L 255/22 *as amended by* Directive 2013/55/EU of the European Parliament and of the Council of 20 November 2013 amending Directive 2005/36/EC on the recognition of professional qualifications and Regulation (EU) No 1024/2012 on administrative cooperation through the Internal Market Information System ('the IMI Regulation'), [2013] OJ L 354/132.

[256] For which a dedicated recommendation was adopted. See Council Recommendation of 16 June 2022 on a European approach to micro-credentials for lifelong learning and employability, [2022] OJ C 243/10 and Sect. 4.2.2 of this chapter.

4.2.1 Credits & Quality Assurance: The 2020 VET Recommendation

The 2020 VET Recommendation was adopted with the objective to support the EEA-2025 by developing a genuine European learning space which is not restricted by borders and removes obstacles to recognition while also working towards a smoother cross-border validation of training and lifelong learning outcomes.[257] VET in the context of the recommendation is defined as education and training which equips persons with knowledge, skills, and competences to prepare them for particular professions or the labour market more broadly speaking.[258] Apart from covering both formal and non-formal training, it also covers all levels of the EQF (including higher education). Flexibility of learning pathways, suitability to drive innovation and the twin transitions, digitalisation, equality, and quality assurance are core pillars of the 2020 VET Recommendation. As far as recognition is concerned, the points on flexibility and quality assurance are particularly important. The former embodies the previous ECVET and connects to the EU's approach on micro-credentials, while the latter consolidates the EQAVET.

Regarding ECVET, the new recommendation notes that while ECVET widely contributed to a better quality mobility experience through units of learning outcomes, the concept of ECVET points was not generally applied.[259] Originally, the ECVET Recommendation had the objective of facilitating the"transfer, recognition and accumulation of assessed learning outcomes of individuals who are aiming to achieve a qualification".[260] This was to be achieved through a common methodological framework through which the transfer of credit for learning outcomes was to be facilitated.[261] Learning outcomes were central to the ECVET and measured by means of units which again were components of a qualification, consisting of a coherent set of knowledge, skills and competence (i.e. learning outcomes).[262] A qualification subsequently consists of several units and is made up of a whole set of units.[263] This unit-based approach was intended to advance flexible individual learning pathways through which learners could accumulate units of learning outcomes over time in

[257] Recital 15 Council Recommendation of 24 November 2020 on vocational education and training (VET) for sustainable competitiveness, social fairness and resilience, [2020] OJ C 417/1 (hereinafter: 2020 VET Recommendation).

[258] Accordingly, VET programmes at higher EQF levels are to be encouraged, see point 11 and Recital 2020 VET Recommendation.

[259] Recital 19 2020 VET Recommendation.

[260] Recital 6 Recommendation of the European Parliament and of the Council of 18 June 2009 on the establishment of a European Credit System for Vocational Education and Training (ECVET), [2009] OJ C 155/11.

[261] Proposal for a Recommendation of the European Parliament and of the Council on the establishment of the European Credit system for Vocational Education and Training (ECVET), COM(2008) 180 final, p. 8.

[262] Annex I point c Recommendation of the European Parliament and of the Council of 18 June 2009 on the establishment of a European Credit System for Vocational Education and Training (ECVET), [2009] OJ C 155/11 (hereinafter: 2009 ECVET Recommendation).

[263] Annex II 2009 ECVET Recommendation 1.

different countries and in different modes to achieve a qualification.[264] Credits would ultimately follow on learning outcomes and could be transferred between Member States through Memoranda of Understanding between participating partners.[265]

ECVET was particularly relevant in two scenarios. First, in the situation where learning outcomes were to be transferred in the context of an organised agreement in the context of formal learning, basically constituting academic recognition by substitution (i.e. the situation where a learner goes abroad temporarily to study certain subjects that become an integral part of the home State's education and training). Second, ECVET was to facilitate recognition of learning outcomes acquired through non-formal and informal learning.[266] In either scenario, ECVET could be applied on all levels of the EQF, thereby comprising also the upper levels overlapping with the three cycles of the QF-EHEA—while still constituting its own credit system next to the ECTS.[267]

However, despite its objectives and possible uses ECVET was also subject to criticism. In the relation with higher education it was for example found to be difficult to relate higher education qualifications to ECVET.[268] Furthermore, ECVET was not considered generally useful, especially not for those countries which already had VET credit systems or VET systems centred on workplace-based training.[269] Ultimately, in 2019, an extensive study showed that only few Member State systems were ready for the ECVET and moreover that its impact in terms of system-level changes was low.[270] This report was ultimately the cause for the introduction of the 2020 VET

[264] Proposal for a Recommendation of the European Parliament and of the Council on the establishment of the European Credit system for Vocational Education and Training (ECVET), COM(2008) 180 final, p. 8.

[265] The partnerships/networks themselves would consist of competent institutions allowed to award qualifications, units or credits to learning outcomes; see Annex II 2009 ECVET Recommendation.

[266] Recital 8 2009 ECVET Recommendation.

[267] Although the two systems were designed from a different starting point, both shared the same basis, namely learning outcomes. Nevertheless, differences pertained to the sectoral vs. overarching character of the systems, the relationship they had with programmes and curricula, and regarding implementation. Indeed, whereas the ECTS focuses on higher education, the ECVET focused on any type of qualification obtained in formal, informal, and non-formal learning. Lastly, both initiatives had different implementation trajectories. Whereas the ECTS has long been in an advanced stage and is mostly applied by higher education institutions, the application of the ECVET was to occur gradually and involved various competent institutions depending on the national system. See recitals 8 and 10 2009 ECVET Recommendation; Cedefop, Linking credit systems and qualifications frameworks: An international comparative analysis, Working Paper No. 5, 2010, p. 41.

[268] Cedefop, Monitoring ECVET implementation strategies in Europe, Working Paper No. 18, 2013, p. 46; PPMI, Implementation of the Recommendation of the European Parliament and of the Council of 18 June 2009 on the establishment of a European Credit System for Vocational Education and Training (ECVET)—Final report 4 July 2014, European Commission, p. 78.

[269] Ibid., p. 10.

[270] For Belgium ECVET impact was measured separately for Flanders and Wallonia, thereby bringing the total count of Member States to 29 (instead of 28); European Commission, Study on EU VET instruments (EQAVET and ECVET), January 2019, pp. 45–46.

Recommendation and consolidation of the ECVET in it.[271] While ECVET as a separate credit system therefore ceased to exist, its principles and some of its technical aspects are still incorporated in the 2020 VET Recommendation.[272] In particular, this concerns the units of learning outcomes, learning agreements, and memoranda of understanding. Point 6 of the recommendation indicates Member States are to base their VET programmes on modules or units of learning outcomes while ensuring validation mechanisms are in place to ensure recognition. The use of learning outcomes is furthermore important for the development of micro-credentials.[273]

Regarding quality assurance, the 2020 VET Recommendation came to replace the ECVET's sister recommendation containing the EQAVET. Originally, EQAVET was introduced as a "reference instrument to help Member States to promote and monitor continuous improvement of their VET systems based on common European references".[274] The use of EQAVET was voluntary and paired with participation in the European Quality Assurance Reference Framework Network (EQAVET Network).[275] In this context, Member States were encouraged to create National Reference Points (NRPs) for quality assurance in VET.

As far as the content of the EQAVET framework goes, the previous framework was taken up in the 2020 VET Recommendation in its entirety and supplemented to address certain shortcomings.[276] The EQAVET particularly consisted of indicative descriptors as well as quality indicators Member States and VET providers could choose from to make their quality assurance systems more transparent.[277]

Apart from having consolidated the ECVET and EQAVET the 2020 VET Recommendation can be considered a first in a line of instruments which has instituted greater coherence and interconnection to pre-existing initiatives for transparency and recognition. In particular, the new recommendation recommends that Member States make the best use possible of tools such as the EQF, ECTS, and ESCO.[278] Efforts should also be undertaken to realise automatic mutual recognition of qualifications and learning periods, especially by making use of the Automatic Recognition Recommendation.[279] In a similar vein, coherence is achieved with Europass by encouraging the use of those tools to facilitate mobility and learning of those holding VET qualifications. In this context, the Commission is also given the task to support the Member States in establishing so-called European Platforms of Centres of Vocational Excellence and even exploring European Vocational Core Profiles—all again

[271] Ibid., p. 11.

[272] Recital 19 2020 VET Recommendation.

[273] Auzinger and Luomi-Messerer (2021, p. 20).

[274] Recital 9 Recommendation of the European Parliament and of the Council of 18 June 2009 on the establishment of a European Quality Assurance Reference Framework for Vocational Education and Training, [2008] OJ C 155/1 (hereinafter: 2009 EQAVET Recommendation).

[275] Paragraph 3 2009 EQAVET Recommendation.

[276] Recital 18 2020 VET Recommendation.

[277] Ibid.

[278] Point 23 2020 VET Recommendation.

[279] Discussed in Sect. 4.3.1 of this chapter.

in the context of Europass and ultimately aimed at facilitating learning mobility as well as transparency and recognition of qualifications.[280] Especially the mention of core profiles is relevant to advancing the last objective. The development of such profiles at the European level could help to emphasise commonalities in VET, which tends to be more varied across Member States than higher education (which was subject to structural harmonisation through the Bologna Process).

A final element of the 2020 VET Recommendation to touch upon is found in point 29 and calls for the Commission to explore the concept and use of micro-credentials in VET. Such credentials are particularly relevant for one of the key objectives of the 2020 VET Recommendation, namely the flexibility of learning pathways and possibility to build these through modules, units of learning outcomes as well as validation and recognition thereof.[281] This exploration of micro-credentials ultimately resulted in a new recommendation dedicated exclusively to these credentials.

4.2.2 The EU's Approach on Micro-Credentials

Whereas the 2020 VET Recommendation provided a general framework for the creation and emphasised the importance of an approach on micro-credentials, a dedicated recommendation on this topic soon followed in 2022.[282] This recommendation is located at the intersection of employment, education, and VET policies in the EU.[283] Accordingly, its objectives range from increasing relevant skills and facilitating flexible learning paths to ultimately contributing to an effective culture of lifelong learning. The Recommendation fills a gap since before its inception no common definition existed for micro-credentials, nor standards regarding their issue. By providing such a framework the Recommendation helps to build trust in micro-credentials. The Micro-credentials Recommendation defines micro-credentials as follows[284]:

> 'Micro-credential' means the record of the learning outcomes that a learner has acquired following a small volume of learning. These learning outcomes will have been assessed against transparent and clearly defined criteria. Learning experiences leading to micro-credentials are designed to provide the learner with specific knowledge, skills and competences that respond to societal, personal, cultural or labour market needs. Micro-credentials are owned by the learner, can be shared and are portable. They may be stand-alone or combined into larger credentials. They are underpinned by quality assurance following agreed standards in the relevant sector or area of activity.

Considering their wide nature, providers of micro-credentials are not only education and training institutions, but also parties such as social partners, employers,

---

[280] Point 30 2020 VET Recommendation.

[281] See points 5 and 6 2020 VET Recommendation.

[282] Council Recommendation of 16 June 2022 on a European approach to micro-credentials for lifelong learning and employability, [2022] OJ C 243/10 (hereinafter: Micro-credentials Recommendation).

[283] Its legal basis being, among others, article 149, 165 and 166 TFEU.

[284] Point 5(a) Micro-credentials Recommendation.

national and regional authorities.[285] Portability is also central to the definition of a micro-credential and revolves around the ability to store the credentials in a system of choice, share them easily, and have them be understood and verified for their authenticity in a facilitated manner.[286] In terms of use, the recommendation reflects the connection to education as well as employment policies. Regarding education, Member States are, for example, recommended to use these credentials to facilitate flexible learning pathways between different types of education and to integrate them in degree programmes.[287] In the context of employment, micro-credentials are connected to efforts related to addressing skills mismatches, as well as up- and re-skilling.[288]

Next to creating a common concept of micro-credentials, another core element of the Micro-credentials Recommendation is the European standard elements to describe micro-credentials and issue them. These are elaborated in point 6 of the Recommendation and its Annexes. Micro-credentials are to contain information such as the identification of the learner, title of the credential, awarding bodies, learning outcomes, workload (where possible in ECTS), and type of assessment. This information is to be included in a European data model available to providers of micro-credentials to support interoperability and exchange—something that could also greatly benefit recognition in the end. The development of this model itself is embedded within Europass. Following Articles 6(1)(c)(d) and 6(2)(b) of the 2018 Europass Decision, the Commission is tasked to develop the European data model for micro-credentials as part of its tasks in managing the Europass online platform.

Moreover, the Recommendation also determines European principles for the design and issuance of micro-credentials in Annex II. Quality, transparency, recognition, and portability are some of the core principles here. For example, external quality assurance is encouraged and use is to be made of pre-existing initiatives such as the EHEA's Standards and Guidelines for Quality Assurance (ESG) and EQAVET framework. To encourage transparency, emphasis is placed on comparability as expressed through workload (ideally ECTS, alternatively EQF), reference to the national qualifications frameworks (which themselves are again referenced to the EQF and QF-EHEA), and reliable and retrievable information (e.g. through quality assurance registers and Europass). In relation to recognition, the Recommendation indicates that micro-credentials should be recognised by competent authorities for academic, training or employment purposes—thus signalling relevance for all recognition types both professional and academic. In terms of procedures, micro-credentials issued by formal education providers should be recognised following standard recognition procedures for foreign qualifications. In the EU, this will most likely be in accordance with the LRC or other national recognition procedures.

Core elements of the Micro-credentials Recommendation are nevertheless still laced with subsidiarity concerns. This is unsurprising considering its legal basis

---

[285] Point 5(b) Micro-credentials Recommendation.

[286] Point 5(g) Micro-credentials Recommendation.

[287] Point 11(c)(d) Micro-credentials Recommendation.

[288] Point 12(a)(i)(ii) Micro-credentials Recommendation.

and limited competence in these areas. Nevertheless, the Recommendation should be welcomed for its greater cohesion to other initiatives on recognition. Indeed, the Micro-credentials Recommendation is deeply embedded in existing employment and education (including VET) initiatives.[289] Connection is also made to the EHEA and the ambitions expressed by ministers in that context to explore the use of smaller flexible units of learning (including micro-credentials).[290] With this, the Micro-credentials Recommendation can be considered to signify a different trend of strengthened coherence with other instruments. For example, it already became clear above that the EQF and—if relevant—QF-EHEA levels are part of the standard elements to describe micro-credentials.[291] The same applies to the ECTS, which is to be used where possible to describe the workload associated with a micro-credential.[292] The ENIC and NARIC centres are furthermore included as bodies to develop transparent recognition procedures—all of which should occur in correspondence with the Automatic Recognition Recommendation.[293]

Regarding the PQD, the Micro-credentials Recommendation also positively discerns itself in terms of coherence. While the standard phrase is included to signify that the Recommendation is without prejudice to the Directive,[294] point 12(g) of the recommendation recommends that Member States integrate micro-credentials into their employment policies to support professional development and meet mandatory requirements for reskilling and upskilling. The Recommendation itself here mentions licences, required training, and permits—something that is often highly relevant for professionals exercising regulated professions. This makes it clear that micro-credentials could also play a role to facilitate recognition under the PQD—which is especially relevant for those using their free movement rights later in their careers and who will likely also have to demonstrate having kept their qualifications up-to-date.

4.3 Academic Recognition & Higher Education in the EU

Earlier in this chapter it was already established that EU action on higher education constitutes one of the core pillars of the EEA-2025.[295] The Commission had

[289] See, for example, recital 10–13 and 18 Micro-credentials Recommendation.

[290] Recital 14 Micro-credentials Recommendation and Rome Ministerial Communiqué, 19 November 2020; Tirana EHEA Ministerial Conference, 29–30 May 2024 (Tirana Communiqué).

[291] Point 6(b)(viii) and Annexes I and II Micro-credentials Recommendation.

[292] Point 6(b)(vii) Micro-credentials Recommendation.

[293] See Sect. 4.3.1 of this chapter and point 13 Micro-credentials Recommendation.

[294] Recital 23 Micro-credentials Recommendation.

[295] Communication from the Commission to the European Parliament, the Council, the European Economic and Social Committee and the Committee of the Regions on achieving the European Education Area by 2025, COM(2020) 625 final, p. 5; Council Resolution on a strategic framework for European cooperation in education and training towards the European Education Area and beyond (2021–2030), [2021] OJ C 66/1.

furthermore expressed the ambition to speed up and intensify cooperation in the Bologna Process in the EU context.[296] These ambitions were given follow-up in a Recommendation on building bridges for effective European higher education cooperation. This Recommendation considers higher education institutions to be essential to realise the twin transitions and boost competitiveness through inter-institutional cooperation and co-creation. Accordingly, advances to the European University Initiative play a central role in the Recommendation, an initiative considered crucial to advancing the EEA-2025, European Research Area, and EHEA—as well as the synergies between these areas.[297] Much importance is awarded to the instruments of the Bologna Process, which are often referred to as means to achieve the Recommendation's objectives. These include, advancing transnational cooperation between higher education institutions, tackling differences in quality assurance, mitigating uneven implementation of the Automatic Recognition Recommendation, and advancing the provision of joint degrees.[298]

The Recommendation also shows more clearly how the EU intends to become a front-runner in the Bologna Process. For example, it seeks to foster innovation by improving cooperation among higher education institutions—a plan which includes possibilities to explore a legal status for inter-institutional cooperation of higher education institutions.[299] In relation to improving recognition, the Recommendation focuses on effectuating automatic recognition,[300] creating a European degree, and developing a European-level quality assurance system.[301]

4.3.1 Achieving Automatic Academic Recognition in the EU

The earlier sections on the EHEA and Benelux Decisions already showed the importance of automatic academic recognition in the context of the Bologna Process, where this type of recognition was introduced on the policy agenda with the 2015 Yerevan Communiqué.[302] Soon after, automatic academic recognition was also taken over as

---

[296] Communication from the Commission to the European Parliament, the Council, the European Economic and Social Committee and the Committee of the Regions on achieving the European Education Area by 2025, COM(2020) 625 final, p. 11.

[297] See, for example, point 5 Council Recommendation of 5 April 2022 on building bridges for effective European higher education cooperation, [2022] OJ C 160/1.

[298] Recitals 9 and 10 and points 2 and 12 Council Recommendation of 5 April 2022 on building bridges for effective European higher education cooperation, [2022] OJ C 160/1.

[299] Point 1 Council Recommendation of 5 April 2022 on building bridges for effective European higher education cooperation, [2022] OJ C 160/1.

[300] For which efforts were initiated through Council Recommendation of 26 November 2018 on promoting automatic mutual recognition of higher education and upper secondary education and training qualifications and the outcomes of learning periods abroad, [2018] OJ C 444/1, discussed in Sect. 4.3.1 of this chapter.

[301] See Recital 4 and points 2 and 12(a) on the European Degree and point 7 on quality assurance Council Recommendation of 5 April 2022 on building bridges for effective European higher education cooperation, [2022] OJ C 160/1.

[302] Yerevan Communiqué, 14–15 May 2015.

a policy objective in the EU context.[303] These ambitions ultimately led to a dedicated Automatic Recognition Recommendation,[304] which is the result of an intertwining of efforts in the EHEA and EEA-2025.[305]

The Recommendation works towards automatic recognition for the purpose of further studies and concerns both higher education qualifications and those giving access thereto,[306] as well as outcomes of learning periods abroad (i.e. both types of academic recognition, by substitution and by accumulation).[307] However, a distinction is made in the intensity of work towards automatic recognition between those qualifications giving access to higher education on the one hand, and higher education as well as outcomes of learning periods abroad on the other hand. This distinction in levels of ambition can be explained through the harmonisation having taken place through the Bologna Process in the structure of higher education. While higher education qualifications follow the three-cycle structure, those giving access thereto are much more varied and rooted in national educational systems and traditions. While harmonisation has not taken place for these types of qualifications yet, the LRC does provide for principles on recognition of qualifications giving access to higher education, meaning a culture of recognition already exists for such qualifications. The question may be raised here why the objective of full automatic recognition was not included for secondary education and training qualifications. Assumedly, answers to such questions are again to be found in limited competences and subsidiarity concerns. However, this difference in levels of ambition for different qualifications is also indicative of different speeds and intensity of cooperation on higher education having taken place in the realm of the EHEA versus that of the EU (although this appears to be more balanced since the advent of the EEA-2025 and its associated initiatives).

The Automatic Recognition Recommendation suggests a step-by-step approach to support Member States with the achievement of such recognition.[308] At its core, this approach consists of the use of the Copenhagen and Bologna Processes and centres on increasing the level of ambition progressively. The Recommendation is therefore very much coherent with other pre-existing initiatives originating from

[303] Communication from the Commission to the European Parliament, the Council, the European Economic and Social Committee and the Committee of the Regions, Strengthening European Identity through Education and Culture—The European Commission's contribution to the Leaders' meeting in Gothenburg 17 November 2017, COM(2017) 673 final. This initiative took place around the same time when the French president Emmanuel Macron held a speech on the EU and its education systems. In it, he presented a vision foreseeing a combination of harmonisation and mutual recognition. The Recommendation mainly reflects the latter topic. Indeed, the Union's competences as they are currently specified in Article 165(4) TFEU exclude any harmonisation in the area of education, challenging the first part of Macron's vision. See Macron (2017).

[304] Council Recommendation of 26 November 2018 on promoting automatic mutual recognition of higher education and upper secondary education and training qualifications and the outcomes of learning periods abroad, [2018] OJ C 444/1 (hereinafter: Automatic Recognition Recommendation).

[305] Recitals 4 and 5 Automatic Recognition Recommendation.

[306] Meaning upper secondary education and training qualifications.

[307] Paragraph 1(a)(b) Automatic Recognition Recommendation.

[308] Recital 14 Automatic Recognition Recommendation.

both the EHEA as well as the EU. Indeed, recognition facilitating tools such as the ECTS, EQF, and the QF-EHEA are particularly mentioned in this context in relation to higher education qualifications.[309] For upper secondary education and training qualifications (i.e. those giving access to higher education), the proposed measures concern, among others, referencing NQFs to the EQF, and applying the EQAVET.[310] The Recommendation can therefore be seen as a way to ensure the full implementation of the Bologna Process, Lisbon Recognition Convention, and Copenhagen Process instruments.[311] Since criticism has frequently been expressed regarding the correct and full application Bologna and Copenhagen tools,[312] a lot of ground may be gained by correctly applying existing instruments and initiatives. Nevertheless, optimal functioning of instruments and tools puts the objective of automatic recognition in the hands of the Member States which can lead to different levels of ambition, something reflected in the 2023 evaluation of the Recommendation.[313]

Apart from the implementation of Bologna and Copenhagen instruments not being optimal yet, the Recommendation is also cause for another point of critique: it does not result in an effective *right* to automatic recognition for individuals. In 2023, the EEA-2025 midterm review process report recognised the importance of ensuring that automatic recognition is learner-centred and seen as a right, mentioning awareness of this right among individuals and possibilities for appeal.[314] This is very important indeed, especially considering the important role that is awarded to automatic academic recognition in relation to free movement. However, while certain rights are associated with automatic recognition an individual right awarded to holders of qualifications is still missing.

It is important here to examine the concept of automatic recognition covered by the Recommendation more closely. The Commission's initial work on the Recommendation mentioned the term "full automatic recognition". However, in the final version of the Recommendation "full automatic recognition" was replaced with the term "automatic mutual recognition".[315] This definition shows that the automatic

---

[309] Recitals 6–8, Paragraph 2–4 Automatic Recognition Recommendation.

[310] Paragraphs 5 and 6 Automatic Recognition Recommendation.

[311] Paragraph 11 Automatic Recognition Recommendation.

[312] See European Commission, EACEA, Eurydice, The European Higher Education Area in 2018: Bologna Process Implementation Report; European Commission, Study on EU VET instruments (EQAVET and ECVET), January 2019.

[313] See Report from the Commission to the Council on the implementation of the Council Recommendation on promoting automatic mutual recognition of higher education and upper secondary education and training qualifications and the outcomes of learning periods abroad, COM(2023) 91 final.

[314] European Commission, European Education Area—midterm review process report (2023), pp. 15–16.

[315] The definition reads: "*automatic mutual recognition of a qualification: the right for holders of a qualification of a certain level that has been issued by one Member State to be considered for entry to a higher education programme in the next level in any other Member State, without having to go through any separate recognition procedure. This shall not prejudice the right of a higher education institution or the competent authorities to set specific evaluation and admission criteria for a specific programme. It does not prejudice the right to check, if the qualification is*

recognition referred to in the Recommendation relates to the *level* of a qualification and not to *content*. In particular, this observation follows from the fact that higher education institutions retain a right to set specific evaluation and admission criteria for programmes—i.e. they remain free to set substantive criteria.

In this context, it is necessary to distinguish different rights associated with the recognition process. First, there is the right of the Member States' authorities (in this context often educational institutions) to maintain specific criteria for admission,[316] i.e. the actual possibility to pursue studies after having been admitted. This is confirmed in the 2023 evaluation of the Automatic Recognition Recommendation which indicates that academic recognition falls within the competence of the Member States and that the LRC is the only legally binding text in this context.[317] Second, there is the right of the individual who holds a certain qualification. In light of the monitoring mentioned report above and the discussion on different types of recognition, the right referred to in relation to the Automatic Recognition Recommendation is a right to *level* recognition—which should become automatic in light of the Recommendation. In this context the use of the term right is particularly interesting. The 2023 evaluation report of the Recommendation and the EEA-2025 midterm report both seem to imply that automatic level recognition originating from the Recommendation is a right held by individuals. Nevertheless, the Recommendation lacks the binding force to effectuate such a right. From the 2023 evaluation report it may be deduced that such a right should perhaps arise from national law,[318] however, the Recommendation itself only reads that the steps necessary to effectuate automatic recognition shall be put in place in accordance with national and EU legislation.[319] As was mentioned before, the steps referred to here primarily consist of correctly implementing the existing Bologna and Copenhagen instruments. Therefore, there seems to be a lack of clarity following from the Recommendation on what exactly is to be translated into national legislation. A close reading of the Recommendation's text nevertheless does not suggest the creation of an individual right to automatic mutual recognition.

While the lack of clarity concerning the rights of individuals is one of the main critiques to be expressed in relation to the Recommendation, its continued and deepened efforts to adequately implement the Bologna and Copenhagen tools constitutes a solid approach to improving automatic recognition. However, another element of

authentic and, in case of an upper secondary education and training qualification, if it really gives access to higher education in the Member State of issuance or, in duly justified cases, if the granted qualification meets the requirements for accessing a specific higher education programme in the receiving Member State." See: Annex Automatic Recognition Recommendation.

316 Report from the Commission to the Council on the implementation of the Council Recommendation on promoting automatic mutual recognition of higher education and upper secondary education and training qualifications and the outcomes of learning periods abroad, COM(2023) 91 final, p. 2.

317 Ibid., p. 1.

318 Ibid., p. 3.

319 See (the introduction to) point 1 Automatic Recognition Recommendation.

the Recommendation perhaps shows the most potential to drastically alter recognition—despite its modest mentioning. In particular, this concerns the use of new technologies such as blockchain.[320] Technologies such as these have the potential to result in more drastic advances in recognition. Nevertheless, time will have to tell what the ramifications of this inclusion will be since no reports were made in this area in the 2023 evaluation of the Recommendation.

4.3.2 Higher Education Quality Assurance & Working Towards a European Degree

Apart from automatic recognition, the ambitions for the EEA-2025 also concern the development of a quality assurance system for higher education and work towards a European degree. These initiatives are explored jointly in the present section due to their strong interconnection. Indeed, more cooperation on quality assurance is to pave the way for a European degree.

To start with quality assurance, a proposal was issued by the European Commission in 2024 for a Council Recommendation on a European Quality Assurance *and Recognition* System in Higher Education. With this proposal the Commission builds on a previous recommendation on cooperation in quality assurance dating back to 2006.[321] The content of this Recommendation was strongly directed at the initial setting up and development of quality assurance systems, something of no surprise considering that this Recommendation is almost 20 years old. At its core, it called Member States to also apply the ESG developed in the context of the Bologna Process. Finally, the 2006 Recommendation called for the creation of a European register in which nationally recognised quality assurance agencies were united.[322]

Recognition of qualifications as a result of the mutual trust strengthened by cooperation of quality assurance was already recognised in the 2006 Recommendation—a trend that is strengthened by the 2024 Commission proposal.[323] According to that proposal, here was a need to update action on quality assurance due to uneven implementation and to make use of the opportunity to better link quality assurance with recognition of qualifications and learning periods, subjects which have developed separately thus far.[324] The proposal considers quality assurance to lay "the

---

[320] Paragraph Automatic Recognition Recommendation.

[321] Recommendation of the European Parliament and of the Council of 15 February 2006 on further European cooperation in quality assurance in higher education, [2006] OJ L 64/60.

[322] Currently the European Quality Assurance Register for Higher Education (EQAR). This organisation is in charge of the Database of External Quality Assurance Results (DEQAR) in which decisions by EQAR registered agencies are taken up to promote transparency. The EQAR was originally adopted in the context of the EHEA as (so far the only) official organisation. There is therefore a parallel between the call in the 2006 Recommendation for a register and the EQAR created in the context of the Bologna Process.

[323] Proposal for a Council Recommendation on a European Quality Assurance and Recognition System in Higher Education, COM(2024) 147 final.

[324] Ibid., p. 2.

groundwork for trust between education systems, which is the condition for the automatic recognition of qualifications and ultimately learning mobility".[325] The proposal shows coherence with previous action taken in the context of the Bologna Process, but again emphasises the EU's ambitions to go further.[326] The proposal particularly seeks to simplify existing quality assurance processes for transnational cooperation,[327] move from programme based approaches to institutional approaches while introducing dedicated quality assurance processes for alliances of higher education institutions cooperating transnationally, and automating recognition procedures.[328] The move to an institutional approach then appears to be specifically aimed at higher education institutions engaged in joint transnational programmes. These types of institutions would normally have to go through different quality assurance procedures in each of the Member States involved thus leading to multiple quality assurance procedures and a considerable administrative burden.[329] Ultimately, alliances of higher education institutions should set up their internal quality assurance system and, in the mid- to long-term, be able to undergo external quality assurance at a cross-institutional level in the context of a European framework.[330]

Considering its legal basis being Article 165(4) TFEU, it is unsurprising that all action in the context of the present proposal is voluntary.[331] Nevertheless, the proposed quality assurance recommendation has important innovative potential. Indeed, whereas the proposal suggests general advances to national quality assurance systems in line with the Bologna Process' ESG, its innovative character particularly lies in its approach for higher education institutions engaged in transnational cooperation. This by recommending the development of a European framework for an overarching quality assurance process for alliances of higher education institutions they

[325] Ibid., p. 1. Automatic recognition in this context is again understood as automatic recognition of the level of a higher education qualification (or one giving access thereto) as defined in the Council Recommendation of 26 November 2018 on promoting automatic mutual recognition of higher education and upper secondary education and training qualifications and the outcomes of learning periods abroad, [2018] OJ C 444/1 discussed in Section 4.3.1 of this chapter.

[326] See Proposal for a Council Recommendation on a European Quality Assurance and Recognition System in Higher Education, COM(2024) 147 final, pp. 3–4 9, 11–13, 15. Also see Communication from the Commission to the European Parliament, the Council, the European Economic and Social Committee and the Committee of the Regions—a blueprint for a European degree, COM(2024) 144, p. 3.

[327] For example, in the context of the European University Alliances, Erasmus Mundus Joint Masters, Marie Sklodowska-Curie (MSCA) Joint Doctoral Programmes, European Institute for Innovation and Technology programmes, and specialised education programmes under the Digital Europe Programme.

[328] Proposal for a Council Recommendation on a European Quality Assurance and Recognition System in Higher Education, COM(2024) 147 final, pp. 3–4.

[329] Although an alternative is proposed for Member States employing a programme approach, namely to use the European Approach for Quality Assurance of Joint Programmes (an initiative developed in the context of the EHEA).

[330] Proposal for a Council Recommendation on a European Quality Assurance and Recognition System in Higher Education, COM(2024) 147 final, p. 4.

[331] Proposal for a Council Recommendation on a European Quality Assurance and Recognition System in Higher Education, COM(2024) 147 final, p. 6.

would complete only once to have their joint programmes accredited.[332] The road to such a cross-institutional and external quality assurance approach is to be based on robust internal quality assurance processes by, for example, limiting programme accreditations to initial accreditations for new programmes to be followed up by repeated self-accreditation processes. The proposal therefore appears apt at mitigating subsidiarity concerns, while advancing cooperation for those higher education institutions that face difficulties due to the transnational nature of their cooperation.[333]

However, the proposal's innovative potential is not limited to quality assurance alone. The proposal also strengthens the connection between quality assurance and recognition of qualifications, encompassing measures to make recognition automatic through, among others, quality assurance and the adoption of a learning outcomes approach in admission procedures.[334] Whereas such measures build on the Automatic Recognition Recommendation, the proposal also introduces a European degree to facilitate issues of accreditation of joint programmes which clearly hold a central role in the EEA-2025.[335] The idea for the European degree originates from the disparities connected to the issue of degrees challenging the issue of joint degrees.[336] This European degree is proposed as a new type of qualification to be enshrined in national legislation that would make it easier for universities engaged in transnational cooperation to develop joint programmes leading to joint degrees.[337] This means another instrument is introduced to advance transnational higher education cooperation. It also explains the initiative's inclusion in the proposed quality assurance recommendation.

The European degree is considered as another way to deepen cooperation in the Bologna Process and hence builds on the Bologna tools.[338] It maintains the

[332] See Proposal for a Council Recommendation on a European Quality Assurance and Recognition System in Higher Education, COM(2024) 147 final, p. 14 and Annex I to the proposal.

[333] Proposal for a Council Recommendation on a European Quality Assurance and Recognition System in Higher Education, COM(2024) 147 final, pp. 9–10.

[334] This means Member States are to focus on the outcomes of qualifications instead of the specific content of the curriculum. Especially regarding the level, they should therefore focus on the level of the degree that was ultimately awarded and not on the substantive components to determine such a level. See Proposal for a Council Recommendation on a European Quality Assurance and Recognition System in Higher Education, COM(2024) 147 final, pp. 15–16.

[335] Proposal for a Council Recommendation on a European Quality Assurance and Recognition System in Higher Education, COM(2024) 147 final, p. 10.

[336] Communication from the Commission to the European Parliament, the Council, the European Economic and Social Committee and the Committee of the Regions—a blueprint for a European degree, COM(2024) 144, p. 8.

[337] Communication from the Commission to the European Parliament, the Council, the European Economic and Social Committee and the Committee of the Regions on a European strategy for universities, COM(2022) 16 final, p. 5; Communication from the Commission to the European Parliament, the Council, the European Economic and Social Committee and the Committee of the Regions—a blueprint for a European degree, COM(2024) 144, p. 1.

[338] Communication from the Commission to the European Parliament, the Council, the European Economic and Social Committee and the Committee of the Regions—a blueprint for a European degree, COM(2024) 144, p. 3 and 9.

voluntary character and embeddedness in national educational systems, but does entail a set of European-level criteria for its issue—and its level is to be automatically recognised across the EU.[339] These criteria are included in Annex II to the proposed quality assurance recommendation and constitute requirements to a variety of aspects connected to transnational education such as the institutions involved, the delivery of the degree, quality assurance, interdisciplinarity, labour market relevance, student mobility, evaluation of theses, and multilingualism.[340] This means joint programmes have to fulfil all these criteria in order to be awarded the European degree (label) status. It also further attests to European degrees being new types of qualifications issued as the result of the pursuit of higher education that is truly transnational in nature.

In order to arrive to the European degree, Member States have the possibility to determine their level of ambition since a gradual approach is proposed.[341] In its lighter version, the Commission has proposed a European label which can be awarded by quality assurance bodies to joint programmes. The European degree would be awarded jointly by higher education institutions in different Member States and integrated into national legislation as a new qualification. Furthermore, its coherence with existing initiatives such as the Bologna Process, PQD, EQF, and Europass is also emphasised.[342] While this trajectory was proposed in a 2024 Commission communication containing a blueprint for the European degree, the proposed quality assurance recommendation mentions a European label which is awarded by quality assurance agencies to joint degree programmes matching the aforementioned pre-defined criteria.[343] Alternatively, EQAR-registered quality assurance agencies can grant higher education institutions the possibility to award the European label to joint programmes or grant alliances that same power.[344]

Apparently, the immediate introduction of a European degree as such was still too advanced. The introduction of a European label nevertheless appears an attempted first step towards a European degree. Indeed, the European degree's scope being

---

[339] Communication from the Commission to the European Parliament, the Council, the European Economic and Social Committee and the Committee of the Regions—a blueprint for a European degree, COM(2024) 144, p. 4.

[340] See Annex II Proposal for a Council Recommendation on a European Quality Assurance and Recognition System in Higher Education, COM(2024) 147 final.

[341] See Communication from the Commission to the European Parliament, the Council, the European Economic and Social Committee and the Committee of the Regions—a blueprint for a European degree, COM(2024) 144, p. 12.

[342] Communication from the Commission to the European Parliament, the Council, the European Economic and Social Committee and the Committee of the Regions—a blueprint for a European degree, COM(2024) 144, p. 17.

[343] See Annex II of the Proposal for a Council Recommendation on a European Quality Assurance and Recognition System in Higher Education, COM(2024) 147 final.

[344] Proposal for a Council Recommendation on a European Quality Assurance and Recognition System in Higher Education, COM(2024) 147 final, p. 15.

limited to a new type of qualification issued as result of transnational higher education manages to respect national education systems while diminishing administrative hurdles for universities—thus advancing the EEA-2025. Nevertheless, we may question the added value of the proposal for a European degree since, in its currently proposed format, it does not actually amount to a degree which is directly accepted into national legal systems. While the sensitivity of the area of education requires caution and a gradual approach, the question is whether this will be successful—and in what term—since such approach ultimately does not (yet) deliver what its name implies.

4.4 Education in the CJEU's Case Law

Over the course of this chapter it has become apparent that a variety of actors is active in the field of education and academic recognition. It is important not only to understand that the variety of actors is mainly due to the restricted competence on education of Article 165 TFEU, but also that education in the EU is strongly intertwined with other areas of EU law. In the early days of European cooperation, education became entrenched with the freedom of movement seen in the internal market when students encountered restrictions to their free movement. However, both the importance and particular nature of education ultimately culminated in the introduction of a supporting competence with the Maastricht Treaty. Indeed, education is a particular area due to its inherent contradiction associated with the achievement as grand as large-scale student mobility while the competence to legislate on education is limited.

Student mobility is often considered one of the main achievements of the EU in relation to education. However, viewed from a legal perspective this achievement is the result of the interconnectedness of education to other areas of EU law, most notably the free movement of persons and EU citizenship, both areas associated with a strong catalogue of rights awarded to mobile EU citizens. This interconnection with other areas of EU law has enabled a strong individual dimension to arise. This individual dimension is associated with educational rights developed through case law from the Court of Justice of the EU (CJEU) and must be distinguished from a more systemic dimension, which covers all legislative and policy action undertaken to advance education in the EU at the level of national systems of education and qualifications (as discussed in the previous sections of this Chapter).[345] The present section, however, discusses this individual dimension and the interconnection between education, the freedom of movement and EU citizenship as apparent from the CJEU's case law. Indeed, the interface among these three areas is particularly evident in the Court's case law on access to education and the financing thereof.[346]

---

[345] See Kortese and Garben (2025), Kortese (2024).

[346] For a detailed account of student mobility from a European law perspective, see Hoogenboom (2017).

Earlier in this chapter, the *Gravier* judgment was already discussed.[347] The case concerned a French student who objected to having to pay an enrolment fee students of Belgian nationality did not have to pay when enrolling for studies in Belgium. This case allowed the Court to confirm that education falls within the scope of the Treaties by ruling on the meaning of vocational education and training. The Court further held that even though education was not a Treaty competence, this did not mean education bore no connection to Community law.[348] According to the Court, the common vocational training policy referred to in Article 128 EEC Treaty (current Article 165 TFEU) constituted an indispensable element of Community activities and vocational training was considered especially likely to promote free movement.[349] The Court therefore held that vocational training was a concept including "any form of education which prepares for a qualification for a particular profession, trade or employment or which provide the necessary training and skills for such a profession, trade or employment [...], whatever the age and the level of training of the pupils or students, and even if the training programme includes an element of general education".[350]

While *Gravier* therefore confirmed education in general to be within the scope of EU law, *Blaizot* clarified which types of education exactly fell within the scope of the concept of vocational training—and notably answered the question whether higher education would fall within its scope. The case concerned a group of students enrolled in veterinary medicine in Belgium who had to pay a supplementary enrolment fee in addition to the regular enrolment fees. Something Belgian students again did not have to pay. According to the Court, there were no indications in Article 128 EEC Treaty indicating that the concept of vocational training was to exclude higher education *and* some university studies were in fact intended to prepare students for particular occupations.[351] Furthermore, since there were differences between Member States regarding what constituted university studies, excluding those from the scope of the Treaties would result in an unequal application of the Treaty.[352]

Cases such as *Gravier* and *Blaizot* therefore opened the way to consider conditions related to access to education as falling within the scope of EU law. Access to education is to be understood as any aspect prior to the actual pursuit of an educational programme. Initially, access to education primarily concerned financial matters such as the registration and enrolment fees referred to above. Indeed, in *Gravier* and *Blaizot* registration fees and supplementary enrolment fees imposed on foreign students were ultimately prohibited in light of the Treaties due to the nationality-based discrimination they maintained. Over the course of time, the concept of access to education has nevertheless come to cover various aspects related to education that do not concern its financing. For example, access to education also covers a

---

347 See Sect. 4 of this chapter; Case 293/83 *Gravier*, ECLI:EU:C:1985:69.

348 Ibid., para. 19.

349 Ibid., para. 23–24.

350 Ibid., para. 30.

351 Case 24/86 *Blaizot*, ECLI:EU:C:1988:43, para. 17.

352 Ibid., para. 18.

right of residence since a denial of such a right could lead to the inability to attend education (i.e. a restriction to free movement).[353] Similarly, limitations on numbers of foreign students have been considered restrictions, although in the *Bressol* case public health considerations could potentially lead to a justification.[354] This was the case here since Belgium imposed this limitation on foreign students to guarantee a sufficient presence of trained professionals in relation to medical and paramedical programmes of study. An abundance of foreign students would risk them returning to their home Member States upon completion of their studies, leaving the Belgian healthcare system depleted. While the Court did accept public health reasons as justification for this restriction, the Court considered that this justification could only hold up if the national judge concluded that there was a genuine risk to the protection of public health and the measure was proportionate.[355]

Finally, access to education has also come to cover entrance qualifications from other Member States, thus creating a link between access to education and recognition of qualifications. In a line of infringement proceedings against Belgium and Austria, the CJEU concluded that Member States were not allowed to maintain stricter access criteria to other nationals.[356] In *Commission v. Austria*,[357] for example, students with qualifications from other Member States had to demonstrate that their qualifications met the entrance requirement for the course they were signing up for in the country in which they obtained their diploma.[358] According to the Court, the opportunities to free movement provided by the Treaties would be rendered ineffective if a person was penalised for using them.[359] Austria brought forward several justifications, one of which referred to compliance of this rule with the LRC.[360] The Court did not accept any of the justifications. In respect to the LRC it argued that the LRC could not be invoked as a justification because it was concluded after Austria acceded to the EU.[361] Therefore, the effect of these cases was that the principle of non-discrimination on the basis of nationality became applicable to EU citizens requiring recognition of their qualifications when seeking access to education in another Member States.[362]

---

353 Furthermore, any grant of study financing related to access to education could not be made dependent on the possession of a residence permit by the student. See Case C-357/89 *Raulin*, ECLI:EU:C:1992:87.

354 Case C-73/08 *Bressol*, ECLI:EU:C:2010:181.

355 Ibid., para. 71 and 75.

356 See Case C-42/87 *Commission v. Belgium*, ECLI:EU:C:1988:454, Case C-65/03 *Commission v. Belgium*, ECLI:EU:C:2004:402, and Case C-147/03 *Commission v. Austria*, ECLI:EU:C:2005:427.

357 Discussed previously in Sect. 3.1 of this chapter.

358 Case C-147/03 *Commission v. Austria*, ECLI:EU:C:2005:427, para. 6.

359 Ibid., para. 44.

360 Ibid., para. 56.

361 Ibid., para. 72–73.

362 However, it did not make further specifications as to the applicable law in this area. This means that the case law on education maintains the current use of instruments for recognition such as the LRC. See Sect. 3.1 of this chapter for more on the Commission v. Austria case and its relation to the LRC.

These cases therefore show that access to education is a broad concept. Nevertheless, it is not limitless. In order to understand the delineation of the concept, measures regarding the financing of education need to be examined more closely by examining the interconnection with the free movement of workers. In this context, one line of early cases ensured that the children of mobile EU citizens could access educational grants. In particular, the (former) worker status of the parents led to the existence of a right of access to education in the context of Regulation 1612/68.[363] A different line of cases concerned persons who were themselves economically active (i.e. workers) and looking to pursue studies. These cases solidified the distinction between access to education (comprising educational grants) and maintenance grants. Whereas educational grants comprise financial support such as tuition, enrolment or registration fees, maintenance grants concern all financial matters related to supporting the cost of living during studies.[364] In particular, the latter were considered more closely associated to social policy, meaning the right to maintenance grants was more restricted than rights associated with access to education.[365]

Initially, the Court opened the possibility for maintenance grants for studies only to those who were economically active and fulfilled the CJEU's definition of a worker.[366] In particular, the Court prioritised the existence of a link between the status of worker and the maintenance grant, which would be the case if there was continuity between the work previously conducted and education to be pursued.[367] Therefore, work that was either marginal or ancillary in relation to the education to be pursued could not lead to a maintenance grant.[368] However, matters started to change once the Court determined that the freedom of movement also covered economically inactive persons.[369] Subsequently, the introduction of EU citizenship in the Treaty of Maastricht enabled the expansion of rights related to maintenance grants. In *Grzelczyk* the Court produced its famous quote indicating that EU citizenship was "destined to be the fundamental status of nationals of the Member States, enabling those who find themselves in the same situation to enjoy the same treatment in law irrespective of their nationality, subject to such exceptions as are expressly provided for".[370] However, the Court also clearly distinguished Grzelczyk's situation from previous case law,[371] indicating that the combination of the advent of EU citizenship together with the codification of a provision on education in the Treaties (i.e. the education competence) meant that it could no longer be inferred from EU

[363] Case 9/74 *Casagrande*, ECLI:EU:C:1974:74; Cases 389/87 and 390/87 *Eternach and Moritz*, ECLI:EU:C:1989:130.

[364] These can even comprise reduced fares on public transport provided to students. See Case C-75/11 *Commission v. Austria*, ECLI:EU:C:2012:605.

[365] Case 39/86 *Lair*, ECLI:EU:C:1988:322, para. 15–16.

[366] Case 53/81 *Levin*, ECLI:EU:C:1982:105; Case 66/85 *Lawrie-Blum*, ECLI:EU:C:1986:28.

[367] Case 39/86 *Lair*, ECLI:EU:C:1988:322, para. 37.

[368] Case 197/86 *Brown*, ECLI:EU:C:1988:323; Case C-357/89 *Raulin*, ECLI:EU:C:1992:87.

[369] Case C-85/96 *Martinez Sala*, ECLI:EU:C:1998:217.

[370] Case C-184/99 *Grzelczyk*, ECLI:EU:C:2001:458, para. 31.

[371] Most notably Case 197/86 *Brown*, ECLI:EU:C:1988:323.

law that maintenance grants should be limited to economically active persons.[372] From then on maintenance grants were therefore also considered to be within the scope of EU law.

However, *Grzelczyk* and subsequent case law did not lead to an unequivocal right to maintenance grants. In *Bidar* the Court determined that while a certain degree of financial solidarity could be expected from Member States, maintenance costs of foreign students should not become an unreasonable burden to Member States. The Court therefore allowed Member States to require a certain level of integration into society, also referred to as the genuine link between a student and the host Member State.[373] Following this case law, the Court was soon confronted with questions on the determination of this degree of integration.[374] In *Förster*, the Court ultimately determined that a five-year residence requirement could be considered a proportionate means of determining this genuine link.[375]

The previous paragraphs therefore show the relationship between education and other fields of EU law, in particular the free movement and EU citizenship. The case law in this area has developed from the early days of European integration when the Court ruled that even though the Member States are competent to establish the content of teaching and the organisation of their education systems, their competence to do so had to be exercised in compliance with Community law.[376] Whereas such a line could be suspected of leading to an expansive reading of education in favour of the mobility rights of EU citizens, later case law on maintenance grants is indicative of a consideration for the Member States. While criticism has been expressed in relation to various aspects of the case law discussed here,[377] in relation to the present discussion on the recognition of qualifications it serves to show the relatively strong dimension of individual rights related to education as opposed to the more limited legal nature of the system of EU education law and policy.

In fact, even in the case law of the CJEU we may find examples to prove that addressing education-related matters from an institutional perspective is challenging under the current EU legal framework. And again, that addressing such matters under EU law takes place where education meets freedom of movement. Here, reference is to be made to the CJEU judgments in *Neri* and *Commission v. Hungary (CEU)*. In *Neri*, certain degrees issued by private educational establishments were not recognised. While the Court accepted the Italian Government's justification for the non-recognition concerning the desire to ensure high standards of university education,

[372] Case C-184/99 *Grzelczyk*, ECLI:EU:C:2001:458. See also Case C-244/98 *D'Hoop*, ECLI:EU:C:2002:432.

[373] Case C-209/03 *Bidar*, ECLI:EU:C:2005:169, para. 56–57.

[374] For example, Cases C-11/06 and 12/06 *Morgan and Bucher*, ECLI:EU:C:2007:626.

[375] Case C-158/07 *Förster*, ECLI:EU:C:2008:630.

[376] See for example Case 9/74 *Casagrande*, ECLI:EU:C:1974:74, para. 12; Cases C-11/06 and 12/06 *Morgan and Bucher*, ECLI:EU:C:2007:626, para. 24.

[377] See, for example, Hoogenboom (2017), Vėlyvytė (2023).

the lack of any possibility to recognise the degrees at stake was considered disproportionate.[378] However, the most important aspect of the *Neri* case in the present discussion concerns the Court's finding that the organisation for remuneration of university courses was to be considered an economic activity.[379] This allowed the Court to adjudicate on the matter in the context of the freedom of establishment, i.e. the fact that it concerned a private institution allowed for the education provided to be considered a service. This educational matter was therefore pulled into the scope of EU law through the freedom of establishment.

Similar reasoning also enabled the Court to examine Hungary's amendment complicating the operation of foreign educational institutions in light of the freedom of establishment. In particular, the amendment of the relevant national law required that foreign educational institutions could only operate in Hungarian territory if Hungary had a treaty with the country of origin of the foreign institution *and* that foreign institution also organised educational activities in the home State. Despite its general formulation, the rule mainly affected the Central European University. The Court ultimately ruled that the amendment was in violation of Article 49 TFEU and Article 16 of the Services Directive, finding that the restriction caused by the amendment could not be justified on grounds of public policy. This since Hungary had not proven there to be a genuine, present, and sufficiently serious threat affecting a fundamental interest of society.[380] As was the case in *Neri*, the Court was able to resolve the case on the basis of the free movement provisions by categorising the educational activities as economic activity—something it was primarily able to do since the case again concerned a private institution. While the Court did introduce a line of reasoning based on Article 13 of the Charter on academic freedom,[381] the main body of the *Commission v. Hungary* case is rooted in economic law (on free movement). The question remains whether a different conclusion was reached had both cases concerned public educational institutions. These cases therefore demonstrate the far-reaching effects of the EU's original economic orientation which continues to be the entry point to bring other subjects within the scope of EU law. This is an important consideration to keep in mind when considering a potential alternative approach to the EU competences on recognition.[382]

The present section has therefore provided an overview of CJEU case law related to education. These case show that a distinction can be made between an individual dimension (concerning rights EU citizens making use of their free movement hold in respect to education) and a systemic dimension (concerning legislative and policy instruments on education). Furthermore, they show that many education-related rights are either rooted in EU citizenship or freedom of movement. While these cases made clear that the individual dimension is quite strong in granting individuals

---

[378] Case C-153/02 *Neri*, ECLI:EU:C:2003:614, para. 46–52.

[379] Ibid., para. 39.

[380] Case C-66/18 *Commission v. Hungary*, ECLI:EU:C:2020:792, para. 157–190 and 191–207.

[381] See Ibid., para. 208–243.

[382] For more on this point, see Chapter "Re-Imagining the System for the Recognition of Qualifications in the EU", Sect. 3.

a right of access to education, it also showed that this mostly concerns an application of the principle of non-discrimination on the basis of nationality. As far as recognition of qualifications is concerned, these cases therefore show that non-discrimination on the basis of nationality requires equality of treatment regarding which qualifications are required from Member State nationals and of holders of foreign qualifications. Further provisions on recognition of qualifications nevertheless still need to be derived from other legislation and policy.[383]

5 Conclusion

The objective of this chapter was to explore the variety of initiatives on academic recognition. As the chapter has demonstrated, initiatives and instruments on academic recognition originate from within and outside the EU legal framework. The chapter also shows that the field is much more dispersed than that for professional recognition. This variety of actors active in the field of academic recognition may be traced to the EU's limited competence in Article 165 TFEU. Accordingly, action parallel to that of the EU has taken place in the context of the Bologna Process, Council of Europe and UNESCO, and regional initiatives such as the Benelux. In fact, the Bologna Process was highly exemplary for the development of the field of academic recognition. It resulted in transparency instruments such as qualifications frameworks, common documentation formats, a credit system, and cooperation on quality assurance—something mirrored in the EU's Copenhagen Process. The Bologna Process furthermore served as the catalyst for activities on academic recognition such as the Benelux Decisions and later Automatic Recognition Recommendation adopted in the EU context. Nevertheless, in recent years the level of ambition in the EU has been increased, leading it to propose and adopt a variety of instruments strengthening previous action.[384] Reference here is to be made to the aforementioned Automatic Recognition Recommendation, Micro-credentials Recommendation, 2020 VET Recommendation and proposed recommendation on quality assurance and recognition, including plans for a European degree. While all instruments discussed in this chapter either came into existence due to the legal basis of Article 165 TFEU or could be maintained due to its limited nature, it is important to consider that these instruments also explicitly and inexplicitly relate to facilitated mobility for labour market purposes. Furthermore, the section on the Court of Justice's case law showed that the topic of education is inextricably linked to free movement and EU

[383] Such as that discussed in Chapters "Professional Recognition" and "Academic Recognition" of this contribution.

[384] It will be particularly interesting to see how these increased ambitions will materialise further in the upcoming years. At the time of conclusion of this manuscript, the Commission had just launched consultations for an upcoming Skills Portability Initiative bringing together, among others, efforts on digitalisation, increased transparency, and improved recognition procedures in relation to both skills and qualifications. The introduction of such plans under the Skills Portability Initiative was foreseen for Q3 of 2026.

citizenship—thus further demonstrating a connection between the fields of education and internal market. The question therefore becomes how the instruments for professional and academic recognition interrelate and what the resulting system for recognition looks like. This question will be explored further in Chapter "Re-Imagining the System for the Recognition of Qualifications in the EU".

References

Auzinger M, Luomi-Messerer K (2021) The European credit system for vocational education and training. Publications Office of the EU, Luxembourg

Benoît-Rohmer F, Klebes H (2005) Council of Europe law: towards a pan-European legal area. Council of Europe Publishing, Strasbourg

Bergan S (2009a) Academic recognition: status and challenges. Assess Educ: Princ, Policy & Pract 16:39–53

Bergan S (2009b) Substantial differences: exploring a concept. In: Hunt ES, Bergan S (eds) Developing attitudes to recognition: substantial differences in an age of globalisation. Council of Europe Publishing, Strasbourg, pp 15–29

Bergan S, Divis J, Rauhvargers A (2000) Bridges over troubled waters: Bologna and the recognition of qualifications. J Stud Int Educ 4/2:11–20.

Bergan S, Rauhvargers A (2005) The Council of Europe/UNESCO (Lisbon) Recognition Convention—what it is and how to use it. In: Bergan S, Rauhvargers A (eds) Standards for recognition: the Lisbon Recognition Convention and its subsidiary texts. Council of Europe Publishing, Strasbourg, pp 25–40

Bohlinger S (2012) Qualifications frameworks and learning outcomes: challenges for Europe's lifelong learning area. J Educ Work 25:279–297

Bouder A (2008) European qualifications framework: Weighing some pros and cons out of a French perspective. J Eur Ind Train 32:114–126

De Bruin L (2014) With both feet on the ground: EAR projects, instruments for recognition. In: Bergan S, Blomqvist C (eds) The Lisbon Recognition Convention at 15: making fair recognition a reality. Council of Europe Publishing, Strasbourg, pp 207–224

Deane A (2005) Transparency of qualifications: are we there yet? Eur J Educ 40:279–293

Devaux A , Fleury S, Howat C, Schaepkens L (2013) Evaluation of the implementation of the European Qualifications Framework Recommendation.

Garben S (2011a) On recognition of qualifications for academic and professional purposes. Tilburg Law Rev 16:127–156

Garben S (2011b) EU higher education law: the Bologna process and harmonization by stealth. Kluwer Law International, Alphen aan den Rijn

Grimonprez K (2020) The European Union and education for democratic citizenship: legal foundations for EU learning at school. Nomos, Baden-Baden Nomos eLibrary

Hoogenboom A (2017) Balancing student mobility rights and national higher education autonomy in the European Union. Brill Nijhoff, Leiden

Juncker J-C (2006) Council of Europe—European Union: A sole ambition for the European continent. Council of Europe, 11 April 2006

Kelo M (2014) Quality assurance as an element of international recognition. In: Bergan S, Blomqvist C (eds) The Lisbon Recognition Convention at 15: making fair recognition a reality. Council of Europe Publishing, Strasbourg, pp 145–156

Kortese L (2024) Education in the EU. In: Garben S et al (eds) Oxford encyclopedia of EU law. Oxford University Press, Oxford. https://opil.ouplaw.com/display/10.1093/law-oeeul/law-oeeul-e233.

Kortese L, Garben S (2025) Post-Brexit cooperation in higher education and research: the changing EU-UK relationship. In: Guinchard E, Panara C (eds) The new relationship between the United Kingdom and the European Union. Springer, Cham, pp 405–427

Macron E (2017) Discours d'Emmanuel Macron pour une Europe souveraine, unie, démocratique. https://www.elysee.fr/emmanuel-macron/2017/09/26/initiative-pour-l-europe-discours-d-emmanuel-macron-pour-une-europe-souveraine-unie-democratique

Mohay A (2017) The status of international agreements concluded by the European Union in the EU legal order. Prav Vjesn 33:151–163

Rauhvargers A (2009) Recognition and qualifications frameworks. Assess Educ: Princ, Policy & Pract 16(2009):111–125

Ravinet P (2008) From voluntary participation to monitored coordination: why European countries feel increasingly bound by their commitment to the Bologna Process. European Journal of Education 43:353–367

Rosas A (2011) The status in EU law of international agreements concluded by EU member states. Fordham Int J 34:1304–1345

Terpan F (2015) Soft law in the European Union—the changing nature of EU law. Eur Law J 21:68–96

Terry LS (2008) The Bologna process and its impact in Europe: it's so much more than degree changes. Vanderbilt Journal of Transnational Law 41:107–228

Vėlyvytė V (2023) Competence creep in EU free movement case law. European Law Review 48:323–342

Verbruggen MLW (2003) De Bolognaverklaring kritisch getoetst aan het Europees onderwijsbeleid. SEW 6:199–212

Wächter B (2004) The Bologna process: Developments and prospects. Eur J Educ 39:265–273

Zgaga P (2014) The Lisbon Recognition Convention as a paradigmatic shift and a change of the philosophy of recognition: between reflection and sentiments. In: Bergan S, Blomqvist C (eds) The Lisbon Recognition Convention at 15: making fair recognition a reality. Council of Europe Publishing, Strasbourg, pp 19–30

A Question of Our Time, A Question of All Times?

Re-Imagining the System for the Recognition of Qualifications in the EU

1 Introduction

The topic of the recognition of qualifications in the EU has been explored in depth throughout this contribution. The long history of the topic was explored in Chapter "The Long History of the Recognition of Qualifications in the EU". Chapter "Challenging Convention: Theory, Competences & The Grey Area of Recognition" showed the typology of recognition, how this was translated into EU competences, and how it could be challenged by exploring the grey area of recognition. Chapters "Professional Recognition" and "Academic Recognition" subsequently provided an in-depth analysis of the different instruments contributing to or effectuating recognition of qualifications in the EU. To recall, the Professional Qualifications Directive (PQD)[1] and the Proportionality Test Directive[2] concern *de jure* professional recognition and are the only instruments adopted on the basis of the Article 53 TFEU competence. By contrast, the academic recognition competence of

[1] The term "Professional Qualifications Directive" is used to refer to Directive 2005/36/EC of the European Parliament and of the Council of 7 September 2005 on the recognition of professional qualifications, [2005] OJ L 255/22 as amended by Directive 2013/55/EU of the European Parliament and of the Council of 20 November 2013 amending Directive 2005/36/EC on the recognition of professional qualifications and Regulation (EU) No 1024/2012 on administrative cooperation through the Internal Market Information System ('the IMI Regulation'), [2013] OJ L 354/132. The consolidated version of the Professional Qualifications Directive can be accessed at: https://eur-lex.europa.eu/legal-content/EN/TXT/?uri=CELEX%3A02005L0036-20251029.

[2] The term "Proportionality Test Directive" is used to refer to Directive (EU) 2018/958 of the European Parliament and of the Council of 28 June 2018 on a proportionality test before adoption of new regulation of professions, [2018] OJ L 173/25.

L. S.J. Kortese, *Effectuating Free Movement in the EU through Recognition of Qualifications*, https://doi.org/10.1007/978-3-032-21335-8_6

Article 165 TFEU was used to adopt the EQF,[3] Europass,[4] Automatic Recognition Recommendation,[5] 2020 VET Recommendation,[6] and Micro-credentials Recommendation[7]—even though most of these instruments also concern (some form of) professional recognition. The limited nature of Article 165 TFEU furthermore provided space for action outside the EU legal framework to be taken in the context of the Bologna Process, Lisbon Recognition Convention (LRC),[8] and Benelux Decisions.[9]

The examination of these instruments demonstrates how multi-faceted the instruments on recognition of qualifications truly are. Despite its vastness, we may question the extent to which the resulting system for recognition is comprehensive thus providing possibilities for recognition at any stage in accordance with common principles defined at EU level. With a view to the future, questions may furthermore be raised as to whether the current system can facilitate ambitions set for the development of the Internal Market and European Education Area (EEA-2025). The objective of the present chapter is to demonstrate that, while the system for recognition as constituted by the different instruments is generally coherent, weaknesses can be identified challenging its comprehensiveness to guarantee recognition at any stage in line with common principles applicable at EU level. In this context, improvements

[3] The term "EQF Recommendation" is used to refer to Council Recommendation of 22 May 2017 on the European Qualifications Framework for lifelong learning and repealing the recommendation of the European Parliament and of the Council of 23 April 2008 on the establishment of the European Qualifications Framework for lifelong learning, [2017] OJ C 189/15.

[4] The term "Europass Decision" is used to refer to Decision (EU) 2018/646 of the European Parliament and of the Council of 18 April 2018 on a common framework for the provision of better services for skills and qualifications (Europass) and repealing Decision No 2241/2004/EC, [2018] OJ L 112/42.

[5] The term "Automatic Recognition Recommendation" is used to refer to Council Recommendation of 26 November 2018 on promoting automatic mutual recognition of higher education and upper secondary education and training qualifications and the outcomes of learning periods abroad, [2018] OJ C 444/1.

[6] The term "2020 VET Recommendation" is used to refer to Council Recommendation of 24 November 2020 on vocational education and training (VET) for sustainable competitiveness, social fairness and resilience, [2020] OJ C 417/1.

[7] The term "Micro-credentials Recommendation" is used to refer to Council Recommendation of 16 June 2022 on a European approach to micro-credentials for lifelong learning and employability, [2022] OJ C 243/10.

[8] The term "Lisbon Recognition Convention" is used to refer to the Convention on the Recognition of Qualifications concerning Higher Education in the European Region, Council of Europe and UNESCO, 11 April 1997, ETS—No. 165.

[9] Beschikking van het Benelux Comité van Ministers betreffende de automatische wederzijdse generieke niveauerkenning van diploma's hoger onderwijs, M(2015) 3; Beschikking van het Benelux Comité van Ministers tot aanvulling van beschikking M(2015) 3 betreffende de automatische wederzijdse generieke niveauerkenning van diploma's hoger onderwijs, M(2018) 1; Verdrag betreffende de automatische erkenning van diploma's in het hoger onderwijs (14 September 2021).

can be suggested to increase legal certainty and ensure that future objectives[10] may be better attained. To support this argument, this chapter first examines the interrelationships between and core characteristics of the different instruments for recognition. However, before focusing on interrelationships attention needs to be given to identifying different approaches in legislation and policy which contribute to recognition. This exercise results in a three-tier hierarchy which can be used to better explain the roles of the instruments included in this contribution. Next, the examination of the interrelationships will confirm the overall coherence of the system while also allowing for the identification of weaknesses in the current system for recognition. The chapter concludes by taking the identified weaknesses in the system for recognition as a starting point to make suggestions on how to improve recognition of qualifications and render it more future-proof.

2 The System for Recognition of Qualifications in the EU: Interpreting Interrelationships & Exposing Weaknesses

The instruments contributing to or effectuating recognition included in this contribution do not exist independently of one another. Instead, they come together to form the system for recognition of qualifications in the EU. Mapping and interpreting the interrelationships existing among the different instruments has several objectives. First, the exercise will confirm the growing coherence among instruments—and therefore of the system for recognition. Second, this examination plays an essential role in exposing weaknesses of the current system for recognition. The exercise is conducted by focusing on the extent to which the recognition instruments are legally binding, who they are directed at, and how recognition is effectuated or contributed to.

However, before turning to this exercise, attention needs to be given to understanding the roles each of the instruments have to play in recognising qualifications. Indeed, this contribution focuses on instruments contributing to or effectuating recognition of qualifications. Three approaches can thereby be distinguished. First, there are instruments directly effectuating recognition. Indeed, only the PQD, LRC, and Benelux Decisions directly provide rights and duties to individuals seeking recognition and the parties recognising them. Second, other instruments contribute to recognition by enhancing transparency. Here, we may particularly group the instruments adopted in the context of the Bologna and Copenhagen Processes, which aim to enhance transparency by establishing qualifications frameworks (EQF & QF-EHEA), common documentation formats (Europass & Diploma Supplement), credit systems (ECTS), and quality assurance processes (ESG). Next to these more established instruments, newer EU initiatives were also explored in the form of

[10] See Chapter "Introduction", Sect. 4. Some ambitious future ambitions have been drawn up related to recognition in the EU. These can be summarised as increasing automatic recognition, decreasing unnecessary regulation, and increasing flexibility of learning pathways.

the Automatic Recognition Recommendation, Micro-credentials Recommendation, 2020 VET Recommendation, and proposals for a EU quality assurance and recognition system for higher education, and European degree. These instruments can be designated as "booster instruments" for their role in deepening the implementation and application of pre-existing instruments adopted in the context of the Bologna and Copenhagen Processes—and can therefore be considered a sub-category of transparency instruments.

Apart from achieving recognition through recognition instruments and by increasing transparency, a third way of achieving recognition can be identified. Some instruments enhance understanding, transparency, mutual trust, and ultimately recognition by harmonising education and training. Indeed, if education and training is the same across countries and is provided under similar circumstances, qualifications are much less likely to be called into question. This increased familiarity and trust means that swift and unconditional recognition is more likely to occur. In the EU, harmonisation of education and training has occurred to a limited extent. There are two prime examples here: first, the Bologna Process which harmonised the structure of higher education into short-cycle higher education degrees, bachelors, masters, and doctorates. Second, the system for automatic recognition within the PQD. Containing the legacy from the 1970s,[11] that system allows for recognition without substantive assessments of professional qualifications since minimum training conditions were determined ensuring that the core of education and training for the professions of doctor, nurse, veterinarian, midwife, dentist, pharmacist, and architect is the same across Member States. Since 2013, automatic recognition can be extended to other professions through the adoption of common training frameworks or tests. A common training test has since been adopted for ski instructors which are now also subject to automatic recognition.[12] Despite this advanced harmonisation, the standards included in the PQD are general in nature, meaning that requirements are made only in relation to duration of training and general knowledge, skills, and competences needed to carry out a profession.[13] Therefore, this automatic recognition under the PQD is the result of harmonisation combined with the principle of mutual recognition. Indeed, mutual recognition under secondary EU law often goes hand in hand with harmonisation.[14] In such situations mutual recognition has a semi-automatic nature and provides a middle path between integration and harmonisation.[15] Accordingly, if harmonisation of laws takes place in combination with the principle of mutual recognition, this can result in automatic recognition,[16] as is the case for the sectoral

[11] See Chapter "The Long History of the Recognition of Qualifications in the EU" of this contribution for the historical development of the recognition of qualifications in the EU.

[12] See Commission Delegated Regulation (EU) 2019/907 of 14 March 2019 establishing a Common Training Test for ski instructors under Article 49b of Directive 2005/36/EC of the European Parliament and of the Council on the recognition of professional qualifications, [2019] OJ L 145/7.

[13] See Chapter III Section 2 of the Professional Qualifications Directive.

[14] Möstl 2010, pp. 413–414).

[15] Hoogenboom (2014, p. 238).

[16] Möstl 2010, pp. 413–414).

professions under the PQD. Alternatively, when there is little or no harmonisation, mutual recognition may take the form of limiting grounds for refusal (something that can be perceived under the PQD's general system).[17]

It goes without saying that harmonisation, transparency, and recognition instruments respectively serve a different purpose in ultimately recognising qualifications. Harmonisation may take away the need for in-depth substantive recognition procedures by rendering qualifications more similar. Transparency instruments are crucial to enhance mutual trust and familiarity with foreign qualifications. Ultimately, recognition instruments comprising rights and duties are essential to provide legal certainty and procedural safeguards. A critic may disagree with the focus on the term recognition in this contribution remarking that recognition of qualifications ultimately only concerns instruments such as the PQD, LRC, and Benelux Decisions. However, the role of transparency instruments in recognition is not to be underestimated since transparency is a necessary precondition for recognition, the latter being the end-result of sufficient transparency between two qualifications originating from different educational systems. Transparency instruments and procedural recognition instruments can subsequently each be considered an expression of a different principle ultimately essential to achieving freedom of movement. While transparency instruments enhance mutual trust, recognition instruments effectuate mutual recognition.

Mutual trust and mutual recognition were previously remarked to be strongly interrelated, trust thereby serving as a prerequisite for recognition.[18] Qualifications will ultimately be recognised on the basis of trust in another Member State's education and professions. Nevertheless, the opposite also applies: positive experiences regarding successful application of the principle of mutual recognition also result in increased mutual trust.[19] Indeed, the relationship between trust and law can be considered recursive.[20] Trust acts as a precondition for successful legal rules, while at the same time legal rules promote trust when they are consistent, coherent, predictable, and efficient. Between the two, mutual trust can nevertheless be considered the more foundational since trust requires a stable and advanced relationship.[21] This is particularly true in the area of the recognition of qualifications because acceptance of a qualification is more likely to be the result of a belief in its suitability for the exercise of a profession or the pursuit of studies. The principle of mutual recognition in itself, though foundational, is insufficient to realise free movement especially since it constitutes a balancing act between the freedoms and rights of individuals on the one hand, and the legitimate pursuit of public interests of Member States on the other.[22] Mutual recognition combined with a lack of trust indeed likely results in the (perceived) need to rely on public interest grounds to limit recognition and/or make

[17] Ibid.

[18] Cambien (2017, p. 114).

[19] Ibid., p. 102.

[20] Wischmeyer (2016, p. 348).

[21] Cambien (2017, pp. 99–100).

[22] Möstl (2010, p. 407).

it conditional upon additional measures with which a person proves their suitability to work or study in a host Member State.

Furthermore, mutual trust is to be considered the more foundational of the two principles in the context of the recognition of qualifications because mutual trust—unlike mutual recognition—is both a concept operating outside the law, as well as a legal principle.[23] Indeed, mutual recognition may not always be enforced, as qualifications are not recognised formally only by Member State actors. For example, for non-regulated professions employers take the final decision on whether or not to employ a holder of foreign qualifications. Although the Court of Justice of the EU ruled that the *Vlassopoulou* doctrine also extends to non-regulated professions,[24] an employer may still consider a nationally trained person more suitable for the job especially if they cannot gain sufficient understanding of a foreign qualification. In this case, there are no public interest considerations preventing recognition and the issue relates more to the unfamiliarity of the employer with foreign qualifications—and ultimately a lack of trust.[25]

Following these considerations on the different ways to achieve recognition, these can be ordered into a three-tier hierarchy providing an overview of how recognition is achieved (see Fig. 1). Harmonisation of education and training is thereby considered the most foundational, thus constituting Tier 1, for its capacity to take away the need for recognition and providing the most advanced form of trust due to the similarity instituted. Indeed, it has been argued that (especially full) harmonisation takes away the need for mutual trust, as Member States are obliged to apply the same rules.[26] Arguably, this tier is also the hardest to achieve due to the strong connection of education and national identity[27]—and therefore interference with the autonomy of Member States. Tier 2 consists of transparency instruments for their capacity to enhance mutual trust, which above was designated more foundational than mutual recognition. Apart from transparency instruments, we may also group booster instruments in Tier 2 since they will not only enhance mutual trust by enhancing transparency instruments, but can also enhance trust in recognition procedures where they boost their functioning and uniform application. Lastly, Tier 3 consists of procedures effectuating mutual recognition.

This three-tier hierarchy of ways to effectuate recognition is instrumental to re-imagining recognition and ensuring it is future-proof. At present, action in the EU taken across the three tiers has not occurred following a consistent approach. Accordingly, the current system for recognition is most elaborate in Tier 2 with regard to enhancing mutual trust, but relatively weak in Tier 3 on mutual recognition. To better

---

[23] Cambien (2017, pp. 112–113).

[24] Case C-234/97 *Fernández de Bobadilla*, ECLI:EU:C:1999:367, para. 28 and 31–33; Case C-164/94, *Aranitis*, ECLI:EU:C:1996:23, para. 30–32. See also Case C-586/08 *Rubino*, ECLI:EU:C:2009:801.

[25] Communication from the Commission on recognition of qualifications for academic and professional purposes, COM(94) 596 final, p. 5.

[26] Schoenmaekers (2010, p. 86).

[27] Walkenhorst (2008, p. 567; and the literature cited), Walkenhorst (2005, p. 2).

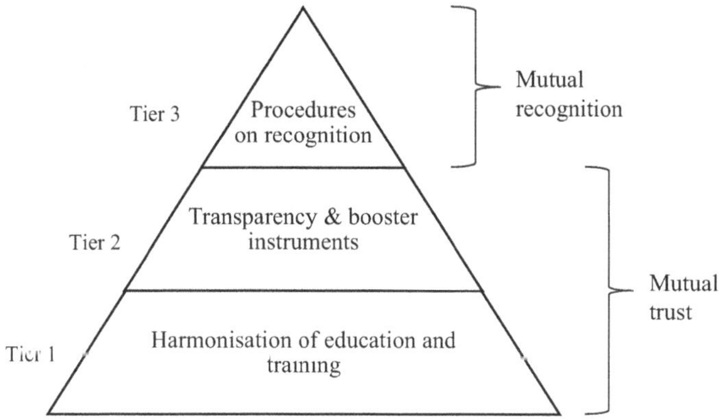

Fig. 1 The three tiers of recognition

understand why, the interrelationships between the instruments need to be examined more closely. This exercise serves to expose weaknesses in the current system for recognition. This examination first focuses on the recognition instruments in Tier 3 (PQD, LRC, and Benelux Decisions) after which the transparency and booster instruments in Tier 2 are examined.

2.1 *Recognition Instruments: The PQD, LRC, and Benelux Decisions*

Taking the PQD, LRC, and Benelux Decisions together we may see quite a comprehensive system starts to arise providing procedures and legal safeguards on recognition. The LRC and Benelux Decisions are thereby connected to one another since they both concern higher education qualifications and are related to the Bologna Process. The Benelux Decisions contribute to facilitate recognition in the context of the Bologna Process because they automate recognition of the level of higher education degrees in the Benelux. As to the PQD, the Decisions explicitly state that they do not concern recognition of professional qualifications as intended by the PQD.[28] In particular, the Benelux Decisions are not relevant for recognition for regulated professions since the PQD itself contains a provision stating that authorities must accept the level of the qualification attested to by the home Member State.[29] The

[28] Preamble Beschikking van het Benelux Comité van Ministers betreffende de automatische wederzijdse generieke niveauerkenning van diploma's hoger onderwijs, M(2015) 3; Preamble Beschikking van het Benelux Comité van Ministers tot aanvulling van beschikking M(2015) 3 betreffende de automatische wederzijdse generieke niveauerkenning van diploma's hoger onderwijs, M(2018) 1.

[29] Article 13(3) Professional Qualifications Directive.

Benelux Decisions can therefore be considered to achieve a similar effect in respect to the LRC (in the Benelux countries) as this provision in the PQD.

Next, the focus needs to be directed to the relationship between the PQD and LRC. While the PQD concerns *de jure* professional recognition, the LRC can concern all types of recognition. Indeed, the LRC can also be considered to concern professional recognition since it also foresees provisions on recognition in relation to labour market access.[30] The LRC can thereby be understood as also concerning regulated professions. However, one must take into account here that the LRC applies to many States outside the EU where there may not be an initiative for recognition of qualifications for regulated professions like that of the PQD. Similarly, the LRC can be relevant in the case of regulated professions in the relation between an EU Member State and another Party to the LRC (to which the PQD does not apply).[31] In the case of the EU Member States, these countries of course take part in both the LRC and PQD. An area of overlap can therefore come into existence in relation to regulated professions for EU Member States. This particularly due to Article XI.4 of the LRC under which assessments of higher education qualifications can lead to advice to competent authorities. However, major incoherencies are avoided. Indeed, the LRC's 2010 Revised Recommendation on Criteria and Procedures for the Assessment of Foreign Qualifications clarifies that the relationship between the PQD and the LRC is to be understood as a *lex specialis*. In particular, the PQD is to take precedence over the LRC in a recognition procedure for a regulated profession in the EU.[32] The only area of overlap between the LRC and the PQD therefore occurs via the activities of ENIC/NARICs when they advise competent recognition authorities which take the final decision on a recognition procedure for a regulated profession.[33] Whereas the competent authority will consider the application in light of the PQD, an ENIC/NARIC can assess the higher education qualification making up part of the professional qualifications of the individual concerned in the context of the LRC.[34]

---

30 Article VI.3 Lisbon Recognition Convention.

31 See Case C-147/03 *Commission v. Austria*, ECLI:EU:C:2005:427, para. 72–73.

32 The Recommendation stipulates that competent authorities determine which national and international legal texts are relevant to a case. These authorities also determine whether a specific decision must be reached or whether a specific procedure must be applied. Examples of such specific legal texts are national laws and regulations concerning the exercise of gainful employment, including regulated professions, and EU directives, including those on professional recognition. See: Paragraph 33 Revised Recommendation on Criteria and Procedures for the Assessment of Foreign Qualifications (adopted by the Lisbon Recognition Convention Committee at its fifth meeting, Sèvres, 23 June 2010); Explanatory Memorandum—Revised Recommendation on Criteria and Procedures for the Assessment of Foreign Qualifications (adopted by the Lisbon Recognition Convention Committee at its fifth meeting, Sèvres, 23 June 2010), p. 20.

33 Article VI.4(a)(c) Lisbon Recognition Convention; Section II Joint ENIC/NARIC Charter of Activities and Services, Council of Europe and UNESCO, 9 June 2004.

34 This approach is also coherent with the case law of the CJEU in which the Court determined that procedures for recognition of academic qualifications need to be taken into account for professional recognition as well. See Chapter "Challenging Convention: Theory, Competences & The Grey Area of Recognition", Sect. 5 and Chapter "Professional Recognition", Sect. 6 of this contribution as well

A similar role may exist for these organisations in the context of *de facto* professional recognition.[35] In this case, an overlap exists with the case law of the CJEU. Chapters "Challenging Convention: Theory, Competences & The Grey Area of Recognition" and "Professional Recognition" previously showed that when it comes to EU law on *de facto* professional recognition, this is primarily governed by the case law from the CJEU on freedom of movement. To recall, this line of cases initiated with *Vlassopoulou* and its core doctrine requires authorities to take into account all diplomas, certificates and other evidence when recognising professional qualifications.[36] Under the doctrine, Member States must make a comparison between the home and host Member State qualifications to see if recognition is possible.[37] If this is not the case, the applicant should be given the opportunity to demonstrate the lacking knowledge.[38] The *Vlassopoulou* doctrine was also recognised by the Court in relation to non-regulated professions (i.e. to *de facto* professional recognition).[39] In light of the shared nature of the Internal Market competence action conflicting with the interpretation given to directly effective Treaty provisions is in principle pre-empted.[40] Nevertheless, in the case of the *Vlassopoulou* doctrine and LRC we may ask to which extent there is a conflict: both sets of norms are based on (an iteration of the principle of) mutual recognition with possible exceptions in case of substantial differences. Nevertheless, some element of conflict is found since the *Vlassopoulou* doctrine requires a consideration of all evidence of qualifications while the LRC focuses on higher education qualifications. Nevertheless, it may be recalled that the Court had ruled in *Brouillard* that all evidence of qualifications is to be considered—even if academic equivalence procedures are used for professional purposes.[41] This reasoning further diminishes the overlap between the LRC and EU action on professional recognition and creates synergy between both realms.

Returning to the comparison of the PQD and LRC, both instruments share the trait that they provide procedures for recognition of qualifications. The LRC relates primarily to higher education qualifications and the PQD to any qualification provided it is necessary to exercise a regulated profession. Both instruments are similar in the sense that they include provisions for both temporary mobility as well as long(er)

---

as the case law in Case C-313/01 *Morgenbesser*, ECLI:EU:C:2003:612; Case C-298/14 *Brouillard*, ECLI:EU:C:2015:652.

[35] Explanatory Memorandum—Revised Recommendation on Criteria and Procedures for the Assessment of Foreign Qualifications (adopted by the Lisbon Recognition Convention Committee at its fifth meeting, Sèvres, 23 June 2010), p. 21.

[36] Case C-340/89 *Vlassopoulou*, ECLI:EU:C:1991:193, para. 16.

[37] Ibid.

[38] Ibid.., para. 19.

[39] Case C-234/97 *Fernández de Bobadilla*, ECLI:EU:C:1999:367, para. 28 and 31–33; Case C-164/94, *Aranitis*, ECLI:EU:C:1996:23, para. 30–32. See also Case C-586/08 *Rubino*, ECLI:EU:C:2009:801.

[40] Gallo (2022, p. 593).

[41] Case C-298/14 *Brouillard*, ECLI:EU:C:2015:652, para. 60 and 67. See also Chapter "Challenging Convention: Theory, Competences & The Grey Area of Recognition", Sect. 5 of this contribution.

term mobility. Indeed, the PQD covers both the freedom of services and of establishment. The LRC concerns higher education qualifications in four different situations: (1) recognition of qualifications giving access to higher education, (2) recognition of periods of study, (3) recognition of higher education qualifications, and (4) recognition of qualifications held by refugees.[42] While a further difference in respect to both instruments concerns the PQD's determination of substantive criteria in the system for automatic recognition, both the PQD and LRC provide for general provisions on recognition that may be applicable to anyone fulfilling the scope of the respective instrument. Despite the differences, the PQD's general system has a similar way of achieving recognition as the LRC. This predominantly concerns the fundamental concept underlying both instruments.

Although they originate from different legal orders, both the PQD's general system and LRC operate on the basis of mutual recognition—or, in the case of the LRC, a principle that resembles it. The LRC's fundamental concept can be found in Articles IV.1, IV.3, V.1 and VI.1 which provide that recognition will be granted *unless* substantial differences can be shown. Whereas under the LRC, this "principle of substantial differences" is used to describe the instrument's fundamental concept,[43] its essence is quite similar to the EU principle of mutual recognition as found in the PQD which centres on the presumption that recognition must be granted, unless substantial differences can be shown.[44] Arguably, the formulation of this principle in the LRC can be considered weaker due to its focus on substantial differences as opposed to mutual recognition.

It is clear that the term "substantial differences" plays an important role in recognising qualifications. The PQD defines substantially different matters as those for which knowledge, skills, and competences are essential to pursue the profession and where the applicant's training is significantly different.[45] Under the LRC, substantial differences are not defined in the Convention itself, but rather in its subsidiary texts.[46] The concept is essential in recognition procedures under each of the respective instruments since a finding of substantial differences delays recognition. Indeed, a finding of substantial differences will likely result in the imposition of additional measures to overcome those differences. Here, we may again perceive a similarity between the two instruments: both provide opportunities to overcome knowledge shortages. In the case of the PQD, it is clear that this may occur through compensation measures, which may consist of an adaptation period of up to three years or an aptitude test.[47] In general, applicants have a right to choose between either

[42] Sections IV through VII Lisbon Recognition Convention.

[43] Rauhvargers (2009, p. 112).

[44] Article 13 and 14(1)(a) Professional Qualifications Directive.

[45] Article 14(4) Professional Qualifications Directive.

[46] Council of Europe and UNESCO, Explanatory Report to the Convention on the Recognition of Qualifications concerning Higher Education in the European Region, 11 April 1997, ETS—No. 165, p. 14; Paragraphs 36–37 Revised Recommendation on Criteria and Procedures for the Assessment of Foreign Qualifications (adopted by the Lisbon Recognition Convention Committee at its fifth meeting, Sèvres, 23 June 2010).

[47] Article 14(1) Professional Qualifications Directive.

of the two options. It is only in exceptional cases that Member States may dictate either one of the compensation measures or even impose both.[48] Article III.5 of the LRC subsequently prescribes that the competent authority must inform the applicant of the reasons why recognition was refused and what possible measures they may take to still obtain recognition. The authority here has a duty to assist the applicant in identifying measures to be able to benefit from recognition at a later point.[49] Possible measures here may involve additional education, examinations or other measures.[50]

In terms of procedures, professionals needing to get their qualifications recognised under the PQD can expect to obtain a decision on their application within three months of submission of their full application.[51] In select cases, the recognition of qualifications may be extended by one month,[52] meaning that the maximum assessment period is four months under the PQD.[53] Under the LRC, Article III.5 indicates that decisions on recognition are to be taken within a reasonable time limit specified beforehand. Parties to the LRC are encouraged to maintain a maximum of four months for recognition procedures.[54] Furthermore, this reasonable time starts to run from the moment all necessary information has been provided, meaning in terms of time limits both instruments are also similar. The same cannot be said for the documentation required, however. Article 50(1) of the PQD allows the competent authorities to require a list of documents as specified in Annex VII of the Directive.[55] Under the LRC, Article III.3(2) requires applicants to provide adequate information. The Recommendation on Criteria and Procedures for the Assessment of Foreign

[48] Article 14(2)(3) Professional Qualifications Directive.

[49] Paragraph 44 Revised Recommendation on Criteria and Procedures for the Assessment of Foreign Qualifications (adopted by the Lisbon Recognition Convention Committee at its fifth meeting, Sèvres, 23 June 2010).

[50] Council of Europe, Explanatory Report to the Convention on the Recognition of Qualifications concerning Higher Education in the European Region, Lisbon 11.IV.1997, ETS no. 165, p. 14.

[51] Professionals thus have to transmit all necessary documents to the competent authority for the assessment period to commence. Article 51(2) Professional Qualifications Directive.

[52] Article 51(2) Professional Qualifications Directive.

[53] This four-month period applies for the "traditional" recognition procedure under the PQD. Directive 2013/55/EU introduced the European Professional Card. This card is not a physical card but entails the digitalisation of the regular recognition procedures. Due to the fact that the Internal Market Information System is used, the regular recognition procedure can be expedited meaning that the maximum duration of the recognition procedure decreases. However, the European Professional Card is not available to all professionals. Currently, only physiotherapists, general care nurses, real estate agents, pharmacists, and mountain guides can benefit from this expedited form of recognition. See Articles 4a through 4e Professional Qualifications Directive and Chapter "Professional Recognition", Sect. 4.2 of this research.

[54] Paragraph 16 Revised Recommendation on Criteria and Procedures for the Assessment of Foreign Qualifications (adopted by the Lisbon Recognition Convention Committee at its fifth meeting, Sèvres, 23 June 2010); Council of Europe, Explanatory Report to the Convention on the Recognition of Qualifications concerning Higher Education in the European Region, Lisbon 11.IV.1997, ETS no. 165, p. 13.

[55] Documents indicated on the list include proof of nationality, copies of the qualifications, attestations of professional experience, proof of physical or mental health, proof of insurances, and an attestation confirming the absence of suspensions from exercising a profession.

Qualifications subsequently only mentions the Diploma Supplement or comparable documents.[56] This difference is nevertheless unsurprising since recognition under the LRC focuses on an academic qualification while under the PQD the whole body of qualifications a person possesses is assessed.

In conclusion, the PQD on the one hand and LRC together with the Benelux Decisions on the other can be said to be mirror initiatives in their respective realms of professional and academic recognition. Accordingly, they can be considered to constitute a full system for recognition of qualifications covering all recognition types in the EU. Nevertheless, several weaknesses can be identified meaning that these recognition instruments cannot be considered to create an encompassing system for recognition. First, the Benelux Decisions obviously only concern the Benelux. While the initiative for automatic mutual generic level recognition has been extended to the Baltic countries—and is open to accession of other States part of the EHEA and LRC, thereby thus including the other EU Member States—its principles are currently not yet applicable EU-wide.[57] Of course there is the Automatic Recognition Recommendation which seeks to achieve such recognition at the EU-level, however, that instrument is non-legally binding. This means that, as of yet, there is no EU-level legally enforceable instrument applicable to guarantee the automatic recognition of the level of higher education degrees across the EU.

Another obvious lacunae concerns the lack of an instrument providing procedures for academic recognition for holders of vocational education and training (VET) qualifications. Although the PQD applies regardless of level of education, it focuses exclusively on regulated professions. The LRC and the Benelux Decisions subsequently relate to any qualification belonging to the field of higher education. While the Bologna Process therefore has the LRC as its only legally binding text establishing procedures on recognition, no such corresponding overarching instrument can be identified for VET. The lack of such an instrument means holders of VET qualifications are subject to procedures determined at national level. In turn, this also means that not only are VET qualifications themselves much more diverse than higher education qualifications,[58] but that holders of VET qualifications are subject to a patchwork of recognition procedures determined nationally should they pursue education or work elsewhere. Of course the EU has the 2020 VET Recommendation, Micro-Credentials Recommendation, and a further Recommendation on

[56] Paragraph 13 Revised Recommendation on Criteria and Procedures for the Assessment of Foreign Qualifications (adopted by the Lisbon Recognition Convention Committee at its fifth meeting, Sèvres, 23 June 2010).

[57] Treaty on the Automatic Recognition of Higher Education Qualifications, Brussel 14 September 2021.

[58] Contrary to higher education in the EU, VET qualifications have not been subject to any harmonisation regarding their structure. While the Bologna Process and the QF-EHEA have therefore ensured that the structure of higher education degrees in the EU has become similar, such an exercise has not occurred for VET meaning it is much more diverse. See, for example, Donlevy et al (2016, p. 17).

the validation of non-formal and informal learning,[59] but these instruments do not establish common procedures for recognition of formal qualifications as is the case in the LRC for higher education.

2.1.1 Conceptual Overlaps in Recognition Instruments: What is Recognition?

The examination of the recognition instruments (PQD, LRC, Benelux Decisions) allows for the identification of another general weakness regarding what actually constitutes recognition. Over the course of the present contribution the term recognition has been mentioned many times already. Rauhvargers provided for an apt general definition of the term when he described it as a process through which a foreign qualification has to be interpreted in terms of a host country's education or employment system.[60] While this term provides us with a general idea of what recognition consists of, there are some overlaps in concepts related to recognition which are important to discern.

Starting with automatic recognition, this form of recognition is sometimes considered as a quasi-holy grail of recognition, implying that qualifications are understood and accepted without any need for further procedural steps. In particular, its immediate nature can be considered particularly desirable—especially when intra-EU mobility in the context of the Internal Market or EEA-2025 is at stake. However, different instruments show that this term can be understood in various ways. In particular, automatic recognition is pursued in the context of the EU through the PQD and the Automatic Recognition Recommendation and in the EHEA (in this contribution expressed primarily in the form of the Benelux Decisions).

Starting with the EHEA, it may be recalled that the dedicated pathfinder group developed the concept of automatic recognition as a form of recognition in which the *level* of a qualification is recognised automatically. Indeed its report, the pathfinder group clarified "automatic recognition of a degree leads to the automatic right of an applicant holding a qualification of a certain level *to be considered for* entry to a programme of further study in the next level in any other EHEA-country", i.e. access.[61] In the Lisbon Recognition Convention (and accordingly in the EHEA) a distinction is maintained between access and admission. Whereas access is the right of applicants to be considered for a higher education programme, admission entails that the applicant is considered qualified and is actually allowed to pursue the higher education programme he or she applied for. The fact that automatic recognition concerns access (and not admission) means the content of one's prior qualifications

---

[59] Council Recommendation of 20 December 2012 on the validation of non-formal and informal learning, [2012] OJ C 398/1.

[60] Rauhvargers (2009, p. 111).

[61] Article I of the Lisbon Recognition Convention and EHEA Pathfinder Group on Automatic Recognition, Report by the EHEA Pathfinder Group on Automatic Recognition: To present to Ministers of the European Area of Higher Education for the Bologna Ministerial Conference 14–15 May 2015 Yerevan, Armenia, January 2015, p. 5.

can very much still be examined. Accordingly, what is automated is the recognition of the level of the degree, meaning no additional steps are taken to decide whether a prospective student can be considered to possess, for example, a bachelor degree. Subsequently, the Benelux Decisions can be considered an example of a legal instrument that enforces the automatic level recognition foreseen in the EHEA. Indeed, the Benelux Decisions concern "automatic mutual generic level recognition", which—in short—entails that the level of higher education diplomas may no longer be disputed.[62] Because the Bologna Process set ranges for the cycles of education established in the QF-EHEA, differences exist between the Benelux countries that had previously been used as an argument not to consider a diploma to be of the same level.[63] When the 2015 Benelux Decision was adopted, automatic level recognition was realised for all bachelor's and master's degrees in the Benelux countries. With the 2018 Decision, automatic level recognition was extended to cover all forms of higher education, thereby including doctorates and short-cycle higher education degrees.[64] The Benelux Decisions have as their main advantage that no additional steps need to be taken, neither by students nor administrators—and have therefore managed to achieve the coveted immediateness often presumed to coincide with automatic recognition.

In essence, the Automatic Recognition Recommendation strives to achieve the same goal as the Benelux Decisions do in terms of achieving the automatic recognition of the level of degrees. However, the Recommendation is wider in scope since it also strives to achieve progress towards automatic recognition of upper secondary education and training qualifications (i.e. those qualifications giving access to higher education). Despite this broader reach in scope, the Recommendation nevertheless also reflects the limitations of an instrument adopted under Article 165 TFEU since it does not prescribe legally binding commitments.

This action taken in the context of the EHEA, Benelux, and Automatic Recognition Recommendation shows that the automatic recognition of qualifications for study purposes (i.e. academic recognition) shares a main trait: it is focused on the level of a qualification. Automatic recognition in the context of the PQD (concerning *de jure* professional recognition) is different in this respect. The Directive contains a system for automatic recognition since it is based on harmonised standards of education and training.[65] Here, the principle of automatic recognition consists of a combination

---

[62] Article 1(b) Beschikking van het Benelux Comité van Ministers betreffende de automatische wederzijdse generieke niveauerkenning van diploma's hoger onderwijs M(2015) 3.

[63] This situation for example occurred in the past between the Netherlands and Belgium. Whereas master's degrees are typically 60 ECTS credits in the Netherlands and last one year, they are typically 120 ECTS credits and last two years in Belgium. Under the Bologna Process, both are master's degree programmes as the range for this cycle is set at 60 to 120 ECTS credits; See Bologna Working Group, A framework for qualifications of the European Higher Education Area, Copenhagen, 2005, p. 72.

[64] See Article 1 Beschikking van het Benelux Comité van Ministers tot aanvulling van beschikking M(2015) 3 betreffende de automatische wederzijdse generieke niveauerkenning van diploma's hoger onderwijs, M(2018) 1.

[65] This system is the legacy of the transitional and vertical approaches maintained in the 1960s and 1970s—and that have since been consolidated in the aforementioned directive. While formally

of measures.[66] First, minimum training conditions have been adopted for doctors, nurses, veterinarians, dentists, midwives, pharmacists and architects. All education and training leading to a qualification in these professions in the EU Member States needs to fulfil these standards.[67] Second, these minimum training conditions are supplemented with lists of diplomas in the Annex to the Directive containing the titles which benefit from automatic recognition. This combination of harmonised education and training and lists of "pre-approved" qualifications ensures that automatic recognition can take place. Nevertheless, the big caveat with this system is that automatic recognition here does not mean without procedure: professionals still need to obtain recognition, i.e. apply and complete a procedure at a competent authority. The automatic nature of recognition for these professions is therefore to be found in the facilitation of recognition procedures since an in-depth examination of a person's qualifications is not necessary anymore.

This reference to in-depth checks regarding the content of certain qualifications then refers us to the next form of recognition, namely mutual recognition. Here is where another general weakness may be perceived in terms of conceptual overlaps. To recall, the legislative approach to mutual recognition was developed in the 1980s in the EU context with the horizontal approach—and can still be found present-day in the general system of the PQD. On the one hand, Member States cannot refuse recognition if professionals possess a qualification at one of the levels of Article 11 of the PQD.[68] On the other hand, Member States are allowed to require the applicant to complete an adaptation period or to take an aptitude test if the matters covered by the home and the host Member State education and training differ substantially.[69] Because of the general obligation to recognise qualifications paired with compensation measures we can say that the Directive presumes recognition, i.e. the result of an application for recognition must in principle have recognition as an end-result.[70]

only the vertical approach is considered to have resulted in automatic recognition, the transitional approach can be considered to have similar effects. In this case, Member States must recognise qualifications that have been pursued in a certain capacity (e.g. as manager of an undertaking or self-employed person) for a certain number of years. Recognition can be said to follow from the combination of these two factors. However, important to note is that this (automatic) recognition based on professional experience is restricted to certain sectors such as, for example, commerce, industry and manufacturing (see Annex IV of the Professional Qualifications Directive for the full list of activities).

[66] See Article 21 of the Professional Qualifications Directive.

[67] Case C-110/01 *Tennah-Durez*, ECLI:EU:C:2003:357, para. 54.

[68] These levels are broader in scope than the ones determined in the context of the EHEA, although bachelor's and master's degrees make up the levels in Article 11(d)(e) of the Professional Qualifications Directive. See Article 13(1) Professional Qualifications Directive.

[69] Article 14 Professional Qualifications Directive.

[70] There is only one exception to this documented in Article 13(4) of the Professional Qualifications Directive: recognition may be refused if the difference in levels of qualifications is too great, namely when a person possesses a qualification that can be categorized under article 11(a) while the required level is that of Article 11(e).

It may be recalled, however, that the 1980s not only saw the development of mutual recognition through legislation, but also through CJEU case law.[71] In particular, the formula that was initially introduced through the *Vlassopoulou* case requires competent authorities to take into account all diplomas, certificates, and other evidence of qualifications to make a comparison with the required knowledge to exercise the profession in the host Member State. If sufficient correspondence is found, qualifications are to be recognised. If only a partial overlap is found, the host Member State can require the individual concerned to show that they have acquired the lacking knowledge and qualifications. The principle of mutual recognition expressed in this case law continues to be used and can be said to have developed into a fallback system applying to those who are outside the scope of the PQD, but still subject to the free movement provisions of Article 45 and 49 TFEU.[72] Those who may find themselves outside the scope of the Directive are likely to be non-fully qualified professionals.[73] For them, the *Vlassopoulou* doctrine provides legal certainty since they can be sure that they are subject to EU law and a common approach to the recognition of their qualifications, instead of, for example, being subject to varying national practices. Whereas the *Vlassopoulou* doctrine originally provided no clarity on what was to happen in the event of great differences between the qualifications held by the individual concerned and those required in the host Member State, later case law confirmed that the Directive's provisions on compensation measures could be applied by analogy in these situations.[74]

Whereas the principle of mutual recognition is a concept that can be considered very particular to the EU legal framework, a similar approach to recognition is taken under the LRC. In the Convention, the obligation to recognise qualifications meeting its general requirements is combined with the principle of substantial differences and therefore results in a similar situation as under the general system of the PQD: qualifications shall be recognised unless substantial differences can be shown.[75] Whereas authorities are encouraged to remain flexible when assessing whether or not qualifications differ substantially, non-recognition is a possibility. Nevertheless, this is certainly not encouraged under the LRC. In fact, if recognition cannot be granted, authorities should consider alternative means for recognition or partial recognition.[76] Accordingly, despite the conceptual difference where the LRC's main principle is considered that of substantial differences,[77] its practical functioning is quite similar

[71] Case 120/78 *Rewe-Zentral AG (Cassis de Dijon)*, ECLI:EU:C:1979:42; Case C-340/89 *Vlassopoulou*, ECLI:EU:C:1991:193.

[72] See Chapter "Professional Recognition", Sect. 6 and the case law discussed there.

[73] See Kortese (2023).

[74] Case C-634/20 A v. Sosiaali- ja terveysalan lupa- ja valvontavirasto, ECLI:ECLI:EU:C:2022:149.

[75] See Articles IV.1, IV.3, V.1 and VI.1 of the Lisbon Recognition Convention.

[76] Paragraph 8 Revised Recommendation on Criteria and Procedures for the Assessment of Foreign Qualifications (adopted by the Lisbon Recognition Convention Committee at its fifth meeting, Sèvres, 23 June 2010).

[77] Rauhvargers (2009, p. 112).

to that of the principle of mutual recognition expressed in the PQD's general system and CJEU case law.

From these conceptual differences related to recognition it may ultimately be deduced that in terms of recognition instruments three approaches are employed: automatic substantive recognition (PQD's system for automatic recognition), automatic level recognition (Benelux Decisions and Automatic Recognition Recommendation), and mutual recognition (PQD's general system, *Vlassopoulou* doctrine and LRC). These different approaches are crucial to consider when creating recognition instruments, also in relation to the expectations they produce with individuals ultimately undergoing recognition procedures. The use of the term "automatic recognition" can be expected to produce the highest expectations, meaning clarification of its actual scope (related to level, substance or both) is essential.

2.2 *Transparency Instruments & Their Contribution to Recognition*

Having concluded the examination of the recognition instruments (PQD, LRC, and Benelux Decisions), the question now becomes how we should consider the role of the other instruments included in this contribution. As mentioned above, these do not directly effectuate recognition by providing legal provisions concerning procedures. In principle, they do not award rights to individuals nor designate the duties of competent authorities. Instead, they are aimed at Member States urging them to put in place mechanisms to increase transparency by enhancing the understanding and readability of foreign qualifications.[78] Accordingly, these instruments are generally legally non-binding.[79] Ultimately, these instruments play a crucial role in enhancing mutual trust in qualifications from other Member States. This section explores how transparency and mutual trust are enhanced by exploring the interrelationships among these transparency instruments—and their relationship to the recognition instruments (i.e. PQD, LRC, and Benelux Decisions).

To start with the most prominent interrelationship between the transparency instruments, attention must be turned to the Bologna Process which bears a strong connection to the LRC and Benelux Decisions. It may be recalled that while the LRC is a legal instrument in its own right established under the auspices of the Council of Europe and UNESCO, it was also incorporated into the Bologna Process as its only legally binding text.[80] Equally, the Benelux Decisions are strongly connected

[78] Exception is the Europass Decision which provides common documentation formats for individuals, although the use of some of the documents (notably the Diploma Supplement and Certificate Supplements) requires involvement of educational institutions meaning a role is also reserved for Member States to ensure such documents are issued by national educational institutions to their graduates.

[79] Indeed, most instruments included here are adopted or proposed as recommendations. Europass is the exception (see the previous footnote).

[80] Zgaga (2014, p. 25), Blomqvist (2014, p. 227).

to the Bologna Process because of their codification of automatic level recognition,[81] the basis for which was laid in the QF-EHEA and further promoted by the Ministers for Education in several Communiqués.[82] Although the significance of the Bologna Process was already clear for higher education, the Process can also be said to have been exemplary for the development of instruments contributing to recognition beyond higher education. Many of the instruments adopted in the EU context on the basis of Article 165 TFEU originate from the Copenhagen Process which was introduced to mirror the achievements of the Bologna Process for VET.[83] This also meant that there are several points of convergence between the two processes, most notably where it concerns qualifications frameworks, common documentation formats, quality assurance, and credit systems.

First, both Copenhagen and Bologna Processes indeed contain qualifications frameworks (EQF and QF-EHEA) which are linked because the structure of the Bologna Process constitutes the upper four levels of the EQF. Indeed, EQF level 5 equals the EHEA's short cycle degrees, EQF level 6 is equal to the QF-EHEA's bachelor's degree, EQF level 7 to the QF-EHEA's master's degree, and EQF level 8 equals a doctorate under the QF-EHEA.[84] Apart from being interlinked, the QF-EHEA and EQF are also connected to the PQD. For example, the QF-EHEA levels of bachelor and master are represented in Article 11(d)(e) of the PQD.[85] Equally,

---

[81] Gemeenschappelijke memorie van toelichting bij beschikking M(2015) 3 van het Benelux Comité van Ministers betreffende de automatische wederzijdse generieke niveauerkenning van diploma's hoger onderwijs, M(2015) 3; Preamble Beschikking van het Benelux Comité van Ministers tot aanvulling van beschikking M(2015) 3 betreffende de automatische wederzijdse generieke niveauerkenning van diploma's hoger onderwijs, M(2018) 1.

[82] Making the Most of Our Potential: Consolidating the European Higher Education Area, Bucharest Communiqué, 26–27 April 2012; Yerevan Communiqué, 14–15 May 2015; Paris Communiqué—Paris, May 25th 2018; EHEA Pathfinder Group on Automatic Recognition, Report by the EHEA Pathfinder Group on Automatic Recognition: To present to Ministers of the European Area of Higher Education for the Bologna Ministerial Conference 14–15 May 2015, Yerevan, Armenia January 2015.

[83] Presidency Conclusions Barcelona European Council 15 and 16 March 2002, p. 19; Council Resolution of 19 December 2002 on the promotion of enhanced European cooperation in vocational education and training, [2003] OJ C 13/2; Declaration of the European Ministers of Vocational Education and Training, and the European Commission, convened in Copenhagen on 29 and 30 November 2002, on enhanced European cooperation in vocational education and training—"The Copenhagen Declaration".

[84] See Annex II Council Recommendation of 22 May 2017 on the European Qualifications Framework for lifelong learning and repealing the recommendation of the European Parliament and of the Council of 23 April 2008 on the establishment of the European Qualifications Framework for lifelong learning, [2017] OJ C 189/15.

[85] According to Directive 2013/55/EU, "higher education institutions have adapted the structure of their programmes to a […] Bachelor's and Master's degree system. In order to ensure that the five levels outlined under Directive 2005/36/EC are consistent with this new degree structure, Bachelor's degree should be classified under level d and Master's degree under level e". As of yet, these are the only levels included in the PQD meaning no convergence is achieved yet with short cycles and doctorates although arguably such qualifications may still be categorised in one of the levels of Article 11 PQD. Recital 11 Directive 2013/55/EU of the European Parliament and of the Council of 20 November 2013 amending Directive 2005/36/EC on the recognition of professional

a connection with the EQF is established, which is understood as an additional source of information for the competent authorities examining professional qualifications.[86] Nevertheless, under the general system levels should only serve as a reference point or benchmarking tools, meaning EQF levels should not be a ground to constitute substantial differences.[87] Turning to the LRC, its consistency with the QF-EHEA levels and EQF levels 5–8 follows from its focus on higher education and its subsidiary texts.[88] Lastly, the 2015 and 2018 Benelux Decisions are also in line with the EQF and the QF-EHEA due to their focus on higher education. While the 2015 Decision related to bachelors and masters (EQF levels 6 & 7), the 2018 Decision focused on associate and doctorate degrees (EQF levels 5 & 8).[89]

Second, both processes contain common documentation formats (Europass and the Diploma Supplement) which are connected because the European Commission, Council of Europe, and UNESCO jointly created the Diploma Supplement which is also one of the Europass documents.[90] As far as further interrelationships go, very little reference is made to transparency documents in the instruments on recognition since, beyond the LRC, none of the other recognition instruments (i.e. PQD and Benelux Decisions) refer to Europass or the Diploma Supplement. Interestingly, when it comes to the target audience, the Europass Decision focuses on individual end-users, on the one hand, and on "relevant stakeholders, such as education and training providers, guidance practitioners, employers, public employment services, social partners, youth work providers, youth organisations and policy makers" on the other.[91] Although no explicit mention is made of competent authorities (i.e. those evaluating qualifications in the context of a regulated profession), these could

qualifications and Regulation (EU) No 1024/2012 on administrative cooperation through the Internal Market Information System ('the IMI Regulation'), [2013] OJ L 354/132.

[86] Recital 11 Directive 2013/55/EU. Recital 20 Council Recommendation of 22 May 2017 on the European Qualifications Framework for lifelong learning and repealing the recommendation of the European Parliament and of the Council of 23 April 2008 on the establishment of the European Qualifications Framework for lifelong learning, [2017] OJ C 189/15.

[87] Proposal for a Directive of the European Parliament and of the Council amending Directive 2005/36/EC on the recognition of professional qualifications and regulation on administrative cooperation through the Internal Market Information System, COM(2011) 883 final, p. 5 and 8.

[88] Paragraph 36 Revised Recommendation on Criteria and Procedures for the Assessment of Foreign Qualifications (adopted by the Lisbon Recognition Convention Committee at its fifth meeting, Sèvres, 23 June 2010); Recommendation on the use of Qualifications Frameworks in the Recognition of Foreign Qualifications, the Committee of the Convention on the Recognition of Qualifications concerning Higher Education in the European Region, 19 June 2013, p. 5.

[89] Article 1(a) Beschikking van het Benelux Comitė van Ministers tot aanvulling van beschikking M(2015) 3 betreffende de automatische wederzijdse generieke niveauerkenning van diploma's hoger onderwijs, M(2018) 1.

[90] Bergan et al. (2000), p. 15; Articles 2(b)(c) and 5 Decision (EU) 2018/646 of the European Parliament and of the Council of 18 April 2018 on a common framework for the provision of better services for skills and qualifications (Europass) and repealing Decision No 2241/2004/EC, [2018] OJ L 112/42.

[91] Article 1(3) Articles 2(b)(c) and 5 Decision (EU) 2018/646.

also benefit from increased transparency through the Europass common documentation. By referring to Europass documents/tools especially in the context of the LRC and PQD, Europass could be more widely used as the documents/tools could be appointed as the preferred form of documentation in a formal recognition process. This enhanced use could then result in better readability and understanding of authorities and education institutions recognising qualifications as they are more familiar with the structure in which evidence on qualifications is presented.

Third, both Processes initially included an instrument on quality assurance (ESG and EQAVET).[92] At present, the legacy of EQAVET is continued in the 2020 VET Recommendation. At the same time, the proposal for a recommendation on quality assurance and recognition in higher education calls for full alignment with the ESG, meaning coherence is at least foreseen between those instruments.[93] When it comes to convergence with the recognition instruments, differing levels of convergence can be identified. In the PQD, convergence with quality assurance principles is indirect since the Directive is focused on qualifications issued by Member State authorities in accordance with national law.[94] As long as a Member State implements the EQAVET[95] and the ESG in its national legal system and qualifications are issued by education institutions whose quality was assured under those instruments, quality assurance as such is indirectly connected to the PQD. Quality assurance could nevertheless constitute a useful addition to the PQD where it concerns the principle of mutual recognition since common standards on quality assurance decrease the chance that general interest considerations related to the quality of a qualification prevent recognition.[96] Quality assurance nevertheless takes a more prominent role in the LRC where a full section is dedicated to it.[97] Under the LRC, quality assurance processes are described

[92] ENQA et al., Standards and Guidelines for Quality Assurance in the European Higher Education Area (ESG), Brussels 2015; Recommendation of the European Parliament and of the council of 18 June 2009 on the establishment of a European Quality Assurance Reference Framework for Vocational Education and Training, [2008] OJ C 155/1.

[93] Proposal for a Council Recommendation on a European Quality Assurance and Recognition System in Higher Education, COM(2024) 147 final, p. 12.

[94] Article 3(1)(c) Professional Qualifications Directive.

[95] Now as represented in the 2020 VET Recommendation.

[96] The Court of Justice of the EU was confronted with a question related to a check of the quality of professional qualifications in the *Kohll* case. The case revolved around the question whether it was permissible for social security institutions to require authorisation before persons could receive care abroad. Luxembourg, the home Member State in the case, argued that the reimbursement of services provided abroad should be subject to authorisation by the home country social security institution. According to Luxembourg, the underlying reason was related to the protection of public health: the authorisation served to guarantee the quality of medical services in the neighbouring country. Although protection of health has been accepted as a justification for a restriction to free movement, the Court of Justice of the EU did not accept the argumentation brought forward by Luxembourg. In particular, it argued that the conditions for access to and exercise of the profession of doctor are harmonised at the EU level (in the PQD). Therefore, doctors in all EU Member States offer guarantees equivalent to those offered by nationally established doctors, meaning that quality assurance of medical services from other Member States must be regarded as an unjustified restriction of the free movement of services. See Case C-158/96 *Kohll*, ECLI:EU:C:1998:171.

[97] Section VIII Lisbon Recognition Convention.

in the context of assessments of institutions or programmes.[98] The definitions of the LRC in Article I state that such an assessment is "the process for establishing the educational quality of a higher education institution or programme". Furthermore, qualifications under the LRC can be recognised if they belong to a Party's higher education system, a requirement which allows those recognising qualifications to confirm whether the quality justifies recognition.[99] Despite this importance for quality assurance, no explicit reference is made to the ESG[100] in the LRC nor its subsidiary texts. The Benelux Decisions, by contrast do have a strong connection to the ESG since both the 2015 and 2018 Decisions connect automatic level recognition to the quality of a diploma. Both the course as well as the institution have to be recognised as part of the higher education system of the Benelux countries, which is based on regular evaluations by a quality assurance organisation that adheres to the ESG.[101]

Fourth, each of the Processes contained a credit system, though compatibility of the ECVET and ECTS was considered limited.[102] Indeed, this point of convergence no longer exists present-day since the ECVET in its previous format has ceased to exist. At the same time, the Micro-credentials Recommendation is not yet sufficiently developed to consider it a credit system similar to the ECTS and, instead, focuses on providing a common definition for micro-credentials. Furthermore, ECTS is mentioned as a possible element forming part of a micro-credential meaning the Micro-credentials Recommendation is to be seen as a different type of instrument than a credit system similar to the ECTS. Nevertheless, the ECTS is compatible with the PQD, LRC, and Benelux Decisions. Since 2013, the PQD includes explicit reference

[98] Council of Europe and UNESCO, Explanatory Report to the Convention on the Recognition of Qualifications concerning Higher Education in the European Region, 11 April 1997, ETS—No. 165, p. 7.

[99] Article VIII.1 Lisbon Recognition Convention; Revised Recommendation on Criteria and Procedures for the Assessment of Foreign Qualifications (adopted by the Lisbon Recognition Convention Committee at its fifth meeting, Sèvres, 23 June 2010), p. 8.

[100] Primarily relevant due to the higher education focus of the LRC.

[101] Gemeenschappelijke memorie van toelichting bij beschikking M(2015) 3 van het Benelux comité van Ministers betreffende de automatische wederzijdse generieke niveauerkenning van diploma's hoger onderwijs, p. 3; Article 2(3)(a)(b)(4) Beschikking van het Benelux Comité van Ministers tot aanvulling van beschikking M(2015) 3 betreffende de automatische wederzijdse generieke niveauerkenning van diploma's hoger onderwijs, M(2018) 1. In the case of doctorates, no requirements are made in regard to quality assurance due to the "specific nature" of these degrees. The lack of requirements on quality assurance for these degrees may be explained by the fact that doctorates are usually individualised trajectories and not training courses, meaning that no quality assurance exists for these types of degrees. See Gemeenschappelijke memorie van toelichting bij beschikking M(2018) 1 van het Benelux Comité van Ministers tot aanvulling van beschikking M(2015) 3 betreffende de automatische wederzijdse generieke niveauerkenning van diploma's hoger onderwijs, p. 4.

[102] See for example BFUG Working Group on Qualifications Frameworks, National Qualifications Frameworks: Development and Certification, May 2007, pp. 9–10; PPMI, Implementation of the Recommendation of the European Parliament and of the Council of 18 June 2009 on the establishment of a European Credit System for Vocational Education and Training (ECVET)—Final report 4 July 2014, European Commission, p. 78.

to ECTS.[103] Since ECTS were already used by many EU higher education institutions and were found to support recognition assessments, it had to be possible to express the duration of a programme in ECTS.[104] When it comes to the LRC, no reference on the ECTS is taken up in the Convention itself despite the fact that the credit system preceded the adoption of the LRC. The convergence between these initiatives nevertheless follows from Article IX.1 of the LRC calling for "transparent systems for the complete description of the qualifications obtained", a term clarified in the explanatory report as extending to the ECTS.[105] The subsidiary texts further promote the use of ECTS to support recognition under the LRC.[106] Arguably, the connection between the LRC and ECTS can be considered weaker than perhaps expected from two Bologna Process instruments. The modest references to credits and the ECTS can nevertheless be explained by the fact that the LRC's primary focus in an assessment for recognition is on learning outcomes.[107] The ECTS Users' Guide nevertheless seems to support the stance that credits are primarily of importance in relation to mobility within the context of a study programme (i.e. academic recognition by substitution).[108] Moving on to the Benelux Decisions no references are made to the ECTS. Nevertheless, such a reference can be considered redundant due to the automatic recognition the Decisions realise.

Transparency is therefore enhanced by these instruments through qualifications frameworks, common documentation formats, cooperation on quality assurance, and through credits for units of learning. While the instruments adopted in the context of the Copenhagen Process initially mirrored those of the Bologna Process, the advent of the Automatic Recognition Recommendation, 2020 VET Recommendation, Micro-credentials Recommendation, and proposals for quality assurance and recognition in higher education and a European degree signifies a distinct turn on behalf of the EU. In particular, the level of ambition had been increased in achieving previously

---

[103] See Article 3(1)(n), Article 11(d)(e), Article 24(2), Article 31(3), Article 34(2), Article 38(1), Article 41(1)(a-c), Article 44(2), and Article 46(3) Professional Qualifications Directive. Furthermore, ECTS may also be used to describe common sets of knowledge skills and competences when developing common training frameworks. EHEA, Bologna Process and European Commission, *ECTS Users' Guide* (Publications Office of the European Union, 2015), p. 33.

[104] Recital 17 Directive 2013/55/EU; Howat et al. (2011, p. 48).

[105] Council of Europe and UNESCO, Explanatory Report to the Convention on the Recognition of Qualifications concerning Higher Education in the European Region, 11 April 1997, ETS—No. 165, p. 22.

[106] Preamble and point III, paragraph 4(d) Recommendation on the use of Qualifications Frameworks in the Recognition of Foreign Qualifications, the Committee of the Convention on the Recognition of Qualifications concerning Higher Education in the European Region, 19 June 2013; Preamble & paragraph 19(b) Revised Recommendation on Criteria and Procedures for the Assessment of Foreign Qualifications (adopted by the Lisbon Recognition Convention Committee at its fifth meeting, Sèvres, 23 June 2010).

[107] See point V, paragraph 40 Revised Recommendation on Criteria and Procedures for the Assessment of Foreign Qualifications (adopted by the Lisbon Recognition Convention Committee at its fifth meeting, Sèvres, 23 June 2010).

[108] EHEA, Bologna Process and European Commission, *ECTS Users' Guide* (Publications Office of the European Union, 2015), p. 75.

determined objectives, many of which were initially set in the context of the Bologna Process.[109] What these instruments share in common is their convergence with pre-existing initiatives and their capacity to serve as a "booster instrument" for previous initiatives. These instruments can therefore be considered particularly valuable to advance coherence between both recognition and transparency instruments.

In the case of the Automatic Recognition Recommendation, it may be recalled that the instrument seeks to put in place automatic level recognition for degrees and learning periods (i.e. academic recognition by accumulation and by substitution). Considering its focus on academic recognition, no connection is made to the PQD. Instead, the Automatic Recognition Recommendation has an objective similar to the Benelux Decisions, but at the EU level and for qualifications beyond higher education since the Recommendation also foresees automatic recognition for qualifications giving access to higher education. Another considerable difference between the Benelux Decisions and the Recommendation is that the former have resulted in an enforceable right to automatic recognition. Whereas the Automatic Recognition Recommendation seeks to ultimately achieve the same, the instrument itself is not legally binding meaning it is mostly meant to encourage Member States to implement automatic recognition in their national legal systems.[110] At present, this can be considered to constitute a weakness in the EU-level system for recognition since a potential right to automatic level recognition is still subject to a patchwork of legislation at the national level. Beyond this weakness, the Recommendation is nevertheless welcome for its convergence with other initiatives. Indeed, the Recommendation encourages Member States to reference their national systems to the EQF and QF-EHEA (and make sure all Bologna Process cycles are in place), to ensure quality assurance is in line with the ESG, to advance use of the diploma supplement and ECTS, to ensure full implementation of the Bologna Processes *and* LRC, and to explore further synergies between the aforementioned instruments.[111]

The categorisation of a "booster instrument" certainly also extends to the Micro-credentials Recommendation. The objective of that Recommendation is to, among others, enhance transparency and flexibility of learning offering to complement and enhance education and employability.[112] Other instruments such as the ECTS, EQF, QF-EHEA, and quality assurance processes are to be used as elements describing

[109] For example, a 2020 Commission Communication explicitly determined that the EU should become a front-runner in relation to activities undertaking in the context of the Bologna Process; Communication from the Commission to the European Parliament, the Council, the European Economic and Social Committee and the Committee of the Regions on achieving the European Education Area by 2025, COM(2020) 625 final, p. 11; Communication from the Commission to the European Parliament, the Council, the European Economic and Social Committee and the Committee of the Regions—a blueprint for a European degree, COM(2024) 144 final, p. 3.

[110] Point 1 Automatic Recognition Recommendation; Report from the Commission to the Council on the implementation of the Council Recommendation on promoting automatic mutual recognition of higher education and upper secondary education and training qualifications and the outcomes of learning periods abroad, COM(2023) 91 final, pp. 5–7.

[111] Point 2–3, 5–6, 11 and 14 Automatic Recognition Recommendation.

[112] Point 1 and 4 Micro-credentials Recommendation.

a micro-credential thus ensuring coherence with those instruments.[113] Considering their unique nature compared to formal qualifications, micro credentials may require their own quality assurance processes. Hence the Recommendation provides for general principles at EU level to guide the development of such processes, which should occur in line with the ESG and EQAVET.[114] The unique nature of micro-credentials also means use of instruments such as the PQD, LRC, and Benelux Decisions may not be suitable. Accordingly, recognition of micro-credentials remains in the hands of the Member States, although the ENIC/NARIC network is relied upon to help develop suitable recognition procedures—which ideally should also be in line with the Automatic Recognition Recommendation.[115] A certain level of convergence with the PQD—or rather *de jure* professional recognition—is assured since the use of micro-credentials is foreseen to also support professional development of workers by helping them to meet skills-related requirements where licences and permits (highly relevant for regulated professions) are concerned.[116]

The 2020 VET Recommendation can also be said to boost existing EU initiatives related to recognition although it is primarily aimed at boosting other transparency instruments discussed in this section and less to the recognition instruments (PQD, LRC, and Benelux Decisions).[117] While in relation to recognition the Recommendation has primarily replaced the previous ECVET and EQAVET Recommendations,[118] it also calls for the full use of other tools such as the EQF, ECTS, and Europass.[119] A link is furthermore made to the Automatic Recognition Recommendation and Micro-credentials Recommendations. As far as automatic recognition is concerned, the 2020 VET Recommendation requires this form of automatic recognition to be facilitated in accordance with the aforementioned Recommendation. Work on micro-credentials is also advanced by requiring the Commission to cooperate with the Member States to explore the concept and use of such credentials for VET.[120]

The last of the instruments included in this section are both still in initial stages and are strongly interconnected. In fact, the communication on a European degree is related to the proposal on a European quality assurance and recognition system in

[113] The recommendation also suggests a possible adaptation of the ECTS to accommodate and advance the use of micro-credentials in a higher education setting and supports implementation in relation to Europass. See point 6.vii, 6.viii, 6.ix, point 16, point 18 and Annex 1 Micro-credentials Recommendation.

[114] N.B. the EQAVET was integrated into the 2020 VET Recommendation. See also Point 9(a) and Annex 2 point 1 Micro-credentials Recommendation.

[115] Point 13 and Annex 2, point 6 Micro-credentials Recommendation.

[116] Point 12(g) Micro-credentials Recommendation.

[117] Indeed, the 2020 VET Recommendation is said to be without prejudice to the PQD (recital 24 2020 VET Recommendation). Furthermore, its focus on VET means the LRC and Benelux Decisions are less relevant since these are focused on higher education.

[118] Indeed, Annex II now includes and updates the former EQAVET framework which should be used in national quality assurance systems. See points 20–21 and Annex II 2020 VET Recommendation.

[119] Points 16, 23 and 30 of the 2020 VET Recommendation.

[120] Point 29 2020 VET Recommendation.

higher education.[121] Both instruments continue the trend as booster instruments for other pre-existing initiatives. For the European degree this occurs by advancing the implementation of Bologna tools.[122] Beyond its correspondence to these initiatives, the plans for the European degree also entail ensuring consistency with the EQF, Europass, Automatic Recognition Recommendation, and—surprisingly—exploring synergies with the PQD.[123] In regards to the proposal on quality assurance and recognition, its designation as a future "booster instrument" is also confirmed. The proposal seeks to facilitate quality assurance processes in the EU moving from dual programme and institutional level processes to a single procedure aimed at the institutional level in line with the Bologna Processes' ESG.[124] In the context of improving quality assurance, the proposal also calls for an extension of such processes to education leading to micro-credentials—for which the Micro-credentials Recommendation is leading.[125] In relation to recognition, the proposal is considered as the suitable moment to create a stronger connection with the Automatic Recognition Recommendation.[126] In particular, quality assurance is to encourage the implementation of automatic recognition of the level of higher education degrees. Automatic recognition is thereby defined as a right to enter higher education at the next level without a separate procedure.[127]

A few particularities and weaknesses can be defined in the (planned) instruments discussed above. First, the use of the term right to automatic recognition is interesting since the question may be posed how such a right is to be effectuated through a recommendation. Likely, the right is to be realized through the national systems of the Member States, who cooperate voluntarily in this area. Nevertheless, the question can be raised at what point it would be desirable to also ensure automatic level recognition is effectuated as a right at EU level. Instituting such a right at EU level would have the benefit of allowing EU citizens to rely on that right in court and to ensure the uniform interpretation thereof by the CJEU. Another potential weakness inferred from both the European degree and proposal on quality assurance and recognition is its focus on higher education. This is not so much a weakness related to higher education, which is rather advanced through these plans, but for VET for which there are no corresponding initiatives. Arguably, the EQAVET (as taken up in the 2020 VET Recommendation) already applies in this area and VET is often considered of a different nature, meaning it is much more dispersed than

[121] Proposal for a Council Recommendation on a European Quality Assurance and Recognition System in Higher Education, COM(2024) 147 final, p. 15; Communication from the Commission to the European Parliament, the Council, the European Economic and Social Committee and the Committee of the Regions—a blueprint for a European degree, COM(2024) 144 final, p. 2.

[122] Communication from the Commission to the European Parliament, the Council, the European Economic and Social Committee and the Committee of the Regions—a blueprint for a European degree, COM(2024) 144 final, pp. 10–11, 17.

[123] Ibid., 5–6, 13, 16–17.

[124] Proposal for a Council Recommendation on a European Quality Assurance and Recognition System in Higher Education, COM(2024) 147 final, pp. 1, 4, 12–13.

[125] Ibid., p. 13.

[126] Ibid., pp. 2, 4–5.

[127] Ibid., pp. 2, 16–17.

higher education. Nevertheless, the question can be raised in light of these new developments in the area of higher education as to what effects different developments for VET and higher education will have—especially considered in light of ambitions to significantly upskill the EU's population.[128]

To conclude, these sections have explored the interrelationships of various instruments on recognition and some weaknesses in the resulting EU system for recognition. While the recognition as well as transparency instruments are generally coherent with one another, some concerns can be inferred from the much more advanced stage of recognition and transparency instruments in relation to higher education as opposed to VET. Furthermore, some weaknesses could be identified in terms of legal certainty and protection which particularly apply in relation to the CJEU's case law on professional recognition (affecting non-fully qualified professionals and non-regulated professions) and the development of a right to automatic level recognition at the EU level (which currently takes place through national legal systems). Recognition of qualifications continues to be an area where the balance needs to be struck between Member States' autonomy and core EU objectives such as the creation of the EEA-2025 and further development of the Internal Market. While these sections reflected increasing ambitions on recognition in these contexts, attention should now be turned to the future development of the system for the recognition of qualifications.

3 The Way Forward: Improving Recognition of Qualifications in the EU

The objective of the present contribution was to examine to which extent the current system for recognition of qualifications is comprehensive so that recognition at any stage of a person's life may run smoothly in accordance with common principles applicable at EU level. This objective is to be considered particularly important in light of the EU freedom of movement as well as ambitions set for the Internal Market and EEA-2025 that concern recognition. The secondary objective is thereby to examine how future-proof the current system for recognition is. This section builds on the weaknesses identified in the previous sections relating to the instruments contributing to or effectuating recognition to improve the system for recognition of qualifications in the EU and render it more future-proof.

So far, this chapter has shown that there are different approaches to recognition either enhancing mutual trust (harmonisation or transparency instruments) or mutual recognition (procedural recognition instruments). In the EU, extensive action has been undertaken in developing transparency instruments based on Article 165 TFEU. In recent years, the advent of booster instruments such as the Automatic Recognition Recommendation, Micro-credentials Recommendation, and 2020 VET Recommendation have sought to further deepen pre-existing transparency and recognition instruments. In terms of enhancing transparency, efforts are therefore considerable

[128] See Chapter "Introduction", Sect. 4 of this contribution.

and contribute to increasing mutual trust in the EU. However, recognition instruments must not be neglected, since they provide procedural safeguards on how recognition is to ultimately be effectuated. Considering the EU's objectives related to the Internal Market and EEA-2025 as areas without internal borders where professionals and students can work and study freely, a system at EU level providing common provisions on recognition of qualifications appears highly necessary. Common provisions determined at EU level are furthermore important to ensure uniformity of procedural rules for recognition—which should be guaranteed by the CJEU which would have jurisdiction to uniformly interpret such rules. While transparency is therefore essential to build trust, legal provisions remain necessary to effectuate recognition.

To help in the development of an encompassing system for the recognition of qualifications at EU level the typology of recognition can be conducive. The system for recognition should in any case include provisions on professional recognition as well as provisions for academic recognition. Chapter "Challenging Convention: Theory, Competences & The Grey Area of Recognition", Sect. 5 of course extensively examined the limitations to this typology by exploring the grey area of recognition types. That exercise mainly showed that challenges related to the typology of recognition could mainly arise in relation to the distinction between *de jure* and *de facto* professional recognition and academic recognition by accumulation. Taking this into consideration, an encompassing recognition system would be one that offers provisions on recognition for those cases clearly falling within one of the four recognition types, while not neglecting those whose situation can be considered to fall under the grey area of recognition types. Challenges in the typology can nevertheless be said to have found their way into the instruments on recognition. Indeed, this chapter also showed that the system for recognition here contains some weaknesses.

At present, it can be questioned whether it is appropriate to even speak of an EU system for recognition of qualifications since the only recognition instrument containing procedural rules located within the EU legal framework is the PQD. Going back to the typology on recognition,[129] this means that the EU system for recognition currently only covers *de jure* professional recognition. In itself, this can be considered a weakness of the current system for recognition. Nevertheless, it has also become clear that when it comes to academic recognition in the EU (both by accumulation and by substitution), the LRC is the main instrument. Section 2.1.1 above furthermore made clear that the PQD's general system and LRC's different sections operate on the basis of a similar principle which requires recognition to be provided unless substantial differences can be shown. While Sect. 2.1.1 above also showed that the LRC's Section VI on Recognition of higher education qualifications can concern *de facto* professional recognition, clashes in this area are prevented due to the CJEU's case law on the *Vlassopoulou* doctrine. Indeed, applied in the area of non-regulated professions, the doctrine requires qualifications to be compared and the applicant to be given the opportunity to demonstrate lacking knowledge if their qualification

[129] See Chapter "Challenging Convention: Theory, Competences & The Grey Area of Recognition" of this contribution.

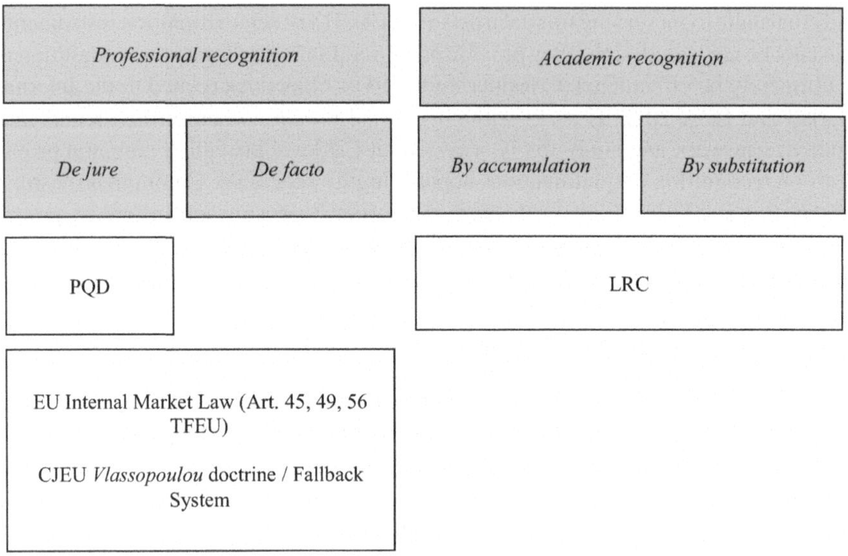

Fig. 2 The current system for recognition of qualifications in the EU

is different from the required one.[130] In light of the shared nature of the Internal Market competence on professional recognition[131] and the direct effect of, among others, article 49 TFEU on freedom of establishment, we may raise the question whether further action beyond the EU on *de facto* professional recognition is pre-empted because of this.[132] The *Vlassopoulou* doctrine is furthermore important since it was elaborated further by the CJEU in respect to non-fully qualified professionals, meaning they can also rest assured to obtain recognition under EU law.[133] This means that the system for recognition of qualifications is currently to be construed as follows (see Fig. 2):

A weakness in respect to the LRC viewed from the perspective of EU law is that it is located outside the EU legal order, meaning its application mainly takes place at national level leaving it subject to different interpretations across the Member States.

[130] Case C-340/89 *Vlassopoulou*, ECLI:EU:C:1991:193, para. 16 and 19; Case C-234/97 *Fernández de Bobadilla*, ECLI:EU:C:1999:367, para. 28 and 31–33; Case C-164/94, *Aranitis*, ECLI:EU:C:1996:23, para. 30–32. See also Case C-586/08 *Rubino*, ECLI:EU:C:2009:801; Case C-298/14 *Brouillard*, ECLI:EU:C:2015:652.

[131] Article 53 TFEU.

[132] Gallo (2022, p. 593).

[133] Chapter "Professional Recognition", Sect. 6 elaborates on the fallback system created by the CJEU's case law in, among others, Case C-313/01 *Morgenbesser*, ECLI:ECLI:EU:C:2003:612; Case C-345/08 *Peśla,* ECLI:ECLI:EU:C:2009:771; Case C-298/14 *Brouillard*, ECLI:ECLI:EU:C:2015:652; Case C-166/20 *BB v. Lietuvos Respublikos sveikatos apsaugos ministerija,* ECLI:EU:C:2021:554; Case C-577/20 *A v. Sosiaali- ja terveysalan lupa- ja valvontavirasto*, ECLI:ECLI:EU:C:2022:467; Case C-634/20 *A v. Sosiaali- ja terveysalan lupa- ja valvontavirasto*, ECLI:ECLI:EU:C:2022:149.

An option explored in Chapter "Academic Recognition", Sect. 3.1 was for the EU to accede to the LRC, a possibility provided in Article XI.3(3) of the Convention. Successful completion of such accession would render the LRC an integral part of EU law and subject to observance by the CJEU and uniform interpretation of the Convention.[134] Opponents of this suggestion could immediately refer to Article 165 TFEU and the limitations therein regarding harmonisation in the field of academic recognition. Indeed, the text of that provision is unequivocal in that respect. Nevertheless, cooperation with the Council of Europe is particularly promoted in relation to education in Article 165(3). Furthermore, the route to EU accession to the LRC runs fully via the Member States—and not via EU procedures associated with more elaborate competences. Indeed, Article XI.3(3) LRC prescribes that EU accession is dependent on a request from its Member States. This avenue would therefore only be open upon the express desire of the Member States, meaning concerns of exceeded competences on behalf of the EU in this respect are mitigated. EU accession to the LRC would therefore constitute a voluntary transfer of the Member States to the EU legal order.

Arguably, questions may be raised at the likelihood of this transfer taking place. One matter concerns direct effect. Indeed, inclusion would also result in the possibility of the provisions of the LRC having direct effect—if sufficiently clear, precise, and unconditional. This may be questioned since the LRC provides for general concepts which are elaborated more extensively in its subsidiary texts. Furthermore, EU accession to the LRC may also cause other disruptions in the system. To start, introducing the LRC into the EU legal order would have as a consequence that it would rank below primary EU law and above secondary legislation.[135] Although this could result in a strange positioning in respect to the PQD which is a source of secondary legislation, conflicts should in principle be avoided in this area due to the different scopes of the respective instruments (*de jure* professional recognition vs. academic recognition). However, a clash may come to arise in the area of *de facto* professional recognition and the CJEU's case law on the *Vlassopoulou* doctrine. Matters needing to be resolved here concern a confirmation that—in the case of assessments for the labour market—not only higher education qualifications, but all evidence of qualifications needs to be considered.[136] Furthermore, the situation of non-fully qualified professionals preparing to exercise a regulated profession would have to be clarified.

In a more general sense, it should be considered whether legislative action on the basis of Article 53 TFEU is desirable regarding the *Vlassopoulou* doctrine and fallback system. In relation to non-fully qualified professionals, the *Vlassopoulou* doctrine can indeed be considered to have developed into a fallback system providing an alternative route to recognition under EU law for those not covered by the PQD.[137] Two routes could be considered here: inclusion in the PQD, or adoption of separate

[134] Grimonprez (2020, p. 184).

[135] Mohay (2017, p. 157).

[136] In line with Case C-298/14 *Brouillard*, ECLI:EU:C:2015:652.

[137] See Chapter "Professional Recognition", Sect. 6.

legislative action based on Article 53 TFEU. Considering the extent of the PQD's legal framework and the fact that recent CJEU case law has become more aligned with the PQD on compensation measures,[138] preference is to be given to inclusion in the PQD.

For non-regulated professions, it should be considered whether the status quo is to be maintained or whether some legislative action would benefit freedom of movement in this respect. Such a suggestion appears to run counter to efforts undertaken to lessen regulation foreseen for the future development of the Internal Market.[139] Efforts can still be continued in the context of the Proportionality Test Directive to critically examine formal regulation of professions. Nevertheless, in conducting such efforts account should be taken of the concerns expressed in Chapter "Professional Recognition", Sect. 2.1.1 of this contribution. In particular, it should be avoided that less formal regulation on professions leads to non-regulatory barriers and thereby detracts from legal certainty of professionals undergoing recognition procedures. This may particularly occur where a profession is no longer formally regulated by law (i.e. no longer subject to *de jure* professional recognition), but the gap left by the formal regulation is filled in by actors on the labour market (e.g. employers or professional organisations) who may still require certain particular qualifications and desire completion of certain procedures to be sure of the adequacy of the qualifications of mobile professionals. In such situations, the extension of the *Vlassopoulou* doctrine to non-regulated professions ensures that in any case the whole body of qualifications a person possesses needs to be considered.[140] In its current fragmented format, questions may be raised whether there is sufficient awareness of the application of the doctrine in situations beyond the PQD. An avenue to be explored is therefore to increase the doctrine's familiarity.[141] Such an approach would still be consistent with calls to lessen regulation since it does not result in more regulation or the maintenance thereof, but rather in a general requirement to take adequate account of foreign qualifications (i.e. ensure that they are not dismissed without proper examination).

---

[138] See Case C-166/20 *BB v. Lietuvos Respublikos sveikatos apsaugos ministerija*, ECLI:EU:C:2021:554; Case C-577/20 *A v. Sosiaali- ja terveysalan lupa- ja valvontavirasto*, ECLI:ECLI:EU:C:2022:467; Case C-634/20 *A v. Sosiaali- ja terveysalan lupa- ja valvontavirasto*, ECLI:ECLI:EU:C:2022:149.

[139] Indeed, the PQD's mutual transparency and evaluation exercise of Article 59 sought to map professional regulation as a first step to subsequently critically assess its use in the context of the Proportionality Test Directive. Equally, the Letta and Draghi reports considered regulation an obstacle to mobility and argued for a diminution of unnecessary regulation: Letta (2024, p. 102), Draghi (2024, p. 265).

[140] Case C-19/92 *Kraus*, ECLI:ECLI:EU:C:1993:125; Case 71/76 *Thieffry*, ECLI:ECLI:EU:C:1977:65; Case C-164/94, *Aranitis*, ECLI:ECLI:EU:C:1996:23; Case C-234/97 *Fernández de Bobadilla*, ECLI:ECLI:EU:C:1999:367; Case C-313/01 *Morgenbesser*, ECLI:ECLI:EU:C:2003:612; Case C-298/14 *Brouillard*, ECLI:ECLI:EU:C:2015:652; Case C-285/01 *Burbaud*, ECLI:ECLI:EU:C:2003:432.

[141] Although in terms of legal certainty, the first option is certainly more desirable.

In keeping with the focus on future ambitions for the EU, it may be recalled that these constituted—apart from tackling excessive regulation—a desire for more automatic recognition and greater flexibilization of learning.[142] Chapter "Professional Recognition" showed that opportunities exist for more automatic recognition under the PQD in the discussion of common training principles. While these have not yet been used extensively, they provide a viable option to pursue more automated recognition under the PQD.

In terms of both flexibilization and automatic recognition in the academic recognition sphere more limitations can be identified from an EU perspective. While more flexible learning paths are underway with efforts done on micro-credentials, their recognition may face similar challenges as can be identified for automatic academic recognition. Indeed, here we have encountered the last two weaknesses in the system for recognition. These primarily concern the current activities in relation to automatic level recognition and lack of action on recognition procedures for VET. In relation to the latter, action on academic recognition in the form of the LRC only creates recognition procedures for higher education qualifications. This also means VET qualifications remain subject to a patchwork of national legislation. In his report, Letta remarked that, at present, the freedom of movement mostly provides opportunities for a minority of EU citizens,[143] not providing unified procedures for recognition of VET qualifications can be considered a contributing factor to limiting the benefits of the freedom of movement to those with higher education qualifications by only providing similar procedural safeguards for them. In this context, the gap in relation to higher education can be considered to increase where recognition of qualifications is concerned. Of course, the Copenhagen Process and 2020 VET Recommendation aim to improve transparency and ultimately recognition, but their potential for advances are more limited than the instruments for higher education which concern the Bologna Process, Automatic Recognition Recommendation, proposal for quality assurance and recognition at higher education level, proposed European degree, and even the Micro-credentials Recommendation.[144] It can be considered that efforts related to VET are located more in the realm of skills and validation of non-formal and informal learning, but the focus on higher education in relation to recognition of qualifications is undeniable. Nevertheless, the way forward here is less clear. Attempting the development of an instrument similar to the LRC but for VET would immediately encounter the confines of Article 165 TFEU for its focus on academic recognition. Furthermore, the varied nature of VET in the EU may lead to issues in the determination of the scope of such an instrument—something exacerbated by the fact that VET also covers higher education in the EU.[145] Nevertheless, some solace may again be found in the *Vlassopoulou* doctrine. Due to its need to take into account all evidence of qualifications and experience, this may

[142] Letta (2024, p. 102), Draghi (2024, pp. 270–273). See also Chapter "Introduction", Sect. 4.

[143] Letta (2024, p. 102).

[144] While the Micro-credentials Recommendation concerns VET, it is equally relevant to higher education.

[145] Case 293/83 *Gravier*, ECLI:EU:C:1985:69 and Case 24/86 *Blaizot*, ECLI:EU:C:1988:43.

prove a solid basis to develop an approach to recognition in the area of VET—or even in the context of micro-credentials.

Turning to initiatives concerning automatic level recognition as foreseen by the Benelux Decisions and the Automatic Recognition Recommendation an opportunity may exist. While evidence can be found in Commission documents of the desire to institute a right to automatic level recognition,[146] it can be questioned how this is to be achieved if legally binding action at the EU level is not possible in this area. Essentially, the Benelux Decisions provide the answer: the route is to be found through the Member States or regional agreements. The Benelux Decisions themselves provided for an avenue for more unity on automatic recognition in higher education. In 2021, the scope of automatic mutual level recognition was extended to the Baltic States by way of a Treaty.[147] Article 13 of that Treaty allows all states who have ratified the LRC and are members of the EHEA to accede to it, as long as they have adequate quality assurance systems, implemented the QF-EHEA, and referenced their national qualifications framework to the EQF. This avenue is therefore open to Member States of the EU since they are also participants in the LRC and EHEA. While this would then ultimately create a situation similar to that of the LRC, i.e. being outside the scope of EU law, at least it would achieve automatic level recognition in a legally binding way. Continuing the current trajectory, however, means that the same concern needs to be expressed here as in the case of recognition of VET qualifications, namely that resulting legislative provisions remain fragmented at national level and levels of implementation may vary.[148]

These examples of the challenges related to potential EU instruments containing procedural rights related to recognition of VET qualifications and automatic recognition ultimately come back to the way the typology on recognition was connected to competences in the TFEU. Article 53 TFEU is the competence offering the possibility to create binding legislation on mutual recognition, while Article 165 TFEU allows for supporting measures on academic recognition. Ultimately, this distinction allowed for the vast landscape on recognition to arise without creating a system for recognition under EU law. Nevertheless, as Chapter "Challenging Convention: Theory, Competences & The Grey Area of Recognition" showed, article 53 TFEU never explicitly referred to professional recognition alone. Accordingly, that provision was ultimately confined to only concern *de jure* professional recognition through introduction of Article 165 TFEU and its use over the years. Indeed, Chapter "Challenging Convention: Theory, Competences & The Grey Area of Recognition" showed that Article 165 TFEU can be considered to be over-extended in use since instruments

[146] See, for example, Proposal for a Council Recommendation on a European Quality Assurance and Recognition System in Higher Education, COM(2024) 147 final, p. 18.

[147] Treaty on the Automatic Recognition of Higher Education Qualifications, Brussel 14 September 2021.

[148] See, for example, Report from the Commission to the Council on the implementation of the Council Recommendation on promoting automatic mutual recognition of higher education and upper secondary education and training qualifications and the outcomes of learning periods abroad, COM(2023) 91 final, pp. 5–7.

adopted on the basis of that legal basis certainly also concerned professional recognition. By contrast, Article 53 TFEU can be considered under-used. Indeed, it should not be forgotten that Article 53 TFEU contains a possibility to coordinate laws, regulation, and administrative action concerning the taking-up and pursuit of professions—a clause used to harmonise education and training in dedicated professions in the past.[149]

In a broader sense, Garben has previously convincingly argued that action on education could also be taken in the context of the Internal Market. This because the EU is endowed with the functional power to ultimately create the Internal Market, meaning other policy fields not initially intended to be handled at EU level could be affected by it.[150] Reference is to be made here to early case law which already indicated that although education was not included in the Treaties, powers conferred to the EU are not limited if they affect such areas.[151] Of course, article 165(4) TFEU prohibits harmonisation on academic recognition. Nevertheless, consultation of the *Tobacco Advertisement* judgment would lead to the observation that harmonising measures in areas subject to a prohibition of harmonisation are not as such prohibited, rather that other legal bases are not to be used to circumvent the prohibition.[152] This reasoning could indeed be employed to argue that recognition ultimately benefits the functioning of the Internal Market. Indeed, the discussion of the education-related case law in Chapter "Academic Recognition" already showed that the development of individual rights related to education often occurred in conjunction with other areas of EU law, most notably the freedom of movement. A similar argument can be made on the basis of Chapter "Challenging Convention: Theory, Competences & The Grey Area of Recognition", Sect. 4 where it was discussed which types of recognition each of the instruments included for analysis. Many of the transparency or booster instruments adopted on the basis of Article 165 TFEU also contributed to one or both forms of professional recognition and therefore to also positively affect employment and thereby the Internal Market.

Another interesting point raised by Garben is that for certain measures to be subject to the prohibition of harmonisation of Article 165(4) TFEU they would have to initially constitute harmonisation.[153] In relation to recognition of qualifications, it is here important to refer back to a distinction made in Chapter "Introduction" where recognition was said to face challenges of multitude in two respects: the first, the variety of national education systems and professions, and the second, the variety of instruments contributing to and effectuating recognition. While the former touches upon national identity, which is protected under EU law for example by Article 4(2) TEU and of course Article 165 TFEU, the latter does not—and certainly not in the

---

[149] I.e. the professions under the system for automatic recognition in the PQD. See Schneider (1995, p. 445).

[150] Garben (2011, p. 186).

[151] Case 9/74 *Casagrande*, ECLI:EU:C:1974:74, para. 12.

[152] Case C-376/98 *Germany v. European Parliament and Council*, ECLI:ECLI:EU:C:2000:544. Garben (2011, p. 192).

[153] Garben (2011, p. 184).

form imagined here. The core argument here is to arrive at an encompassing system for recognition of qualifications that can benefit EU citizens at all stages of their lives, by ensuring the *procedures* for recognition are common and anchored in EU law. Ultimately, the suggestion is that EU citizens exercising their rights to free movement should be able to do so under *a single set of rules*. This should therefore not concern harmonisation of education or professions at the national level, but rather of differing administrative practices on recognition procedures.

Article 165 TFEU could then very much continue to be the standard course of action for areas where more substantive cooperation is desired. In fact, a scenario may even be imagined where Articles 165 and 53 TFEU would have a progressive relationship with one another to build towards an EU system for recognition of qualifications. A measure affecting both academic and professional recognition could be introduced in the context of Article 165 TFEU to initiate action and enhance transparency and ultimately mutual trust. Once sufficient experience is gained, follow-up action could be taken on the basis of Article 53 TFEU to achieve the situation where EU citizens may benefit from common procedural rights to recognition.

The reasoning regarding the use of Internal Market competences in other fields is therefore not new. Nevertheless, it should be given new consideration due to the lack of an encompassing EU system for recognition of qualifications and the importance of the recognition of qualifications in effectuating free movement. This reasoning indeed provides an avenue to continue to progress in effectuating the Internal Market and EEA-2025 under current competences. This is particularly necessary since more drastic changes to competences are not to be expected, although an interesting avenue was briefly explored in 2023 when a number of Members of the European Parliament submitted proposals to reform the EU Treaties and thereby also proposed to review the competence on education. In particular, transnational issues such as mutual recognition of qualifications were suggested to be moved to a shared competence.[154] This is a particularly interesting avenue to consider in the future and consistent with the explanation given above that creating a system for recognition of qualifications at EU level should be primarily aimed at establishing common procedures streamlining national administrative practices.

4 Conclusion

This chapter has combined findings from the previous Chapters "Introduction", "The Long History of the Recognition of Qualifications in the EU", "Challenging Convention: Theory, Competences & The Grey Area of Recognition", "Professional Recognition", and "Academic Recognition" to examine the weaknesses in the system for recognition of qualifications in the EU. The chapter showed that there are different ways in which instruments contribute to or effectuate recognition. These can be sorted

[154] European Parliament Report on proposals of the European Parliament for the amendment of the Treaties (2022/2051/INL)), A9-0337/2023, p. 5.

into approaches enhancing mutual trust (through harmonisation and transparency instruments) or by effectuating mutual recognition (recognition instruments). Interrelationships between different instruments were furthermore mapped to identify weaknesses. The system for recognition shows an overall weakness since attention is mainly given to transparency instruments, while there seems to be no consistent approach to recognition instruments. Indeed, a core objective of this contribution is to examine to which extent there is an encompassing system for recognition of qualifications. Based on the typology of recognition and its grey area an encompassing system would consist of provisions for all recognition types, thereby including avenues to recognition for non-fully qualified professionals.

This chapter showed that existence of an EU system for recognition could be questioned since the PQD is the only instrument within the EU legal framework which effectuates recognition. The existence of the LRC outside the EU legal framework also means uniformity of procedures is more limited than in the situation where it was located within the EU framework. The area of *de facto* professional recognition is subsequently subject to the case law of the CJEU which, supporting recognition of non-fully qualified professionals and providing instructions for how to assess qualifications on the non-regulated part of the labour market, may also suffer from issues of fragmentation. Similar issues of fragmentation could also be perceived when examining current action on automatic academic recognition. A further weakness in the system came from the fact that much action is undertaken to advance recognition in the sphere of higher education, creating a gap with action on VET.

The chapter subsequently examined different solutions to tackle fragmentation ranging from EU accession to the LRC or extension of the Benelux' automatic mutual generic level recognition to undertaking legislative action for non-fully qualified professionals on the basis of Article 53 TFEU. While these measures may ensure more legally binding action on recognition can be taken to ensure migrating professionals are offered legal certainty regarding the recognition of their qualifications, they are remedial measures that do not result in an encompassing system for recognition. To achieve such a system, the solution is to ultimately be sought in a different interpretation—or alteration…—of Treaty competences on recognition.

References

Bergan S, Divis J, Rauhvargers A (2000) Bridges over troubled waters: Bologna and the recognition of qualifications. J Stud Int Educ 4/2:11–20. SAGE Journals

Blomqvist C (2014) Recognition in a broader policy context. In: Bergan S, Blomqvist C (eds) The Lisbon Recognition Convention at 15: making fair recognition a reality. Council of Europe Publishing, Strasbourg, pp 227–238

Cambien N (2017) Mutual recognition and mutual trust in the internal market. Eur Pap 2:93–115

Donlevy V, Curtarelli M, McCoshan A, Meierkord A (2016) Study on obstacles to recognition of skills and qualifications: final report. Publications Office of the European Union, Luxembourg

Draghi M (2024) The future of European competitiveness: Part B – In-depth analysis and recommendations

Gallo D (2022) Rethinking direct effect and its evolution: a proposal. Eur Law Open 1:576–605
Garben S (2011) EU higher education law: the Bologna process and harmonization by stealth. Kluwer Law International, Alphen aan den Rijn
Grimonprez K (2020) The European union and education for democratic citizenship: legal foundations for EU learning at school. Nomos, Baden-Baden
Hoogenboom A (2014) Origin and meaning of mutual recognition as foundational principle in the European integration process. Eur Tidskr 17:237–265
Howat C, Ulicna D, Harris P, GHK, DTI (2011) Revised final report — Study evaluating the Professional Qualifications Directive against recent educational reforms in EU Member States. DG Internal Market and Services - European Commission
Kortese L (2023) Erkenning van beroepskwalificaties van beginnende professionals in Zaak C-577/20. NtER 1(2):1–6
Letta E (2024) Much more than a market: speed, security, solidarity – empowering the Single Market to deliver a sustainable future and prosperity for all EU citizens
Mohay A (2017) The status of international agreements concluded by the European Union in the EU legal order. Prav Vjesn 33:151–163
Möstl M (2010) Preconditions and limits of mutual recognition. Common Market Law Review 47:405–436
Rauhvargers A (2009) Recognition and qualifications frameworks. Assess Educ: Princ, Policy & Pract 16(2009):111–125
Schneider H (1995) Die Anerkennung von Diplomen in der Europäischen Gemeinschaft. MAKLU Uitgevers, Antwerpen—Apeldoorn
Schoenmaekers S (2010) The regulation of architects in Belgium and the Netherlands. Datawyse / Universitaire Pers Maastricht, Maastricht
Walkenhorst H (2005) The changing role of eu education policy – a critical assessment. Paper for the EUSA 9th Biennal International Conference
Walkenhorst H (2008) Explaining change in EU education policy. J Eur Publ Policy 15:567–587
Wischmeyer T (2016) Generating trust through law? Judicial cooperation in the European Union and the "Principle of Mutual Trust." Ger Law J 17:339–382
Zgaga P (2014) The Lisbon Recognition Convention as a paradigmatic shift and a change of the philosophy of recognition: between reflection and sentiments. In: Bergan S, Blomqvist C (eds) The Lisbon Recognition Convention at 15: making fair recognition a reality. Council of Europe Publishing, Strasbourg, pp 19–30

Conclusion

1 Conclusion

This contribution has extensively examined the recognition of qualifications in the EU. Recognition of qualifications plays an important role in facilitating mobility, since a denial of the use of one's qualifications can deter a move to another Member State. In the EU, the facilitation of intra-EU mobility is particularly important considering the freedom of movement and associated rights held by EU citizens. Despite the importance of recognition, it is often perceived as an obstacle. The importance of recognition for mobility and known status as obstacle have made that extensive action has been taken on recognition of qualifications by an equally large variety of actors. Focusing on the EU, it is not only the EU itself that has acted on recognition of qualifications since other parties such as the Council of Europe and UNESCO, Bologna Process, regional cooperation initiatives, and Member States in their own capacities are also active in this area. While extensive action can be said to attest to the topic's importance, the core question may be raised whether such extensive action by various actors results in a system for the recognition of qualifications that is able to support recognition—and ultimately mobility—at all stages of life. Furthermore, recent years have seen a considerable increase in ambitions for the EU's Internal Market and European Education Area (EEA-2025) which also affected recognition of qualifications. In particular, calls were made to lessen restrictive forms of professional regulation, increase flexibility of learning, and increase opportunities for automatic recognition in the EU. In light of the perceived fragmentation of instruments contributing to or effectuating recognition and the ambitions set, the present contribution sought to examine to which extent the existing system for recognition of qualifications is not only encompassing but also future-proof.

In order to uncover the system for the recognition of qualifications in the EU and its functioning, attention was first given in Chapter "The Long History of the Recognition of Qualifications in the EU" to exploring the topic's vast history. Indeed, the topic was already tackled in the context of the EU since the early days of European

L. S.J. Kortese, *Effectuating Free Movement in the EU through Recognition of Qualifications*, https://doi.org/10.1007/978-3-032-21335-8_7

integration when directives (predecessors of the Professional Qualifications Directive—PQD) were first adopted to facilitate the recognition of professionals moving to other Member States. Over the course of time, the EU's approach changed from adopting directives targeted at particular professions (i.e. the vertical approach) to a more general (i.e. horizontal) approach based on the principle of mutual recognition. Nevertheless, Chapter "The Long History of the Recognition of Qualifications in the EU" also showed, that while the EU was the primary actor on recognition of qualifications for a long time, this ended in the 1990s. A host of developments on recognition came together leading to the quick emergence of other actors on recognition—and to the introduction of a divide in recognition types that would come to deeply affect the future development of the system for recognition. While action on recognition was therefore originally initiated for professionals on the labour market, the 1970s and 80s saw developments calling for action to also be taken concerning education. The latter area became subject to action by many different parties. While the EU itself took action to facilitate recognition in the context of studies, more significant advances were made in the context of the Bologna Process, an intergovernmental cooperation initiative located outside the scope of EU law. The late 1990s also saw the introduction of the Lisbon Recognition Convention, the instrument that up until today continues to be the most important for recognition in the context of higher education. In more recent years, other actors also took the stage for this type of recognition. In this contribution, an example of a regional cooperation agreement was included by way of the Benelux Decisions on automatic mutual generic level recognition, which ensured that the levels of higher education instituted by the Bologna Process (bachelor, master, doctorate) were henceforth considered the same across the Benelux.

While Chapter "The Long History of the Recognition of Qualifications in the EU" already showed that recognition had different purposes that were guiding for its development, Chapter "Challenging Convention: Theory, Competences & The Grey Area of Recognition" turned the attention to discussing the typology of the recognition of qualifications in-depth. Following the typology, two main types and four subtypes of recognition were identified. Professional recognition was used to describe recognition in the context of work. A further distinction could be made here between *de jure* professional recognition and *de facto* professional recognition, ultimately signifying the distinction between regulated and non-regulated professions. Next to professional recognition, academic recognition was used to describe recognition in the context of education. This type of recognition could be divided further into academic recognition by accumulation and by substitution. The former concerns recognition needed when a person has finalised studies at one institution and wishes to continue pursuing education at another institution. The latter concerns recognition needed when a person temporarily attends education at another institution, for example, in the context of an exchange. While the distinction between professional and academic recognition logically reflected the realities of needing recognition for work or educational purposes, Chapter "Challenging Convention: Theory, Competences & The Grey Area of Recognition" also showed that the distinction in recognition types could be challenged. In particular, situations where academic qualifications are recognised for labour market purposes in the case of non-fully qualified professionals could be considered the prime example of the grey area between recognition types.

Discussing the typology of recognition and its grey area was furthermore of importance to better understand how the topic developed in the EU. As Chapter "The Long History of the Recognition of Qualifications in the EU" had shown previously, professional and academic recognition had developed relatively separately from the 1990s onwards. The answer to this development can be found in the EU's competences. Indeed, the division between professional and academic recognition was not merely theoretical, as it was paired with a distinction in competences: one shared on internal market (professional recognition—Article 53 TFEU) and the other supporting on education (academic recognition—Article 165 TFEU). This distinction enabled the current pluriform legal and policy landscape to arise mostly due to the more limited nature of the education competence which was paired with a prohibition of harmonisation. The typology and competences were subsequently used to examine the main instruments contributing to or effectuating recognition.[1] What this examination for the instruments' purpose in light of typology and competences mainly showed is that the use of competences has not followed the strict delineation between professional and academic recognition types since existing instruments affect recognition types secondary to those they were primarily created for. This means that the instruments themselves also contribute to the grey area between recognition types.

To gain a deeper understanding of the different instruments on recognition, attention was subsequently diverted to examining the instruments in-depth in Chapters "Professional Recognition" and "Academic Recognition". Chapter "Professional Recognition" was mainly aimed at discussing the Professional Qualifications Directive (PQD) due to its focus on professional recognition. It became clear that the Directive contains the legislative history previously discussed in Chapter "The Long History of the Recognition of Qualifications in the EU" and provides various routes to recognition with its system on automatic recognition for certain professions and general system based on mutual recognition. The chapter explored the various additions introduced to the Directive by Directive 2013/55/EU such as the European Professional Card (EPC) and the mutual evaluation and transparency exercise aimed at tackling superfluous and/or ineffective forms of professional regulation. Regarding the latter point, caution was expressed in preventing non-regulatory barriers from arising upon a removal of formal regulation for a certain profession. Doing so would no longer render a profession regulated and subject to the PQD. While the more general provisions on freedom of movement should still guarantee access to another

[1] To recall, these instruments were the Professional Qualifications Directive, Proportionality Test Directive, European Qualifications Framework for lifelong learning, Europass, the 2020 VET Recommendation, Automatic Recognition Recommendation, Micro-credentials Recommendation, Proposal for a recommendation on quality assurance and recognition, blueprint for a European degree, Lisbon Recognition Convention, Qualifications Framework for the European Higher Education Area, Diploma supplement, ECTS, and Standards and guidelines for quality assurance in the EHEA.

Member States' labour market, qualifications requirements may come into existence that, although not legally imposed, may limit market access.

Nevertheless, the chapter also explored the case law of the CJEU which provided some remedy in this respect. It may be recalled that while the PQD concerns *de jure* professional recognition, case law from the CJEU also showed that some guidelines may be inferred for *de facto* professional recognition (non-regulated professions). The case law from the CJEU thereby developed considerably from its ruling in *Vlassopoulou.* A case that led to the formulation of the *Vlassopoulou* doctrine which would come to guide recognition practices in the non-regulated part of the labour market as well as providing non-fully qualified professionals with a fully-fledged fallback system alternative to the PQD meaning they would not fall outside the scope of EU law for their recognition. A question left open was whether there is a general awareness of the existence of the *Vlassopoulou* doctrine and fallback system beyond the scope of the PQD.

Chapter "Academic Recognition" subsequently turned to the discussion of initiatives for academic recognition in the EU. This chapter can be considered the most extensive since it included action from the EU, Council of Europe and UNESCO, Bologna Process, and Benelux. The chapter started with the discussion of the Bologna Process and elaborated on the exemplary role it instituted for transparency and recognition of higher education qualifications. In particular, the Bologna Process led to the development of a qualifications framework, common documentation formats increasing transparency, a credit system, and standards on quality assurance. While not directly regulating recognition, all of these aspects contribute to the effectuation of recognition by increasing transparency and mutual trust. Recognition in the process was then achieved by ensuring convergence with the Council of Europe and UNESCO by incorporating the Lisbon Recognition Convention (LRC) as the Bologna Process' only legally binding text. Further legislative follow-up was also given to action initiated in the Bologna Process at the regional level. From 2012 onwards, an important objective in the Bologna Process became to strive for automatic recognition of the level of higher education degrees issued in accordance with its three-cycle structure. Follow-up to this initial development at the European level in the EHEA was given in the Benelux which adopted two Decisions on automatic mutual generic level recognition, thereby giving legal expression to the intergovernmental action taken in the Bologna Process.

The Bologna Process furthermore also had effects for the EU legal order. The different transparency instruments mentioned above also served as inspiration for the EU's action on academic recognition, which initiated similar action in the context of the Copenhagen Process leading to the EQF, and Europass. Nevertheless, in recent years the EU can be said to have taken a marked turn. While its action in the Copenhagen Process first mirrored that of the Bologna Process, the EU had set itself the objective to further develop the EEA-2025 and to become a frontrunner in the Bologna Process. Accordingly, this led to the adoption of instruments such as the 2020 VET Recommendation, Automatic Recognition Recommendation and Micro-credentials Recommendation and to the further introduction of proposals on a quality assurance and recognition system for higher education and blueprint for a European degree.

Having examined recognition typology, EU competences on recognition, and the various instruments contributing to or effectuating recognition in depth, attention was then turned to examining the resulting system for recognition of qualifications in the EU in Chapter "Re-Imagining the System for the Recognition of Qualifications in the EU". Central to this chapter was an examination of the interrelationships between the different instruments contributing to or effectuating recognition to expose weaknesses in the system for recognition of qualifications in the EU. The chapter also provided a categorisation of approaches to recognition which could be deduced on the basis of the instruments. At its most fundamental level, recognition can be achieved through harmonisation of education and training which facilitates recognition since differences are taken away. In the EU, limited harmonisation has taken place but the main examples constitute the system for automatic recognition under the PQD and the harmonisation of the structure of higher education effectuated by the Bologna Process. Next, recognition also greatly benefits from increased transparency of qualifications. Increasing transparency and understanding of qualifications ensures that mutual trust can be strengthened, which in turn provides the basis for swifter recognition. Here is where the majority of instruments can be placed, namely the EQF and QF-EHEA, Europass and Diploma Supplement, ECTS, and ESG. Furthermore, next to the transparency instruments we may also add a new category which may be described as booster instruments. These are the Automatic Recognition Recommendation, Micro-credentials Recommendation, and 2020 VET Recommendation—and therefore constitute the instruments the EU has adopted since having increased its ambitions in the Internal Market and EEA-2025. These instruments are particularly useful to not only increase transparency, but also to enhance coherence with other instruments since they include calls for the deepening of cooperation on existing instruments. Finally, the last category of instruments are those providing procedures and/or legal provisions on recognition, thereby effectuating mutual recognition. Here, we may find the PQD, LRC, and Benelux Decisions.

The subsequent examination of the interrelationships between these different instruments contributing to or effectuating recognition showed that the resulting system is generally coherent (and can be considered increasingly so due to the booster instruments). Nevertheless, this assessment did result in the identification of a number of weaknesses that challenge the creation of an encompassing system for recognition of qualifications providing for recognition in accordance with common European principles at all stages of a person's life. Based on the typology of recognition and its grey area an encompassing system could be construed. In particular, this would consist of provisions for all recognition types (*de jure* and *de facto* professional recognition and academic recognition by accumulation and by substitution).

Nevertheless, the analysis in Chapter "Re-Imagining the System for the Recognition of Qualifications in the EU" also showed several weaknesses in the current system for recognition in the EU. An overall weakness was identified in the system for recognition since attention is mainly given to contributing to recognition of qualifications through transparency instruments, instead of effectuating recognition through instruments providing procedures and other legal safeguards to persons undergoing recognition processes. Mutual trust therefore appears to be prioritised over mutual recognition whereas the latter may be easier to achieve in the short-term through legislative action whilst the former takes time to build gradually. This can even lead to the question of whether we can speak of an EU system for recognition of qualifications since very limited procedures on recognition can be perceived at the EU level. Furthermore, where these exist they are usually aimed at particular qualifications thus taking away from the existence of a system for recognition able to support recognition at all stages. Looking more closely at the instruments, the PQD is the only legally binding instrument within the EU legal framework which effectuates recognition. And compared to the typology of recognition its scope is relatively limited to *de jure* professional recognition. Considering the importance of recognition of qualifications in realising free movement—a right EU citizens have—the lack of a legally embedded system for recognition is to be considered particularly problematic. Of course, the LRC does provide for provisions on academic recognition, but its location outside the EU legal framework means its application mainly takes place at the national level where practices may again differ. Furthermore, its focus is limited to recognition in the context of higher education. The benefit of instruments within the EU legal framework is to be found in the direct effect such instruments could have and the possibility for the CJEU to guarantee the uniformity of the system. In this context, Chapter "Re-Imagining the System for the Recognition of Qualifications in the EU" also explored the possible accession of the EU to the LRC. Though a possibility, such route would not be without obstacle since the Member States would have to invite the EU to accede. Furthermore, certain matters regarding the application of that Convention under EU law and its overlap with some of the case law of the CJEU concerning the *Vlassopoulou* doctrine would have to be clarified. Nevertheless, a potential accession of the EU would have as a consequence that the Convention was brought within the EU legal framework and would indeed enable its uniform application to be guaranteed within the EU's institutional structure.

Continuing with the *Vlassopoulou* doctrine, another weakness could be identified here especially where non-fully qualified professions are concerned. As of yet, non-fully qualified professionals are outside the scope of the PQD and therefore subject to what can be described as a fallback system resulting from the CJEU's case law in *Vlassopoulou*. Through this line of cases, the CJEU has ensured that non-fully qualified professionals can still acquire recognition of their qualifications under EU law. Questions can nevertheless be raised regarding the familiarity of this case law in practice and therefore whether non-fully qualified professionals actually enjoy the safeguards provided by the *Vlassopoulou* doctrine. Therefore, codification of this case law would be desirable to enhance legal certainty and uniform application of this case law. Use of Article 53 TFEU to integrate these professionals into the PQD appears the most straightforward option here.

To continue with the *Vlassopoulou* doctrine, further attention is to also be given in respect to its relevance for professions outside the scope of the PQD. In principle, recognition through a procedure should not be necessary for such professions since the employer would be the primary party deciding on whether or not to recognise qualifications by employing a person. Nevertheless, optional procedures may exist at national level (some originating from the sphere of academic recognition). Either way, where qualifications are assessed on the non-regulated part of the labour market account is also to be had of the *Vlassopoulou* doctrine, meaning all qualifications have to be taken into account and the person has to be given the opportunity to demonstrate knowledge which is found to be lacking. The same question as above may again be posed here namely whether this doctrine is sufficiently known to find its application in practice. Ensuring this is the case may be of particular importance in light of ambitions to lessen unnecessary or excessive professional regulation. Removal of such regulation would mean professions move from being regulated and subject to the PQD to being non-regulated and subject to conditions on the labour market. While in some cases this may lead to a lifting of barriers to mobility, the situation to be prevented is one where labour market actors will take over qualifications requirements formerly embedded in legislation and maintain them in practice. Since this may not occur in a consistent, transparent, nor clearly defined manner, it could pose new restrictions to market access for those with foreign qualifications. While the Proportionality Test Directive therefore ensures Member States should thoroughly consider whether or not to regulate professions, the *Vlassopoulou* doctrine should also be taken into account by labour market actors in the case of non-regulated professions to prevent that foreign qualifications cannot be used effectively.

Tackling excessive regulation was considered one of three future Internal Market and EEA-2025 ambitions on recognition. The other two concerned increased automatic recognition and more flexible learning paths. While good opportunities exist to enhance automatic recognition under the PQD by expanding the use of common training principles, enhancing automatic academic recognition may encounter more difficulties. Of course, work in this area is being done through the Automatic Recognition Recommendation. However, the prohibition of harmonisation in Article 165(4) TFEU seems to prevent legally binding action to be taken here in the EU context. Despite this limitation, a possible avenue explored in this context consisted of accession of individual Member States to the Benelux Treaty concluded with the Baltic States on automatic mutual generic level recognition. This would be positive since a legally enforceable right would be created for holders of higher education qualifications. Nevertheless, it would again result in a situation similar to the LRC where legally binding provisions are provided outside the EU legal order. The core of this weakness is therefore again located in the use of competences. Here we also touch upon a last major weakness of the system for recognition, namely its focus on higher education. While action on higher education in itself is to be considered positive, it also exposes a weakness since VET qualifications are not subject to similar advances in relation to recognition.

As a last avenue to arrive at a system for recognition of qualifications under EU law a different interpretation of current competences was explored. Indeed, Chapter "Challenging Convention: Theory, Competences & The Grey Area of Recognition" already showed that the internal market competence of Article 53 TFEU did not contain an explicit reference to professional recognition and was furthermore used to harmonise education and training for certain professions under the PQD. In a similar vein, that chapter showed that instruments contributing to or effectuating recognition do not adhere to the strict delineation of recognition types, i.e. many of the instruments adopted on the basis of Article 165 TFEU also concern professional recognition. Previous scholarship and case law was relied on to suggest a different reading of the competences. For an important part this depends on approaching the topic from an Internal Market perspective: as long as the functioning of the Internal Market is improved and reliance on that competence is not such as to circumvent other more limited legal bases, it should be possible to use Internal Market legal bases.[2] As mentioned previously, since many of the instruments adopted on the basis of Article 165 TFEU are said to also positively contribute to professional recognition, they can also be considered to improve the functioning of the Internal Market.

In this context, an important consideration is related to harmonisation and whether this is actually the case when seeking to create a system with procedures and provisions on recognition. Here, it is important to refer back to the two different challenges related to recognition identified in the introduction to this contribution: (1) the variety of national education systems and professions, and (2) the variety of instruments contributing to and effectuating recognition. While the former is to be considered to touch upon national identity, the latter does not. In particular, the present contribution argues in favour of an encompassing system for recognition of qualifications that can benefit EU citizens at all stages of their lives by ensuring that *procedures* for recognition are common and anchored in EU law. Ultimately, the suggestion is that EU citizens exercising their rights to free movement should be able to do so under *a single set of rules*. Proposed action is therefore aimed at achieving common administrative practices on recognition.

Attempts have been made—and continue to be made—to achieve recognition by touching upon subjects that concerned the way education systems and professions were shaped (challenge 1 above). Attempts that were previously abandoned (e.g. in the vertical approach) or were of limited success (e.g. the use of common training principles so far). A trend seems to exist where more advanced forms of recognition—notably automatic recognition—are strived for without sufficient political will to realise them or the legal capacity to do so (e.g. Automatic Recognition Recommendation). Accordingly, the resulting system for recognition reflects a piecemeal approach as opposed to a long-term, encompassing, and coherent strategy to improving recognition. The question may be raised why attempts were not made to initially create a general framework for recognition based on the principle of mutual recognition (as reflected in the *Vlassopoulou* doctrine). Such framework could indeed be applicable to any type of recognition, be it for professional or educational purposes (as attested to by the PQD's general system and LRC). Furthermore, it could also contribute to recognition in the context of more flexible learning paths—a subject of which it is not yet clear how the current framework contributes to this. More targeted and advanced actions could then be taken for professions, courses of study, or types of education for which there was a particular willingness or gain of having more advanced forms of recognition.

[2] Garben (2011); Case 9/74 *Casagrande*, ECLI:EU:C:1974:74; Case C-376/98 *Germany v. European Parliament and Council*, ECLI:ECLI:EU:C:2000:544.

Maintaining the status quo will mean that the current multitude of instruments on recognition of qualifications will be maintained in the future—and perhaps even exacerbated. This jeopardises advances in both the Internal Market and EEA-2025 by inhibiting smooth recognition at any stage. While recommendations were made in the context of this contribution to improve the system for recognition, many of these are remedial in character. Furthermore, many of these are forced to be formulated along the current understanding of competences on recognition in the TFEU where Article 165 can be said to be over-extended in use while Article 53 under-used. The answer to the quest for a more integrated and long-term approach to recognition may lie in a different approach to EU competences on recognition to ultimately develop an EU-level system for recognition of qualifications that is both encompassing in the sense that it provides common rules for recognition at any stage of a person's life as well as future-proof.

Annex—Glossary

Glossary providing brief explanations of the terms used in this contribution

2020 VET Recommendation Term used to describe Council Recommendation of 24 November 2020 on vocational education and training (VET) for sustainable competitiveness, social fairness and resilience, [2020] OJ C 417/1.

Academic recognition Recognition for the purposes of study consisting of two sub-types: academic recognition by accumulation and by substitution. Academic recognition by accumulation concerns recognition occurring after completion of one course of study and needed to progress to the next. Academic recognition by substitution concerns a temporary stay at another educational institution which contributes to completing education at the original institution in the home Member State (e.g. exchanges).

Automatic Recognition Recommendation Term used to describe Council Recommendation of 26 November 2018 on promoting automatic mutual recognition of higher education and upper secondary education and training qualifications and the outcomes of learning periods abroad, [2018] OJ C 444/1.

Benelux Decisions Term used to describe Beschikking van het Benelux Comité van Ministers betreffende de automatische wederzijdse generieke niveauerkenning van diploma's hoger onderwijs, M(2015) and Beschikking van het Benelux Comité van Ministers tot aanvulling van beschikking M(2015) 3 betreffende de automatische wederzijdse generieke niveauerkenning van diploma's hoger onderwijs, M(2018) 1. Both instruments achieve mutual generic level recognition of higher education degrees in the Benelux.

Bologna Process Process located outside the EU legal framework consisting of several measures to enhance the coherence of education systems across Europe.

Common documentation formats Formats created as a result of cooperation between different international organisations providing a common format for

L. S.J. Kortese, *Effectuating Free Movement in the EU through Recognition of Qualifications*, https://doi.org/10.1007/978-3-032-21335-8

documentation attesting to qualifications thereby helping to enhance their transparency (e.g. Europass, Diploma Supplement).

Competence Following from the principle of conferral of Article 5(1)(2) Treaty on European Union. According to this principle EU action is limited to what is prescribed in the Treaties. If a competence is not conferred to the EU, it remains with the Member States. Competences are found in the Treaty on the Functioning of the European Union.

Copenhagen Process Process located within the EU legal framework consisting of several measures to enhance the quality and attractiveness of vocational education and training.

Credit system System expressing learning experiences and their duration in credits (e.g. ECTS).

Diploma Supplement Document to enhance the transparency and understanding of higher education qualifications.

Europass Platform providing common documentation formats (e.g. a CV or certificate supplement) to enhance transparency and understanding of qualifications. Europass is found in Decision (EU) 2018/646 of the European Parliament and of the Council of 18 April 2018 on a common framework for the provision of better services for skills and qualifications (Europass) and repealing Decision No 2241/2004/EC, [2018] OJ L 112/42.

European Credit Transfer and Accumulation System (ECTS) System employed in the context of the European Higher Education Area to make the pursuit of courses of study at higher education level more transparent by expressing learning experiences and their duration in credits.

European Education Area (EEA-2025) Located within the EU context and allowing Member States to cooperate to improve education at all levels (from early childhood education to adult learning).

European Higher Education Area (EHEA) Resulted from the Bologna Process and comprises 49 countries (including the EU's Member States).

European Qualifications Framework for lifelong learning (EQF) Transparency instrument following from the Copenhagen Process helping to make national qualifications more understandable by sorting these into eight different levels. The EQF can be found in Council Recommendation of 22 May 2017 on the European Qualifications Framework for lifelong learning and repealing the recommendation of the European Parliament and of the Council of 23 April 2008 on the establishment of the European Qualifications Framework for lifelong learning, [2017] OJ C 189/15.

Harmonization In the EU context: (legislative) process through which differing national legal systems are rendered (progressively) more similar.

Higher education Education taking place after upper secondary education at universities or similar educational establishments.

Lisbon Recognition Convention (LRC) Term used to describe the Council of Europe and UNESCO Convention on the Recognition of Qualifications concerning Higher Education in the European Region (ETS No. 165) laying down procedures for recognition in the context of higher education.

Micro-credentials Recommendation Term used to describe Council Recommendation of 16 June 2022 on a European approach to micro-credentials for lifelong learning and employability, [2022] OJ C 243/10.

Professional Qualifications Directive (PQD) Term used to describe EU Directive 2005/36/EC as amended by Directive 2013/55/EU laying down procedures for *de jure* professional recognition.

Professional recognition Recognition for the purpose of work consisting of two sub-types: *de jure* and de facto professional recognition. *De jure* professional recognition concerns professions for which qualification requirements are laid down through legislative provisions (i.e. regulated professions). De facto professional recognition relates to the use of qualifications on the non-regulated part of the labour market (i.e. non-regulated professions) and generally concerns the decision of the employer.

Proportionality Principle of EU law limiting EU action to what is necessary to achieve Treaty objectives. Found in Article 5(4) Treaty on European Union. Alternatively, proportionality constitutes a test applied in the context of the freedom of movement to examine the suitability and necessity of measures restricting free movement maintained for reasons in the general interest.

Proportionality Test Directive Term used to describe Directive 2018/958/EU guiding Member States in conducting a proportionality test generally relating to the suitability and necessity of all new and amended regulation of professions. Directive connected to the Professional Qualifications Directive.

Qualification Diplomas, certificates or other evidence attesting to certain education being completed or professional experience gained.

Qualifications framework Instrument that categorises education, training and/or qualifications into different levels based on particular knowledge, skills, and competences to increase transparency thereof (e.g. QF-EHEA, EQF).

Qualifications Framework of the European Higher Education Area (QF-EHEA) Instrument connected to the Bologna Process and European Higher Education Area consisting of descriptors based on learning outcomes and ECTS for different cycles of higher education (bachelor, master, and doctorate).

Quality assurance Process involving evaluation of various aspects of education and training to guarantee a sufficient level of quality thereof (Standards and guidelines for quality assurance in the EHEA & 2020 VET Recommendation).

Recognition Process through which qualifications are examined to see if they are suitable to be used in the context of an education system or profession in another Member State.

Reverse discrimination Situation occurring in the context of the EU freedom of movement where non-mobile citizens of an EU Member State are treated less favourably than mobile EU citizens. Consequence of EU law not affecting purely internal situations, which are considered subject to national law and therefore outside the scope of EU law.

Standards and guidelines for quality assurance in the EHEA (ESG) Instrument to guide quality assurance processes in the European Higher Education Area.

Subsidiarity Principle of EU law ensuring that EU action is only taken if the result of such action cannot be sufficiently achieved at the national level. Found in Article 5(3) Treaty on European Union.

Vocational education and training (VET) Education preparing for the exercise of a profession starting at the level of upper secondary education.

The manufacturer's authorised representative in the EU is Springer Nature Customer Service Centre GmbH, Europaplatz 3, 69115 Heidelberg, Germany. If you have any concerns regarding our products, please contact ProductSafety@springernature.com

Printed and bound by CPI Group (UK) Ltd, Croydon, CR0 4YY
07/10/2026
02229352-0005